D0761409

Privatism and Urban Policy in Britain and the United States

Privatism and Urban Policy in Britain and the United States

TIMOTHY BARNEKOV
ROBIN BOYLE
and
DANIEL RICH

OXFORD UNIVERSITY PRESS
1989

Oxford University Press, Walton Street, Oxford OX2 6DP
Oxford New York Toronto
Delhi Bombay Calcutta Madras Karachi
Petaling Jaya Singapore Hong Kong Tokyo
Nairobi Dar es Salaam Cape Town
· Melbourne Auckland
and associated companies in
Berlin Ibadan

Oxford is a trade mark of Oxford University Press

Published in the United States
by Oxford University Press, New York

© Timothy K. Barnekov, Robin Boyle and Daniel Rich, 1989

All rights reserved. No part of this publication may be reproduced,
stored in a retrieval system, or transmitted, in any form or by any means,
electronic, mechanical, photocopying, recording, or otherwise, without
the prior permission of Oxford University Press

This book is sold subject to the condition that it shall not, by way
of trade or otherwise, be lent, re-sold, hired out, or otherwise circulated
without the publisher's prior consent in any form of binding or cover
other than that in which it is published and without a similar condition
including this condition being imposed on the subsequent purchaser

British Library Cataloguing in Publication Data
Barnekov, Timothy
Privatism and urban policy in Britain and the United States.
1. Urban regions. Social planning. Economic aspects
I. Title II. Boyle, Robin III. Rich, Daniel
307'.12
ISBN 0–19–823275–6
ISBN 0–19–823274–8 (pbk.)

Library of Congress Cataloging in Publication Data
Barnekov, Timothy K. (Timothy Kiel)
Privatism and urban policy in Britain and the United States.

Bibliography Includes index.
1. Urban policy—Great Britain. 2. Urban policy—
United States. 3. Privatization—Great Britain.
4. Privatization—United States. I. Boyle, Robin.
II. Rich, Daniel. III. Title.
HT133.B26   1989   307.7'6'0941   88–33029
ISBN 0–19–823275–6
ISBN 0–19–823274–8 (pbk.)

Set by Colset Private Limited, Singapore

Printed and bound in
Great Britain by Biddles Ltd,
Guildford and King's Lynn

*To J. Barry Cullingworth who
created the link between the
University of Delaware and
the University of Strathclyde*

PREFACE

THE term privatism was first used by Sam Bass Warner, Jr. to denote the dominant cultural tradition influencing urban development in America. It is a tradition that has equal importance in Britain. Privatism signifies an underlying confidence in the capacity of the private sector to create the conditions for personal and community prosperity. It also indicates a belief in the legitimacy of market values as the appropriate standard for community choice. Privatism has been central to the historical growth of cities in Britain and the United States, and it remains central to the development and implementation of contemporary urban policy in both countries.

In this book, we examine the relationship of privatism to urban policy in Britain and the United States. We seek to evaluate the meaning and implications of the pursuit of the private city in both countries. This subject gained considerable salience in the 1980s as conservative governments in the US and Britain were outspoken in their enthusiasm for privatizing urban policy. National policies sought to enlarge the role of the private sector in urban change and to limit public interventions in local development. The apparent complementarity of urban policy perspectives provided a strong catalyst for popularized cross-national comparisons and contributed to a substantial transatlantic traffic in policy salesmen anxious to transplant ideas and program experiments. Part of the stimulus for this book was our judgment that too much attention was being devoted to selling the virtues of the private city on both sides of the Atlantic and too little to the impact and implications of efforts to privatize urban policy. But our interest in the influence of privatism on urban policy extends beyond particular political incumbencies in either country. Indeed, to appreciate the meaning and implications of the recent enthusiasm for privatism on both sides of the Atlantic, we must place current events in a broader historical context.

Our objective is to evaluate the experience with privatism as a foundation for urban policy. The primary emphasis is not on comparing and contrasting British and American styles of urban policy; it is to identify the common themes and outcomes of a particular policy orientation, which we call privatism, in two quite different institutional and political contexts. In our view, the lessons from experience with privatism have been consistent but poorly understood and rarely accepted by the architects of policy in either country—although the resistance to learning has been more continuous in the US where privatism has always been at the center of urban policy. Precisely because privatism has been a dominant tradition in both countries, its achievements have generally been exaggerated while its failures have been ignored or excused. Our purpose is to apply a more critical perspective. While we do not dismiss the achievements of privatism, we do seek to more clearly explicate and document its limits. Beyond this, we hope that our account will help readers recognize that the influence of privatism on urban policy has been a political choice which is expressed through public decisions and public actions.

Our research collaboration was made possible by a valuable institutional link between the University of Delaware and the University of Strathclyde, a link forged by J. Barry Cullingworth, to whom this book is dedicated. It was given encouragement, guidance, and financial support by Urlan Wannop, head of the Centre for Planning at Strathclyde; John Byrne, Director of the Center for Energy and Urban Policy Research at Delaware; and David Ames, Dean of the College of Urban Affairs and Public Policy at Delaware. Beyond their institutional support, these colleagues have helped to shape our ideas, for which we are grateful, and they have provided us with substantial advice—some of which was accepted! We also received useful criticism of the manuscript from Michael Keating, Greg Lloyd, Janet Johnson, John Stapleford, and Peter Roberts. In addition to John Byrne, Michael Keating, and Urlan Wannop, we have collaborated on related research with Robert Warren and Jack Dustin. All of these colleagues will see their imprint on these pages—hopefully in a manner they will find satisfying.

We also wish to give our thanks for the support of the Nuffield Foundation in Britain, the Carnegie Trust for the Universities of Scotland, and Provost L. Leon Campbell of the University of Delaware.

And to all those family, friends, and colleagues alike, who, with incredible patience and remarkable good spirit, paid the price of our endless revisions, we offer thanks and, finally, liberation!

T.B.
R.B.
D.R.

CONTENTS

LIST OF TABLES

LIST OF ABBREVIATIONS

US

ACIR	Advisory Commission on Intergovernmental Relations
AFDC	Aid to Families with Dependent Children
AWOL	Absence Without Leave
BEDCO	Baltimore Economic Development Corporation
CAP	Community Action Program
CBD	Central Business District
CCIHM	Charles Center–Inner Harbor Management, Inc.
CDBG	Community Development Block Grant
CED	Committee for Economic Development
CETA	Comprehensive Employment Training Act
CUED	National Council for Urban Economic Development
EDA	Economic Development Administration
EO	Executive Office of the President
FHA	Federal Housing Administration
FY	Fiscal Year
GAO	General Accounting Office
GBC	Greater Baltimore Committee
GPM	Greater Philadelphia Movement
GPO	Government Printing Office
HHFA	Housing and Home Finance Agency
HUD	Department of Housing and Urban Development
ICMA	International City Management Association
IRB	Industrial Revenue Bond
JEC	Joint Economic Committee of the US Congress
JOBS	Job Opportunities in the Business Sector
LPA	Local Public Authority
NAB	National Alliance of Businessmen
NOCDC	New Orleans Citywide Development Corporation
NRC	National Resources Committee
MDTA	Manpower Development and Training Act
OMB	Office of Management and Budget
OTA	Office of Technology Assessment
PC	President's Commission for a National Agenda for the Eighties
PSE	Public Service Employment Program
PHA	Public Housing Administration
SIP	Special Impact Program
UDAG	Urban Development Action Grant
URA	Urban Renewal Administration
URPG	Urban and Regional Policy Group
USHUD	US Department of Housing and Urban Development

BRITAIN

BBC	British Broadcasting Corporation
BIC	Business in the Community
CATs	City Action Teams
CDP	Community Development Project
DE	Department of Employment
DCC	Docklands Consultative Committee
DoE	Department of the Environment
DTI	Department of Trade and Industry
FIG	Financial Institutions Group
HMSO	Her Majesty's Stationery Office
JDAG	Joint Docklands Action Group
LDDC	London Docklands Development Corporation
LEG-UP	Local Enterprise Grants for Urban Projects
NAO	National Audit Office
NHS	National Health Service
MDC	Merseyside Development Corporation
PAG	Property Advisory Group
PSMRU	Public Sector Management Research Unit
RSG	Rate Support Grant
SDA	Scottish Development Agency
TCPA	Town and Country Planning Association
UDC	Urban Development Corporation
UDG	Urban Development Grant
UPMI	Urban Programme Management Initiative
URG	Urban Regeneration Grant

1

The Pursuit of the Private City

PRIVATISM is the dominant cultural tradition affecting urban policy in the United States and Britain. It is a tradition that encourages a reliance on the private sector as the principal agent of urban change. Privatism stresses the social as well as economic importance of private initiative and competition, and it legitimizes the public consequences of private action. Its legacy is that both personal and community well-being are evaluated largely in terms of the fulfillment of private aspirations and the achievements of private institutions.

While privatism draws inspiration from capitalist institutions and justification from capitalist doctrines, its pervasive influence as a cultural tradition extends beyond any particular institution or set of principles. In this sense, privatism constitutes a framework of social expectations within which the institutions of political economy have developed and operated. By the eighteenth century, these expectations had already become the dominant cultural tradition in the US and Britain. According to Sam Bass Warner, Jr. the essence of privatism:

lay in its concentration upon the individual and the individual's search for wealth. Psychologically, privatism meant that the individual should seek happiness in personal independence and in the search for wealth; socially, privatism meant that the individual should see his first loyalty as his immediate family, and that a community should be a union of such moneymaking, accumulating families; politically, privatism meant that the community should keep the peace among individual money-makers and, if possible, help to create an open and thriving setting where each citizen would have some substantial opportunity to prosper (Warner 1987: 3–4).

In both Britain and the US, the content of this cultural tradition continued to evolve throughout the nineteenth and twentieth centuries. The individualistic emphasis was moderated reflecting changes in the scale and structure of social organization and political economy. At the same time, greater emphasis was given to the institutional dimensions of privatism and these became more prominent, more fully elaborated, and more influential. As a result, in the twentieth century, privatism encompasses a distinctive set of expectations about the social functions and responsibilities of private firms and public bureaucracies, private markets and public policies. Underpinning these expectations is an assumption that the private sector is inherently dynamic, productive, and dependable; a belief that private institutions are intrinsically superior to public institutions for the delivery of goods and services; and a confidence that market efficiency is the appropriate criterion of social performance in virtually all spheres of community activity.

1

Privatism has exerted a persistent influence on urban development and urban policy in both the US and Britain. To a significant extent, cities in Britain and the United States are private cities: places where privatism is the prevailing community standard. Privatism has stimulated the growth of cities and shaped their physical forms, their politics, and their economic and social structures. As Warner has argued, it also has been greatly responsible for the achievements and failures of urban development (1987).

In America the private sector has always been the central force in urban change. Despite the growth of federal intervention in urban affairs over the past half century, private decisions continue to determine the pattern of urban development. Public interventions have accommodated the requirements of a private system of production and exchange, but they have never supplanted nor, for the most part, seriously challenged the dominance of the private sector in matters of community choice. National urban policy has thus been designed to facilitate the private sector's role in guiding urban development. For forty years federal urban programs, under Democratic and Republican administrations alike, have sought to mobilize the private sector to take a more active role in urban development through tax credits, contract incentives, location subsidies, appeals to corporate social responsibility, and a wide variety of public–private partnerships.

In Britain there is also a long tradition of promoting private sector guidance of urban development, but in the twentieth century there has been a strong countervailing tradition of direct public involvement in the shaping of urban change. In the post-war period, the provision of urban services and infrastructure, the patterns of urban growth, and much of the funding for urban programs were directed and implemented to a significant extent by the public sector. Thus, the influence of privatism on urban policy in Britain has been less uniform and the use of public power to regulate urban growth more common and more continuous than in the US. But even in the periods of public-sector activism, the influence of privatism was not eliminated; privatism continued to affect the general pattern of British urban development.

The cultural tradition of privatism does not encompass or explain all of the urban experience in either the US or Britain, but it is not possible to fully account for that experience without an assessment of the influence of privatism. Moreover, while privatism historically has been influential in British and American urban development, there was a resurgence of enthusiasm for privatism in the 1980s that increased its salience for urban policy. In both Britain and the United States, the pursuit of the private city was greatly invigorated by conservative governments that were committed to strengthening the role of the private sector in effecting urban change.

The Pursuit of the Private City in the 1980s

For both the Thatcher and Reagan governments efforts to privatize urban policy were part of a general reorientation of domestic policy. Political rhetoric encouraged greater fidelity to the tradition of privatism and recalled well-known themes of conservative political and economic theory: government is too big, too expensive, and too involved in economic and social affairs; the market is intrinsically more sensitive and more responsive than the state to social and economic change; and the removal of government supports and controls allows firms and families alike to rediscover the traditional values of enterprise, initiative, and self-reliance.

In the 1980s, proposals to halt the growth of government and introduce a new era of privatism gained widespread popular support in both countries and clearly contributed to the electoral victories of the conservative leaders. E. S. Savas, Assistant Secretary at the US Department of Housing and Urban Development during the early years of the Reagan administration, expressed the conservative sentiment of the 1980s in the introduction to his book *Privatizing the Public Sector*:

reconsidering the roles and responsibilities of government, the individual, the family, voluntary organizations, private firms, and the marketplace . . . can bring about more limited and more sensible government—and hence greater freedom, justice and efficiency—without sacrificing the advances of the last half century (Savas 1982: 6).

Seeking to act upon this sentiment, both British and American governments supported privatization programs to expand the role of the private sector by shifting from public sector provision of goods and services to private sector alternatives. While the specific justifications for these initiatives varied, there were a number of frequently cited objectives which included: the improvement of the economic performance of public assets or service functions; the depoliticization of economic decisions; the generation of budget revenues through the sale of public assets; the cutback in public expenditures and taxes; the reduction of the power of public-sector unions; and the promotion of popular capitalism through the wider ownership of assets (Hanke 1987: 2). In promoting these objectives, privatization initiatives took several forms in both the US and Britain: the elimination of a public function or its transferral to the private sector; the shift of production and delivery of goods and services from the public to the private sector while maintaining public financing; the sale of assets such as public lands, infrastructure, and public enterprises; and the deregulation or removal of controls on the private provision of goods and services (Pack 1987: 523–5; Starr 1987: 125).

The relative emphasis on one or another dimension of privatization sometimes has been quite different in the US and Britain, reflecting not only variations in political priorities but also in policy traditions. A central feature of British government initiative during the first half of the twentieth century was the nationalization of services in the areas of health, education, transport, communications, and utility operations. After World War II, the state also nationalized numerous private companies in declining industries—steel, shipbuilding, motor vehicles—and, for strategic and ideological reasons, took a controlling interest in oil, airways, telecommunications, and some financial services. Moreover, in housing and in local services for welfare facilities, recreation, the arts and more, local government took a major role. This is in marked contrast to the US where there is no comparable basis of direct public control across as wide a range of services and functions, and, therefore, no opportunity for comparable privatization initiatives. Thus, the British government's commitment in the 1980s to rolling back the state and returning business and services to the private sector was intended to reverse a pattern of public control and direction that has no equivalent, in either scope or magnitude, in the US. In Britain, for example, much of the large public housing sector was targeted for privatization by the Conservative Government. In the US, public housing always has been a minor element in a largely private housing market. By contrast, in the case of contracting with the private sector for services, there is extensive experience in the US with a variety of arrangements across a whole array of service areas which in Britain are almost exclusively direct public functions.

To advocates, any list of privatization initiatives will always be incomplete since privatization reflects a general policy orientation rather than a finite set of policy alternatives. In this sense, privatization is an effort to restrict the functions of government in accord with the beliefs and expectations that buttress the cultural tradition of privatism. As Robert W. Bailey points out, 'despite the confusion of what exactly is meant by the term privatization, there is a clear unifying thread in all its uses: maximization of efficiency. The assumption among advocates is that, inherently, private managers can deliver at lower costs services similar or superior to those of public managers' (Bailey 1987: 141). In this context, privatization involves not only actions that transfer ownership and control of public goods and services to the private sector, but also, and sometimes more importantly, the public sector's emulation of the private sector as a model of efficient performance. Public organizations in the US and Britain have been encouraged to adopt a more businesslike approach to both the definition of responsibilities and the operation of programs. Emphasis has been on cost containment, on adoption of private sector methods of program management and financial control, and, to use the British phrase, on value for money. For the advocates of privatization, the superiority of the private sector is more than an operational hypothesis to be tested through experiments with different public–private arrangements for the production and delivery of services. Rather, it is a normative imperative that arises from the tradition of privatism and links particular privatization proposals to a systematic political preference for market institutions in decision making and policy implementation.

In the 1980s, in Britain and the United States, there were at least four important and mutually reinforcing policy dimensions of this political preference. First, in virtually all areas of domestic activity, priority was to be given to economic considerations and the requirements for market efficiency.

Second, wherever possible, private markets were to be relied upon in preference to public policies in making allocative social choices. Third, where public intervention was necessary, it was to be designed to augment market processes and to elicit the greatest possible private sector participation. Finally, when direct public programs were undertaken, they were to be organized in a manner that corresponded to the administrative, financial, and evaluative methods of the private sector.

In both Britain and the United States the reinvigoration of the private sector was pursued as the key to long-term national economic growth. Pronouncements on both sides of the Atlantic manifested an ideological commitment to a smaller role for government and suggested that retrenchment of the public sector was the only viable national response to the problems of economic stagnation. The most urgent goal of government was to reverse the processes of industrial decline. This required a rapid transition from an industrial to a post-industrial society; a general realignment of institutional and technological infrastructure away from the intensive focus on industrial manufacturing and towards a new and more globally competitive service-oriented economy. To accomplish the transition, the urban landscape had to be rearranged to allow for increasing mobility and spatial deconcentration of population and economic activities.

The facilitation of the post-industrial transition was a national priority in Britain and America throughout the 1980s. Achievement of this priority was believed to require an extensive reliance on a marketplace that was as free as possible from governmental restraint. To this end, the British and American governments sought to reduce the scope and financing of domestic public sector involvements, to deregulate industrial and commercial markets, to transfer services and responsibilities to the private sector, and to create a policy environment that favored the growth of private investment.

Accompanying the vision of a market-led path to post-industrial society was a general rethinking of the relationship between local and national prosperity. Urban regeneration was regarded largely as a process of local adaptation to national change. There was an expectation—though not frequently articulated—that national economic development might occur at the expense of areas and communities that were not in the wealth-producing sectors of the post-industrial economy. In this regard, the traditional pattern of government aid to cities was seen to slow the process of adaptation and thereby delay national economic recovery. On occasion there was even the assertion that the national government can or should do little to insulate particular urban places from the effects of economic change.

National government programs for cities, when justified, the argument continued, are best directed at stimulating local economic development by assisting the private sector either directly or through partnerships with local authorities. The mandate for cities was clear: establish economic development as the central focus of local attention and as the basic function of local institutions, stimulate new public-private alliances, and abstain from public actions which distort the efficient operation of the marketplace or constrain the locational choices, investment decisions, and operational plans of firms. The prosperity of cities, it was proposed, depends on effective competition for industry, jobs, and investments in a dynamic national economy that is shaped largely by the spatial and sectoral needs of private enterprise.

In the US, the translation of this logic into program initiative led the Reagan administration to prescribe a new era of privatism for cities that included proposals for federal disengagement from local affairs, consolidation of urban programs, cutbacks in social and environmental expenditures, turning back responsibility for resolving urban problems to the states and cities, and dismantling public bureaucracies in favor of public–private partnerships. While rhetoric often exceeded implementation, there is little doubt that the Reagan administration tried to shift the direction of urban policy. Urban development had to proceed in concert with the processes of economic growth brought about by private initiative and market efficiency. *The President's 1982 National Urban Policy Report* proclaimed: 'Governments alone can do little to solve problems without the direct and strong involvement of the people' (USHUD 1982b: 9).

Local and State leaders have begun making creative and productive use of the special expertise, wisdom and dedication found in private firms, civic groups and neighborhood associations to spur community development and to address specific problems. The administration seeks to build on this positive trend by employing private sector initiatives, creating Enterprise Zones and pursuing other approaches and experiments that can help revitalize urban America and improve the quality of life in all our communities (USHUD 1982b: 9).

Within this context, the Reagan administration encouraged municipal competition for economic growth and sought to restrict or roll back federal aid programs—even those focused on stimulating local economic development. David Stockman, former Director of the Office of Management and Budget, argued that even when federal economic development aid to a community works, it does so only at the expense of overall economic growth. By inducing firms to locate or remain in a particular city, government aid imposes economic costs on private investment decisions by 'shifting investments to high-cost or less economically efficient areas' (*National Journal*, 21 Mar. 1981: 495).

The Reagan urban policy, argued Myron Levine, must be understood in terms of a hierarchy of goals. National economic growth was pursued in preference to local economic development and local economic development was favored over 'spending for social purposes which represents an even greater diversion of potential investment resources from the area of national economic growth' (Levine 1983: 18). The growth in national budget deficits added pragmatic justification to the more ideological rationale for reduced federal assistance. Cities, it was said, must accept responsibility for their own salvation. As E. S. Savas put it, 'no national government can assure eternal life for all its cities at their historically highest level of prosperity' (Savas 1983: 450). The most prudent course for both prosperous and declining urban areas was to 'form partnerships with their private sectors and plan strategically to enhance their comparative advantages relative to other jurisdictions' (USHUD 1982*b*: 3).

In Britain, the Thatcher Government expressed similar enthusiasm for the benefits of private enterprise, individual initiative, and personal self-reliance. Encouragement of the private sector became a keynote of national urban policy throughout the 1980s. At the center of these efforts was a commitment to increase reliance on market institutions in local and national economic development. This commitment resulted in efforts to deregulate economic activity, to selectively dismantle public planning machinery and remove local planning controls, and to leverage local private investment through public–private partnerships. In effect, urban policy in the 1980s sought to restore the influence which the private sector exercised on urban development in earlier periods of British history. John Patten, at one time Minister for Housing, Urban Affairs and Construction, articulated the Conservative Government's market-based strategy:

The public sector dominated municipal solutions of the past have simply not worked. They made things worse because they were based on a misunderstanding of what makes cities—and other areas—successful. We should draw a line under them. Cities grew and flourished because of private enterprise and civic pride; it is private enterprise, backed by helpful, direct and concerted government action, that will renew them (Patten 1987).

One observer noted that the government considered 'privatising practically everything that is run by the State short of the Falklands Task Force' (Keegan 1982). Urban policy was no exception.

The perception is widely shared in Britain that the cities are in trouble because of the country's declining economic fortunes and that to rebuild them one must first address the larger economic question. Even the prestigious Town and Country Planning Association, long an advocate of government control over land development, has come to the conclusion that trying to prevent the forces of decentralization at work in Britain's metropolitan areas is futile and costly. Instead, the government should support private enterprise in its move to decentralize (Heidenheimer *et al.* 1983: 224–5).

The main factors of urban change—land, housing, and local services—all were targeted for privatization. Enterprise Zones, financial assistance to private developers, the removal of planning restrictions on development activity, the release of public land holdings, and the sale of public housing and other public assets were proposed and pursued in order to change the post-war balance of public–private responsibilities. The central theme was that 'top priority must be given to economic regeneration and environmental improvements, either directly linked to private sector investment . . . or aimed at creating the conditions in which the private sector and private individuals will invest' (Environment Committee 1983: 27). Jeffrey Jacobs reports that:

Since 1979, government policy in running the Urban Programme had been increasingly turning towards economic regeneration and, in particular trying to bring public

and private sectors together to secure that objective . . . Initiatives . . . were aimed at
. . . bringing the private sector back into inner cities and of using public money to
lever greater private investment (Jacobs 1985: 191).

The direction of Conservative urban policy was in fundamental accord
with the tradition of privatism; it was 'clearly rooted in the firm belief that a
thriving private sector will eventually stimulate the economic expansion of
cities' (Lawless 1981: 174). Michael Heseltine, former Secretary of State for
the Environment and one of the chief architects of the privatization of
British urban policy, proclaimed with obvious satisfaction that by 1983 the
privatization of urban change was already becoming a reality.

I believe it is now self-evident that on a very exciting scale the private sector is being
persuaded and 'incentivised' to come back into urban programmes . . . the private
sector is now willing to be involved and is prepared to provide very substantial
financial support in pursuit of profits in urban areas, providing the mechanisms for
evolving them are developed . . . (Heseltine 1983: 13).

Privatism and the Transatlantic Transfer

The similarities in urban policy rhetoric and programs in the US and Britain
in the 1980s were extensions of parallels in British and American urban
policies over the previous forty years. In the post-war era both countries
launched major efforts directed towards the physical redevelopment of cities.
Later, policies focused on comprehensive programs to address the multi-
faceted problems of social deprivation among the urban poor. These parallels
have not been accidental. The economic, political, and social changes
influencing patterns of urban development and decline in industrialized
nations affected urban areas on both sides of the Atlantic. Both countries
experienced the diffusion of urban growth outward from central cities, the
deterioration of central city infrastructure, the inadequacies of urban and
suburban housing stock, and poverty as a chronic problem of inner-city
areas.
    Clearly there was some direct transfer of ideas and experiments to address
or redress these conditions. For example, in commenting on the origins of the
British Community Development Projects, A. H. Halsey wrote of 'ideas drift-
ing casually across the Atlantic, soggy on arrival and of dubious utility'
(Halsey 1973), and similarly Peter Marris criticized the Americans for
handing on an idea, the Community Action Program, with which they were
already largely disillusioned (Marris 1987: 15). Urlan Wannop observed that
'since the late 1960s, it has been possible to see a broadening stream of
methods of urban planning and of urban policy initiatives flowing from the
United States to the United Kingdom, running between political and
administrative environments divided by more than a common language'
(Wannop 1985: 176). In a wider frame of reference that incorporates British
influence on American planning concepts and policies, the transatlantic

traffic has been two-way. 'There has always been a close link between US and British planning,' argues Charles Haar; 'not only in the United States' adoption of British statutes and judicial opinions, the powerful impact of Blackstone's commentaries on US notions of property, and the common heritage of the laws of nuisance and waste, but also in more recent developments in urban design, master planning, and citizen participation' (Haar 1984: p.xiii).

Despite some dissatisfaction with the results of earlier transfers, the exchange of urban policy concepts and experiments has continued and no doubt contributed to similarities in American and British urban policy initiatives in the 1970s and 1980s. Wannop has argued that 'many of the urban policy initiatives we have been taking in the United Kingdom since the early 1970s have so considerably borrowed from initiatives taken earlier in the United States' (Wannop 1985: 176–7). Indeed, he points out that the ways in which many developments in urban policy have been managed and financed, as well as the objectives they have been intended to pursue, 'tend towards older United States styles rather than to those we have been more accustomed to in Britain over the past period of 30 years or so' (Wannop 1985: 177).

For the most part, interest in policy transfer throughout the 1980s sharply focused on initiatives to induce or cajole private institutions into a more active role in urban areas. With few exceptions, notably urban Enterprise Zones, attention focused on transfers from the US to Britain reflecting, on the one hand, the predominant direction of transfer over the previous forty years and, on the other, the longer and more continuous US policy experience with stimulating private sector involvement in urban development. In 1980, for example, leading members of the British government, senior civil servants, and representatives from industry met in Britain with counterparts from the United States to review recent American experience with corporate social responsibility in urban affairs. The occasion for the meeting was the confluence of forces shaping the political economy of urban change in both countries and the similar policy orientations towards such change.

The unmistakable enthusiasm for private sector involvement in urban development on both sides of the Atlantic created a heavy traffic of 'salesmen' from American arriving in Britain to portray the superior virtues of a market way of urban life and to help unlock the mysteries of effective local development marketing strategies. Even the language of urban policy was shared: public–private partnerships, Enterprise Zones, privatization, leverage, urban development grants, and corporate social responsibility. After Mrs. Thatcher's election for a third term in 1987, this transatlantic traffic reached new levels. Senior ministers were ushered to the United States to learn more about the 'successes' of business involvement in urban affairs in areas as disparate as industrial regeneration, education, and 'workfare'. Impressed by the US model of corporate responsibility, Mrs. Thatcher played host to the launching of the British equivalent of the US 'Per Cent Club', where corporate members pledge to contribute a portion of pre-tax profits to the community. Even the Prince of Wales joined the mobile sales force. Shortly after his return from a trip to Pittsburgh, he extolled the virtues of corporate social responsibility in his capacity as president of Business in the Community (BIC). At a meeting of US and British business leaders, jointly sponsored by BIC and the US Presidential Office of Private Sector Initiative, the Prince proposed that 'for those who take the decision to invest in the regeneration of communities . . . there are big opportunities there, I can assure you' (*Guardian*, 4 May 1988). In urban affairs at least, the British maxim for the 1980s appeared to be, 'Follow America and all will come right' (Watkins 1988).

Evaluating Privatism

Government efforts to enlarge the role of the private sector have stimulated general debate about the benefits of privatism but, to a significant extent, the initiative has been taken by advocates of privatism who have rehearsed and rehashed ideological doctrines with little substantive analysis of the strengths and weaknesses of efforts to privatize public policy. In urban policy, the promotion of privatism often has been subjected to even less critical assessment than in other policy areas. For advocates, the merits of privatism as a framework for urban policy are a given. The focus of policy attention has been confined to the question of how the private city may be most effectively promoted.

Substantial effort has been devoted to selling the virtues of the private city in the US and Britain but despite the complementarity of political rhetoric and program initiative in the 1980s, the conclusion that the pursuit of the private city has the same meaning and implications in Britain and the United States is unwarranted without a thorough examination of the similarities and differences in the content of urban policy. Furthermore, policy orientations in the 1980s need to be evaluated against the background of earlier urban policy traditions and very different political and institutional frameworks for the formulation and delivery of urban policy.

This book examines and evaluates the relationship of privatism to urban policy in the United States and Britain. It considers how urban policy has been designed to promote privatism and what similarities and differences exist in this endeavor between the two countries. Considerable attention is devoted to examining the pursuit of privatism by conservative governments in the 1980s but the objective here is broader than to provide a review of privatism's influence during specific governmental tenures. We are concerned with evaluating the strengths and weaknesses of efforts to privatize urban policy and with assessing the impacts of privatism upon cities and citizens in Britain and the United States.

In pursuing this objective we recognize that the influence of privatism on urban policy and on cities in the United States and Britain cannot be understood apart from the institutional conditions which define the political economies of both countries, or separate from the balance of power between central and local government. There is a rich analytic, theoretical, and critical literature that has addressed these underlying structural conditions: the intersection of public and private authority in decision making and policy and the institutionalized patterns of urban development (Pahl 1975; Molotch 1976; Barnekov and Rich 1976; Saunders 1979; Mollenkopf 1983; Fainstein *et al.* 1986; Stone and Sanders 1987*a*; Cummings 1988; Judd 1988; Molotch 1988); the political and economic arrangements and conflicts that structure relationships between the national state, the local community, and the urban system (Castells 1977, 1978; Clark and Dear 1984; Gurr and King 1987); and the dynamics of political and economic power that operate within the local state and between the central state and local community (Cockburn 1977; Dunleavy 1981; Saunders 1986; Duncan and Goodwin 1988). Our evaluation of privatism has been informed by this general theoretical dialogue on the urban question. Our central concern is more focused, however, and substantially less ambitious than the efforts to forge a viable conception of the urban system as a whole or even to provide a comprehensive framework for assessment of central–local relations. In this respect, we do not deal at great length with analysis of the institutional conditions which give rise to privatism or which sustain it as a cultural tradition. Our attention is on the expression of that tradition through policy and with the impacts of policy on urban areas and their residents.

We concentrate our analysis on three related dimensions of privatism that have been central to urban policy development and implementation in both countries. Privatism is used as an instrument of urban policy, a strategy of urban regeneration, and a standard of community performance. As an instrument of urban policy, privatism encourages a reliance on the private sector as the principal agent of urban change and promotes a greater involvement of private institutions in the formulation and implementation of policies for cities. As a strategy of urban regeneration, privatism ties the fortunes of cities to the vitality of their private sectors and concentrates community attention and resources on economic development and private investment. As a community standard, privatism establishes market efficiency as the criterion for judging the appropriateness of any action, public or private.

Each of these dimensions raises important issues that need to be addressed in evaluating the strengths and weaknesses of efforts to privatize urban policy. What are the types and distribution of costs and benefits that result from a reliance on privatism as an instrument of urban policy? When privatism is pursued as a strategy of urban regeneration, does it enhance opportunities for the development of urban communities in general and distressed cities in particular? What are the impacts on urban governance when privatism is adopted as a community standard? And when governments adopt privatism as a national policy standard, what are the long-term implications for the process of urban change and for the role of cities in the national political economy? These questions form the guideposts for our analysis.

Our analysis begins with a consideration of the historical influence of privatism on urban development in the United States and Britain. We consider the traditions of urban privatism in Britain and America and point to important differences in the urban policy traditions of the two countries. We then turn to the American experience with privatism. Precisely because privatism has been a consistent feature of US urban policy, the American experience is instructive of the consequences that can be expected from a dedicated pursuit of the private city. In assessing these consequences we consider the role of the private sector in urban redevelopment in the immediate post-war period and review the influence of privatism on policy responses to the urban crisis of the 1960s. The roots of what may be called the 'new privatism' in US urban policy pre-date the Reagan administration. These roots are traced to a shift in the environment of urban policy and politics in the 1970s; a movement away from the social policy concerns of the 1960s and an increasing focus of both national and local attention on issues of urban economic growth. But, while the roots of the 'new privatism' may be traced to the 1970s, it is nonetheless true that it was the Reagan administration which most enthusiastically embraced the private city and promoted an urban policy framework intended to fully accommodate market-driven spatial and economic reconfigurations. We demonstrate that much of what was proposed in the pursuit of the private city had been proposed before, if not always with the same level of ideological consistency and zeal. What was new were the objectives of privatism and the prevailing view of the role of cities in the national economy. The overriding purpose of the 'new privatism' was not the regeneration of cities but rather the adaptation of the urban landscape to the spatial requirements of a post-industrial economy.

Our review of urban policy in Britain begins with a discussion of the policy redirection that took place in the 1970s. We suggest that the enthusiasm for privatism emerged before the election of the Thatcher Government in 1979 and was supported by an extensive critique of traditional, welfare-based, urban policy. Inner-city policy evolved from a concern with the social problems of the city to a concentration on economic development and this evolution set the stage for the Thatcher Government's efforts to redesign urban policy to accord more closely with a free-market philosophy of governance. At the center of the government's efforts was a commitment to deregulation of economic activity, selective dismantling of the public planning machinery, and increased reliance on market institutions and central agencies sympathetic to commercial interests. In acting upon these commitments, there was a consistent interplay between the strategy of privatization and the urban policy emphasis on economic regeneration. This interplay was accompanied by a centralization of urban policy oversight and initiative and a sustained effort by the Thatcher Government to remove, or at least dramatically reduce, the powers of local government. In this context we examine the meaning and implications of the new arrangements for public–private partnership that were promoted by the government to transform Britain's ailing urban areas.

We conclude our analysis with an overall assessment of the strengths and weaknesses of privatism as an instrument of urban policy, a strategy of urban regeneration and a standard of community performance. We argue that the influence of privatism on urban policy is the result of political choice expressed through public decisions and public actions and that the political character of privatism needs to be evaluated against alternative standards of community performance.

2

Urban Policy Traditions in the United States and Britain

IN both the US and Britain privatization policies are often portrayed as measures to counteract government pre-emption of private initiative. Rarely are these policies evaluated with reference to the role that privatism traditionally has played in American or British urban development or on the basis of what can be learned from that experience. Unfortunately, history is generally ignored in contemporary discussions of urban policy.

Profiles of the traditions of urban privatism in the US and Britain are subject to the danger of over-simplification and the temptation to translate diverse and complex urban experiences into one-dimensional historical summaries. Some of these tendencies are unavoidable short of a comprehensive urban history of Britain and America. It is not our intention to present such an account here but rather to identify aspects of urban history and political culture that help us understand the role of privatism in urban development and urban policy in each nation. Recognizing that historians and theorists disagree about how to interpret urban history, we believe, nonetheless, that proposals for privatization are expressions of long and enduring urban traditions in both countries. The meaning and implications of the search for the private city should be understood in the context of earlier experiences with urban privatism in Britain and America.

The Private City in America

Sam Bass Warner, Jr. has said that privatism is the 'quality which above all else' characterizes America's 'urban inheritance' (Warner 1987: 202). Private institutions have played the dominant role in urban change, and private decisions have largely determined the pattern of American urban development. The tradition of privatism has meant that community performance is judged primarily by a standard of economic productivity.

City-Building and the Economic Calculus of Value

American cities developed first and foremost as economic entities. Their location, activities, and their very existence most often were a function of economic factors. In Europe, 'cities were proverbially the centers of institutions,' writes Daniel Boorstin, 'where records were kept and the past was chronicled, hallowed and enshrined. They were sites of palaces, cathedrals, libraries, archives, and great monuments of all kinds' (Boorstin 1967: 121).

14

By contrast, Americans have perceived their cities as places with no history, emerging in an environment 'free of vested interests, guilds, skills, and "No Trespassing" signs' (Boorstin 1967: 121). The image of America as an urban wilderness has not been confined to the early period of American history; rather, it has been a persistent feature of a distinctively American outlook towards urban life. Though they are predominantly an urban people, Americans have refused to accept the city as their home.[1]

Entrepreneurs were the true American 'frontiersmen'. They urbanized new regions and stimulated the growth and expansion of existing urban centers (Wade 1959). In the early nineteenth century, there was broad public support for their efforts to stimulate municipal growth. On the eastern seaboard, entrepreneurs formulated complex and expensive schemes for transportation networks that would give one city or another an advantage over its rivals (Goodrich 1960). The necessary public financing and legislative sanction were justified by claims that these schemes would enhance the general well-being of the community (McKelvey 1963: 7; Livingood 1947). A railroad or canal was desired 'not just by this or that group of aggressive Baltimore or Philadelphia businessmen but by "Baltimore" or "Philadelphia" ' (Glaab and Brown 1976: 36). When New York City penetrated the West by building the Erie Canal, costly canal projects were launched by Philadelphia and the state of Pennsylvania and later by other cities seeking to establish dominant positions within their trading areas (Kantor 1987: 499).

Municipal mercantilism and urban rivalry also shaped the development of the cities of the interior and the West. These communities were founded as speculative enterprises and, as such, did not just grow—they were promoted. They owed their initial success to commerce and their growth stemmed from commercial expansion (Wade 1958: 16; Kantor 1987). 'The promotional activities of the original speculator-founders', wrote Bayrd Still, 'were only the beginning of a long-time program in which newspaper editors, merchants, and citizens at large combined their efforts to attract settlers and business to a given city and away from its neighboring rivals' (Still 1941: 197).

The dominance of privatism ensured that the institutions of the city were directed towards the enrichment and expansion of the local economy. In early nineteenth-century cities, the institutions of government were only minimally developed, and for the most part these cities were hardly governed at all. In Philadelphia, 'most streets went unpaved', notes Warner; 'the public wharves little repaired. There were no public schools, no public water, and at best a thin charity' (Warner 1987: 10). The wealthy made their own arrangements for police and fire protection, contributing money to buy water-pumping equipment for volunteer fire companies and establishing common funds to pay for night-time police protection. While a few larger cities developed publicly financed systems for police, fire protection, and other services, reliance on the private provision of services was typical for most municipalities. By the end of the nineteenth century, the pressures of industrial expansion and urban population growth forced most large municipalities to provide a broad array of publicly supported services. Even so, the

United States lagged behind other urbanized nations, notably Britain, in public financing of municipal services. Indeed, it was not until the last two decades of the nineteenth century that most American cities were policed. By contrast, Britain had regular police patrols in both rural and urban places by the mid-nineteenth century (Monkkonen 1985: 442). Private involvement in local service delivery has remained a distinctive feature of twentieth-century American cities despite the substantial growth in municipal services. 'Do-it-yourself government', says Norton Long, 'has a long history in the United States' (Long 1967: 247). Contemporary calls for the privatization of muni-cipal functions ranging from snow removal, to fire protection, to social services, even to prisons, need to be understood in the context of a tradition that, in the broad historical perspective, was only briefly, and never entirely, supplanted by the public delivery of municipal services.

The tradition of privatism has meant that the politics of American cities depended for its actors and for a good deal of its subject-matter 'on the changing focus of men's private economic activities' (Warner 1987: 4). Throughout the nineteenth century and well into the twentieth century, the influence of businessmen in civic affairs was unequalled and usually decisive. Leading businessmen frequently viewed the local community as an exten-sion of their personal commercial interests and sought to 'fuse themselves and their destiny with that of their community' (Boorstin 1967: 121). William Ogden, a wealthy land speculator and the first mayor of Chicago, recognized, as one of his fellow businessmen observed, 'that everything which benefitted Chicago, or built up the great West, benefitted him' (Boorstin 1967: 117). As a result there was hardly a public improvement in which Ogden and his private capital did not play a leading role. Similarly, during periods of industrial growth, businessmen often viewed themselves, and were viewed by others, as builders of communities 'where personal and public growth, personal and public prosperity intermingled' (Boorstin 1967: 119).

For much of the nineteenth century, governmental authority at the local level remained diffuse. The exercise of local authority was largely channelled to growth-promoting activities, and local business leaders, particularly mer-chants, generally occupied the key community positions which defined the meaning and direction of growth (Dahl 1961; Schulze 1961; McKelvey 1963; Kantor 1987). Business dominance of local affairs remained largely unchallenged throughout the nineteenth century. Despite basic changes in the American political economy, city council lists read 'like the local business directory' (Wade 1959: 78).

Throughout the period of rapid industrialization, city-building remained largely an economic enterprise. Indeed, the principal function of the industrial city was to serve as a vehicle of economic expansion. The complementarity of industrial technology and urban form was so extensive that the phenomena of industrialization and urbanization were virtually indistinguishable. In the late nineteenth century, 'the actual physical building of cities supplied a fundamental generative factor in the growth of the economy' (Glaab and Brown 1976: 136). The leadership of this growth came to rest with those who represented the large corporation, the institution that symbolized the new industrial order.

Rationalizing the City in the New Industrial Order

By the latter part of the nineteenth century, the changes brought about by rapid industrialization created pressures for a redefinition of the meaning of privatism. The doctrines of *laissez-faire* no longer provided an adequate rationale for the structure and operations of the new industrial order and specifically for the increasing concentration of economic wealth and power in large-scale corporations. The accumulating pressures of industrialization—class divisions, labor strife, unemployment, intense competition and fluctuating profits, and the human misery that accompanied the concentration of the poor in large cities—made some form of community action inescapable. In the five decades from 1890 to 1939, government involvement in economic affairs increased enormously. While it often appeared that this activity was directed against the private sector—attacks on monopolies and trusts and efforts to ameliorate the hardships experienced by low-income groups—the appearance is misleading: few government reforms were enacted without at least the tacit approval, if not the guidance, of the leaders of large corporations. At the national level, corporate leaders played a direct role in fostering a major change in the functions of the American state by promoting federal regulation of the economy—regulation that was supported by serious reformers but 'was invariably controlled by the leaders of the regulated industry towards ends they deemed acceptable or desirable' (Kolko 1963: 3). Government intervention in economic matters served to protect the large corporations from 'irresponsible business conduct and to assure stability in marketing and financial affairs' (Long 1960: 202).

A new conception of privatism emerged which accepted the need to expand the scope of state activity but retained the essence of the earlier tradition by conceiving of state activity as necessary to fulfill the needs of the private marketplace and to protect established interests against change. Government intervention provided stability, order, and predictability in the economic environment so that the private sector could continue to function efficiently without undue risk. In part, corporate leaders recognized that the nature and scope of business enterprise in the new industrial order required an activist and 'positive' state that could intervene to stabilize the marketplace and provide the services needed for the operation of geographically dispersed business operations.

Efforts to utilize the powers of the public sector to create an environment that was conducive to the efficient and profitable operation of large-scale enterprise occurred first at the local level. As a result of the expanded geographical scope of business affairs, some businessmen promoted the creation of local political structures that would centralize the processes of local decision making and respond more effectively to the needs of large corporations.

These efforts to reform local governmental structures occurred in many American cities beginning in the last decade of the nineteenth century. They were stimulated by the development of a form of local government that was not consistent with the needs of large-scale business enterprise.

The tradition of privatism left the American city without institutions capable of alleviating the problems of persistent and pervasive poverty that resulted from industrialization and rapid urbanization. To fill this vacuum, political bosses and party organizations in the big cities provided the expanding urban proletariat with services and a level of responsiveness which were not available from the formal structures of local government (Judd 1979: 52–5). These included jobs, emergency aid to the needy, protection from conflicts with the police, and a wide range of informal social services. This system, known as 'machine politics', maximized representation of neighborhoods. City councilmen and party leaders spoke for their local areas, defending the economic interests, residential concerns, and those educational, recreational, and religious perspectives that mattered most to the constituencies they represented. It was a decentralized system of political life based on an organizational style that concerned itself largely with local and particular interests rather than with the substantive problems of the city as a whole.

The relationship between the political machine system and the business community was complex. On the one hand, there was uneasiness among the older business groups who found themselves circumvented in the making of basic economic and political decisions. The older merchant and manufacturing class was 'less important and they knew it' (Hofstadter 1955: 137). On the other hand, some businessmen found the machine acceptable and, in fact, profited from the provision of municipal services and facilities to meet the needs of a growing urban population. Local government, even under the rule of political party bosses, depended upon the private sector to construct new streets, develop new transportation systems, and build bridges, sewers, water systems, power plants, and energy transmission networks. Despite the benefits that the machine provided for some businessmen, the system of machine rule was not organized to be responsive to growing business institutions which required a political environment that was reliable and predictable and delivered services on a scale that matched the scope of their expanding markets. As a result, business leaders were often in the forefront of the initiatives for municipal reform that sought to replace urban political machines with 'apolitical' systems of city government; systems guided by principles of civic efficiency which could provide a range of services more responsive to the needs of economic enterprises that increasingly were city-wide or regional in scope.

The business leaders active in promoting a more 'businesslike' municipal government represented the emerging industrial, manufacturing, and retail corporations which had 'come to dominate the city's economic life' (Hays 1964: 160). These business leaders were all involved in the rationalization and systematization of modern life; they wished a form of government which would be more consistent with the objectives inherent in those developments. The most important single feature of their perspective was the rapid expansion of the geographical scope of affairs which they wished to influence and manipulate, a scope which was no longer limited and narrow, no longer within the confines of pedestrian communities, but was now broad and city-wide, covering the whole range of activities of the metropolitan area (Hays 1964: 161).

The American municipal reform movement was an attempt to adjust the range and functions of public institutions to the enlarged domain and emerging needs of new industrial enterprises central to continued economic development. It was 'an effort by leading members of the business community to bring order, stability, and predictability to the competitive chaos of the emerging industrial order' (Greenberg 1974: 88).

The ideas of the reform era—rationalization of the scope, scale, and functions of municipal services and promotion of a more businesslike mode of urban government—are themes that recur in American urban politics and policy throughout the twentieth century. Indeed, Richard Hofstadter defined the age of reform as the period running from about 1890 to World War II (Hofstadter 1955: 3). In fact, reform ideas have continued to influence urban politics and policy throughout the post-war period. The movement to create metropolitan governments and regional service areas in the 1950s, for example, was an attempt to match the boundaries of public service institutions to the spatial dispersion of economic activity and population. Similarly, there have been continuing efforts to invoke the model of the business corporation as the ideal for rational city government. The enthusiasm for the city manager movement was only the first of periodic calls for the use of business management techniques to run the municipal enterprise in a manner that would exhibit the same efficiency and professionalism attributed to commercial enterprise. In the 1960s the Rand Corporation and others spent considerable resources to instruct cities like New York on how they could use the techniques of systems management to deliver basic services and so emulate the purported efficiencies of the aerospace corporations. In the 1970s, cities faced with diminishing revenues and growing service obligations were encouraged by both public and private officials to learn how to live within their means by adopting business methods for cost containment. Calls for the privatization of local government services in the 1980s represent another expression of faith in the capacities and efficiencies of the private sector. The era of reform has left an enduring imprint on the politics and policy of urban America—it is the image of the city as a commercial establishment.

The City, the Corporation, and Social Responsibility

The efforts to rationalize city government and city politics by no means resolved the question of the appropriate relationship between major economic institutions and the communities in which they operated. Throughout the twentieth century this relationship continued to evolve, sometimes in seemingly contradictory manners. On the one hand, changes in political economy associated with the increasing mobility of economic activity diminished the dependence of the corporation on the local community and ultimately created an incentive for business to abandon any urban site that did not provide a sufficiently favorable environment. On the other hand, the growth of corporate power created pressures for greater business account- ability and stimulated claims, often by corporate leaders themselves, that they must accept wider social responsibility by taking a more active role in ameliorating the social impacts of the economic changes they often initiated.

The disengagement of large corporate enterprises from community affairs was first evident when the expansion of commercial markets combined with growth in the size of business corporations brought about an increase in absentee ownership. The emergence of institutions which were regional and national in scope meant that the city was less important to business leaders, and in response they abandoned its politics. Their local involvements became more selective and focused on specific issues of direct economic interest. The manager of an absentee-owned corporation viewed the city very differently from the owner of a local enterprise.

He was far less dependent on local sales or real estate values and thus less concerned with growth itself. His was a contingent investment in the community . . . His partici- pation in the allocation of community resources, while potentially great was infre- quent and discontinuous. He was concerned only to protect his relatively narrowly defined corporate interests, not a generalized pattern of influence (Salisbury 1964: 781).

To understand the impact of absentee ownership on businessmen's partic- ipation in local affairs, it is necessary to distinguish between civic participation and community power. While it may be true that the managers of absentee- owned firms withdrew from associational involvements and from shoul- dering the burdens of political office, it does not follow that there was a decline in the ability of the corporation to influence community affairs. Indeed, the corporation had to be involved in community affairs to protect its investment. The influence of the corporation in the community does not derive from formal participation of corporate leaders in politics but 'from the fact that [it] controls valued and scarce resources, mobilizes large numbers of people, and provides them with income' (Mott 1970: 172).

Between 1880 and 1940, the locus of power in American communities often appeared to be bifurcated between political and economic élites. Busi- nessmen in this period were less likely to maintain a continuous and general- ized interest in community affairs than they had in earlier periods. While some local business leaders played an active role in the civic reform move- ment, the general pattern of business participation in local affairs was special- ized, and this was often especially true of the managers of the emerging absentee-owned corporations, whose activities were directed primarily towards influencing public policy that affected the specific economic interests of their enterprises. The more selective focus of the new corporate business leaders with regard to issues of local politics did not diminish the power of their institutions within the civic political economy or limit their capacity to induce local governments to rearrange parts of the social structure as a condition of their continued operation within the municipal boundaries.

The mobility of economic activity and an attendant shift in population and demographics contributed to a pattern of urban deconcentration throughout much of the twentieth century. This pattern has fundamentally altered the shape of the urban landscape and has created in its wake some of the most serious problems faced by American cities and, indeed, cities throughout the world. Dislocations initially created by metropolitan decentralization from the central cities to the suburbs were subsequently followed by major regional shifts most notably from the industrial cities of the frostbelt to the newer urban areas of the sunbelt and further by international realignments made possible by the growing mobility of production systems and markets. The out-migration of business enterprises in search of more favorable economic climates left many cities without a viable economic base and stimulated the decline of older industrial centers. More recently, the mobility of economic activity has become the catalyst for a new era of municipal mercantilism which ties the prosperity of municipalities to their ability to compete with other areas in attracting and keeping business capital. Mobile capital and footloose corporations have broken the bond between business institutions and the city that was forged throughout the period of industrialization. How much can cities rely on the private sector as major instruments of urban regeneration when major corporate institutions no longer have a rationale for sustained responsibility to particular urban places? In this context the influence of privatism on urban development has generated new issues for urban policy at both the local and national level in the mid- and late-twentieth century. These issues center on concerns about keeping and attracting business investment in central city areas and enlisting business participation in urban redevelopment. What must a local, or for that matter a national urban policy, offer to generate active business involvement in efforts at civic revitalization?

While the increasing mobility of economic activity weakened the attachment of business institutions to the communities in which they operated, other changes in political economy have acted as countervailing forces that strengthened that attachment. The growth of corporate capitalism has given rise to efforts to redefine the meaning of privatism to accommodate and justify the growing power of corporate institutions and to match that power with an equivalent scope of responsibility. Throughout the mid-twentieth century business leaders have preached a gospel of social responsibility that sought to define the corporation as an institution with community-wide interests—one that could be relied upon to act voluntarily in the service of a broad social constituency and that, acting alone or in partnership with public institutions, would seek out ways to address community concerns.

The idea that corporations have a social responsibility was in part a response to the recognition that the economic power of the modern corporation could not be effectively justified by the classical doctrine of the business firm as a private-property institution. The modern corporation is an entity which does not remotely correspond either to the old legal model of proprietorship or to the economic model of the atomistic firm in the competitive market (McKie 1974: 27). Indeed, the corporation exhibits few of the historic features of traditional capitalism so that the older rubrics 'no longer furnished an adequate intellectual system for explaining the social consequences of business activities' (Frederic 1960: 55). With the rise of the corporation the atom of property has been split and the integrity of property ownership has thereby been undermined. Indeed, in most cases, ownership is a legal fiction—the corporation remains a private enterprise institution, but it is no longer a private-property institution (Berle and Means 1932; Bell 1971). Control rests with a new class of professional managers. If it is no longer possible to justify responsiveness to only one constituency—the owners—then what interests are legitimate and how are these interests to be balanced?

Such questions focus on what Richard Eells called the 'constitutional crisis in the corporation' (Eells 1962: 16). The idea of corporate social responsibility is clearly intended as a means of addressing, or perhaps more accurately, circumventing that crisis. It is an attempt to 'seek legitimacy, to gain sovereign approval of an awkward, if bountiful, *de facto* status that is a natural by-product of big corporations with dispersed stock ownership' (Cheit 1964: 8). In the absence of a new justification, corporate economic power is vulnerable to political challenge, and there is the danger that dissatisfaction with the performance of the social and economic system will focus upon the corporation as the most visible institution other than government. It is only realistic then for the new managers of business enterprise 'to understand that they must assume some responsibilities just because the corporations are there, because large corporations are such prominent features of the social landscape and have control over such a large aggregation of resources and managerial talent' (McKie 1974: 31).

Corporate social responsibility also represents an attempt to find a new and viable rationale for the complex relationships of interdependence which evolved between corporate institutions and the public sector in the twentieth century. The rise of the activist state and its acceptance of responsibility to stabilize the economic system were instrumental to the growth of corporate capitalism. At the same time, the acceptance of such activism made it more difficult to argue that the state should not also intervene in a widening variety of social and economic domains that were traditionally left to the private sector or that the state should not regulate corporate power and wealth to achieve the goals of social and economic stability. Corporate social responsibility is an attempt by businessmen to constrain the scope of government economic regulation and to ensure their own participation in shaping the economic and social order. If society accepts the need to engage in collective efforts to resolve public problems, some business leaders argued that it is better for business to act voluntarily to lead these efforts or to form a partnership with government than to run the risk of having programs and policies put forth that are antithetical to the basic interests of the business community.

In the context of urban affairs, the impact of corporate social responsibility was slow in materializing. Definition of the sphere of community responsibility of the business firm remained quite limited until after World War II.[2] The managers of large firms accepted a broader conception of their responsibilities to society in the 1920s than their counterparts in the 1890s, but the issues of minority rights, consumerism, and the environment, as aspects of business responsibility, remained unexamined (McKie 1974: 27). For the most part, businessmen confined themselves to community service, manifested by extensive participation in community charities and voluntary social service associations. Nevertheless, this represented a change from the traditional involvement of individual businessmen in personal charity and philanthropy (M. Heald 1970). A slowly emerging model of corporate citizensip was being promoted which led to the contribution of company funds as well as the services of business executives to efforts directed towards community service. But the activities followed no consistent organizational or policy direction.

By the mid-1950s, testimonials to corporate responsibility had become so common that Peter Drucker chided American businessmen: 'you might wonder, if you were a conscientious newspaper reader, when the managers of American business had any time for business' (Drucker 1954: 67). Essentially, the main current of this thought was that businessmen would voluntarily act as trustees of the community interest, that what was good for business would be congruent with the welfare of the community and, therefore, they should be relied upon to exercise leadership in urban development and in addressing community problems. The rhetoric of corporate social responsibility often exceeded its performance. Even so, corporate social responsibility became the rallying cry for a new style of privatism. In the decades following World War II, urban policy at both the local and national levels was most often guided by an expectation that the solution to urban problems lay in mobilizing the power, wealth, and managerial skills of American corporations. This expectation resulted in continuing efforts to launch public–private partnerships for urban change and, at times, particularly in the late 1960s, led to a reliance on the corporation as a major social welfare institution—one that was able and willing to address the problems of urban distress and social deprivation. While the calls for corporate social responsibility have been persistent they have provided no credible resolution of the evolving relationship between large business corporations and the cities in which they reside. The mobility of economic activity has intensified and the scope of modern business enterprise has continued to transcend the boundaries of urban places. While the thrust of urban policy was to rely as fully as possible on the private sector as the agent of urban change and development, the operations of that sector were frequently bypassing those cities in most distress. Social responsibility, both public and private, might dictate active efforts at urban revitalization, but the primary calculus affecting the fortunes of cities was, as it had always been, economic. Under that calculus many cities were judged to be poor investment risks.

Privatism and the Context of Urban Policy

The modern American city is based on a non-regulatory and growth promoting model which developed in the mid-nineteenth century (Monkkonen 1985: 444). Its spatial form and many of its functional characteristics arose in response to the dynamics of an unregulated urban land market dominated by 'profit seeking builders, land speculators, and large investors' (Warner 1987: 4). In 1975 Robert Wood, former Secretary of Housing and Urban Development, wrote: 'the plain fact is that now as before, the main force in our process of urban development is the private land developer' (Wood 1975: 51). Private decisions have determined the principal features of the urban landscape: the patterns of residence, the characteristics of the housing stock, the nature and location of cultural, educational, and economic institutions, and the configuration of communications and transportation networks. The result has been the development of cities with two sides:

Their attractive side includes productive manufacturing, innovative service industries, striking architecture, and experimental programs on the frontiers of social policy. Their unattractive side features slum housing, grinding poverty, widespread crime and attendant social programs that seem unable to cope with people's needs and occasional disorder that threatens the political fabric (Sharkansky 1975: 71).

To a significant extent this bifurcated, dualistic character of American cities is a feature of urban life in many societies. In America, however, the contrasts have been especially acute and persistent and have resulted in large part from the mixed consequences of privatism. Privatism promoted the rapid growth of American cities as centers of productivity and wealth—cities that were often distinctive for the rate and scale of technological innovation and for their adaptability to changing economic priorities. At the same time, privatism meant that 'essentially American cities developed as money mining camps with the mentality characteristics of such camps: a sense of impermanence and an indifference to the despoiling of the environment' (Blumenfeld 1969: 141). When entrepreneurship succeeded, urban development flourished and local economies boomed. When the economic incentive was absent, urban development stagnated. An area's economic value was transient and largely determined by speculative potential. When such potential was exhausted, economic motivations dictated that it was prudent to move on to new opportunities at more advantageous sites. Moreover, the pre-eminence of economic over political institutions within local areas meant that when the market bypassed a city, there was often little in the way of local public authority to fill the void.

The dominance of privatism has sustained a system of American city governance in which public authority has remained diffuse. This has often meant that the functional politics of American cities—the politics of growth and development of the civic economy—lay outside of the domain and beyond the scope of the formal politics of municipal government. Norton Long has said that the emphasis on the city as an open economy contributed to its subordination as a polity (Long 1983). The exercise of public power has been restrained in the interests of economic growth. Diffuse local authority has allowed business institutions to periodically organize to fill the political vacuum and occasionally to operate as private governments—circumstances which have led to a long debate about the extent to which American communities are dominated by a power élite whose influence is concentrated among those who control major economic institutions. But the locus of influence within American cities may be less important than the more general subordination of local government to the demands of economic change. That subordination has contributed to a politics of limited commitment in what Scott Greer has described as communities of limited liability, where there is an absence of investment in the city as a whole, a vision of local identity as transient, and a regard for local political boundaries as impermanent, and often trivial (Greer 1962: 139).

The ease of adaptation to the increasing decentralization of economic activity and the continuing dispersal of metropolitan regions throughout the twentieth century is a testimony to the amorphous nature of local political commitments in America and the primacy of an economic calculus of value. Gerald Frug argues that this condition is not accidental—America has chosen 'to have powerless cities' and 'this choice has largely been made through legal doctrine' (Frug 1980: 1059–60). The powers of the municipal corporation have been consistently restrained by state and federal laws while, at the same time, the freedom of action of the business corporation has been broadly extended. Moreover, rather than being accepted as a political choice, the rejection of local power is conventionally understood as a necessary and desirable feature of modern life and an inevitable condition for a mobile, national economy.

In part as a response to the weaknesses of local government and the need to cope with the pressures of urbanization at a national scale, the federal government has become a more active participant in urban affairs over the last half century. Federal urban programs, from the New Deal legislation of the 1930s to the Great Society legislation of the 1960s, transformed the relationship between cities and the national government and, at times, created a dependency of cities on federal patronage. The emergence of explicit federal urban policies represented a belated recognition of the national importance of urban places—an environment in which more than two-thirds of the people resided. This in itself was a radical departure from earlier periods of US history in which the acknowledgement of urban America, much less its support, remained outside of the domain of accepted federal government responsibilities (Mark Gelfand 1975). Nevertheless, as we demonstrate in the following chapters, it would be wrong to conclude that the growth of federal activism signified a diminution in the importance of privatism for American urban development. While acknowledging the United States as an urban nation, and recognizing that a number of dimensions of urban life are truly national in scope and implications, there has been no sustained effort to use the powers of the federal government to displace the initiative of the private sector. Government intervention has been consistently directed towards stimulating and supporting private development activities. It has attempted to complement the processes of national economic change and create a stable environment for continued economic growth. In this process, the priorities and perspectives of the business community continue to determine the range of public actions that are feasible and desirable. The policy debate has focused on the style of privatism that should be pursued and on the objectives that it should serve.

Privatism and the Planning Response in Britain

Like America, Britain has had extensive familiarity with urban privatism. Unplanned, market-led urban growth was dominant until the early twentieth century, but following World War II the British government attempted to play a leading role in shaping urban change. British urban policy in the 1980s needs to be recognized, at a rhetorical level at least, as an attempt to break away from the planning regime that shaped urban Britain in the earlier post-war period. In some respects, the current pursuit of the private city in Britain symbolizes a repudiation of the recent past and a return to a much earlier tradition of private sector domination of urban development.

The Legacy of Privatism

From the second half of the eighteenth century onwards the growth and development of British towns was shaped by spatial and demographic changes induced by economic transformations accompanying industraliza-tion. The urban landscape largely reflected the uneven and frequency disorderly processes of economic expansion. Economic progress was irregular and investment in industrial plant and dwellings occurred spasmod-ically. 'Boom years and depressions followed each other in quick succession,' notes Gordon Cherry; and 'development took place piecemeal, both spatially as well as over time. There was no sustained logical pattern of building' (Cherry 1972: 4).

Yet, even during the early stages of the British Industrial Revolution, urban development was not fully left to the operation of unplanned economic forces. 'The inherited tradition of town building,' says Cherry, 'where towns developed to a conscious pattern or design, was a long one in this country, and never quite died out from the 13th century, the time of Edward I, onwards' (Cherry 1972: 4). Principles of estate development as well as com-prehensive planning and design gave character to a number of towns in Britain, even as the Industrial Revolution gathered momentum and created serious problems for the new manufacturing towns. The tradition of town building 'was never lost and extended into the nineteenth century to exist side by side with the result of the more usual, uncoordinated urban development of the day' (Cherry 1972: 4). Nonetheless, the impact of this tradition of town building was highly circumscribed in the industrial towns of the early nineteenth century. As, H. L. Beales points out, 'the industrial towns were willing to give their central areas a dignified façade, but not to deal with the poorer quarters' (Beales 1967: 83). There the speculative builder was left to deal with housing the constant influx of people as cheaply as possible. It was the speculative builder 'who rushed up houses in unpaved and undrained streets and courts: he had to crowd them together to make a profit at all, as rents were advancing rapidly. The time had not yet come for the establishment of a social code protective of that rather helpless body, the community' (Beales 1967: 84).

In the midst of a general pattern of neglect and indifference to the conditions of the working class in industrial towns, a few early industrialists experimented with planned urban communities. From Robert Owen's New Lanark in Scotland to Lord Lever's Port Sunlight on Merseyside, there are monuments—some museum pieces, some living entities—to planned town and estate development based on a vision of the beautiful, efficient, profitable, and morally wholesome city. These early examples of corporate enlightenment stemmed, in part, from a recognition of the harsh circumstances endured by the working class in the large industrial cities and a genuine desire to improve the quality of life in urban areas. Nevertheless, these motives were secondary to the overwhelming desire to improve industrial productivity, produce a compliant work-force, and control urban activities. The vision of harmony between profitable industry and urban improvement beyond the 'stinking cities' was at the heart of the Victorian Garden City Association, founded to promote Ebenezer Howard's utopian ideal of balanced new communities—based on ideas contained in his book, *Garden Cities of Tomorrow*, first published in 1898 (Howard 1965). The Association was instrumental in creating the first new towns at Letchworth (1904) and Welwyn (1920). These were essentially private residential ventures with little direct involvement by local governments and no initial public subsidy.

The Association expanded into the Town and Country Planning Association (TCPA). Throughout the inter-war years, the TCPA lobbied government to adopt Howard's principles and introduce a state program of new town construction principally as a means of relieving the housing problems of the larger industrial cities. Their efforts were rewarded in 1945 when the New Towns Act authorized the funding and construction of new communities throughout Britain. As of 1980, twenty-eight new towns had been built, providing a mix of public and private housing for more than two million people in England, Scotland, and Wales (TCPA 1980: 370–1). Despite their modest contribution to post-war housing and the mixed consequences of using new towns as agents of regional development, the British new towns remain a monument to the ambition and optimism of state planning and development that existed in the period immediately following World War II.

The countervailing, though by no means equally balanced, influences on urban development in Britain were readily apparent throughout the Victorian period. Asa Briggs aptly characterizes the Victorian city as a testimony to the difficulties of reconciling economic individualism with a concern for common civic purposes (Briggs 1963). For the most part, however, urban Britain in the Victorian period represented an instructive model of the successes and failures of *laissez-faire* ideals. Indeed, the idea of cities in the nineteenth century took shape through the new doctrines of political economy and competitive individualism. The controversy about cities largely centered on the strengths and limits of new economic doctrines—doctrines that were 'identified with the defence of the industrial towns, and the whole argument became entangled with questions of capitalist industrialism, competition and the factory system' (B. Coleman 1973: 5). Progressive images focused on the city of 'invention' and its proven instrumentality in the creation of new wealth, new culture, and expanded economic freedom. Critics, by contrast, pointed to the city as the most apparent symbol of the chaos and social decay brought about by industrial civilization and the callous indifference of its ruling class. According to Coleman:

The main case for the city became the assertion of the values of economic competition and social individualism, while opponents attacked such theories and practices as mere palliatives of the city's evils, if not the cause of them. . . . The case for the city's commercial civilization lay mainly in material achievement and aggregation; the critics rejected such criteria as pernicious or irrelevant and stressed less tangible matters of social relationships and pyschological conditions (B. Coleman 1973: 5, 7).

Despite a continuing undercurrent of social criticism and sporadic calls for social reform, the predominant pattern throughout the early and mid-Victorian years reflected the self-assurance of those who saw the city as a tangible achievement of economic progress. 'There was to be little or no outside interference with the economic and social processes which were shaping the cities,' continues Coleman. 'Even sanitary reform, which required the action of municipal goverment, left business enterprise substantially unregulated, imposed no alien ideal or authority upon urban society and did not call into question the totality of city civilization. The cities were to be left to work out their own salvation' (B. Coleman 1973: 9).

Similarly Briggs argues that 'the priority of industrial discipline in shaping all human relations was bound to make other aspects of life seem secondary,' and to result not only in 'a paucity of social investment but a total indifference to social costs' (Briggs 1963: 18). Others, like Mumford, are even less generous in their assessments of the primacy of economic values and argue that cities in the new industrial age were often no more than a 'fortuitous concourse of atoms . . . held together temporarily by motives of self-seeking and private profit' (Mumford 1961: 454). Capitalism, with its emphasis on speculation rather than on security and on profit-making institutions rather than on value-conserving traditions and continuities, 'tended to dismantle the whole structure of urban life and place it upon a new impersonal basis: money and profit' (Mumford 1961: 416). While denying that Victorian cities were the 'insensate' man-heaps and machine warrens characterized by Mumford, Briggs nonetheless acknowledges that the arguments for social reform of the Victorian city rested largely on the expectation that 'it would actually save money in the long run, not squander it' (Briggs 1963: 20).

Within the industrial cities of Britain, as within the industrial cities of the United States, civic leadérsip was heavily concentrated among business leaders. Just as in the United States, proprietors of large businesses appeared in the mid-Victorian period as the most numerous and most influential group among town councillors and their 'legitimacy rested firmly on their financial expertise, on their proven ability to "run a business" ' (Elliott and McCrone 1982: 69). Indeed, it appears that Victorian Britain was obsessed by a desire to ensure that the burgeoning cities would be managed by, in the words of E. P. Hennock, 'fit and proper persons' (Hennock 1973). The early Victorians, as he eloquently describes:

generally agreed that ideally town councillors possessed two or possibly three crucial characteristics. They were men of *station* or *respectability*, they were men of *substance* or *property* or *wealth*, and they were men of *intelligence* or *education*. They were never merely intelligent without being also men of station and substance. It was station or respectability that appeared on all occasions as the indispensable criterion, and it was substance or property that was most commonly linked with it (Hennock 1973: 308).

Throughout the Victorian period, civic philanthropy, industrial and commercial entrepreneurship, and an unbridled confidence in the natural synchronization of markets combined to produce a familiar urban landscape of social and physical contrasts. At the end of the period,

cities were confused and complicated, a patchwork of private properties, developed separately with little sense of common plan, a jumble of sites and buildings with few formal frontiers, a bewildering variety of heights and eye-levels, a profusion of noises and smells, a social disorder with districts of deprivation and ostentation, and every architectural style, past and present to add to the confusion (Briggs 1963: 22).

Yet, this was only one side of the picture. Throughout the Victorian period there was pérsistent pressure to control social change and there were frequent manifestations of genuine civic pride. Occasionally, as in the case of Joseph Chamberlain's leadership of Birmingham, there was also a belief in the capacity to transform civic pride into active and creative municipal government. As mayor in the 1870s, he was determined to put an end to neglect and misgovernment and initiated efforts to clear slum areas, adopt great housing schemes, acquire and develop gas and water systems, and provide parks and recreation facilities (Hammond 1935: 50).

The growth of industrial cities, and the social problems they engendered, were catalysts for the development of public health and housing policies in the late nineteenth century which were intended to redress some of the more obvious failures of the Victorian period. The experience with unplanned, market-driven urbanization during the nineteenth century stimulated the ideas of Ebenezer Howard, Patrick Geddes, Raymond Unwin, and others who responded to the depredations embodied in industrial cities by postulating the need for a new age of city-building in which human energies would be harnessed, in Geddes' phrase, 'towards house building and town planning, even towards city design; and all these upon a scale to rival—nay, surpass the past glories of history' (Geddes 1971: 71). Clawson and Hall observe that the ideas serving as foundations for British initiatives in planned urban develop-ment in the mid-twentieth century were laid down at the turn of the century and represented a direct response to the shortcomings of the Victorian period. Here 'was a physical evil, with a physical solution' (Clawson and Hall 1973: 33). At the same time, the improvement of sanitary engineering, the construction of urban infrastructure, and the provision of working-class hous-ing was a necessary stimulant to private property development as well as a means of improving the health—and the productivity—of the burgeoning urban proletariat.

A number of cities in late Victorian Britain developed a sophisticated array of public services, offering a range of facilities that the private sector failed to provide. Glasgow, at the turn of the century, the second largest city in Britain, was a case in point:

[In Glasgow a citizen] may live in a municipal house; he may walk along the municipal street, or ride on the municipal tramcar and watch the municipal dust cart collecting the refuse which is to be used to fertilise the municipal farm. Then he may turn into the municipal market, buy a steak from an animal killed in the municipal slaughterhouse, and cook it by the municipal gas stove. For his recreation he can choose amongst municipal libraries, municipal art galleries and municipal music in the municipal parks. Should he fall ill, he can ring his doctor up on the municipal telephone, or he may be taken to the municipal hospital in the municipal ambulance by a municipal policeman. Should he be so unfortunate to get on fire, he will be put out by a municipal fireman, using municipal water; after which he will, perhaps, forego the enjoyment of a municipal bath, though he may find it necessary to get a new suit in the municipal old clothes market (Smout 1986: 45, quoting from R. E. C. Lond 1903).

Public provision of gas, water, electricity, and transport introduced new standards of comfort, cleanliness, health, and mobility to the Victorian city (Robson 1935).[3] Much of this activity was based on local responses to local problems (Fraser 1979: 157) and ran in parallel with various national attempts to reform and standardize local government. Nonetheless, these local initiatives were to play an important role in strengthening local government in the twentieth century. So much so that the major national urban planning reforms of the 1944–7 period relied heavily on local government for the implementation of policy. Indeed, up until the 1970s city authorities were viewed as the natural agents for directing and controlling urban change.

The Rise of the Planning Regime

A principal objective of British urban policy in the twentieth century has been to use the instruments of planning to overcome the Victorian inheritance of unplanned and uneven urban development. 'What the private sector had constructed in the industrial revolution of the nineteenth century the state had to rebuild in the twentieth' (Cherry 1979: 296). The urban policy experience of Britain differs most dramatically from that of the US precisely because, in twentienth-century Britain, there has been a strong countervailing tradition of direct public involvement in the shaping of urban development. Haar notes that the British pioneered the planned development of cities while in the US 'planning powers, extensive as they have become, pale before the controls instituted in Britain' (Haar 1984: xii). Controlled land development regulated by public law began in 1909, and the scope of such law was expanded throughout the early twentieth century. It may be true, as Simmie suggests, that the institutional innovations in the first half of the twentieth century did not 'radically alter either the underlying conflicts in British society or the distribution of resources and power which generated this conflict' (Simmie 1974: 74). Nonetheless, the extent and range of the vision of planned urban development in twentieth-century Britain is without parallel in the United States and constitutes as well a sharp contrast with the earlier Victorian allegiance to *laissez-faire* ideals.

While many of the innovations that now distinguish British planning were formulated in the inter-war period, it was not until the post-World-War-II era that a consensus emerged around the idea of planned urban growth. According to Checkland, the state, since 1945, 'accepted a range of responsibilities unthinkable in the nineteenth century, and, indeed, as late as the 1920s' (Checkland 1981: 97). There was considerable enthusiasm for increased state involvement in housing, and, with the war damage to London, Coventry, and other cities, the idea of public planning and reconstruction—within cities and across the country as a whole—gained considerable public support. Cherry notes that the logic of planned urban development seemed inescapable.

> Planning had won the war, so why could it not win the peace? Town planning promised control over land use, co-ordination of physical development, the reconstruction of cities . . . State direction was the way forward; private interests in land and development had to be subservient to the public interest (Cherry 1982: 42).

Massive public intervention intended to redress the worst consequences of market forces became an established feature of British urban policy in the mid-twentieth century. Public planning and social administration were used as the major policy instruments to attack 'the brutality of the inherited Victorian city' (Cherry 1984: 29) and to pursue 'a programme for providing twentieth century amenities in nineteenth century towns' (Cullingworth 1962: 1).

Nowhere was this more clearly evident than in the massive program of housing renewal undertaken a decade after World War II. Aneurin Bevan,

Minister for Health and responsible for housing in the early years of the Attlee Government, summarized the dominant role of the state with the argument that, 'if we are to plan, we have to plan with plannable instruments, and the speculative builder, by his very nature is not a plannable instrument'; the full weight of the housing program rests on local authorities 'because the programme can be planned and because in fact we can check them if we demand to' (quoted in Donnison and Ungerson 1982: 142). In the post-war years, and especially after 1954, British urban renewal was dominated by the activity of residential renewal and in particular the replacement of unfit or below tolerable standard private dwellings by public housing. Addition to the housing stock was accepted as a public sector responsibility, and the postulation and evaluation of public housing targets frequently dominated policy debate. Public agencies were responsible for over 57 percent of all new housing in Britain between 1945 and 1970 and virtually all of it was built as rental property to remain in the public domain. In the US, by contrast, public housing constituted less than 3 percent of non-farm housing starts between 1945 and 1969 (Clawson and Hall 1973: 134–5).

In the immediate post-war period, urban planning initiatives in Britain were guided by a very definite and consistent philosophy. As Clawson and Hall point out, 'the idea of containing urban growth and of creating new communities was fused with the idea of correcting regional economic imbalances by positive government action on industrial location policy'; indeed, 'the whole complex of ideas ... amounted to a demand for radical interventionism on the part of government—interventionism that would probably have been inconceivable before the war' (Clawson and Hall 1973: 38). Moreover, the belief in the desirability of government intervention to shape urban form was, as Cherry notes, matched by an underlying belief that government had the capacity to do so; political will combined with a '*melange* of progressive land, housing, employment and welfare planning would implant a civilising touch to the late twentieth century city' (Cherry 1984: 25) In this view, government should not merely give incentives to industry to locate in depressed areas, it should prohibit location in other areas, especially areas that were congested or suffering from urban sprawl.

government should create a land use planning system with effective negative powers to stop developers building on valuable farmland and on areas of scenic or historic importance. The government should effectively nationalize development rights on all land that was not already built upon. And the government itself should take the lead in building new communities on a large scale, through the medium of public development corporations (Clawson and Hall 1973: 40).

While the means were radical, the ends were fundamentally and explicitly conservative: to maintain the existing distribution of population, contain the invasion of the countryside through speculative investment, and to create new planned communities at chosen locations.

The extension of government activity to control market processes of urban change was fostered by the presentation of town planning as an apparently neutral political concept; 'a device for making the best of all worlds: individualism and socialism; town and country; past and future; preservation and change' (Glass 1959: 402). Conservatives and radicals were attracted to these concepts, a coalition that 'could hardly fail to win the day' (Clawson and Hall 1973: 40). And win they did, at least in the short term, as was evident in the Town and Country Planning Act of 1947 and subsequent legislation. Cullingworth describes the Act as a framework which 'brought almost all development under control by making it subject to planning permission' (Cullingworth 1985: 16). It was a new conception of town and country planning that 'was to be no longer merely a regulative function'. All areas of the country would have development plans:

These were to outline the way in which each area was to be developed or, where desirable, preserved . . . All owners were thus placed in the position of owning only the existing (1947) use rights and values in their land. Compensation for development rights was to be paid 'once and for all' out of a national fund, and developers were to pay a 'development charge' amounting to 100 percent of the increase in the value of land resulting from the development (Cullingworth 1985: 16).

'Good planning principles' would now direct development, and the central government's Board of Trade would take responsibility for 'a proper distribution of industry'.

New industrial projects (above a minimum size) would require the Board's certification that the development would be consistent with the proper distribution of industry . . . New towns were to be developed by *ad hoc* development corporations financed by the Treasury. Somewhat later (in 1952) new powers were provided for the planned expansion of towns by local authorities. The designation of national parks and 'areas of outstanding natural beauty' was entrusted to a new National Parks Commission . . . New powers were granted for preserving amenity, trees, historic building and ancient monuments. Later controls were introduced over river and air pollution, litter and noise. Indeed, the flow of legislation has been unceasing (Cullingworth 1985: 16).

Within the context of the newly empowered planning system, the urban policy framework that emerged in post-war Britain and shaped the ideas of the early post-war years was characterized by a preoccupation with the role of the public sector in urban change and, more specifically, with the containment of change. The planning orientation developed in the immediate post-war period underwent substantial modification and elaboration over the following decades. There were occasional efforts, notably in the period immediately after the election of a Conservative Government in 1951, to shift the balance of urban initiatives towards the private sector. Despite these, the focus of attention, even during the Conservative Governments between 1951 and 1963, was with the rationalization of public motives and public actions that were part and parcel of the welfare-oriented post-war consensus. The dominant urban policy concerns were public housing, planned urban development, government investment in new infrastructure, and state management of urban change.

The emergence of the planning regime in post-war Britain did not mean that private interests in urban development were systematically displaced. Indeed, the chief beneficiaries of planned urban change were often found in the business community. City center redevelopment, motorway construction, and the new town program were conceived and promoted by the planning system as public programs but, as might be expected in a mixed economy, they also served the interests of the private construction industry. Some analysts have argued that, in fact, these programs consistently favored business interests. For example, Dunleavy, proposed that the state tended to:

centralize, corporatise, depoliticise and insulate from traditional representative institutions those areas of policy making which are of direct significance for business interests. There has apparently been a continuous structural pressure on central government to maintain tight social control over policy areas with major implications for capital accumulation and economic development (Dunleavy 1981: 78).

Whether or not state action intentionally and systematically promoted and protected private capital, it is true that in Britain, as in the US, private interests have been served, rather than hindered, by planned urban change. While Britain's post-war planning regime would embody a redefinition of traditional public and private responsibilities in urban change, it was never intended to fully displace private interests. Public motives, public actors, and planned actions would play a more substantial and decisive role in the development of British cities than in any earlier period. The planning regime was a visible symbol of the post-war welfare consensus, and as such it received first the enthusiastic support and later the growing public criticism directed at British performance as a welfare state. In the 1960s and early 1970s there were signs of disenchantment with the benevolent paternalism attributed to the ideals of planned urban development, an expanding catalogue of planning failures, and eventually a more critical attitude towards a planning system that was blamed for the progressive bureaucratization of urban life. The doubts about the efficacy of a planned response to urban change were part of a growing general concern about the welfare state and the inequities that remained. By the mid-1970s, public support for the post-war planning regime had substantially eroded. At the same time there was a growing concentration, at least rhetorically, on the economic decline of urban areas and even before the election of Margaret Thatcher in 1979, this concern was being translated into a need to stimulate greater private sector involvement in British cities.

Urban Policy Orientations in a Comparative Context

Despite a parallel growth in the activist state during the post-war period, there is no US equivalent of the modern British tradition of public planning and control of urban development. Indeed, the underlying premises of the two urban policy and planning systems are quite different. Heap's assessment may be somewhat exaggerated but it is to the point: 'In Britain one can do nothing without permission. In the United States, one can do anything that is not prohibited' (Heap 1984: 7). The use of public power to consciously influence urban growth has been more extensive in Britain than in the US. There is an even more fundamental difference in the way in which public power has been applied. In Britain, planning and urban policy have been pursued as an alternative to, and frequently as a substitute for, reliance on private instruments of service delivery. The objective has been to use the instruments of public planning and policy to rationalize and direct the processes of urban change. In the US, public planning and policy have been pursued to promote, and often to protect, private development activities. Thus, the objective of the American system of land-use zoning is to contribute to the general welfare of the community by protecting private property and facilitating private development.

Indeed, it is not an overstatement to suggest that, in the United States, the primary urban policy and planning system is a private one in the sense that the initiatives and the objectives are largely shaped by and for the private sector. In America the responsibility for rationalizing urban change and growth has been assigned, for the most part, to the marketplace with the public sector playing a supportive role. The overriding objective of urban policy has been to accommodate urban development and land use to the requirements of a private system of production and exchange (Mollenkopf 1977). As we will demonstrate, the increasing reliance on federal policy as an instrument of urban change after World War II did not eclipse 'the power and authority of private institutions to make critical political decisions involving jobs, land use, and investment' (Judd 1979: 1).

As we move from a historical review of urban policy traditions to an assessment of how privatism has been alternatively sustained or rediscovered in the US and Britain, we are mindful of the dangers of underestimating the significant social, governmental, and institutional differences between the two nations. Indeed, we are concerned that British enthusiasm for US urban initiatives has often disregarded these differences. A commonality of language and symbolism, engendered through the mass media, has often served to minimize and confuse rather than illustrate and elucidate important differences.

Clearly the comparison of urban policy orientations in the US and Britain needs to take place in the context of a recognition of the sharply contrasting systems of government. There are the obvious differences of a decentralized federal system versus a highly centralized unitary system, a written versus unwritten constitutional framework, a presidential versus parliamentary form of government, and a party structure which is highly fragmented and almost non-existent at the national level in the US versus one which is centralized and disciplined in Britain. There is no need to belabor these well-known differences here, but it is important to point out that there is a substantially greater predisposition in Britain for the central state to actively and openly direct change in local areas, and in general this predisposition has been supported by the institutional structures of government. Indeed, since the mid-seventies, central government has increased its role in key areas of domestic policy. Despite the well-documented problems of administering public services in Britain—not the least of which are in the areas of housing, education, and health—and the enthusiasm for privatism in the 1980s, the central state and its bureaucracies play a pivotal role in the delivery of public goods. In this context, much of the service delivery system—particularly as it affects cities—remains largely a public enterprise directed by central government.

By contrast, the role of the state in the delivery of services is far less extensive in the US, and this is both reflected in and reinforced by the decentralized character of the governmental system. 'Even when strong pressures for an enhanced federal government exist', notes David McKay, 'the resulting increase in Washington's role has been accepted only reluctantly or even as a temporary, short-term expedient' (1987: 213). In the US, the Jeffersonian model of self-reliant local government never materialized, but there remains a deep-seated belief in local control. This said it does not necessarily follow that local government in the US is more autonomous than in Britain—although this is the common portrayal. M. David Gelfand has warned that simple generalizations about local government in the two countries often do not hold up under scrutiny. Close analysis of four critical factors, Gelfand writes: 'legal status, intergovernmental aid, controls over taxation and spending, and administrative regulation—reveals ... that British local government was actually somewhat more autonomous than US local government until the dramatic changes introduced by the Local Government, Planning and Land Act 1980' (Gelfand 1985: 235–6).

One area of striking difference is the jurisdictional fragmentation of local government found in the US as compared to the more consolidated structure in Britain. The suburbanization of urban America led to increased fragmentation, and the attempts to consolidate local government through reform have largely failed. Indeed, in the post-war period, thousands of new governing authorities have appeared in suburban areas including newly incorporated towns and special districts that provide specific services across different municipalities. This has meant that 'national and state political leaders have a far more difficult task in imposing their priorities upon American cities, counties and districts' (Lee 1985: 55). In Britain, on the other hand, the reorganization of local government in the 1970s reduced the number of local councils in England and Wales from 1,000 to just over 400 (with a similar percentage change in Scotland), eliminating some 15,000 elected positions. These changes have strengthened the hand of central government and created a platform for increasing centralization in the 1980s.

Edward Banfield once summarized the differences in local government in the two political systems as follows: American local government tends to be experimental, contentious, open, demotic, participatory, and pluralist; whereas the British tends to be conservative, placid, closed, deferential, autonomous, and monist (1965: 3). These generalizations have been widely criticized, however, and other analysts conclude that the reality of the two systems is considerably more complicated than Banfield suggests. L. J. Sharpe, for example, points out that while there is a much narrower conception of what are the appropriate limits of local government in the US, 'it would be wrong to conclude with any finality which is the most experimental system'; and while the expression of vehement disagreement in British urban politics seems less frequent, 'it would be wrong to confuse style with content' (Sharpe 1973: 6–7). Class antagonism always lies just below the surface in British society and, Sharpe suggests, in some respects has been more evident in urban local government than in national government.

While recognizing the political, institutional, and cultural differences between the British and American forms of governance, our intention is not to add to the documentation of these differences. Rather, it is to examine the impact of a policy orientation, which we have called privatism, on urban policy in two quite different political and institutional contexts. We believe that, despite the differences between Britain and America, there have been striking similarities in the objectives of urban policy in the 1980s. In addition, as the following chapters demonstrate, a number of common patterns can be discerned in the outcomes of this policy.

Notes

1. Warner has argued that 'Americans have no urban history. They live in one of the world's most urbanized countries as if it were a wilderness in both time and space. Beyond some civic and ethnic myths and a few family and neighborhood memories, Americans are not conscious that they have a past' (Warner 1972: 4).
2. In the 19th cent., there was a form of corporate paternalism that developed in communities which were dominated by a few or only one major business enterprise, usually local and family-owned. In these places, local business leaders found themselves to be 'inescapably accountable for and dependent upon the social conditions which prevailed' (M. Heald 1970: 3). Their feelings of personal responsibility towards the community and its welfare were undoubtedly shaped by a well-developed concern for their own private interests but this was often translated into service to the community (Rogers and Zimet 1968). The most extreme manifestation of this early corporate paternalism was the model industrial community at Pullman, Ill., founded by George M. Pullman of the Pullman Palace Car Company. The physical aspects of the new town—the standards of housing, maintenance, and appearance—were widely praised, but its residents resented their position of dependence on the Pullman Company. The community became a benevolent autocracy and eventually a violent and bitter strike brought an end to this experiment in business paternalism.
3. Public provision of utilities formed a principal topic of debate towards the end of the 19th cent. when the Fabian Society opposed the idea that utilities should be run on a profit-making basis. Sidney and Beatrice Webb and other leading members of the Society were described as 'gas and water socialists' by those who regarded municipal provision as too unimportant to warrant the attention of serious revolutionary socialists (Robson 1935: 311).

3

Urban Redevelopment and the US War on Poverty

URBAN policy in the US since World War II has been designed to stimulate, support, and occasionally supplement private investment. The objectives have been to encourage privatism, to broaden its scope, and at times to channel private resources towards public purposes—the redevelopment of deteriorating central cities, the war against poverty, the efficient delivery of municipal services, the creation of a stable and growing housing market, and the stimulation of local economic development. Congruent with the tradition of privatism, urban redevelopment was predicated upon the expectation that the profit motive could be harnessed to serve the purpose of civic revitalization. Throughout the 1950s and 1960s and into the 1970s, major redevelopment efforts sought to reverse the physical deterioration of city centers by mobilizing the resources and initiative of private developers and local corporate institutions. Redevelopment represents an area of urban policy where the impact of privatism has been clear and where both the costs and benefits have been substantial.

US experience with public-private partnerships extends beyond the sometimes dramatic results of initiatives in the physical regeneration of cities. The urban unrest of the 1960s and the national attention it focused on racial discrimination, economic inequality, and the urban poor generated a new conception of the responsibilities of the public and the private sectors. As part of the War on Poverty, new public-private partnerships were launched with the intent of channeling private, generally corporate, resources towards efforts at urban social rehabilitation.[1]

Privatism and Urban Redevelopment

In some cities, the initiative for urban redevelopment came first from local business leaders. The relatively *ad hoc* and discontinuous involvements which characterized the role of businessmen, particularly corporate managers, throughout much of the early twentieth century were transformed during the post-war era into sustained influence on the overall pattern of urban redevelopment. The impetus for this was a cycle of economic decline stimulated by the progressive decentralization of population and firms outward from the older urban cores. The erosion of the central city's economic base was accompanied by a decline of retail activities, a reduction in local public revenues, a deterioration of physical amenities, a decline in the quality of public services, and a decrease in local private investment. The increasing out-migration of middle-income families, manufacturing, and retail activities to the suburbs directly threatened business institutions that had large financial investments in the city core or depended upon a central city location for services, distribution, and markets. In some cases, the promotion of redevelopment by businesses trapped in economically declining urban centers predated the federal government's urban renewal program which began when the Housing Act of 1949 authorized loans and grants to localities for the clearance and development of inner-city slums. For the most part, however, it was the rising level of federal expenditure for urban renewal during the 1950s that provided the necessary additional impetus for major redevelopment efforts and for the public–private partnerships that guided redevelopment.

The Pattern of Partnership in Urban Renewal

In essence the federal urban renewal program was based on the expectation that center city deterioration could be reversed by public subsidies for private redevelopment of blighted areas. With sufficient patronage from the federal government, private developers could pursue public goals and still make a profit. The urban renewal program depended upon a complex intermixture of private initiative and public authority. In order to acquire an adequate amount of land to carry out a major redevelopment project, a substantial number of independent parcels of property had to be assembled. This was seldom an attractive proposition for private investors. Urban renewal legislation represented a new approach to the problem by establishing an instrument which, in principle, combined the legal powers of government with the development resources of the private sector. The scope of the government's power of eminent domain—a power which traditionally had been used to obtain private property for the construction of public facilities equivalent to the British practice of compulsory purchase—was expanded in the urban renewal program to acquire land for private uses that were purported to be in the public interest.[2] Local government, represented by a Local Public Authority (LPA), selected a redevelopment site and declared it to be blighted. Then using the power of eminent domain, it bought the land, and cleared it for reuse, attracting private developers by pricing the land below its market value. The federal government underwrote two-thirds of the program cost or the difference between what the LPA received for the land from the private developer and the costs the agency incurred in its purchase and clearance. The only stipulation was that the land be used to accomplish a socially desirable purpose. The original objective was to provide low-cost housing but this emphasis was soon modified. Legislation was subsequently revised to authorize the types of redevelopment the private sector was actually prepared to pursue.[3]

The success of urban renewal depended upon a partnership between private enterprise and public authority. Government was to take the initiative using its powers and its resources to prepare the way for private redevelopment. The private sector was to follow-through on implementation, site acquisition, and financing new construction that was in accordance with public objectives. In practice, however, the responsibilities for initiative and response were usually reversed. In most cities, it was the private sector that determined the direction and pace of redevelopment.[4] Indeed, urban renewal often provided a local business community with opportunities for private planning of economic expansion and land-use investment that could never have been secured without the use of public powers. As Chester Hartman notes:

> taking over an entire section of the downtown, evicting its occupants, demolishing the existing structures, and converting the land to a different use—requires careful preparation, specialized skills, and most important, a legal and political base of operations. The federal–local urban renewal program, with its powers of eminent domain, land-cost and clearance subsidies, and battery of planners and other technicians, provided the ideal vehicle for downtown expansion (Hartman 1974: 33).

Local business leaders often looked to renewal programs as a way to protect their investments, improve retail markets and local services, and restore the competitive position of the center city business district. In addition to direct incentives, federally sponsored urban renewal gave local business communities a reason to organize for self-protection to ensure that business interests were reflected in redevelopment initiatives. Nevertheless, despite the obvious benefits that accrued to some business enterprises as a result of redevelopment, some analysts have depicted businessmen as frequently indifferent or hostile to redevelopment and as unable to organize and agree upon redevelopment plans. While it is acknowledged that urban redevelopment appealed to the latent self-interest of the business community, both ideological and pragmatic obstacles are seen as restricting the conversion of latent interest into concrete support. Raymond Wolfinger asserted, for example, that 'a local business community seldom took the lead in formulating, adopting and executing an urban renewal program,' partly because of a generalized ideological opposition to 'spending', 'big government', 'federal interference', and 'socialism', and partly because of divergences of interest among businessmen (Wolfinger 1974: 148–9). Similarly, Charles Adrian and Charles Press observed that the influence of businessmen, while potentially great, was attenuated by the lack of any effective central organization at the local level such that business groups spent 'much of their time opposing one another' (Adrian and Press 1977: 84).

Urban redevelopment had serious costs for some businessmen. Firms forced to relocate lost customers and usually paid higher costs for new quarters; disruption caused by demolition and construction made it difficult for small and marginal businesses to survive during the redevelopment process; and businesses outside the redevelopment area faced competition from new firms located in the project (Wolfinger 1974). As a result, redevelopment generated opposition from some businessmen. Until the mid-1960s, the US Chamber of Commerce, which generally represents small, locally based firms, opposed federal assistance for urban redevelopment. The extent of opposition should not be overstated however. For the most part, it came from small businessmen who were not adequately compensated for the costs of relocation, the disruptions caused by demolition and construction, and the competition from new firms attracted to renewal projects. Even many small businessmen eventually conceived of redevelopment as beneficial once improved compensation arrangements were instituted.

Local business leaders generally have been supportive of redevelopment. To a large extent, the executives of major business institutions considered the long-term benefits of redevelopment as outweighing the short-term costs. The leaders of large corporate institutions, in particular, were attracted by prospects for long-term stabilization of the local business environment that would protect local investments. The chief executives of large firms based in the city were often the major proponents of center city redevelopment and provided the local leadership for federally sponsored programs of urban renewal.

The model for business initiative in the guidance of urban renewal was the Allegheny Conference in Pittsburgh. It was formed in 1943, before the federal renewal program, when Richard Mellon, head of a three billion dollar financial empire convened a small group of businessmen to discuss Pittsburgh's future. Pittsburgh had been in a condition of deterioration for many years. 'No new construction had taken place in its oppressively drab downtown for nearly two decades,' reports Jeanne Lowe. 'Forty percent of the business district was blighted or vacant. This commercial stagnation was reflected in the steady downward slide since the early 1930s of the CBD's assessed valuations of some $18 million a year' (Lowe 1967: 112). Large corporations had difficulty attracting executives willing to live in Pittsburgh and a number began planning to move their offices to other cities. While the difficulties of the city had been apparent for many years, community improvement efforts were stymied by a lack of leadership and continuing quarrels among competing groups about the nature and focus of improvement efforts. By the early 1940s, the leaders of those institutions that had the largest financial stake in the city recognized that: 'No longer could they vacillate, rationalize, compromise . . . Either they would stay and eventually rebuild the core of the central city, or they would get out and take their industries with them' (Lubove 1969: 107).

The decision made by the business leaders convened by Mellon was to form a non-profit, non-partisan civic organization devoted to research and planning and the development of a comprehensive community improvement program. In essence, the strategy was to offer concrete, detailed plans prepared by professionals for the revitalization of the central business district and to ensure the execution of these plans by forging a coalition of businessmen and local politicians. The plans of the Allegheny Conference were subsequently funded and implemented virtually unaltered by the renewal program.

The Gateway Center project, sponsored by the Allegheny Conference, was the most dramatic expression of what came to be known as the Pittsburgh

Renaissance. Between 1950, when construction began, and the mid-1960s, more than 25 percent of the 330-acre downtown area now known as the Golden Triangle was rebuilt. By 1967, 19 renewal projects were completed or were under construction in the area, at a total public cost of $171.5 million (Lubove 1969: 127–8). Gateway Center, as Roy Lubove has noted:

Illustrated the tactics of the civic coalition in generating large-scale environmental change. These included use of the public authority mechanism or any administrative expedient that could link Pittsburgh with government assistance at any level. Gateway Center also depended upon the civic coalition's access to professional and technical skills—architectural, planning, engineering and legal. Finally, Gateway Center was the product of an extraordinary combination of prestige and power, one that could induce Equitable [Life Assurance Society] and local corporations to invest millions in the future of the CBD and break the deadlocks that had obstructed environmental change in the past, (Lubove 1969: 123).

The combination of private influence and public resources to rebuild the downtown area of Pittsburgh became a model for other cities. Philadelphia, Baltimore, St. Louis, Cleveland, San Francisco, San Diego, and many other cities, launched their own versions of the Pittsburgh Renaissance and in each case relied upon the active involvement and guidance of organized local business leaders to shape the pattern of civic redevelopment. By 1972, the International Downtown Executives Association estimated that there were more than 300 downtown associations working to promote redevelopment of central business districts. Chambers of Commerce also became extensively involved in redevelopment despite their early opposition to federal renewal programs. A Chamber of Commerce survey in 1972 found that in 191 communities with urban renewal projects, local chambers actively participated in the planning or implementation of 150 (Chamber of Commerce 1972: 16). But downtown associations and Chambers of Commerce were not the most influential private sector participants in urban redevelopment partnerships. That role was played by businessmen's development committees which were established specifically to promote urban redevelopment. The committees were composed of the chief executives of institutions which represented the economic infrastructure of the city.[5]

Private Governments and Redevelopment Policy

Building upon the model of the Allegheny Conference, businessmen's development committees organized in virtually every major city in the United States between 1945 and 1965: the Greater Philadelphia Movement, Central Atlanta Progress, Inc., Detroit Renaissance, Greater Baltimore Committee, Downtown Lower Manhattan Association, Central City Planning (Los Angeles), Chicago Central Area Committee, Civic Progress Inc. (St. Louis), the Blyth–Zellerbach Committee (San Francisco), Citizens Action Commission (New Haven), San Diegans, Inc., Operation New Birmingham, Greater Hartford Process, Inc., Downtown Council of Minneapolis, Federal City Council (Washington, DC), Central Area Council (New Orleans), Metro 70

(Albuquerque), and the Cleveland Development Foundation among many others[6] The type of business represented on the committees was similar in most cities: manufacturing and service industries, public utilities, banks and insurance companies, large retail stores, contractors, and land developers. As one might expect, 'the businessmen who are most active in city affairs are those whose companies are most directly affected by what the city government does' (Banfield and Wilson 1963: 261). Representation was also skewed in the direction of those businesses which were locally owned or whose corporate headquarters were locally based—those that were locked into the city by investment and tradition and for whom changing locations would have been costly. Most often it was the representatives of these latter institutions who gave the committees their dominant leadership and who co-opted other businessmen who were less likely to participate on their own (Barnekov and Rich 1977). Development committees were often not so much representative of local business as a whole as they were representative of the patterns of dominance within the local business community.

In some cities businessmen's development committees were responsible for virtually all major initiatives in urban redevelopment. In other cities committees responded to the initiatives of public officials.[7] In either case, their organized presence combined with the power of their institutional membership ensured that little redevelopment was undertaken without their approval, oversight, and active participation. Most often, the influence of these committees decisively tilted the balance of the public–private partnerships in urban redevelopment. Petshek's 1965 study of Philadelphia indicated that a series of interlocking directorates had been established in which members of the Greater Philadelphia Movement (GPM) participated more extensively than other businessmen or civic leaders (Petshek 1973). In St Louis, Edgar found that members of Civic Progress, a businessmen's development committee, held 82 board positions and filled half of the officerships in eight major local community organizations (Edgar 1970).

While specific programs differed from city to city, the types of activities sponsored by the post-war partnerships in redevelopment, as well as the results of these activities, were remarkably consistent and this consistency generally reflected the priorities of businessmen's development committees. For the most part, activities focused on physical renewal of central business districts in accord with comprehensive plans sponsored by development committees. Urban social problems were ignored or were relegated to a relatively insignificant status in comparison with other development activities. Obviously this emphasis reflected the overall orientation of national urban policy which, until the mid-1960s, was preoccupied with the physical dimensions of urban regeneration. Even so, the focus on redevelopment for commercial purposes cannot be explained apart from the influence which local business development committees exercised in the redevelopment partnership. The urban renewal program was, after all, conceived initially as a vehicle to increase the availability of low-cost housing and not, as the program became, a means to publicly subsidize commercial expansion and renewal of central business districts. Throughout the urban renewal program, however, local development committees kept the focus of attention on those urban problems, generally physical in nature, which were amenable to solution by mobilizing the managerial and technical skills of the private sector; not surprisingly, these were also the problems highest on the agenda of the local business community.[8] Even during the late 1960s, when federal programs stressed the social aspects of urban development, most of the local development committees remained committed to programs and plans for physical renewal.

A key contribution of the public–private partnerships in the 1950s and 1960s was their sponsorship of comprehensive development plans to guide urban renewal. The emphasis on rational comprehensive planning was congruent with the dominant planning theory in the US (Kaplan 1973): The principal impetus for such plans, however, was less often professional planners than the businessmen's development committees. Although some of the committees viewed the central city, and occasionally even the entire metropolitan region, as the development unit, the objective of these plans was generally the revitalization of the central business district. Transportation services, housing projects, and industrial development programs were pursued as spin-offs of the basic CBD planning objectives.

The planning initiatives of the development committees sometimes had dramatic effects on the overall pattern of redevelopment resulting in 'development spectaculars' on the scale of Pittsburgh's Gateway Center, Baltimore's Charles Center, or Detroit's Renaissance Center. In other cases, however, development committees were more modest in their planning efforts and in a few cases committees formulated plans that met with opposition which delayed, if not precluded, their implementation.[9] But even when a committee was unsuccessful in implementing its plans, the existence of the plans, and an organized body of locally influential supporters, determined what development issues became salient in the community and what ideas dominated the agenda for public action. The expenditure of tens, and sometimes hundreds, of thousands of dollars on a development committee plan forced public officials to consider it seriously, even if they disagreed with it. As Banfield and Wilson pointed out, while a politician may be less than enthusiastic about a committee's plan for civic improvement:

in the end, he usually does endorse it, or something like it, however, for he too believes that something must be done to stop the decline of the central business district and his judgment tells him that whatever the leading businessmen can agree upon is the most feasible place to begin (Banfield and Wilson 1963: 269).

While promoting plans central to the welfare of the business community, the activities of the committees were frequently characterized, by public officials as well as business leaders, as community-wide efforts which served community-wide goals. Reminiscent of the era of boosterism, development committees were often regarded as speaking not only for a particular development interest but for the city as a whole. Often there was an assumption that business interests and community interests were largely compatible and that the central place of businessmen in the community created a special capacity to serve as a catalyst for community development efforts. Such beliefs have been central to the influence of development committees because the mobilization of public support for businessmen's development plans required that these plans be viewed as consistent with the public interest. Moreover, widespread public acceptance of the 'public interestedness' of private development initiatives made it possible to side-step the issues of accountability raised by the concerted and overt application of private power to public policy.

Over two decades ago, Banfield and Wilson recognized that the formation of private development committees and their subsequent partnerships with local public officials might serve to reshape business–government relations (Banfield and Wilson 1963: 267). In many cities this is exactly what happened. The public-private partnerships created to guide redevelopment often established a new locus of authority in their communities. At times these redevelopment partnersips led to a lasting governing coalition which Salibury described as a 'new convergence of power' comprised of business leaders, technical experts, and political élites which governed the political economy as well as guided the physical redesign of the city (Salisbury 1964: 786). Other partnerships were more transitory—surviving only as long as the redevelopment venture was sustained.

In Pittsburgh, Baltimore, Philadelphia, San Francisco, and many other cities, local business élites alternated between periods of broad influence on the general shape of redevelopment and periods of relative inactivity. Successful completion of a major project was sometimes followed by reduced interest on the part of local business élites. Even then, local business leaders participated in whatever programs were taking place and, acting through development committees, exercised influence that was often decisive in determining the pattern of redevelopment. Indeed, in a number of cities, the extensive and sustained influence of private development organizations meant not only that they were influential partners in new political coalitions, and sometimes the principal architects of urban renewal, but also that they served for some period of time as local private governments—institutions which existed apart from public government but exercised decisive power in vital areas of community concern (Lakoff and Rich 1973: 1). To characterize businessmen's development groups as private governments does not mean that they exercised a monopoly of power in urban communities or that the consequences of local policy decisions were always favorable to their interests. Edward Hayes points out the test of a dominant group is not whether it always obtains what it wants.

No ruling group in history fulfills such a requirement. The appropriate test is whether on a majority or disproportionately large number of cases, in which it takes an interest, one social group's wishes become official policy, while the wishes of other groups are not articulated, are ignored, or are successfully combatted (Hayes 1972: 197).

During periods of redevelopment the preferences of local business élites were systematically satisfied while those of other groups in the city were ignored or defeated. Beyond this, as private governments, development committees performed functions which would otherwise be performed by public government or not at all: setting the agenda for public action, planning the pattern of city development, and carrying out their priorities through the use of public authority and public resources. In this sense they exercised what Michael Parenti has referred to as 'the powers of pre-emption': the power to limit the scope of policy consideration and conflict and the power to define the range of policy alternatives that receives serious public attention (Parenti 1970). In a fundamental sense development committees determined the outcome of local political and policy decisions and propagated plans and procedures that operated systematically and consistently to the benefit of certain groups at the expense of others (Bachrach and Baratz 1970).

As private governments, development committees were influential not only as a result of their impact upon the decisions of public government, but also because they commanded such extensive local resources that their actions, and at times their inaction, were in themselves consequential for the community. Although privately constituted and privately controlled, they made decisions and performed functions that were public in scope and in consequences; that pertained to and affected the community as a whole. Indeed, the critical issue posed by private governments in urban redevelopment has been their exercise of power without equivalent accountability. What is impressive, and at the same time disconcerting, is the widespread, ready acceptance of these private governments as the legitimate agents of urban redevelopment.[10] Questions of accountability generally have been ignored or raised in retrospect after the impact of committee activities had become apparent. Moreover, when such questions were raised they tended to be directed at particular programs rather than at the basic legitimacy of these local private governments or at the objectives of the 'partnerships' they frequently dominated.

The Limits of Partnership in Urban Redevelopment

The public–private partnerships stimulated by post-war urban renewal represented a continuation of the American tradition of privatism, albeit in a different form. It was learned from this experience that, with sufficient public patronage, the business community in most cities will mobilize to undertake an active role in urban regeneration and that at times it will take the initiative to deal with urban problems directly affecting its investment interests. Often the physical results of this involvement have been impressive. The development spectaculars that typified CBD renewal in Pittsburgh and other cities are clear testimonials to what public–private partnerships can achieve when influential businessmen work with energetic and ambitious political leaders. The successes of these projects were as much symbolic as practical. They sustained, or more often rekindled, local pride and enthusiasm,

projected a positive image of the local business community as progressive
and civic-minded and demonstrated the commitment of local public officials
to creating a favorable climate for business. Frequently the road to urban
revival was perceived as beginning with a reconstruction of the image of the
city and its leaders. The long-term, overall economic impacts on cities are
more difficult to gauge and these clearly have varied dramatically from one
urban center to another. Nonetheless, it is undoubtedly true that the public–
private partnerships in redevelopment over the past forty years have contributed to the economic regeneration of central commercial districts in a
number of older industrial cities or at least they have helped to arrest some
facets of physical decline and economic out-migration that inhibited such
regeneration. The Urban Renewal Administration estimated that property
values increased from $464 million to $1,675 million in the 708 project areas
on which land acquisition had been completed by 1971 (US Senate 1973: 63).
Redevelopment helped cities to hold on to businesses that might otherwise
have migrated to the suburbs or the sunbelt, to attract new businesses to
redeveloped sites, and to lure suburbanites and tourists back to the city to
enjoy the new cultural amenities brought about by an urban renaissance.

Nevertheless, despite achievements in downtown redevelopment and
civic imagery (and in part because of them), there are now numerous pain-
fully detailed documentations of the failures of public–private partnerships in
urban redevelopment (Wilson 1966; Jane Jacobs 1961; Anderson 1964;
Abrams 1965; Greer 1965; Wolfinger 1974). The urban renewal program in
particular has been an object of criticism for three decades. While urban
renewal bolstered central business districts and may even have contributed
indirectly to a city's economic vitality, it also dislocated neighborhoods and
often created more urban blight than it removed. Lawrence Friedman
pointed out that, 'urban renewal takes sides; it uproots and evicts some for
the benefit of others' (Friedman 1968: 166). Urban renewal benefited some
center city businessmen and the upper-middle class but frequently at the
expense of the urban poor. As Hartman suggests, 'the aggregate benefits [of
urban renewal] are private benefits, and accrue to a small, select segment of
the city's elite "public", while the costs . . . fall on those least able to bear
them' (Hartman 1974: 183). Anthony Downs estimated that households displaced by urban renewal suffered an average uncompensated loss
amounting to 20 to 30 percent of one year's income (Downs 1970: 223).
Moreover, while originally conceived as a means of increasing the supply of
low-cost housing, American urban renewal actually exacerbated the urban
housing problem. 'At a cost of more than three billion dollars', the urban
renewal program by 1965 'succeeded in materially reducing the supply of
low-cost housing, in American cities' (Greer 1965: 3). In subsequent years the
pattern was no different. Between 1967 and 1971, 538,000 housing units
were razed but only 201,000 replaced (Weicher 1972: 6).

In some respects this result should not have been surprising. In the area of
housing, private developers have been relied upon almost exclusively in the
US. In the initial urban renewal legislation, as in earlier housing legislation,

the government was to build housing only where it was obvious the private sector could not or would not fill the need. For the most part, the renewal program was dependent upon the private sector to implement its housing objectives; there was no intention that there be an active and continuing role for the federal government in the direct provision of housing. Indeed, the limited experience with public housing in the US has so thoroughly discredited the concept that it is rarely regarded even as an option (Hartman 1980: 131). In direct contrast with the post-war experience in Britain, US policies have sought to keep the government removed from a public housing program. What to build, where to build, and for whom to build are matters that have been left to the private market even when government funds have been used, as they were in urban renewal, to stimulate private housing investment. One observer concluded that America's housing policy is 'to have no housing policy and rely on private enterprise' (Headey 1978: 175). This has meant that, in contrast to modern Britain, there is virtually no public housing sector in the US to privatize.

Public–private partnerships in urban redevelopment tend naturally to focus on items high on the agenda of local business leaders but low on the agenda of other city residents, particularly the poor and minorities. The very success of redevelopment ventures has often been made possible only by publicly subsidizing the investment interests of local business élites and, at times, by turning over a good portion of the responsibilities for civic govern-ance to local corporate institutions. Lubove characterized the Pittsburgh Renaissance as a program of public paternalism for private economic gain.

The foundation of the entire Renaissance effort was the use of public power and resources to preserve the economic vitality of the central business district (CBD) and, more broadly, the competitive economic position of the Pittsburgh region. In essence, the Pittsburgh Renaissance represented a response to a crisis situation, one that precipitated a dramatic expansion of public enterprise and investment to serve corpor-ate needs; it established a reverse welfare state (Lubove 1969: 106).

The situation in Pittsburgh may have been extreme but later experience with public–private partnerships in urban renewal suggests that it was typical of a pattern that has exhibited variance in degree but not in kind. In the late 1970s Detroit unveiled its Renaissance Center consisting of five office towers, a 70-story hotel, as well as other projects. Soaring costs had raised the price of construction from $237 million to $337 million dollars, but Henry Ford II, a member of Detroit Renaissance which initiated the projects, succeeded in 'finding' the additional money to complete the job. Such are the advantages of public–private partnerships. Partly because of its striking contrast to the rest of Detroit, the Renaissance Center raised important questions about the beneficiaries of redevelopment. Critics saw 'the project as a self-contained white island that will absorb thousands of affluent suburbanites by day, disgorge them to the freeways at night—and do little to pep up a dispirited downtown' (quoted in Judd 1979: 383). The critique was not greatly dissimilar from those made about the products of earlier public–private part-nerships under urban renewal.

Heidenheimer, and others, point out that the nature of urban renewal projects is market determined; what is undertaken depends largely on what the private sector sees as its priorities and is willing to accept as an invest-ment risk.

No clearer example exists than New York State's Urban Development Corporation, created in 1968 as the most powerful renewal agency in the nation. A decade later its mission had shifted dramatically from building housing for low- and moderate-income families to building high-priced apartments, luxury hotels and a convention center, and supporting industrial expansion. The reason was simply that the development corporation could not attract sufficient investment to carry out its socially desirable but financially risky projects. It's director admitted, 'The projects we now select to do are ones which the private sector can almost do without government participation' (Heidenheimer *et al.* 1983: 246–7).

These shifts in priorities indicate the types of imbalances in influence which have consistently characterized public–private partnerships in urban redevelopment. The results have sometimes been rationalized by claims that what is good for business is inevitably good for a city and its residents. Such rationalizations are reminiscent of a long history of reformist thinking in American cities which postulated the existence of a community of common goals and values and the possibility of establishing a standard level of muni-cipal services beneficial to all residents. Nearly 100 years of US experience with the results of this approach should convince even the most committed advocate of privatism that urban development goals are central matters of political dispute and that a favorable business climate often means public subsidy for the pursuit of private benefit. Experience suggests that it has been relatively easy to induce the private sector to participate in efforts at urban renewal in America, but far more difficult to channel that participation towards public objectives. The profit motive may be powerful but it has not been easily harnessed. This became all the more apparent in the effort to mobilize public–private partnerships in response to the urban crisis of the 1960s.

Privatizing the War on Poverty

Prior to 1961 urban renewal and public housing were the only major federal programs targeted especially to cities. With the election of John F. Kennedy as President, tentative steps were taken towards a commitment of increased federal support for urban areas. Poverty and race had become national issues as a result of the civil rights movement, and there was growing recognition that some sections of America, particularly the inner-city ghettos of older industrial cities, were suffering from rates of unemployment and deprivation that exceeded those experienced in the great depression of the 1930s. The evidence of decline was difficult to ignore. The old urban core was 'physically obsolete, financially unworkable, crime-ridden, garbage-strewn, polluted, torn by racial conflicts, wallowing in welfare, unemployment, despair and official corruption' (Raskin 1971). Michael Harrington's best seller, *The Other America*, vividly described the massive poverty that existed in an otherwise affluent America and was instrumental in convincing President Kennedy that a national program to combat poverty was needed (Harrington 1962).

The poverty program envisioned by Kennedy was rather small, but the idea was seized upon by Lyndon Johnson and became the basis of his program to create 'The Great Society'. In Johnson's January 1964 State of the Union message to Congress, the President declared 'an unconditional war on poverty' (Johnson 1964: 114) and over the next two years persuaded Congress to enact three major initiatives designed primarily to assist cities and the urban poor. The Economic Opportunity Act of 1964 was made up of a variety of programs, including the Jobs Corps (a job training program), Head Start (a pre-school program for ghetto children), the Neighborhood Youth Corps (a work program for high school students from inner-city neighborhoods), and small business assistance, but the most important component—and eventually most controversial—was the Community Action Program (CAP) (Economic Opportunity Act of 1964, Public Law 88–452, Eighty-eighth Congress). CAP was intended to create a direct link between the federal government and the urban poor. Federally funded local community action agencies, which did not have to answer to state or local governments, were expected to provide and coordinate programs and services in inner-city areas. Not only were local authorities bypassed but there was to be 'maximum feasible participation' of the poor in the development and management of local community action programs. Some of the administrators of these programs interpreted this to mean that the poor were to be mobilized and involved in every phase of the local agencies' operation, and thus, within a few months of their establishment, complaints were heard from mayors and other local officials that these agencies were stirring up trouble in the ghetto and wasting funds.

In early September 1965, President Johnson signed legislation to establish a new cabinet level agency to be named the Department of Housing and Urban Development (HUD). Up until then urban dwellers had been represented by the Housing and Home Finance Agency (HHFA) which administered a collection of programs including the Federal Housing Administration (FHA), the Public Housing Administration (PHA), and the Urban Renewal Administration (URA). The new urban department simply elevated HHFA to cabinet status and by no means contained all of the federal programs that affected urban areas. Nevertheless, a nation—which had been predominantly urban for fifty years—had finally provided a chair at the President's table in the White House for a department responsible for dealing with the problems of its urban areas (McFarland 1978: 19).

The third major urban policy initiative of the Johnson administration, the Model Cities Program, tempered some of the more radical features of CAP.

Established by the Demonstration Cities and Metropolitan Development Act of 1966 (Public Law 89–754, Eighty-ninth Congress), Model Cities was to be a coordinated, comprehensive attack on urban social and physical problems in selected demonstration areas. City Demonstration Agencies, operating under the authority of local government, would receive funding to prepare 'comprehensive development plans' as well as support over a five-year period 'for new and innovative activities, the redirection of existing resources to better use, and the mobilization of additional resources' (Demonstration Cities and Metropolitan Development Act of 1966). Rather than bypassing existing agencies, Model Cities operated under the authority of local government and focused on the need to coordinate services and improve their administration. Learning from the experience of CAP, those who drafted the Model Cities legislation called for 'widespread citizen participation' and 'maximum opportunities for employment of residents of the area' rather than 'maximum feasible participation'. As Marris and Rein have shown, the program 'seemed deliberately designed to restore the initiative in reform to established authority, in reaction against the radical tendencies of community action' (Marris and Rein 1973: 262).

The social welfare orientation of federal urban policy during the 1960s, particularly between 1964 and 1967, represented a shift away from the traditional focus on physical rehabilitation of central business districts. It was a period of interventionist policymaking by the federal government directed at achieving a national purpose, the improvement of the quality of urban life. Nonetheless, these initiatives were never intended to seriously challenge the dominant role of the private sector in urban change and urban development. Marris and Rein have described the conservative underpinnings of the community action projects:

the projects seemed to assume . . . that urban society is essentially a benevolent anarchy. Highly competitive, the city is yet open to all ambitious enough to pit themselves in the struggle. Its harshness is mitigated by social welfare, which should not merely comfort the failures, but encourage them back into the race. And its justice is protected by an educational system which should ensure to every child an equal start. The will to compete is primary, and social agencies are to be judged, above all, by their ability to foster and sustain it (Marris and Rein 1973: 52).

Not only were the War on Poverty programs intended to provide the urban poor with skills and experiences that would enable them to participate in the economic system, some of the programs depended upon private sector support for implementation. The Jobs Corps, for example, sought to remove poor youths from debilitating poverty environments by placing them in residential centers, operated by private contractors, where they would be rehabilitated with educational and vocational training. In May 1967, private firms—including General Electric, IBM, Litton Industries, RCA, and Westinghouse—operated 21 of the 28 urban centers (Levitan and Mangum 1969: 170–1). The remaining seven were administered by universities or non-profit organizations. The Neighborhood Youth Corps was established 'to put idle youth to work constructively and, in some cases, to help prevent high school dropouts by providing part-time work' (*Congressional Record*, 23 July 1964: 16219). Work assignments were initially limited to public and non-profit organizations, but in 1966 they were extended to private industry. CAP also included locally designed employment and training projects as part of community action agency activities and promoted community capitalism through the Special Impact Program (SIP). In 1966 Senators Robert Kennedy and Jacob Javits sponsored an amendment to the Economic Opportunity Act which would promote economic development of inner-city ghettos by concentrating public and private resources on the creation of jobs and businesses. Fully $7 million of the $25 million initially appropriated for SIP went to the Brooklyn's Bedford-Stuyvesant Restoration Corporation to develop new firms and attract branch plants of large corporations. Its most notable achievement was the establishment of an IBM facility which eventually employed 400 Bedford-Stuyvesant residents. The Brooklyn program was successful because of the active involvement of Senators Kennedy and Javits and the support of business leaders including IBM's President Thomas Watson. Unfortunately the experience could not be replicated in the fourteen other community development corporations funded through SIP. These projects were generally unsuccessful because of meager business support or inadequate local leadership (Levitan and Taggart 1971: 13–14).

While CAP, Model Cities, and other War on Poverty programs provided services, funds, and patronage that strengthened ghetto organizations and enhanced the power of black leadership (Piven and Cloward 1971), they were eventually criticized as divisive, expensive, politically naïve, cumbersome and more concerned with bureaucratic politics than with the problems of the urban poor (Frieden and Kaplan 1975). Talk of radical action by minorities, the escalating costs of the Vietnam war, and growing unrest in the cities led to a political backlash which was first apparent in the congressional elections of 1966 when Republicans picked up some seats in the House and Senate. Indeed, Model Cities was very nearly an early victim of the emerging opposition to social legislation. It passed by only a narrow margin in 1966 in contrast to the broad congressional support for the Economic Opportunity Act of 1964.

The growing dissatisfaction with federal activism coincided with increasing racial tension in the cities. In 1965, a section of Los Angeles called Watts was the scene of major rioting. Disorders occurred on the west side of Chicago and in the Hough section of Cleveland in the summer of 1966. But the most extensive rioting took place in the summer of 1967. Nearly 150 cities reported disorders with the most violent occurring in Newark, New Jersey and Detroit, Michigan. It was a national upheaval which gave substance to proclamations of an 'urban crisis'. The problems encountered by the War on Poverty programs, however, had convinced many government officials, business leaders, and often the victims of poverty themselves, that government could not solve this crisis by the sheer force of bureaucratic presence, public patronage, and good will. For some, a new mandate had been created for the establishment of public–private partnerships to deal with inadequate housing, urban decay, and unemployment. In a manifesto written for his 1968 presidential campaign, *To Seek a Newer World*, Senator Robert Kennedy argued that 'to ignore the potential contribution of private enterprise is to fight poverty with a single platoon while great armies are left to stand aside' (Kennedy 1967: 41). Other prominent politicians, including Senators Jacob Javits and Charles Percy, Vice-President Hubert Humphrey, and Governor Nelson Rockefeller, also proposed public–private arrangements to deal with the urban crisis. Business leaders as well, frightened by the threat to their investments posed by continued urban violence, promised to join government and voluntary organizations in efforts to resolve the urban crisis and to take action themselves by setting up their own urban affairs programs. Thus both public and private leaders called for a new privatism that would be inspired by commitments to corporate social responsibility and by a belief that the modern business corporation could and should serve as a major social welfare institution.

Privatism and the Gospel of Corporate Social Responsibility

As shown in Chapter 2, the idea that business firms, particularly large corporations, had a responsibility to actively promote the well-being of society had been a subject of debate throughout the post-war period. In the late 1960s, corporate social responsibility was explicitly used as a rallying cry and justification for business involvement in the resolution of urban problems.

In the aftermath of the urban riots, the problems of the ghetto and of its inhabitants frequently were defined so that their solutions seemed to require mobilization of the resources and the managerial and technical skills of American corporations. The causes of poverty were identified with the characteristics of the poor (their lack of education and skills, their lower-class culture) or with the environmental inadequacies of impoverished areas (lack of jobs, poor housing, inefficient public services, and the like). By locating in the ghetto, by providing jobs and training, by fostering entrepreneurial skills and motivations, and by providing health, education, and transportation services, the corporation was expected to contribute to the rehabilitation of the poor and the revitalization of depressed areas. A. J. Cervantes, former mayor of St. Louis, argued that:

It is primarily up to private enterprise, and not to the government, to upgrade the disadvantaged, to provide training for the unemployed, to break down the complexities of job components, to employ the willing, to make them able, to push for social betterment, to dissolve the ghettos, to break through the vicious cycle of welfarism, to integrate the poor into an affluent economy, and to rebuild the cities (Cervantes 1967: 56).

These arguments reflected a widespread belief that it was the private sector, particularly large corporations, that possessed the creative leadership and economic resources necessary to help the poor. But why should the business community have been expected to respond? Indeed, to some, private sector investment in social welfare functions appeared economically unrealistic. Investment in the ghetto was a bad business risk. Further, the corporation's role as a social welfare institution was incompatible with the profit motive; insofar as that role was taken seriously, social welfare activities would have a fundamentally subversive impact upon a system of private property. Milton Friedman argued that the very idea of 'corporate social responsibility' is a myth and a delusion; if it is not pure rhetoric, it must mean that corporate management is to act in some way that is not in the interest of its employers. This amounts to managerial irresponsibility since, Friedman argued, in a private property system, management's only responsibility is to its employers: 'there is one and only one social responsibility of business—to use its resources and engage in activities designed to increase its profits so long as it stays within the rules of the game, which is to say, engages in open and free competition, without deception or fraud' (Friedman 1962: 133).

Friedman's concerns were at least partially unfounded. There is no evidence that corporate willingness to become involved in social welfare activities reflected a lessening of self-interested motivation or a lack of desire for profits. Indeed, Jules Cohn's 1970 survey of 247 major corporations indicated that, without exception, corporate leaders saw involvement in urban problem-solving as consistent with the profit motive (Cohn 1971: 4). Virtually all of the executives interviewed in the study saw their urban affairs programs as expressions of enlightened self-interest. Corporate managers hoped to enhance their company's reputation and image; to demonstrate compliance with government equal opportunity requirements in employment and in the awarding of contracts; to discourage boycotts, violence, and other threats to company well-being; and to promote a frank profit-making interest in attracting black customers or in selling services for urban affairs projects (Cohn 1971: 6–7). David Rockefeller said, 'Our urban affairs work is good for Chase Manhattan [Bank] in a strictly business sense' (Cohn 1971: 4). That 'business sense' frequently involved a long-term perspective on profitability.[11] The Committee for Economic Development (CED), a group composed of major corporate leaders, argued for a comprehensive conception of profit. 'Current profitability, once regarded as the dominant if not exclusive objective, is now often seen more as a vital means and powerful motivating force for achieving broader ends, rather than as an end in itself' (CED 1971: 22). As a permanent institution in society, the corporation was expected to look upon long-term security and stable growth as more important than immediate economic returns. It was no surprise, therefore, that the rhetoric of corporate management emphasized the compatibility of social responsibility and 'enlightened self-interest'.

In support of this view, minority representatives and some government leaders pointed out that the conditions of poverty and urban deprivation often reflected the chronic failures of the wealth producing sector of American society. It was now up to enlightened business institutions to actively undertake to reduce, if not fully remove, the conditions of economic inequity and racial discrimination which they had helped to create and sustain. At the same time, some corporate spokesmen warned their brethren that the absence of concerted social investment was likely to increase government activism and regulation and ultimately might fuel demands for greater corporate accountability. Moreover, business leaders recognized that the eruption of urban violence and racial conflict not only threatened current business investments but, more importantly, pointed to basic institutional failures that undermined the long-term stability of the political economy in which they held a major stake. Since business depends on conditions of social stability, they felt 'that it was only common sense to try to solve social problems that could threaten their future' (Cohn 1971: 4). Business involvement in the War on Poverty was justified by claims that the exercise of broad corporate social responsibilities was essential for political and economic progress. At the same time it was held to be consistent with enlightened self-interest. Business institutions could serve as trustees of the public interest and still offer a return to investors. According to the CED, corporate involvement in urban affairs signified the beginning of an alliance of public and private institutions that offered 'a new means for developing the innate capabilities of a political-economic system capable of managing social and technical change in the interest of a better social order' (CED 1971: 59).[12]

Support for broader corporate social responsibility and greater business involvement in resolving urban problems was not universal. Objections to corporate involvement in social welfare activities were based on both pragmatic and ideological arguments. Some critics suggested that there were widespread misconceptions of the nature of urban problems and an over-inflated image of the capacity of business institutions and public–private partnerships to play a role in their resolution. It was pointed out that proposals for government-private enterprise alliances in urban affairs often found their inspiration, and justification, in the real and anticipated contributions of such alliances in the areas of space exploration and national defense. Impressed by the achievements of the space program, some advocates of public–private alliances, according to Richard Nelson, sought to apply the moon-ghetto metaphor to programs that would 'launch the aerospace companies on problems of garbage collection, education and crime-control' (1977: 17). Others drew their inspiration from the proclaimed successes of the defense industry. Just as a mobilization of scientific, technical, and managerial skills through an alliance of government and industry had provided for defense against external threats by making possible the development of sophisticated weapons systems, it was expected that this alliance could help win the domestic wars: 'the war on poverty, the war on crime, and the war on blight' (Sapolsky 1969: 2). These expectations about the defense policy approach to center city resurrection were characterized by Harvey M. Sapolsky as the 'ballistic missile solution to the urban crisis' and were judged by him and others as grossly unrealistic. The success of a government–private sector alliance in national security affairs resulted from systematic mobilization of scientific and technical skills to achieve goals designated by a centralized authority. There was no agreement, however, as to the nature of the problems of the city, much less about the goals of urban public policy, nor was there a legitimized domestic equivalent of the Department of Defense to provide overall direction. Moreover, as Sapolsky pointed out, the problems that seem most susceptible to solution by the mobilization of managerial and technical skills—water pollution, air pollution, transportation—are essentially middle-class concerns and not the priorities of the core city poor, black or white (Sapolsky 1969: 10).

Some critics suggested that business involvement in the ghetto would take place only as a result of major government subsidies and corporate safeguards. William Tabb pointed out that past experience should raise serious doubts about the use of government incentives to attract industry to locate anywhere in urban areas.

To the extent that industrial location drives real estate prices up, adds to traffic congestion, uproots people from their homes and brings industry into residential areas, the program may have distinctly harmful effects on the neighborhood which may not be offset by the advantage of the additional employment opportunities in the urban poverty areas (Tabb 1969: 399).

Others argued that business involvement in social welfare activities would be detrimental to the poor and therefore the corporation should be excluded from the ghetto, or at least its presence should be rigorously regulated by public authority. Richard Cloward and Francis Piven asserted that corporations entering the ghetto as government subsidiaries would lead to 'corporate imperialism for the poor' (Cloward and Piven 1967: 365). Corporations would become 'new managers' of the ghetto, exploiting opportunities for subsidized profit while remaining insulated from effective political control. Inhabitants of the ghetto would be absorbed within the corporate enterprise—co-opted through token participation in corporate decision making—and, as a result, would become instruments of national corporate power. While the short-term economic conditions of the ghetto may be improved by corporate involvement, long-term prospects were endangered. Corporate involvement was preventing ghetto populations from developing a power base in local government by diminishing the importance of the political process and limiting the ability of local government to control the distribution of rewards and services.

Michael Harrington and others argued that the basic decisions needed to solve the problems of the poor 'are not susceptible to business priorities' (Harrington 1968: 5). Federal subsidies might succeed in prodding industry into the ghetto, but it would be at the cost of excluding the poor and the majority of blacks from the benefits. Federal subsidies to private builders would result in the construction of housing beyond the economic means of the very poor, amounting to what Harrington described as a public subsidy of private profit. Corporate involvement, unless it is subordinate to public decisions, cannot help the poor because it is precisely the pursuit of profit 'that has exacerbated our crisis and can hardly solve it'. What is needed to solve the

problems of the ghetto is 'an "uneconomic" investment of public funds motivated by considerations of social and aesthetic values rather than by the
calculus of private profit' (Harrington 1968: 5–6).

Finally, it was pointed out that the concept of corporate social responsibility was often applied by businessmen to rationalize their independence
from government regulation without addressing the questions of to whom
and for what they were or should be held accountable (Barnekov and Rich
1972).

The Corporation as a Social Welfare Institution

Despite the challenges raised to the gospel of social responsibility, and the
fears expressed that greater reliance on privatism would fail to alleviate and
perhaps might exacerbate the problems of depressed areas and their residents, there was a rapid mobilization of corporate urban involvements in
1967 and 1968. Most large corporations created departments or offices of
urban affairs to stimulate and monitor urban problem-solving efforts (*Business Week*, 17 Aug. 1968). Corporate donation policies were changed to
provide grants for groups involved in efforts to resolve urban problems.
Special outreach programs were set up to recruit blacks and other minorities
for entry-level jobs and several companies, including Aerojet-General, Fair-
child Hiller, Xerox, General Electric, and Mattel, set up subsidiaries meant to
be developed for eventual ownership by neighborhood groups. Cohn's survey in 1970 found that 201 major corporations had some sort of formally
organized urban affairs program and only four of these had been set up
before 1965. Corporate activities included: donations of cash, staff, executive
time, and/or facilities; minority group employment and advancement; hiring
and training the disadvantaged; and assistance to community economic
development, black capitalism, and environmental improvement efforts
(Cohn 1971: 8).

A major emphasis of private sector activity was on programs for the training and hiring of the poor of the central cities. In fact, federally funded
employment training programs pre-dated the War on Poverty. The Manpower Development and Training Act (MDTA), enacted in 1962, was the
first major program to give private industry a direct role in manpower training efforts. The Job Corps reached a peak of 42,000 enrollees in 1967 (*Congressional Record*, 20 Feb. 1975: S2330–5) but proved to be very expensive,
averaging about $8,000 per enrollee (Controller General 1969), and was an
early victim of the Johnson administration's effort to pay for the war in
Vietnam by cutting back on domestic expenditures. In 1968, President
Johnson endeavored to broaden industry's commitment to the training and
employment of the ghetto poor. In his message to Congress announcing the
JOBS (Job Opportunities in the Business Sector) program, he expressed his
hope that a new partnership between business and government 'will help put
500,000 hard-core unemployed into productive business and industrial jobs
in the next three years' (Johnson 1968: 50). He called upon American industry

to establish a National Alliance of Businessmen (NAB) 'to press the attack on the problem of the jobless in our cities' (Johnson 1968: 49). Henry Ford II of the Ford Motor Company and J. Paul Austin of Coca-Cola, named Chairman and Vice-Chairman, respectively, launched an effort to find 100,000 jobs for the hard-core unemployed by June 1969 and 500,000 by mid-1971.

Initial response to the program by the business community exceeded expectations. Forty percent of the firms contacted, primarily major companies, made pledges to hire trainees, and surprisingly two-thirds of these pledges were by firms who sought no federal subsidies (Nemore and Mangum 1969: 69). In March 1969, the Alliance announced that: 'the first year's goal will be reached months ahead of schedule! In the nation's fifty largest cities JOBS is progressing at the rate of thousands of placements per month—more than the anticipated rate. Over 125,000 hard core workers have been hired, and 85,000 remain on the job' (NAB 1969: 96). Moreover, more than two-thirds of these placements, NAB claimed, had been made voluntarily by employers and 'two out of every three hard-core workers have remained on the job—better than the normal rate for all entry level jobs' (NAB 1969: 97).

Despite what appeared to be a record of accomplishment, by 1970 the efforts of the NAB began to show signs of strain. An investigation conducted by the Senate Committee on Labor and Public Welfare revealed evidence disproving many of the inflated figures on job placements cited by the NAB (US Senate 1970). The Committee found that it was difficult to answer the question, 'What is JOBS accomplishing?'

The very desire to enlist the voluntary cooperation of businessmen dictates a handsoff policy in determining the kind of program to be instituted, the supervision of its progress, and the collection of verified data on its results. On a nationwide basis, we simply do not have any certain picture of what NAB/JOBS has done (US Senate 1970: 121).

Employers had been asked no specifics about the date or nature of their intended hiring. Many offered jobs that were listed at employment services and continued to find no takers. Others appeared to consider blacks and the disadvantaged to be synonymous.

While JOBS was initially designed to be a job-creation program there is little evidence that it either created new jobs or modified existing jobs on a significant scale for the long-run benefit of the disadvantaged (Perry 1976: 189). A General Accounting Office study found that a 'significant number of the jobs provided by contractors paid low wages and appeared to afford little or no opportunity for advancement' (Controller General 1971: 47), and a report prepared for the Manpower Administration concluded that 'most jobs offered through the JOBS program are dead end and are likely to be vulnerable to technological change' (Greenleigh Associates 1970).

When the economy began to stagnate in early 1970 the massive layoffs in various industries seriously affected NAB's efforts to locate and keep jobs in the hands of the hard-core unemployed. Many of the local NAB units not only failed to attain their job goals but also were forced to cancel drives to seek more pledges and jobs and it became increasingly difficult to interest top business leaders in the program (*New York Times*, 26 Dec. 1970). Part of the problem was that many businessmen were uncomfortable working with the poor, especially with militant blacks. According to John Gardner, Lyndon Johnson's Secretary of Health, Education, and Welfare, 'We could get a lot more action if we told [businessmen] they didn't have to sit down at a table with anyone . . . but could just raise the money and then lob it over the walls of the ghetto' (*Business and Society Review*, Oct. 1969: 6).

The private sector's other major voluntary organization for dealing with the urban crisis was the National Urban Coalition. Formed in August 1967, just after the Newark and Detroit riots, the Urban Coalition was designed to bring together leaders from business, local government, labor, and the black community—groups that normally did not collaborate—to seek solutions to the urban crisis (Gardner 1968). It immediately set out to establish local coalitions which were to include the same groups as the National Coalition and be committed 'to a comprehensive attack on all of the interrelated community problems—poverty, poor housing, inadequate educational facilities, racial tensions' (Bourne 1973: 30).[13]. John Gardner, who left the Johnson administration to become chairman of the Urban Coalition, reported in December 1968 that 39 local coalitions:

have gotten in an extraordinary variety of activities. They have formed venture capital corporations to assist black businesses, launched significant housing ventures, supported important new educational activities such as the Street Academies, set up youth councils, tackled local problems of race conflict, and so on (Gardner 1968).

Unfortunately, just over a year later *Business Week* reported that the National Urban Coalition and many of its local affiliates around the country were 'showing strains that could be the harbinger of worse days to come' (*Business Week*, 30 May 1970: 31). Its grand design of 100 local coalitions had fallen sort (only 47 were then in existence and less than half of those were strong) and in some cities such as Cleveland and Boston coalition activity had withered or died completely. Even in New York City, where the local coalition was viewed by the national headquarters as the most creative and productive—business leaders were beginning to lose interest (*New York Times*, 28 Oct. 1969). Top executives went to the initial meetings but began to designate second- or third-level executives as substitutes once the threat of riots diminished. In New York and elsewhere, the local coalition proliferated programs amid an atmosphere of enthusiastic goodwill and, some would add, freshly released guilt, but within a few years the enthusiasm gave way to what Eugene Callender, president of the New York Coalition, described as 'a realistic understanding of just how complicated and difficult urban problems are' (*New York Times*, 11 Nov. 1974).

Corporate Retrenchment and the Redirection of Urban Policy

The enthusiasm for business activism in seeking solutions to the problems of poverty and racism was rapidly drained once the threat of urban violence subsided and the experience with corporate social programs had demonstrated the limits of 'business know-how'. Privatism offered no quick solution to institutionalized problems of social and economic inequity. Similarly, the performance of corporations as social welfare institutions left much to be desired particularly by those who were the purported beneficiaries of corporate largess. The experience with public–private partnerships suggested that the private sector was no better prepared, and often less motivated, than the federal government to tackle the challenges of urban impoverishment and racial discrimination.

The rush of major corporations to participate in urban affairs activities began to subside by the early 1970s. Governmental pressure on corporations to join in efforts to relieve the urban crisis—which was aggressively pursued in the Johnson administration—lessened in the Nixon administration. The recession of 1970–1 also imposed limits on the expenditure of corporate funds for urban affairs activities, and many businessmen acknowledged that they had second thoughts about the role corporations should play in community affairs. According to Cohn, 'most of the board chairmen and company presidents interviewed seem chastened by their experiences as urban do-gooders, as though they had passed through some exotic rites of initiation and are now looking back, trying to understand what happened and why' (Cohn 1971: 1). They learned that urban affairs programs were more costly than they had anticipated and that they sometimes had unwelcome effects such as resentment of older employees to the hiring of disadvantaged minorities or confrontation resulting from direct contact with community groups. They also discovered that these programs frequently required skills which they did not possess. Business 'know-how' is largely managerial, technical, and entrepreneurial; the opportunities to use such skills are limited when, as in the 1960s, the definition of the problem is contested, the relevant constituencies are disparate and shifting, the criteria for evaluating success are uncertain, and the legitimacy of entrepreneurial interventions is questioned. Thus, the public–private alliances promoted in the 1960s resulted in activities which corporate leaders, among others, came eventually to view as poorly conceived and frustrating to implement. Cohn found that businessmen were reluctant to set their hopes too high for future achievement. 'We really didn't know what we were getting into,' said one chief executive officer. 'We were pressed hard to act fast, and unfortunately we did' (Cohn 1971: 3). Efforts to privatize the War on Poverty ultimately convinced many businessmen that they possessed neither the skills nor the incentives to play an active role in the social regeneration of cities. Business institutions, which remained active in city regeneration after the memory of urban violence began to diminish, redirected their efforts to areas that were more familiar: promoting physical redevelopment and economic growth.

Notes

1. At the outset, it is important to distinguish formal from functional urban policies in the US. The focus of this analysis is on the role of privatism in post-war policies intended to directly address the problems of American cities and their residents, but these policies constitute only a portion, and often a less influential portion, of the general domestic policies that have impacted urban America. Some key examples of ostensibly non-urban federal policies that have had significant impacts on cities include federally assisted highway programs that have encouraged population decentralization and suburban sprawl, federal spending for goods and services—particularly for weapons procurement—that have favored growing regions in the South and West, federally insured mortgage loans that stimulated private sector housing development in suburban areas, federal fiscal and monetary policies that have often limited the impact of public housing programs, and federal tax policies that have favored new investment over investment in existing facilities (URPG 1978: I-68–71). As formal urban policy emerged, there were often tensions between its objectives and the spatial impacts of ostensibly non-urban policies. For example, when the federal government launched the urban renewal program in the late 1940s to revitalize inner cities, the mortgage insurance and highway subsidy programs were at the same time encouraging a decentralization of population and economic activity that was contributing to a general pattern of decline in the vitality of the urban core. This tension has continued throughout the post-war period.
2. The Supreme Court upheld this interpretation of the power of eminent domain—*Berman* v. *Parker*, 348 US 26 (1954)—despite objections that it was inappropriate for government to take a person's property against his or her will for the profitable use of another citizen.
3. The Housing Act of 1949 was designed to clear slums and construct low-income housing, but amendments to the legislation in 1954 authorized communities to use 10 percent of project funds for commercial revitalization and in 1960 this proportion was raised to 30 percent. 'In actual practice', according to Dennis Judd, 'half or more of all funds could be diverted away from low-income housing to commercial redevelopment. Any renewal project that allocated 51 percent or more of its funds to housing was designated by the federal administrators as a "100 percent housing" project. By manipulating this definition, local authorities could allocate as much as two-thirds of their funds for commercial development, but still remain within federal guidelines' (Judd 1988: 269).
4. Roger Friedland's analysis of 130 central cities found that high-corporate-power cities (cities with two or more national corporate headquarters were considered high-corporate-power cities) had higher levels of urban renewal than low corporate cities (a mean of 76.9 acres versus 32.5 acres). He concludes that 'in high-corporate-power cities, downtown retail growth, the level of poverty in the city's core, population density, and the city fiscal burden, all have significant positive effects on urban renewal. In low-corporate-power cities, only downtown retail growth has a significant positive effect. In neither group of cities does the quality of the city's housing stock have a significant impact on the level of urban renewal ... [T]he results suggest that corporate power increases the local level of urban renewal, net of local economic conditions' (Friedland 1980: 216–20).
5. Development committees were established as organizations independent of existing business groups—Chambers of Commerce and downtown associations—

because the chief executives of large firms who formed the new committees usually perceived these groups to be sprawling, loosely knit coalitions of competing interests which were often led by small businessmen or second- or third-echelon executives of larger businesses who had to 'check back with Papa' before they could act (L. Peterson 1961: 130; Lash 1973: 46–8).

6. In 1975 Barnekov and Rich conducted a study of development committees in 33 cities using both personal interviews and a written questionnaire (Barnekov and Rich 1977). Information is also available on committees in Pittsburgh (Lowe 1967; Lubove 1969; Stewman and Tarr 1982), Philadelphia (Lowe 1967; Petshek 1973), St. Louis (Edgar 1970), Baltimore (Lyall 1982), New Haven (Wolfinger 1974; Talbot 1967), Chicago (Cafferty and McCready 1982), Minneapolis and St Paul (Brandl and Brooks 1982), Dallas (Claggett 1982), and Atlanta (Henson and King 1982).

7. Perhaps the most skillful was Richard Lee of New Haven who promoted the formation of the Citizen's Action Commission shortly after taking office as mayor in 1953 (Wolfinger 1974: 228). In a somewhat similar fashion, David Lawrence of Pittsburgh, Richardson Dilworth and Joseph Clark of Philadelphia, Joseph Darst, Raymond Tucker, and A. J. Cervantes of St. Louis, and William Schaefer of Baltimore worked closely with businessmen's development committees.

8. Until 1966 most of the committees were concerned almost exclusively with physical improvements, but beginning in 1967 increased efforts were made to deal with economic and social problems (Lash 1973: 46–8). In the Barnekov and Rich study no case was found in which a committee's efforts stressed social programs over physical programs. Moreover, the majority of unsuccessful programs sponsored by businessmen's committees were social programs: low-income housing projects, neighborhood improvement programs, education and job training efforts, and youth employment projects (Barnekov and Rich 1977).

9. Twenty-nine of the 33 committees included in the Barnekov and Rich study had prepared comprehensive plans. All except Ann Arbor Tomorrow, whose plan was under preparation at the time of the study, claimed that their plans had been implemented or were in the process of implementation. Only five committees indicated partial or significant alterations in their plans (Barnekov and Rich 1977).

10. As private governments, development committees have on occasion dominated the public agenda to the point whereby their priorities are systematically subsidized by public funds. This situation developed most dramatically in Pittsburgh during the late 1940s. Another illustration of a development committee assuming the role of a private government is the domination of social welfare policy, particularly the implementation stages, by Civic Progress in St Louis during the 1950s and 1960s. Edgar concluded that 'Civic Progress does not confine itself to the narrow definitions of health and welfare, but rather ranges across a broad spectrum of problems and solutions akin to the Welfare State' (Edgar 1970: 11).

11. As Michael Reagan pointed out, 'managers believe and hope that their good-will expenditures will enhance profits, and so long as they are operating on this premise, profit is still the motive' (Reagan 1963: 136–7).

12. The US experience with corporate involvement in urban affairs in the 1960s and 1970s helped to shape a nation-wide experiment with corporate social responsibility in Britain a decade later.

13. Cited in Bourne from a Coalition brochure, *An Urban Coalition in Your Community* (Bourne 1973).

4

Local Economic Development Policy in the US

IN the 1970s the pursuit of the private city in the US gained new momentum. Some commentators proposed that the urban policies of the 1960s demonstrated the high cost of underemphasizing the economic priorities of the private sector. Once again it was asserted that urban problems resulted from too little private investment and their resolution required an extension of privatism. Within a decade after the urban riots, Robert W. MacGregor, President of Chicago United, a consortium of business leaders, argued:

My criticism is that privatism is waning. Urban strategists should concern themselves with the decline of privatism, or the failure of the private sector to do more. In my judgement, the real failure is that the private sector is not active enough in urban development. We do not have enough business involvement and the conclusion we ought to reach today is that we should broaden the scope—to see that business takes more leadership. Some leading urbanologists believe that the cities are strangled with insolvable problems today, and that the cities of America will die. If privatism is not encouraged, the prophets of doom could be accurate (MacGregor 1977: 467).

In the political and economic environment of the 1970s these sentiments were often well received by both national and local public officials. While the renewal of enthusiasm for privatism was in part a result of disillusionment with costly social programs, it was also a reaction to changing economic conditions at both the national and local levels. Dislocations and unemployment created by national economic recession, continuing out-migration of population and economic activity from central cities—particularly the older industrial cities in the Northeast and Midwest—and chronic municipal fiscal stress resulting from dwindling revenues and expanding service obligations combined to focus attention on the economic dimensions of urban policy. Indeed, for many municipalities a concern with cost containment and with stimulating private investment became a practical necessity.

The shift in attention to economic priorities was also in tune with the more conservative policy orientation of the federal government. The Republican administrations in the early 1970s declared that the urban crisis was over.[1] They embarked on a number of initiatives to reduce the federal role in local affairs including lower subsidies for housing, efforts to cut the cost of welfare and food stamp programs, and policies intended to dismantle the Great Society poverty programs. The Nixon administration's strategy was to disengage the federal government from social programs and to rely increasingly 'upon State and local government to make the multitude of public decisions required in the pursuit of domestic goals' (ACIR 1970: 1). Under the label 'New Federalism', repeated attempts were made to reduce expenditures on social programs while at the same time money was provided to state and localities with few restrictions attached through a new revenue sharing program. Despite the rhetoric, outlays for grants-in-aid to state and local governments, including revenue sharing, rose from $20.3 billion in fiscal 1969 to $59 billion in fiscal 1976 (EO 1980: 237).

Nevertheless, a number of urban leaders viewed the shift in policy orientation with trepidation. The declared 'end of the urban crisis' was regarded as simply a way of justifying federal cost cutting and the benign neglect of cities. 'What they really mean', said Representative Parren Mitchell from Baltimore, 'is that the cities are not burning' (*New York Times*, 23 Mar. 1975). For some, Nixon's 'New Federalism' was a convenient rationale for the reduction of federal responsibilities for cities. Similarly, there was concern that the decentralization of expenditure decisions through revenue sharing would reinforce a historical pattern of neglect of the cities by state governments. Increasingly, federal officials were defining the problems of urban areas as local problems requiring local solutions. In this context, the need for city governments to turn to the private sector was as much a response to national policy withdrawal as a result of local policy design. Louis Masotti articulated the view of many when he argued on pragmatic grounds for a new era of privatism. 'As federal urban dollars fade away, and until the states demonstrate a sincere financially supported commitment to their cities, joint public–private ventures of mutual benefit may be the only game in town' (Masotti 1974: 11–12).

By the mid-1970s, urban privatism was being pursued with renewed vigor. National and local government policies reflected a growing preoccupation with strategies to promote urban economic development and specifically with those that would use limited public resources to stimulate private investment in distressed areas. The emphasis on local economic development gained its fullest expression during the Carter administration. While still a candidate, Carter promised to end the federal government's benign neglect of distressed cities and to restore urban policy to a high priority on the national agenda. Speaking before the United States Conference of Mayors prior to his election, Carter called for 'a coherent national urban policy that is consistent, compassionate, realistic and that reflects the decency and good sense of the American people' (USHUD 1978: 114). After the election in 1976, the new administration set out to develop a comprehensive and multi-faceted urban policy; one which recognized the central importance of cities to the nation as a whole and which established a 'New Partnership to Conserve America's Communities'.

Over the next four years a wide variety of policy instruments were promoted, but much of the Carter urban policy never reached fruition. The promised 'comprehensive' approach failed to materialize. Yet, the administration did succeed in shifting the focus of the urban policy dialogue by concentrating significant attention and resources on efforts to assist distressed cities through programs of economic development. By the late 1970s economic development had emerged as the keynote of both national urban policy attention and local policy initiative. The prevailing expectation was that public–private partnerships would initiate a new era of civic entrepreneurship and economic development programs would promote job creation and help cities capture the general benefits of economic growth.

To understand and evaluate urban privatism in the 1970s one must examine a number of questions about the meaning and impact of local economic development policy. What were the expectations which defined this policy approach and what were the anticipated roles of national and local government in the processes of urban economic change? How were local economic development strategies carried out, what were their outcomes and impacts, and who were their beneficiaries? Finally, what lessons might be learned from experience with efforts to promote local economic development? While the discussion in this chapter focuses on policies and programs that were initiated in the 1970s, many aspects of these policies and programs remained salient in the 1980s; their limitations were also apparent throughout the subsequent decade.

The Evolution of Local Economic Development Policy

Local economic development policies and programs in the 1970s recalled earlier themes of urban privatism. The city was defined largely in economic terms and the fate of urban communities and their residents was linked to local business prosperity. The physical renewal of the central city was re-emphasized and, as a result, a number of the redevelopment projects of the 1970s were as impressive in their scale as the urban renewal projects of the 1950s and 1960s. But, in contrast to urban renewal where elimination of 'blight' was the purported goal, attention was now directed to projects that would achieve revitalization by stimulating general changes in the urban economy. The challenge to the embattled American city was to create a new economic base—one that would transform declining physical and capital infrastructure, attract new firms, new population and new employment, and enable the city to successfully compete for a prominent role in an emerging service society. The key to meeting this challenge was to stimulate private investment in the city.

Local economic development was commonly portrayed as a policy approach with widely dispersed benefits, an approach which would ultimately help the poor while it simultaneously served the interests of the city as a whole (URPG 1978; USHUD 1978). Claims about the general benefits of economic development helped to rationalize the shift in focus away from urban social policy and this rationalization was often reinforced by a revision in the conception of the problems of urban poverty. The view that now came into fashion was that among the many problems faced by distressed cities and their residents, the chief ailment was unemployment.[2]

By the early 1970s many urban scholars as well as government officials were convinced that the problem of unemployment could not be effectively addressed through the kind of social policy interventions into the labor market tried in the past. They concluded that these approaches were too costly and too ineffective in producing major improvements in the economic well-being of low income people, especially minorities. Indeed, the programs often took on the stigma of failure and support for them declined, even among some of their earlier advocates (Aaron 1978). The employment problems of the urban poor were now perceived to be the direct result of an insufficient demand for labor in urban areas. It followed that employment problems—and therefore accompanying problems such as poor housing, urban crime, inadequate health care—could be addressed most effectively by stimulating the demand for labor in low-income areas and this could be achieved by subsidizing one or more of the costs of doing business there (Doolittle 1983: 75).

Where the manpower programs of the 1960s had assumed that companies already located in cities would hire the poor if only they acquired appropriate skills and work habits, it was believed now that the public sector had to take an active role in creating new jobs. This entailed a responsibility to stimulate the growth and development of new economic enterprises. The best way to help the poor was to create jobs and the best way to create jobs was to strengthen the city's economic base. Moreover, success in creating new jobs would produce additional economic reverberations that would strengthen retailing, revitalize neighborhoods, and shore up the tax bases of the nation's cities. This logic had obvious political appeal. By focusing on job creation and income generation rather than on welfare programs and income redistribution, everyone would be made better off. Indeed, economic development programs at times were portrayed as painless ways to help the poor.

By the mid-1970s, local economic development was understood to require active but different roles for federal and local government. The primary responsibility of the federal government was to serve as a catalyst for local initiative. Municipalities in economic distress were to be provided with policy tools and resources that would concentrate efforts on consolidating growth promoting coalitions with the private sector. To be successful, federal policies had to be matched by local government initiatives. City governments had to promote and channel economic change by pulling together and marketing packages of inducements, capital subsidies, and service incentives to influence private investment decisions and locational choices. The idea that dominated local economic development strategies was that limited public resources would have the greatest impact if they were used as leverage to stimulate greater amounts of private investment. The concept of leverage eventually became the common feature of a wide variety of economic development strategies at both the national and local levels and it emerged as a central facet of the urban policy proposals offered by the Carter administration.

The Search for Policy Leverage

A central assumption underlying the Carter administration's concern with urban policy was the belief that good urban policy was good economic policy because national economic prosperity depended upon the prosperity of America's cities. The administration proposed that 'the vitality of American cities [was] crucial to maintaining our nation's economic strength and quality of life' (URPG 1978: P–1). There was nothing new about this economic rationale for federal involvement in urban programs. Indeed, the administration pointed out that the importance of cities for the national economy had been 'recognized more than forty years ago in the first major Federal study of urban problems' (URPG 1978: P–1). That report, issued in 1937 by the Urbanism Committee of the National Resources Committee (NRC), argued that the neglect of the central role of cities in the national economy as well as the continual and cumulative disregard of urban policy at the national level was inhibiting the nation's recovery from the Depression. It called for a recognition of the city as 'the workshop of our industrial society and the nerve center of our vast and delicate commercial mechanism' (NRC 1937: V), and it admonished the federal government to carry out policies that 'take into account the place of the urban community in the national economy' (NRC 1937: X). The Carter administration echoed these themes. It proposed that national economic recovery in the 1970s depended upon the economic renewal of America's urban places. A comprehensive urban policy was an essential part of a national program to address the problems of inflation, unemployment, and declining productivity (URPG 1978: P–6).

It followed from this reasoning that federal policy for cities should concentrate on redressing the conditions of urban economic decline by stimulating local programs that would enhance the prospects of cities while simultaneously contributing to national economic prosperity. It was expected that by focusing national and local resources on economic development it would be possible to redress a myriad of acute urban ailments. In particular, it was pointed out that many of the dimensions of urban distress reflected the cumulative impact of the continuing decentralization and dispersal of population and economic activity.

For some this urban 'thinning out' process has created the special pressures of rapid growth, for others the social and fiscal strain of population and employment decline. No region has a monopoly on the problems of either growth or decline . . . However, the older, formerly industrial cities are afflicted with absolute increases in their poor populations; meanwhile, they are losing middle and upper income population together with employment, particularly manufacturing employment (USHUD 1978: 2).

The decentralization and dispersal of population and economic activity was perceived to be part of a general economic transformation and it signified that the nation had 'entered a new stage of urban development' (USHUD 1978: 2). The need now was for urban policies that matched the new challenges posed by the economics of urban growth and decline. This meant above all else that local economic development should be encouraged in ways that would assist distressed communities to cope with and gain from the process of economic change.

In formulating its urban policy, the Carter administration sought an approach which addressed the city as a whole and was balanced in its efforts to assist both people and places. The President's Urban and Regional Policy Group (URPG), an interdepartmental task force appointed by Carter in early 1977 to develop recommendations for a comprehensive national urban strategy, emphasized that:

urban problems are not only those of people, but also those of places. It is not enough to increase job options for the unemployed if high costs prevent them from securing affordable decent housing. It is not enough to provide basic income assistance to the poor if their neighborhoods and housing are decaying, and if public services remain inadequate. If meaningful improvements in the quality of urban life are to occur, urban policy cannot address the problems of people without addressing the troubles of cities. Put another way, it cannot address problems of places and ignore the hardships of people who live in those places. Dealing effectively with urban problems will require an emphasis on both people and places (URPG 1978: P–5).

In practice, the proposed balance of policies for people and places gave way to an approach which emphasized economic assistance to places and largely omitted policy consideration of social assistance to people. This was most apparent in the approach to the problems of urban unemployment. The administration recognized that the most acute manifestation of distress— particularly in many of the older, industrial cities—was the high rate of unemployment which the URPG reported as increasing from 6 percent among central city residents in 1974 to 9.2 percent in 1976 (URPG 1978: I–43). Therefore, it concentrated a great deal of attention on the problem of urban unemployment. But the policy emphasis was always on job creation stimulated by economic development rather than on direct assistance to the unemployed. According to Stuart Eizenstat, Carter's chief domestic adviser, a decision was made to limit urban policy to 'programs that affect cities as cities, that will make them more livable, encourage their growth, stabilize their tax bases, [and] make them better providers of services' (*New York Times*, 19 Sept. 1977).

The Carter administration believed that government alone could not reverse the powerful economic and demographic trends that had pulled firms, jobs, and middle-class taxpayers from distressed cities. As the *President's National Urban Policy Report* of 1978 proposed, a viable policy should recognize that the private sector must play a pivotal role in urban change. 'No matter how well-conceived public efforts might be to restore and maintain our communities as good places in which to live and find work, the ultimate outcomes depend on private decisions and private investment' (USHUD 1978: 91). In this context, the basic responsibility of the federal government was to provide strong incentives for business to reinvest and relocate in central cities. Washington could best use its limited resources in attempts to mobilize the private sector. Consistent with the concept of policy leverage, properly crafted programs that used small amounts of public money could be expected to generate large amounts of private investment.

Which programs would best express the administration's economic development objectives was a contested issue from the outset. Indeed, one sign of the importance the Carter administration attached to urban policy in general and economic development programs in particular was the vigorous competition among cabinet level secretaries about which Department would provide the leadership for the new urban policy. The Departments of Treasury, Commerce, and Housing and Urban Development each offered an economic development scheme to serve as the key program initiative. Treasury Secretary W. Michael Blumenthal announced the establishment of an Office of Urban Finance to develop financial assistance programs for cities including an urban development bank that would provide low-cost loans for construction of industrial facilities; Commerce Secretary Juanita M. Kreps stressed a new urban focus for the Economic Development Administration to revive sagging local economies and decrease unemployment; and HUD Secretary Patricia Harris proposed to greatly expand the economic development provisions in the Community Development Block Grant (CDBG) program and to set up the Urban Development Action Grant program (UDAG) to stimulate economic recovery in the most distressed urban areas.

The UDAG program, which ultimately became Carter's most fully developed leveraging initiative, was approved early in the administration as part of the Housing and Community Development Act of 1977. A discretionary fund of $400 million was to be distributed to 'distressed' communities to carry out specific economic development projects such as amassing land or providing services necessary to convince a company to stay in a city or to attract a new firm. But while the UDAG program would later be proclaimed as the principal Carter program to strengthen urban economies, early in his administration the President continued to seek a more 'comprehensive' strategy to infuse new economic life into troubled cities. The report of his Urban and Regional Policy Group argued that 'no simplistic "centerpiece" policy will achieve our commitments. Instead a comprehensive policy approach is necessary' (URPG 1978: II–11). This was the keynote when Carter announced his 'New Partnership to Conserve America's Communities' on 28 March 1978. He presented a plan that was intended to be flexible enough to respond to diverse needs of all cities and communities, that was focused on conserving existing communities and, at the same time, recognized that some places require strategic targeting of resources (URPG 1978).

The 'New Partnership' established a broad target group for federal policy attention, and it also included active roles for state and local government, neighborhood groups, and voluntary organizations. But the private sector had the pivotal role as the provider of jobs and the builder of the new urban resource base. To provide the needed leverage to stimulate private investment, the President proposed to establish 'a National Development Bank which would encourage businesses to locate or expand in economically distressed urban and rural areas [and] . . . . would be authorized to guarantee investments totaling $11 billion through 1981' (USHUD 1978: 137).[3] The debate about the National Development Bank foreshadowed problems that would plague Carter throughout his administration in his effort to establish a coherent national urban policy.

The National Development Bank. The concept of a development bank was described as the key to the 'new' Democratic urban strategy (*New York Times*, 7 Sept. 1977). Originally called an 'urban development bank' (nicknamed Urbank[4]), it involved a series of financing incentives to persuade business to locate or expand in depressed urban areas (US Treasury Department 1977). The Treasury experts who proposed the original version of the development bank argued that it would alleviate structural unemployment by inducing the private sector to expand job opportunities in the nation's older cities (US Treasury Department 1977: 1). But skeptics charged that the 'Urbank' was only a catchy name in search of a purpose.[5] Louis Winnick, deputy vice president of the Ford Foundation observed that the country was already well-endowed with credit mechanisms so 'What purpose would a new one serve?' (*New York Times*, 7 Sept. 1977). For others, Urbank was only a re-invention of the discredited urban renewal program. The most serious charge was that the bank did not address the most critical factors affecting the location of economic activity. It was based on the assumption that lack of capital was the principal impediment to renewed private sector investment in declining cities, but a number of studies were showing that other factors were more important (Harrison and Kanter 1978; Schmenner 1978). For example, James M. Howell, senior vice president of the First National Bank of Boston, pointed out that a survey by his bank showed that, when considering a city location, business executives were primarily concerned about crime, high property taxes, and the absence of skilled labor. (Howell 1979: 274). Yet more than half of the $4.4 billion sought by Carter in budget authority for his urban strategy in fiscal 1979 would be directed towards various types of capital assistance to be used by the development bank to encourage firms to remain or relocate in depressed areas.

These criticisms emerged during a lengthy, and ultimately unsuccessful, battle to gain Congressional approval for some version of the development bank idea. One commentator called it Carter's search for a unicorn (*National Journal*, 16 Dec. 1978: 2030). Disagreement about what the development bank should do, conflict between agencies as to who should run it, concern whether it was or was not needed or that it would duplicate the functions of programs already in existence, and criticism that it was an expensive solution to the wrong problem all provided fuel for Congressional opposition to the administration's proposal. The fundamental problem, however, was that in a time of steep inflation, many members of Congress were not willing to spend large sums of money on a narrow urban constituency. Nevertheless, having defined the development bank as the focal point of its urban policy, the White House persisted in its effort to push some version through Congress.

Economic Development Administration. As it became clear that Congress was not going to approve the development bank in the manner originally proposed by the administration, advocates of economic development turned greater attention to the Economic Development Administration (EDA), an organization which had operated within the Commerce Department since 1966 and already had the authority and capacity to stimulate private investment. EDA's basic mission was threefold: to support strategic economic development planning by local governments, to subsidize the construction or renovation of public facilities that would promote economic development, and to provide aid to areas undergoing 'economic dislocation' such as plant closings. However, during its first decade, EDA functioned largely as a rural development agency, providing only 17 percent of all its public works and development funds to cities with populations over 50,000 (Martin and Leone 1977: 47).

The Public Works and Economic Development Act of 1965 mandated EDA to help establish stable and diversified local economies in areas that suffered from persistent unemployment. It was to accomplish this mandate by providing 'financial assistance, including grants for public works and development facilities, to communities, industries, enterprises, and individuals in areas needing development' (Public Law 89–136, Eighty-ninth Congress, First Session). Deficiencies in the local infrastructure were assumed to be the principal cause of community distress. Strengthening of that infrastructure would stimulate self-sustaining growth in the private sector—growth which would continue after federal assistance had been withdrawn. Since the private sector was to be the key remedy to unemployment in depressed areas, support was mobilized for the EDA legislation by emphasizing the role of private development. The economic development tools provided to EDA to fulfill its mission included grants and loans for the construction or improvement of public infrastructure; long-term, low-interest loans for commercial and industrial enterprises willing to locate in a depressed area; technical assistance grants for planning, research, and demonstration projects; and job training programs. Improvements to public infrastructure were emphasized as a means of making depressed areas more attractive to private industry.

In the mid-1970s, growing unhappiness among big city mayors about the responsiveness of EDA to urban problems brought pressure to bear on the agency to change its priorities. From the fourth quarter of 1973 to the first quarter of 1975, the US experienced its worst recession since the 1930s. Concern with persistently high unemployment led Congress in July 1976, to enact, over President Ford's veto, a program of economic stimulants including $2 billion through fiscal 1977 for state and local public works projects. The expectation was that almost all of the construction would be done by the private sector. It was the largest anti-recessionary public works effort since the Great Depression. Administered by EDA, the program was intended to be implemented quickly, and therefore funds were authorized for projects that could be started within 90 days of approval. Under the law, priority was to be given to local governments and to areas with high unemployment.

While the legislation mandated EDA to give greater attention to urban areas, there were still bitter complaints from big city mayors when the first awards were announced in December of 1976. The mayors argued that not enough funds went to areas with the worst unemployment and they were particularly upset that almost half of the 100 largest cities in the country did not receive funding (*National Journal*, 23 July 1977: 247). Almost immediately after taking office, the Carter administration recommended that the program be redesigned so that more funds would go to areas with the greatest amount of unemployment and proposed that its authorization be increased by $4 billion. Carter sought to increase grants to urban areas by 65 percent, and he shifted the agency's priorities in the direction of business assistance (USHUD 1978: 134). For fiscal 1977, the last Ford budget, less than one-fifth of the $407 million EDA budget (excluding the anti-recessionary public works program) went for business loans and loan guarantees. For fiscal 1979, support for business assistance rose to nearly $1.1 billion out of a total EDA budget of $1.5 billion (*National Journal*, 23 July 1979: 1033).

EDA's moment of glory occurred after the administration resolved that Congress was not going to approve the development bank proposal. A new plan was offered which was designed to accomplish the bank's objectives through EDA. If Congress had accepted the plan, EDA would have acquired significant influence in the nation's capital markets, a remarkable transformation for an agency that had been primarily concerned with public works projects in rural areas. But the effort bogged down in a series of disputes in Congress: should EDA assist only distressed communities or let its funds flow freely in a pork barrel fashion to virtually every congressional district; should it support small or large businesses; should it be primarily concerned about manufacturing or also subsidize commercial and retail enterprises? There were also complaints about the expenditure of large sums of money on industrial parks which had failed to attract firms and about the high rate of defaults in the business loan program. However, the principal reason for Carter's failure to get Congressional approval for the transformation of EDA into a high-powered urban agency was an irreconcilable difference between House members who wanted more money to be spent on politically popular construction projects and Senators who were worried about budget deficits. The effort to turn EDA into the principal agency for urban economic development was defeated and just prior to the 1980 election, Congress passed a simple measure allowing EDA to continue spending at the same level for the next fiscal year.

Urban Development Action Grants. In contrast to Carter's other urban policy initiatives, the UDAG program sailed through Congress without a great amount of opposition.[6] Eventually, UDAG would be proclaimed as the principal innovation of the Carter administration's effort to strengthen the economies of ailing cities. The program gained a great deal of popularity among state and local officials as well as in Congress. Indeed, in June of 1979, the *New York Times* described UDAG as the focus of 'a legislative toe dance featuring representatives of Sunbelt and Snowbelt cities attempting to be civilized about the politics of scarcity' (*New York Times*, 8 June 1979).

The primary objective of UDAG was to stimulate private investment in severely distressed communities by providing a capital subsidy for economic development projects where there was a firm commitment of private resources. In order to receive funds, local government officials had to show that a project would be viable if a specific problem were solved—usually a financing gap—and that the Action Grant could solve it. The project had to be 'wired' in that both the local government and the private investor were committed in advance before the project was approved. The grant application also had to estimate how many jobs the project would create, predict how the project would affect the municipality's fiscal position, show how much experience the local government had with similar undertakings, and provide information on physical and economic distress in the community including the condition of its housing stock, its tax base, its median income level, and its population losses (Webman 1981: 191–3).

The distinguishing feature of the UDAG program was its emphasis on the role of the private sector, particularly its requirement that there be a legally binding private commitment to invest in a specific project. This meant that business people were brought directly and publicly into the design of a development project. 'The program not only subsidizes private firms', said analyst Jerry Webman, 'but [it] also brings them into a bargaining process with public officials. The bargains that are struck in this process are the basis for the program' (Webman 1981: 207). UDAG's effect went well beyond the public and private dollars that were authorized for projects; it reshaped policymaking at the local level. The program thrust local government into a proactive role as a deal maker in economic development projects. The attention of local government was shifted towards the consummation of agreements between city hall and private businesses in order to structure financial arrangements which would support economic development projects. The acquisition of a UDAG award was often perceived as evidence of the political and technical proficiency of local officials, as a demonstration of the viability of local public–private partnerships, and as an indicator of renewed economic vitality in the community. It was not unusual for these awards to be hailed in a community as major political accomplishments.

The development strategy of the UDAG program, which emphasized specific projects with binding commitments from private investors, combined flexibility with the ability to tailor assistance to fit the investment needs of specific firms. It differed from the 'cookie cutter' approach of the urban renewal program where local redevelopment agencies used urban renewal funds to buy land and sell it at greatly reduced prices to developers through a process of competitive bidding. They could also provide some indirect aid for infrastructure and public facilities, but they could not directly subsidize a business in return for investment in a renewal area. The result was a mixed record in attracting developers. In fact, in many cities, redevelopment agencies assembled and cleared land but could find no private developer to buy and use it (Webman 1981: 192). On the other hand, in the UDAG program a deal had to be structured with a specific developer or developers before a grant proposal could be submitted to the federal government. Otherwise, there was a great deal of discretion as to how UDAG funds could be used: public facilities related to a project could be financed (parking garages, streets, plazas, etc.); sites could be acquired and prepared and then leased or sold to a developer; houses and businesses in the development area could be relocated; and equity or debt financing could be provided for private facilities. As a development tool, the UDAG program was both more flexible and more precise than urban renewal, and therefore it was not surprising that the private funds required for completion of projects were generally forthcoming.

Municipal Marketing and Civic Entrepreneurship

The *President's National Urban Policy Report* for 1978 pointed out that 'until this decade, economic development was not considered a major responsibility of local government in most cities. That function was left to Chambers of Commerce, downtown associations, and similar organizations' (USHUD 1978: 90). While it is true that, throughout the post-war period, local public officials frequently formed coalitions with private sector élites to promote economic growth (Barnekov and Rich 1976; Molotch 1976; Mollenkopf 1977), increasingly in the 1970s, local governments directly assumed the function of promoting economic development; mayors and city commerce departments took on the roles traditionally played by local businessmen's organizations. 'Mayors are now entrepreneurs,' pointed out David B. Walker, assistant director of the Advisory Commission on Intergovernmental Relations (ACIR). 'They have become master orchestrators of public and private projects. They are no longer just old-style managers' (*National Journal*, 26 May 1979: 868). The change was hardly the result of a recent awakening to the virtues of promoting privatism through local government. Rather, it was the outgrowth of a new vision of the entrepreneurial role of city government and its political leadership that appeared to be demanded by the emerging realities of urban change.

In the 1970s, American cities were engaged in a competition for economic growth. A national transformation was reshaping the urban landscape, and no city could afford to sit on the sidelines unless it was willing to consign its future to chance. The 'urban sweepstakes' underway paralleled 'the one that was played one hundred years ago. During the 1860s and 1870s, cities competed for railroad connections. Those that lost the railroad competition stagnated. In the 1970s, cities compete[d] for economic growth and affluent residents (Judd 1979: 359). The cities in greatest economic distress were those that were losing the competition and their prospects remained dim so long as they failed to obtain a competitive edge in the dynamic national marketplace.

Since it was the private sector that would pace the transformation, the fortunes of particular cities depended upon their ability to capture and retain firms and to induce local investment and therefore jobs in the new growth areas of the economy. It was not enough for city government to be responsive to the priorities of local business institutions; it was now necessary for the public sector to take the initiative in promoting business priorities. Municipal marketing and civic entrepreneurship were responsibilities now lodged firmly in the public domain. Cities that succeeded in their programs of economic development would create a favorable climate for private investment and this, in turn, would place these cities in a preferred position to win the urban sweepstakes. Cities that neglected economic development or failed to provide effective programs would experience continued decline. In this sense, local government support for privatism was often portrayed as more than a preferred policy approach: it was the essential requirement for civic survival.

The belief that what was good for business was good for the city became part of the popular creed of local economic development policy. Under that creed, the civic polity was first and foremost an economic development agent. In the 1970s, the accommodation of many city governments to this role was so complete that local businessmen's development committees which previously performed civic promotion and brokerage functions often became superfluous. In many cities these business organizations closed down or cut back on their promotional functions. What need was there for the private sector to maintain organizations to promote economic development projects when city governments now openly accepted this as their responsibility?

The *President's National Urban Policy Report* of 1978 recognized the changes that were taking place and pointed out that 'some cities and metropolitan areas [were] ... developing highly sophisticated tools and mechanisms to promote their economic redevelopment, nearly always involving joint public and private planning' (USHUD 1978: 72). Departments of Commerce changed from passive complaint bureaus for the business community to active promoters of economic development projects. Cities developed capabilities to simplify local decision making on economic development projects, to hold or assemble land, to provide long-term, low-cost financing for development projects, to share risks through co-venturing, and to provide tax abatements in exchange for desirable development (USHUD 1978: 72).

Quasi-Public Economic Development Corporation. One of the tools that was increasingly used by local government during the 1970s was the quasi-public economic development corporation. While accurate figures have not been compiled, it has been estimated that at least 15,000 of these organizations were operating in communities across the US by 1980 (Levy 1981: 1). Certainly every major city had at least one, and often many, development corporations each with its own combination of public and private participants and funding arrangements. These organizations differed from the businessmen's development committees that were active in the urban renewal program because they were set up by local government, received and administered public funds, and offered public incentives such as land banking and tax abatement schemes. Many different mechanisms were used to support these organizations including CDBG funds, UDAG paybacks, general revenue, and even private debenture sales. They were governed by executive boards made up of public officials, citizens, and businessmen and women and were charged with promoting city goals and objectives for economic development. The advantage of development corporations was that their legal status as quasi-public, non-profit organizations provided them with powers which were difficult or impossible for public agencies to exercise and, even more important, they were insulated from the political process. They could bypass restrictions and procedures which prevent government from entering into partnerships or agreements with the private sector; they could make direct loans to private business; buy, develop, and lease property without public hearings and approvals; issue bonds; and take equity positions in projects. In effect, the city through the development corporation could act as an investor and risk taker in partnership with private business (Kysiak 1983: 20).

In Detroit, for example, public officials created a structure and strategy for economic development that connected several development corporations— the Economic Growth Corporation, the Economic Development Corporation, the Downtown Development Authority, and the Development Corporation— with each other, to private organizations, and to city, county, and state agencies through a series of overlapping memberships (Hill 1986: 103) In New Orleans, Mayor Ernest Morial appointed prominent local business and banking leaders to sit on the board of directors of the New Orleans Citywide Development Corporation (NOCDC). Its purpose was to assist businesses in obtaining credit by arranging joint ventures between the Small Business Administration, private lenders, and the NOCDC (Smith and Keller 1986: 145). In these cities and many others, the development corporation became a principal vehicle for the promotion and implementation of a local economic development agenda.

Industrial Revenue Bonds. Another economic development tool which gained popularity at the local level during the 1970s was the Industrial Revenue Bond (IRB). These were tax exempt bonds issued by state and local governments to provide financing for private sector investment in plants and equipment. Unlike general obligation bonds, revenue bonds were not backed by the taxing power of the state or locality but only by the revenues of the project being financed—the company receiving funds guaranteed repayment. A state or local government issued an IRB 'on behalf of' a non-exempt private borrower, in effect, transferring its tax exempt status to the borrower. Since IRBs yielded tax-exempt returns to bond holders, they were sold to private investors—usually banks—at rates well below the prevailing market rate of interest, generally about 70 percent of the rate for taxable corporate bonds. The debt was amortized from payments made by the private borrower which were passed through the issuer to the holders of the IRB. The local government was simply the conduit necessary to obtain a tax exemption (Woolridge and Gray 1981: 84); it was the federal treasury, in lost tax revenue, that subsidized the borrowing costs of the private investor.

IRBs were first used in Mississippi in the 1930s, but they did not gain widespread application until the 1970s. In addition to rising interest rates, the intensified efforts of local governments to influence industrial and commercial location decisions encouraged increased use of IRBs as a development tool. Proponents argued that bonds represented the only source of investment funds for many small companies. It was also asserted that IRBs 'are productive instruments for promoting economic development by making saving and investment more attractive to individuals and businesses. Their use results in overall gains in capital formation, employment, and output, rather than merely changes in the location of economic activity' (Ture 1980: 517). In 1970, 70 percent of all tax-exempt securities consisted of general obligation bonds, dedicated to financing improvements to local government facilities and backed by local taxing powers (*National Journal*, 18 Oct. 1980: 1749). By 1979, tax-exempt financing for private entities accounted for about 50 percent of the market for new long-term issues and the biggest expansion occurred in the volume of small issue IRBs—from just over $3 billion in 1978 to over $12 billion in 1981 (Rivlin 1983: 304).

The increasing use of IRBs and the growth of locally organized development corporations, along with the availability of other development tools from the UDAG, EDA, and CDBG programs, led to the emergence of a new type of city official whose background more often reflected experience in economic development than in civic governance. Success in urban bureaucracies now depended upon whether one had the training and experience needed to work closely with lawyers, bankers, financial consultants, and business executives to structure complex arrangements of public and private financing. Reputations rested on the capacity to promote growth by eliminating or, at least, reducing regulatory controls on the private sector and on the ability to outbid officials from other cities in providing subsidies for private investment. The new civic entrepreneurs were also learning to be more self-reliant. Instead of focusing exclusively on expanded federal aid to resolve their problems, solutions now were sought in a combination of thrifty city administration, aggressive economic development programs, and new investment partnerships with the private sector that were suited to make the best use of limited funding available from state and federal governments.

The changes in civic leadership were sometimes reflected in new styles of urban development which stressed achievements in urban tourism, civic restoration, and neighborhood self-reliance and which measured success by the ability of cities to attract high-tech industries and to bring back the middle class. But in some ways the new patterns of urban development were twists on familiar themes in the pursuit of the private city: they extended the traditional conception of the American city as primarily an economic entity; they promoted partnerships of local public and private leaders to formulate and implement comprehensive strategies for development; and they defined the problems of cities as largely the problems of private investment.

Pitfalls on the Path to Local Economic Development

It has proved easier to promote the use of local economic development strategies than to deliver the promised benefits. In practice, the path to local economic development is filled with pitfalls. It is difficult to target economic development activities so that the most distressed urban areas or disadvantaged social groups are assisted. Even when economic development occurs within a distressed community, it is far from clear—given the leakage of jobs and investment across municipal boundaries—that local residents necessarily benefit.[7] Furthermore, it is claimed that national and local development tools stimulate—or leverage—private investment in a community. In fact, the private sector often 'leverages' public investment by obtaining various combinations of publicly funded grants and loans, and other types of subsidies, to accomplish its development objectives. Rather than directing investment, local governments often find themselves held hostage by footloose industries which threaten to locate elsewhere if generous support is not forthcoming. Finally, the competition for growth between jurisdictions—each using the same development tools and strategies—leads to diminishing returns for any one jurisdiction. For some cities, the new era of municipal mercantilism means that scarce resources have to be used to embark on programs simply because other cities are similarly engaged. All of these dilemmas became apparent as experience accumulated with the national and local economic development programs of the 1970s, and they continued to plague local economic development efforts throughout the 1980s.

The Dilemmas of Targeting Assistance

One of the central issues is the extent to which the benefits of development projects can be directed to low-income groups, minority groups, or distressed communities as a whole. The first barrier to the targeting of federal programs occurs in the legislative process. Broad political representation in Congress dilutes efforts to direct benefits to particular jurisdictions or social groups. In the area of economic development, there is an additional built-in tension between the goal of assisting disadvantaged groups and communities and the creation of incentives that will attract private funds to a development project. If strict guidelines are established to target the benefits of a project, private investors are less inclined to participate, arguing that they would prefer to invest their resources in situations that are less encumbered. The idea behind local economic development is to attract private investment to locations experiencing physical and economic distress, but it is difficult to create this environment if restrictive and costly obligations are imposed. Thus, there is a tendency for the targeting objectives of an economic development program to be minimized or circumvented by local officials whose central concern is to make a project 'happen' or by private enterprise once the subsidies have been awarded and the project is completed.

Targeting Places. There are powerful political barriers, particularly in the American federal system, and economic obstacles to policies that are explicitly intended to aid specific places or regions. For example, EDA had a mandate to strengthen the economies of depressed areas; one would expect that its allocation of funds would be concentrated in states with low levels of economic development. In fact, Patrick Grasso's analysis of EDA expenditures for fiscal years 1965–78 demonstrates that they were not related to the ostensible goal of relieving long-term economic distress.

There is little evidence that the agency's programs have succeeded in promoting the economic development of chronically depressed areas. Rather, the agency seems to have concentrated on achieving the goal of a wide geographic dispersal of aid, with a disproportionate share of the funds channeled to states with disproportionate representation in Congress (Grasso 1986: 95).

In the case of UDAG, the authorizing legislation was very specific about which communities were to receive grants—severely distressed cities and urban counties'—but it was vague as to how these grants were to alleviate distress (Webman 1981: 90). The contradiction in the UDAG program was that relative city distress was the primary criterion for awarding an Action Grant, but at the same time the extent of private financing was an important factor in deciding which projects received funding. Cities that provided the best investment opportunities—where private funds were more available—were not likely to be severely distressed.

HUD data shows that from 1978 to 1986, out of those cities which met HUD's requirements for UDAG eligibility, the most highly distressed received 59 percent of all large city projects as compared to 26 percent for the moderately distressed and 15 percent for the least distressed cities (USHUD 1987: 75). Furthermore, distressed frostbelt cities of the Northeast and North Central regions received a disproportionate share of grant allocations. While these cities had only 56 percent of the total eligible population, they received 64 percent of total UDAG allocations (USHUD 1983: 103). Nevertheless, the extent to which UDAGs were successfully 'targeted' to the poorest cities has been questioned by some analysts. John Gist and R. Carter Hill point out that HUD studies which show a higher proportion of allocations to the most distressed cities include only funded projects in their sample (Gist and Hill 1984: 160). When all projects applied for, funded and unfunded, are included, the researchers found that for large cities, where individual grants were larger and funds were depleted more quickly, private investment, especially the ratio of private funds to UDAG funds, was the most significant selection factor; whereas, for small cities, distress proved to be the most significant selection factor (Gist and Hill 1984: 170). They concluded that UDAG regulations establishing the extent of private financing as a principal criterion for grant selection gave program officials an opportunity to justify the selection of low-risk projects in less severely distressed cities, particularly when costly projects in large cities were involved.

Another analyst, Jerry Webman, concluded that UDAGs subsidized private investment in America's most distressed cities and that they subsidized this investment more heavily where distress was more severe, but he found that projects followed rather than countered urbanization patterns (Webman 1981: 199). 'The kinds of places where commercial and industrial UDAG projects are locating', said Webman, 'are very similar to the kinds of places where commercial and industrial firms are making unsubsidized investments' (Webman 1981: 201). He argued that this did not mean that businesses received windfall benefits for doing what they would have done anyway, but it did mean that grants influenced the choice of investment location only within the bounds of dominant nation-wide patterns of economic development. If this was the case, it was very unlikely that Action Grants would restore large numbers of jobs to declining urban areas (Webman 1981: 201–6).

An objective of the UDAG program was to enhance the fiscal base of distressed cities by producing additional property taxes as well as other tax sources such as the local part of a sales tax and income tax. Because of the time lag between project inception, construction and the levy of taxes, and the obvious problems of data collection, it has been difficult to measure the impact of UDAG funds on tax revenue. Nevertheless, available data suggests that the UDAG program has not significantly improved the fiscal base of cities and 'received' taxes have been considerably lower than what was planned in the grant agreements. Of the $604 million in annual property and other local taxes anticipated from all projects funded through fiscal year 1986 (Table 4.1), only $187 million (31 percent) in actual benefit was reported as received as of 30 September 1986 (USHUD 1987: 82). In closed out and completed projects, $100 million (47 percent) of total planned annual local tax revenue of $213 million was reported as received (USHUD 1987: 82).

Targeting Disadvantaged Groups. While local economic development is, by definition, place-oriented, most programs are designed to target benefits to low-income groups and/or minorities in distressed areas. The early years of the EDA program illustrate the difficulties of using economic development strategies to benefit these groups. In spite of EDA's initial orientation to rural areas,[8] the first year of the program produced one major urban project— a $23 million dollar package of grants and loans to Oakland, California, for the development of an airport hanger, a marine terminal, a port industrial park, as well as other public works projects and business loans.[9] From the beginning, there was a conflict in the goals of the federal and local participants. Representatives of the Port and airline executives wanted to use federal assistance to improve their capital facilities, but EDA officials were primarily interested in creating jobs for unemployed minorities. A plan was developed whereby applicants for EDA assistance were required to specify what would be done to recruit the hard-core unemployed (Pressman and Wildavsky 1984: 25). The results were disappointing. By 1 December 1970,

TABLE 4.1. *Urban Development Action Grant Program: Planned Investment and Benefits in Funded Projects (M—million)*

Fiscal Year	1978	1979	1980	1981	1982	1983	1984	1985	1986	TOTAL
Number of projects	123	257	285	354	290	462	395	318	280	2,764
Large (no.)	75	121	161	210	180	249	193	172	180	1,541
Small (no.)	48	136	124	144	110	213	202	146	100	1,223
Large (%)	61	47	56	59	62	54	49	54	64	56
Small (%)	39	53	44	41	38	46	51	46	36	44
UDAG funding ($M)	276	420	554	590	347	641	546	437	437	4,249
Proportion received by:										
Large projects ($M)	226	324	429	442	248	487	341	321	331	3,184
Small projects ($M)	50	96	125	148	63	154	205	116	106	1,065
Large projects (%)	82	77	77	75	82	76	62	73	76	75
Small projects (%)	18	23	23	25	18	24	38	27	24	25
Private investment ($M)	1,745	2,557	2,807	3,964	2,057	3,184	2,689	3,569	3,486	26,059
Ratio to UDAG funding	6.3	6.1	5.1	6.7	5.9	5.0	4.9	8.2	8.0	6.1
State and local funding ($M)	195	205	194	331	104	104	165	114	418	1,829
Other federal ($M)	104	130	61	53	51	38	35	30	69	571
Total project investment ($M)	2,320	3,312	3,616	4,939	2,558	3,967	3,435	4,149	4,411	32,708
New permanent jobs	48,416	70,869	75,420	78,642	41,806	67,065	59,690	54,860	54,036	550,790
UDAG funding per job ($)	5,705	5,929	7,346	7,518	8,296	9,564	9,134	7,966	8,090	7,715
Low/moderate income jobs (%)	62	54	59	56	58	44	60	51	57	55
Construction jobs	43,214	59,774	44,816	64,942	31,387	52,546	47,036	53,221	50,703	447,645
Total new annual revenue ($M)	33	86	68	129	33	74	59	51	72	604

Source: USHUD 1987: 97.

The figures in Table 4.1 appear in HUD's 1987 *Consolidated Annual Report to Congress on Community Development Programs (CDBG, UDAG, Rental Rehabilitation, Section 312, Urban Homesteading)* (USHUD 1987: 97). Some descrepancies between the totals of FY 1978 through FY 1986 are the result of rounding off the figures. The total New Permanent Jobs is 550,804 rather than 550,790 reported by HUD. The total New Permanent Jobs is 550,804 rather than 550,790 reported by HUD. HUD's figures are retained in the table and the text.

EDA had dispersed over $13 million for projects that had created only 500 jobs for minorities of which just 65 went to the hard-core unemployed (EDA Report as cited in Pressman and Wildavsky 1984: 68).

Economic development policies are based on the assumption that stimulation of private sector growth, in combination with commitments from assisted firms, will create jobs for minorities and the hard-core unemployed. The dilemma is that the target groups reside in metropolitan regions containing populations that are well-trained, have access to public and private transportation, and experience little difficulty in adapting to changes in job locations. It is not simply a problem of strengthening an economy enough to employ an underemployed population, it is 'one of rigging a strong and well-developed metropolitan economy so as to reduce the disparity between the location and characteristics of jobs available and the location and skills of the distressed population' (Pressman and Wildavsky 1984: 153). Even when new jobs and investment are created, communities face persistent obstacles to appropriating the resulting benefits. Since the boundaries of cities are open and permeable, communities cannot assure that local economic development will enhance levels of investment within their jurisdictions or even provide employment to local residents. As Andrew Kirby explains:

firms will employ residents of any locality, and may often recruit highly skilled employees from entirely different regions or low-wage employees from different countries. Some types of economic development are even predicated on the assumption that regeneration will displace low-income residents and replace them by commuting labor and new, high-income residents (1985: 211).

Improving public infrastructure—airports, industrial parks, port facilities, sewer lines, or roads—might stimulate private development but the incentives for businesses to hire well-trained people with proven work records, as long as they live within commuting distance, remain powerful. Promises may be made to hire hard-core unemployed, but the monitoring of actual performance is complicated and expensive, and, if the promises are not fulfilled, it is difficult to demonstrate bad faith. Moreover, even if bad faith is proven, punitive actions are nearly impossible to carry out once loans are made or facilities built. In the case of the Oakland project, some community representatives recognized these dilemmas before the bureaucrats. In the early stages of the project a black woman said, after being told about the employment plan idea:

Let me get this straight. You have some employer, who files a Plan saying he will employ twenty of our people. We approve his plan, and he starts up with your money. But then he chisels a little bit, and only employs eighteen, and takes two others from outside, maybe his cousins or something. Does this committee then say, 'You fire those two, and take on two of ours'? And if he won't, then you call his loan, and put him out of business, and the other eighteen lose their jobs? I don't like the sound of that (Bradford 1968: 165).

As an economic development program, UDAG was designed to improve job opportunities in selected cities and emphasis was placed on jobs for low-to moderate-income persons and minorities. Performance evaluations, therefore, have concentrated on the number, types, and cost of jobs created by UDAG projects.[10] In the original grant agreements, the 2,764 projects funded through fiscal year 1986 were expected to create 550,790 permanent jobs at a cost of $7,715 UDAG dollars per job (Table 4.1).[11] Fully 55 percent, or 305,093 jobs, were to be for low- to moderate-income persons and 20 percent, or 121,000 jobs, were to be for minorities (USHUD 1987: 84). Since many of the projects had not been completed as of 30 September 1986, the actual number of permanent jobs created by the projects was only 275,000 or 50 percent of total planned employment (USHUD 1987: 80). Of the total new jobs actually created, 165,000 were for low- or moderate-income persons, or 54 percent of the number planned, and just over 69,000 were for minorities, or 62 percent of those planned (USHUD 1987: 84). 'When uncompleted projects are excluded from the calculation', according to a report from HUD, 'the percent of actual jobs created increases significantly. Eighty percent of planned new permanent jobs were actually created in completed or closed out projects and 86 percent of planned new jobs for low- and moderate-income persons' (USHUD 1987: 81).[12] If these rates are maintained for the uncompleted projects, then 440,632 new permanent jobs will result from an expenditure of $4.249 billion of UDAG dollars, a cost of $9,645 per job.[13]

The jury is still out as to the overall impact of the UDAG program, but local politicians and officials obviously supported UDAG as another way of securing resources for their cities. While the actual benefits of the program fell short of the planned targets, the number of jobs associated with projects in distressed cities are not insignificant but the policy issue is not the number of jobs; it is their source and who benefits. Are these jobs new or merely the displacement of employment from one part of a metropolitan area to another? Critics of UDAG argue that the program does not add to the urban economic product, it merely provides an alternative way of dividing the pie. Furthermore, because of the potential for central city employees to reside in the suburbs, the net result may not be a significant job gain for city residents. Although new jobs may be created, high unemployment rates in distressed cities are not likely to be significantly reduced by economic development programs in general or UDAG in particular (Jacobs and Roistacher 1980: 360). The service sector and tourist-oriented businesses that are most viable in the central cities, and therefore most likely to respond to the incentives provided by economic development initiatives, will not have a substantial impact on the job opportunities or income levels of unskilled or low-income city residents.

Private Planning and Reverse Leverage

The principle of 'leveraging'—or the attraction of private funds (and other public funds) by the injection of public money—is at the heart of the economic development strategy. The argument is that government alone cannot solve urban problems. It must have help from the private sector. 'Only it can provide the capital needed for rebuilding and growing; only it can carry out the large scale development necessary to provide healthy local economies' (USHUD 1978: 121). Leveraging private investment with public funds is not a new principle—indeed, urban renewal was based on the same idea— however, it was most fully developed in the UDAG program where private developers were expected to provide at least $2.5 dollars for each dollar of UDAG funds. In practice, HUD officials anticipated that each UDAG dollar would bring along six dollars in private investment (USHUD 1982a: 45). An analysis of the leveraging performance of three economic development programs found that UDAG projects achieved ratios of better than 6 to 1 as compared to 1.4 to 1 for the EDA Business and Industrial Loan Program and 1.3 to 1 for the Farmers' Home Administration Business Loan Program (May 1981; USHUD 1987).[14] By contrast, as of 30 June 1971, the urban renewal program had attracted $9.15 billion in private investment for various projects with $9.03 billion in federal grants and public investment, a leveraging ratio of about 1 to 1 (US Senate 1973: 65).

The ability of UDAGs to leverage private dollars is not very meaningful if those dollars would have been invested anyway. The issue of 'substitution' is not new to policy makers; it is central to all public intervention into a predominantly market economy (Boyle 1983b). Substitution became a key issue in 1979 when Congress passed an amendment to ensure that UDAG did not substitute for or replace other non-federal funds and that projects would be approved only if it was demonstrated that they would not go ahead 'but for' the UDAG award. In a test of the extent to which substitution was taking place, a 1982 HUD evaluation by a panel of real estate finance and development experts concluded that 36 percent of the projects examined involved some degree of substitution (USHUD 1982a: 26). The evidence for substitution was as varied as the projects—the existence of commitments to fund the same project prior to applying for UDAG funding, instances where there was sufficient financial feasibility for the project to have occurred without UDAG, and instances where the developer would have gone ahead with a smaller or different project. Substitution did not occur where there were extraordinary site development costs, where there was a genuine financing gap, where public improvements were necessary to allow the private investment to occur, or where there was an extraordinarily high risk.

It must be said that the determination of whether substitution occurs is a difficult problem which has to take into account 'site history, market conditions, other economic development activities in the area, and the intentions and long-term economic interests of the major project actors' (USHUD 1982a: 23). It is further complicated by the fact that the local participants— public and private—are often biased towards demonstrating that a project will not go ahead without federal funding. In the case of UDAG, the developer was interested in obtaining the Action Grant to reduce project costs. The local official also had a substantial stake in making the case. Not only were there important public relations benefits for local governments but, in addition, the UDAG meant an injection of federal funds into the community which otherwise would not have been obtained. For the local politician or bureaucrat, there is much to gain and little to lose in the marshalling of evidence to support a grant application.

While UDAGs or other economic development programs can leverage private investment in distressed areas, it can also be argued that these programs encourage the private sector to leverage public funds to support private sector development objectives. Given the difficulty of demonstrating beneficial impacts on lower income groups or being certain that public funds are not simply being substituted for private funds, the potential for private leverage of public funds must be considered. To a large extent, the conclusion one reaches on the issue is a question of perspective: for some, the glass is half full, for others, it is half empty.

The dilemma for local public officials is that once the game of economic development begins, it is difficult to avoid playing. The condition of competition between localities for economic growth is exacerbated by the availability of development subsidies. Paul Kantor argues that cities have been driven to adopt programs that reflect their diminished position *vis-á-vis* business (1987: 510–11). As a result, the wide-ranging subsidies have 'socialized' business risk on a continuous and unprecedented scale.[15] Communities which do not use these subsidies jeopardize their ability to attract or retain businesses. Indeed, to some extent, civic entrepreneurship turns the free enterprise system on its head, leaving local government 'in the role of competitor and business as welfare recipient. It is-a process in which the public takes enormous financial risks, while business surveys the willing suitors and moves freely to where the public risk-taking is greatest' (Goodman 1979: 4).

An example from the UDAG program illustrates the extent to which private firms are able to leverage public resources to accomplish their development objectives (Buches 1980). In early 1979, the Hercules Corporation was considering a move from its headquarters in downtown Wilmington, Delaware—a city of 70,000 people located approximately 35 miles southwest of Philadelphia.[16] Hercules needed a facility which would have the capacity for up to 1,600 employees (the company then employed 1,350 personnel at its downtown site) and major consideration was given to a suburban site. The biggest factor in the relocation decision was the cost differential between construction on an urban site versus construction on a suburban site— estimated by company officials to be $32.5 million in favor of the suburban site. The company indicated that it would reconsider a center city location if the cost of development were approximately the same as a comparable building in the suburbs. The city, with the support of the state of Delaware, set out to devise a strategy to reduce the cost differential. The cornerstone of this strategy was an Action Grant.

From one perspective, the $16 million UDAG which was eventually awarded for the Hercules project leveraged $77 million in private investment in a distressed urban area, a ratio of 4.6 private dollars to each public dollar. From another perspective, the Hercules Company obtained a subsidy which significantly lowered its land costs and saved millions in interest on project financing;[17] in addition, it received a substantial abatement of property taxes for eleven years after building occupancy. While the subsidies fell short of the $32 million differential in urban and suburban development costs by $3 to $4 million, other factors, such as poor accessibility and visibility of the suburban site, outweighed the remaining differential and convinced Hercules to remain in the city. An uncharitable interpretation of the situation is that Hercules was never very interested in the suburban site and only talked about relocation as a means of getting as much of its center city development subsidized as possible. In any case, Hercules obtained benefits in addition to the subsidies from the UDAG grant and the abatement of city taxes. The state acquired a facility adjacent to the new Hercules site, demolished the building and developed a park; the city enhanced the project area including street, sidewalk, and traffic improvements; and the Wilmington Parking Authority built an 1,100 space parking facility next to the Hercules office building.

The grant agreement indicated that the project would result in 1,775 new permanent jobs in Wilmington of which almost 900 would go to low/moderate income workers and 70 would go to minorities. These job targets have been difficult to achieve. As of 15 August 1986, a HUD monitoring team found that 1,530 jobs had been directly or indirectly created by the project. These included 730 jobs in the building vacated by Hercules, 95 jobs resulting from the expansion of a company located next to the new Hercules facility which indicated that its plans were influenced by the development, 146 jobs in the retail facilities located in the Hercules building, 424 building maintenance jobs,[18] and 135 jobs attributable directly to Hercules. Hercules had until July 1988 to reach the 1,775 figure but only had to demonstrate a 'best effort'. As a practical matter, there are really no sanctions that can be applied if this goal is not reached. In short, in exchange for keeping its headquarters in the downtown and directly creating 135 new jobs in the City of Wilmington, Hercules received a subsidy of nearly $30 million as well as a number of other benefits.

Despite evidence that the Hercules project did not benefit the low-income or minority residents of Wilmington in any direct way, from the point of view of the city administration it was very beneficial. Not only did the city capture $16 million in UDAG funds (which would result in over $27 million of interest and principal payback to the city over 25 years), it avoided the loss of a major employer and, thereby, retained the wage tax revenues generated by Hercules employees. As far as the city was concerned, the property tax abatement provided to Hercules was not a cost because this tax revenue would have been lost anyway had the company moved to the suburbs. From a broader perspective, however, the economic development process allowed a major corporation to escape paying local property taxes for a period of eleven years.

The Hidden Costs of Economic Development

The perception has been that economic development is without cost to local government. Communities 'win' by being effective at capturing federal resources to leverage local development. But even federally subsidized programs that on the surface appear to be 'windfall' gains for local governments, such as UDAGs or IRBs, contain hidden costs and lead to substantial commitment of local tax revenue. Very often they have to be supplemented by other inducements such as the abatement of property taxes or the improvement of public facilities in order to consummate a development project. They also reduce the federal resources available for other programs. In addition, some subsidy programs help to raise interest rates and thus increase borrowing costs for traditional public activities. In the meantime, federal economic development funds transform the municipal agenda. As federal largess is withdrawn, the argument for economic development turns to the question of survival and pressure increases on communities to use their own tax bases to leverage private investment.

Economic development itself involves substantial costs for roads, sewers, water systems, and other public services and infrastructure which are not paid for by individual firms but by the community. 'When local governments operate to facilitate the location or expansion of pollution-causing firms, or when they retreat from the planning and intervention necessary to deal with the broad service problems created by private profit making,' argues Joe Feagin, 'they actually cooperate in inflicting social costs on the urban citizenry' (1988: 208). Houston offers a striking example of the serious costs that can be imposed on a community as a result of dramatic growth in an environment of limited governmental intervention. Public–private cooperation in major economic development projects from the 1950s to the 1980s meant maintaining 'a good business climate' with low taxes, a limited array of city services, and a weak regulatory bureaucracy. In Houston the result has been major problems in toxic waste and air pollution, routine sewage and garbage disposal, water quality, flood control, auto congestion, mass transit, and road maintenance (Feagin 1988). Houston's economic development has imposed substantial costs on present and future taxpayers.

In addition to the costs that economic development imposes on communities, situations of high unemployment along with competition for private investment often lead, according to Andrew Kirby, to 'Faustian bargains' between corporate capital on the one hand and jurisdictions on the other (1985: 212). The most notable case is Poletown in Detroit in which the construction of a new Cadillac plant in the city 'led to the destruction of 1,021 homes and apartment buildings, 155 businesses, churches, and a hospital, displaced 3,500 people, and all but obliterated a more or less stably integrated community embodying a century of Polish cultural life' (Hill 1986: 11). The irony of Detroit's acquiescence to corporate demands is that the promised number of jobs did not appear (Kirby 1985: 212).

Some of the hidden costs of the economic development strategy are illustrated by the IRB program. While the original purpose of IRB financing was to spur economic activity by creating industrial jobs in economically depressed areas, many states allowed commercial as well as industrial projects—shopping centers, office buildings, and fast food outlets. These uses led to charges that IRBs stimulated the wrong kinds of business or businesses which competed with existing firms. Since federal laws placed no restrictions on IRB use—there were no criteria to direct investments to depressed areas or to specify the types of jobs created—critics argued that local governments did not use IRBs effectively. 'The real abuse is that the issuers have no interest in the project,' said John F. Shirey, legislative council for the National League of Cities. 'In no way do they make sure that the project is central to the goals of their development program. The industry just stops off at city hall or the state house on its way to the bank' (*National Journal*, 15 May 1982: 871).

A study of IRBs issued in Ohio between 1974 and 1978 showed that there was no relationship between unemployment levels in a geographic area and the approval of IRBs. At best the bonds were issued with no regard to unemployment, and at times they appeared to be used more extensively where unemployment was low. In two large Ohio counties it was found that the jobs created by IRB investments were not directed towards low-income workers (Pascarella and Raymond 1982: 83). IRB programs in most states operated similarly. 'More than half of the states issuing IRBs place[d] no restriction on their use and only a few states [made] any attempt to target them geographically, (Pascarella and Raymond 1982: 84).

In fact, local governments had very few incentives to restrict the use of IRBs. Tax-exempt financing provided the local government development official with a great deal of discretion. The federal government could be committed to a tax expenditure quickly without prior consultation. There was no fixed pot of money for which projects had to compete and no ranking or prioritizing of projects. The only requirement was that projects comply with appropriate state law and Internal Revenue Service code provisions and serve a broadly defined public purpose such as providing jobs and increasing the tax base (Levy 1981: 96–7). IRBs allowed local government officials to actively participate in the development process—to provide benefits to their constituents and to claim credit for promoting economic growth. Furthermore, the direct cost of the IRB program to state and local governments was quite small—the legal costs were borne by private firms and the federal government suffered the loss of tax revenue (Pascarella and Raymond 1982: 84). Indeed, many local agencies charged for their services—perhaps 1 percent of the face amount of an issue. On the other hand, if a jurisdiction abandoned its IRB program or tried to limit the use of IRBs to particular areas or industries, then other jurisdictions that continued to use them without restriction might attract industry away from them. For the most part, the only negative voice at the local level came from municipal finance officers who feared that the proliferation of IRBs would drive up the cost of general obligation bonds issued by localities to build sewers and repair roads (*National Journal*, 15 May 1982: 871).

Federal officials also voiced objections. Officials in Republican and Democratic administrations argued that IRBs led to a multi-billion dollar revenue loss to the federal government. In 1983, Alice Rivlin, the Director of the

Congressional Budget Office, predicted in testimony before the House Ways and Means Committee, that 'during the next five years, subsidies to private entities from tax-exempt bonds will cost the federal government an average of about $13 billion a year' (Rivlin 1983: 303). In 1978, the Carter administration had tried to correct some of the alleged shortcomings of IRBs by proposing the elimination of tax exemptions for most small issues while expanding it for projects built in distressed areas. Congress responded by raising the capital spending limit on small issues from $5 to $10 million and up to $20 million for projects receiving a UDAG (*National Journal*, 18 Oct. 1980: 1752). It was clear that IRBs had gained an influential constituency— big and small businesses,[19] state and local development officials, lawyers, and underwriters who specialized in the bonds (*National Journal*, 18 Oct. 1980: 1752). Indeed, during the Reagan administration, the economic development value of these bonds for state and local government increased as other incentives formerly available to states and cities were withdrawn (National Journal, 15 May 1982: 870).[20]

Although IRBs may have had a locational influence when relatively few jurisdictions issued them, the near universal availability of IRBs meant that they functioned more as a general investment subsidy than as an instrument for regional economic development (Marlin 1985: 33). Gregory Squires pointed out the flaw in the logic of IRBs:

IRBs are predicated on the faith that financial incentives for the business community will generate a flow of private capital (and subsequently jobs, tax revenues, and economic revitalization) to those areas most in need, with predominantly minority, inner-city residents benefiting the most. Yet the dynamics of private decision-making encourage the flow of capital in directions that enrich the entrepreneur regardless of the social costs . . . Ironically, the IRB supporters look to precisely those factors that accounted for the decline of urban communities and entire regions of the nation to be the salvation (Squires 1984: 1).

The Problem of Accountability

The main impact of UDAG and other economic programs may be less in their generation of jobs and private investment than in their effect on local policy-making, on the skills and orientation of city officials, and on the willingness of local politicians and bureaucrats to work in partnership with private developers. In the long term, economic development programs helped to create a new breed of city official whose capacity for negotiation, for handling complex financial issues, and for preparing development proposals was significantly enhanced. In essence, these programs fostered the emergence of local government professionals who were more capable of making public–private partnerships work. Whether these partnerships served the interests of a community in a responsive fashion is another matter.

The structuring of development 'deals' is a complicated process that is accessible to a small number of professionals in the public and private sectors. The process is built around confidentiality and the use of proprietary information. It takes place behind closed doors to maximize flexibility and speed in negotiating the development deal and to minimize disclosure of competitive bids and sensitive financial information. As a result, local economic development tends to remove significant actions of local government from public scrutiny. As Paul Kantor points out:

> there are powerful inducements for urban political leaders to insulate the process of economic policymaking from popular involvement . . . [L]ocal government leaders are forced to bargain out conflicts over development within a very limited universe of producers whose systemic economic power accords them a privileged political position . . . [As a result], city governments tend to manage popular control by seeking ways to avoid leaving decisions about development to the uncertainties and preferences of popular opinion, since the latter may well differ from what is acceptable to the private sector (Kantor 1987: 512).

An illustration of this tendency is the network of 24 quasi-public development corporations utilized by Mayor Donald Schaefer in Baltimore in the 1970s to pursue his economic development programs. Critics dubbed them 'Schaefer's Shadow Government' because they operated outside of the constraints of the city charter in their allocation of public resources (Stoker 1987). The three most important development corporations were Charles Center–Inner Harbor Management, Inc. (CCIHM), which directed downtown redevelopment; the Baltimore Economic Development Corporation (BEDCO) which promoted industrial development by arranging financing and location, offering technical assistance, and developing industrial parks; and the most controversial—the Baltimore City Trustees Loan and Guarantee Program, a quasi-public development bank which disbursed or guaranteed over $500 million between 1976 and 1986 by packaging public funds—UDAGs, CDBGs, IRBs—loans, loan guarantees, and subsidies to provide 'gap financing' to leverage private investment in redevelopment projects (Marc Levine 1987: 108). The Trustees bank was a striking example of the political insulation of development corporations as well as an illustration of the ability of these institutions to allocate substantial public resources in the name of facilitating public-private cooperation and leveraging private investment. One of the board members described it clearly: 'The Trustees have the responsibility of determining priorities for the community, deciding what projects come above everything else. This is, in my view, far better than what happens in most cities, where operations are based on who gets there first and who yells the loudest' (US Conference of Mayors 1984: 70).

The assumption implicit in this statement is that, in the arena of development policy, a community of common goals, values, and interests enables a group of 'experts' and business leaders to make decisions that will be beneficial to all the residents of a city. This is the vision of the development process portrayed by Paul Peterson in *City Limits* (1981). Peterson points to the benefits of development 'for all members of the city' (1981: 47) and describes business involvement in development decisions as 'apolitical' (1981: 142) and largely a matter of providing know-how. Peterson views the city as a utility-maximizing entity with a unitary interest in development around which consensus can be built and public action organized. In fact, experience with economic development indicates that it is a political rather than a technical process and laden with the potential for conflict. 'Decisions associated with physical and economic development', argue Susan and Norman Fainstein, 'embody class and racial interests. There are always social groups who win and lose, regardless of whether political conflict becomes overt' (1986*a*: 3). As Heywood Sanders and Clarence Stone point out, 'conflict and the pursuit of particular interests are characteristic of the development arena in city politics' (1987*a*: 521). As the development process moves from promotion to execution, a pattern of winners and losers is brought to the forefront destroying whatever consensus existed in the early stages (Sanders and Stone 1987*a*, 1987*b*).

The Retreat from Social Policy

Perhaps the most injurious outcome of the focus on economic development and public entrepreneurship was its impact on the commitment of local, state, and federal government to the resolution of social problems. As the attention of public officials and the resources of government were increasingly directed to meeting the needs of private enterprise, there was less time and fewer resources to deal with poverty, poor health care, and inadequate education. As cities competed against each other to attract or retain businesses, the size of the public subsidy to private development interests increased and the ability of even large municipalities to direct investment for socially desirable purposes declined (Fainstein and Fainstein 1986*c*: 267). In the 1970s local governments shied away from direct participation in many social programs, arguing that only the state and federal governments had the resources to cope with these problems. Unfortunately, the federal government was also withdrawing its commitment, a process which began with the Nixon administration and continued through the Carter years. The problem with many economic development efforts was that 'instead of identifying community needs and developing programs that expressly address them', argued Gregory Squires (in relation to IRBs), 'public officials strive to create incentives to attract private capital in hopes of achieving economic growth which will resolve the various social problems plaguing their communities' (Squires 1984: 4–5). Evidence to support the contention that this approach benefited low-income residents of cities or resolved social problems is notably lacking.

The redevelopment strategy of Coleman Young's administration in Detroit during the 1970s is an example of the ways in which public resources were diverted from social investments to support private development projects. Richard Child Hill described the strategy as corporate-centered: 'Elected officials offer tax breaks and social investment subsidies to business to succor investment, while reducing social consumption services to residents in Detroit's neighborhoods' (1986: 109). Over a period when some $260 million in tax abatements, subsidies, and federal grants were provided to reconstruct downtown Detroit, the percentage of Detroit's budget devoted to various social consumption services such as transportation, health, and sanitation remained stationary or declined (Hill 1986: 110).

Reshaping the Cinderella City

By the end of the 1970s the skills and instruments of civic entrepreneurship were well-developed in cities across the country, and Baltimore was one of the places where they were most effectively applied. Baltimore's experience with local economic development illustrates the possibilities and limitations of this strategy for urban revitalization.

Once described as the 'Worst American City' (Louis 1975), Baltimore has become the 'Cinderella City' (*National Journal*, 26 Nov. 1983: 2480) by virtue of the apparent renaissance brought about by strategic use of federal grants in the 1960s and 1970s and a long-term local commitment to public–private partnerships. The civic and business commitment to revitalization of the city's economy resulted in two celebrated redevelopment projects: the 33-acre downtown complex of offices and commercial establishments known as Charles Center, completed in 1973, and the transformation of the inner harbor which culminated in the 1980 opening of Harborplace, the Rouse Company's 'festival marketplace'. Baltimore's renaissance has been touted as one of America's most successful examples of the potential of public–private partnerships and civic entrepreneurship; it has become a model for the redevelopment efforts of other cities in the US and Britain.

The story of Charles Center is the familiar one of a partnership between political leaders and an élite organization of corporate chief executives, the Greater Baltimore Committee (GBC), mobilized to promote a 'single dramatic project' that would boost investor confidence in the downtown (Millspaugh 1964). Using city powers of eminent domain, federal urban renewal funds for land acquisition and site clearance, and the first of Baltimore's quasi-public organizations—Charles Center–Inner Harbor Management, Inc. (CCIHM)—to negotiate and package deals between the city and developers, the partnership set out to develop private office towers, a theater, a hotel, a retail square, and a federal building at a cost of $180 million with $145 million from private and $35 million in public sources (Lyall 1982: 32). The project was hailed as 'a vivid demonstration of the merging of public and private interests' (Lyall 1982: 35), but there was virtually no grassroots citizen participation. 'It was produced and managed as a professional exercise,' writes Katherine Lyall, 'and announced to the public as a set of faits accomplis' (Lyall 1982: 46).

The partnership's success with Charles Center encouraged many of the same people and organizations to take on a larger project to reclaim Baltimore's waterfront which, in the early 1960s, consisted largely of abandoned warehouses and deteriorated wharfs. In 1964 'The Inner Harbor Concept' set out a series of projects to convert the waterfront and adjacent areas into 240 acres of office buildings, a marina, cultural facilities, parks, and residences. Drafted by the GBC, the plan was expected to cost $270 million over thirty years, including $180 million in federal funds, $58 million in city resources, and $22 million in private investments (Lyall 1982: 38). While bond issues for land acquisition, site clearance, and public improvements were approved in 1964 and 1966, opposition from neighborhood groups and the 1968 race riots, put the redevelopment program on hold until the election of Schaefer as mayor in 1971. Under Schaefer's leadership, much of the Inner Harbor transformation was completed, downtown experienced an investment boom, neighborhoods around the waterfront were revitalized and gentrified, and Baltimore cultivated a national and international reputation as a 'renaissance city'.

Using the full array of tools available for local economic development—UDAGs, Community Development Block Grants (CDBGs), mortgage bonds, general obligation bonds, IRBs, quasi-public corporations, urban homesteading, city-created tax shelters for developers, loans, loan guarantees—the city and its private partners pursued four priorities for the downtown redevelopment during the 1970s and early 1980s: office development, revitalization of retail and commercial activity, the promotion of tourism and conventions, and residential gentrification around the harbor. The transformation of the Inner Harbor included new office buildings, a World Trade Center, the Baltimore Convention Center, the Maryland Science Center, the National Aquarium, residential development in adjacent neighborhoods such as Fells Point and Federal Hill, and the symbol of Baltimore's turnaround, Harborplace, a $22 million marketplace of small shops, cafes, kiosks, and food stalls.

Once rivalling Philadelphia as the eastern seaboard's most belittled city, Baltimore is now cited as the prototype of successful civic entrepreneurship. The physical improvements are unmistakable. Rather than rotting piers, abandoned buildings, deteriorated warehouses, and a polluted harbor, the visitor to the downtown sees a thriving tourist, convention, and office complex. But to what extent have the benefits of Baltimore's public–private partnership been shared by all segments of the city's population? Marc Levine argues that the spatial, racial, and class impacts have been highly uneven (Levine 1987). The main beneficiaries, he contends, were developers and real estate speculators who profited from the downtown ventures, suburban professionals who disproportionately captured the quality employment opportunities generated by redevelopment, back-to-the-city gentry who took up residence in revitalized neighborhoods and in the up-scale condominiums around the harbor, and tourists who patronized the shopping and recreational facilities.

Levine argues that 'statistical data confirm that for Baltimore's poorer, primarily black neighborhoods, conditions worsened considerably during the Schaefer years' (Levine 1987: 112). He marshals the following evidence to support his conclusion:

- Between 1970 and 1980, 210 of the city's 277 neighborhoods (as designated by the Baltimore City Planning Department) experienced increases in the percentage of their residents living below the poverty line (Goodman and Taylor 1983).
- Between 1970 and 1980, poverty rates increased in 105 of the 117 predominantly black neighborhoods (those in which the black percentage of the population exceeded 90 percent) (Goodman and Taylor 1983).
- Between 1976 and 1983, the percentage of renters experiencing 'high rent burden' increased from 47.4 percent to 57.3 percent. Over 40 percent of renter-occupied dwellings contained one or more structural deficiencies in 1976 and 1983 (US Bureau of the Census 1983).
- The percentage of workers in the CBD who were residents of the city fell from 57.6 percent in 1969 to 46.2 percent in 1979. Suburban residents constituted 53.8 percent of all CBD workers but represented 74.8 percent of all CBD workers earning over $25,000 annually. While CBD employment did jump by 8,000 in the 1970s, the benefits 'leaked' substantially to the suburbs (US Bureau of the Census 1980).

Indicators of the aggregate economic health of Baltimore continue to reflect stagnation or actual decline rather than a thriving city, successfully adjusting to economic change. Retail sales declined precipitously from 1963 to 1983 from $2.019 billion to $0.909 billion as measured in constant 1967 dollars (Peterson, Rabe, and Wong 1986: 65).[21] Levine notes that for all frost-belt cities with 1970 populations between 400,000 and 1.5 million, [22] Baltimore ranked eighth of 12 in service and retail sales growth between 1972 and 1982, eleventh in manufacturing growth, and tenth in per capita income growth (Levine 1987: 111).

On perhaps the key indicator of economic well-being, the per capita income of city residents, the gap between Baltimore and all but two of the cities increased during Baltimore's 'renaissance' years. Small wonder that Baltimore's poverty rate was the highest among all these cities—22.9% according to the latest urban poverty data (Levine 1987: 111–12).

Employment trends corroborate the dismal economic picture. Between 1970 and 1980, Baltimore lost 56,000 jobs and an estimate by John Kasarda indicates that this decline has accelerated—by 1983 employment had fallen another 20,000 (Peterson, Rabe, and Wong 1986: 65; Kasarda 1986). Moreover, the employment losses were particularly severe in areas that are likely to provide opportunities for the urban poor and minorities as well as the working class. Between 1960 and 1980, there were employment losses in the job categories that employ manufacturing and other blue-collar workers—craftsmen/foremen, operatives, and a general category that includes laborers and private household workers (Table 4.2). Kasarda has also shown that between 1979 and 1984, Baltimore lost 73,000 'entry-level' jobs, a decline of 46 percent, while during these same years, it gained 15,000 'knowledge-intensive' jobs, an increase of 56 percent (Kasarda 1985: 50; Levine 1987: 116).

TABLE 4.2. *Employment Trends in Baltimore by Job Classification, 1960–1980*

	1960	1970	1980	Absolute change 1960–80	Percent change 1960–80
Professional/Technical	36,413	45,407	45,386	8,973	24.6
Clerical	60,187	71,955	61,381	1,194	2.0
Craftsmen/Foremen	43,497	44,038	31,017	– 12,480	– 28.7
Operatives[a]	67,838	51,520	64,843	– 2,995	– 4.4
Managers/Administrators	23,358	18,480	23,626	268	1.1
Service	37,099	51,636	57,606	20,507	55.3
Sales	26,313	20,749	20,945	– 5,368	– 20.4
Other[b]	67,606	48,915	1,444	– 66,162	– 97.9
TOTAL	362,311	352,700	306,248	– 56,063	– 15.5

[a] Includes people employed in the manufacture of durable and non-durable goods.

[b] Includes private household workers and laborers except farm and mine (in 1960 and 1970 only), transportation equipment operators (1970 only), and occupation not reported (1960 only).

Source: US Bureau of the Census 1960, 1970, 1980 (as cited in Peterson, Rabe, and Wong 1986: 66).

In sum, despite the downtown investment and signs of restoration around the waterfront, Baltimore's public–private partnership resulted in limited and uneven development.[23]

[T]here is little evidence to sustain the notion of Baltimore as a break-out Frostbelt city. The benefits that have been generated by downtown redevelopment have been unevenly distributed. City neighborhoods continue to deteriorate, city dwellers have been unable to secure quality employment, and city space has been increasingly restructured to meet the various interests of developers, tourists, and upper-income consumers. Along with secular trends in the American economy, such as the rise of services and the decline of manufacturing, Schaefer's policies have helped Baltimore become the archetype of a 1980s 'dual city,' a city of haves and have nots (Levine 1987: 115).

Given national and international economic trends, some would argue that Baltimore's choices in the pursuit of local economic development have been severely constrained. Local policies that conflict with the priorities of the business community run the risk of promoting further decline and impairing the competitive position of the local area in the inter-city rivalry for private investment. Nonetheless, in contrast to its image as a Cinderella city that has overcome industrial decline, Baltimore's redevelopment program has not benefited the majority of city dwellers and its overall economic performance has not matched that of other comparable cities. Despite these shortcomings, Baltimore has achieved undisputed success in image management. It is the town, as Neil Peirce points out, that 'other cities unabashedly seek to copy to revive their own decaying downtowns' (Peirce 1986: 69).

Rethinking Local Economic Development Policy

City officials have offered public rationales for their development policies
that understandably emphasize expected community benefits rather than
political responsiveness to private development priorities. These rationales
were articulated in the 1970s by politicians and public officials at all levels of
government and, despite shifts in federal policy during the next decade, many
continued to be advanced throughout the 1980s. In essence, the rationale for
local economic development links economic development to community
well-being. Social programs are discounted as a focus of urban policy because
they are too expensive, do not work, and put cities at a competitive disadvantage in relation to cities that apply local resources to the stimulation of
private investment. Unemployment is asserted to be the chief urban ailment,
and since the private sector has the pivotal role in job creation, ways have to
be found to stimulate the expansion of private activity in urban areas. The
best strategy is to use public funds—particularly federal funds—to 'leverage'
private investment. Because private investment decisions require technical
expertise, it is important to develop a cadre of local government officials who
are skilled in using the financial tools of economic development and in
negotiating investment packages with the private sector.

The benefits of local economic development are alleged to be widely
distributed. While development efforts can and should be 'targeted' to minority groups, the hard-core unemployed, and distressed communities, ultimately everyone will benefit and the costs of development will not be concentrated in any one segment of the population. Local economic
development is also perceived to have distinct political advantages and
sometimes is portrayed as a painless way to help the disadvantaged through
income *creation* rather than *redistribution*. Business interests can support the
goal of increased employment opportunities for low-income people because
it is pursued through incentives for business rather than sanctions. The
initiation and implementation of economic development projects also provides government with opportunities to gain political support from a diverse
constituency. By contrast, only trouble is in sight when efforts are made to
expand welfare programs or civil rights enforcement (Doolittle 1983: 78).

The focus on economic development in preference to social policy
approaches was well received by many urban leaders, but some critics viewed
it as a way of avoiding urban problems. Efforts to promote economic development were 'doomed to failure', it was argued, without a concomitant effort to
solve the crime, transportation, education, and other social problems that
made cities so unattractive to business. 'Solving the capital problems of
Newark', warned Richard G. Hatcher, the black mayor of Gary, Indiana, 'will
not solve the social problems of Newark' (*New York Times*, 19 Sept. 1977).

In our view the benefits of local economic development generally have
been exaggerated while the costs have been largely ignored. Below we
offer a series of propositions about the limitations of local economic development. Not all of these propositions apply equally to every local economic

development program or strategy. Nonetheless, they challenge assumptions and expectations that conventionally are used to justify the concentration of public resources on local economic development and to support claims about its benefits.

1. Local economic development programs designed to use public funds to leverage private investment frequently result in reverse leverage—that is, private enterprise often leverages public funds to accomplish its own development objectives and, in the process, holds local governments hostage if they do not come forth with generous subsidies.
2. Local public officials and private developers are interested in putting projects in place or in 'capturing' federal or state funds; they often attempt to circumvent requirements to demonstrate that development projects are not viable without subsidies.
3. Targeting of economic development programs to distressed communities is limited by political barriers, by disincentives built into the project negotiation process, and by persistent difficulties in monitoring and enforcing program requirements.
4. Local economic development programs remove significant actions of local government from public debate, reduce political accountability of local officials, and narrow the representativeness of local government.
5. Local economic development programs contain hidden or unanticipated costs to local government by creating pressures to supplement federal funds or state funds with local funds on development projects and by increasing borrowing costs, thereby reducing revenues available for other public programs, or by increasing the need for expenditures on services or infrastructure.
6. Local economic development strategies divert attention and resources of government away from direct efforts to resolve social problems.
7. Communities will not necessarily capture the benefits from local economic development programs because of the leakage of jobs and investment across municipal boundaries.
8. Local economic development does not reflect the interests of the city as a whole; it results in an uneven distribution of benefits, not only for different groups within the urban community but also for different sections within cities and for different cities within the nation.

We will return to these points in the concluding chapter. What is important for present purposes is to recognize that the urban policies and politics of the 1970s in the US were predicated upon an economic conception of the city and these policies were designed and carried out by a coalition of public officials and local business leaders who adhered to a tradition of privatism which has always been the hallmark of American urban development. The Carter administration was successful in developing and channelling a number of policy tools to leverage local economic development. The promised 'comprehensive' urban policy failed to emerge and some of the proposed programs were never enacted, but the administration succeeded in shifting the frame of reference within which urban policy proposals were offered and evaluated. Economic development was now the primary focus of national urban policy and this signified a new stage in the pursuit of the private city.

Notes

1. William Lilley III, Deputy Assistant Secretary of Policy Development at the Department of Housing and Urban Development in the Ford administration said, 'There was an urban crisis at one time but that has changed in the past few years. Oh yes, there are some serious problems—and some cities are in crisis—but now the picture varies from one city to another' (*New York Times*, 23 Mar. 1975).
2. Rates of unemployment during 1975 in cities with populations greater than 50,000 ranged from a high of 18.6 percent to a low of 2.8 percent with a median of 7.4 percent (USHUD 1978: 37).
3. In addition to the development bank, other features of the urban economic development program included: (1) a 5 percent investment tax credit for businesses locating in distressed communities in addition to the 10 percent credit previously proposed for new industrial construction; (2) a $3 billion, three-year public works program to employ disadvantaged workers in the renovation of public facilities; (3) a targeted employment tax credit of $2,000 to encourage businesses to hire disadvantaged young workers; (4) $1 billion of fiscal assistance to communities with above average unemployment rates; (5) $400 million over two years for states which adopted their own comprehensive urban strategies; direct financing of neighborhood revitalization projects which received the approval of city hall; and (6) other grants for urban transit, crime prevention, recreation, and human services programs.
4. It was subsequently renamed to appeal to rural as well as urban interests.
5. These reservations were expressed at a round-table discussion that the Brookings Institution conducted with 20 leading urban experts.
6. There was some amount of skepticism in the Senate about the viability of the program and resistance to the idea of giving the Secretary of HUD the ability to support UDAG projects through a discretionary fund.
7. Friedland's analysis of the 1980 Census shows that there is significant job leakage across city boundaries. Approximately one-quarter of a city's residents typically work outside the city (Friedland 1983).
8. In order to qualify for EDA programs in 1966, a county or municipality had to have an unemployment rate of 6 percent for the most recent calendar year as well as an unemployment rate over the preceding four years which was from 50 percent to 100 percent higher than the national average. Eligibility had to be achieved on the basis of city-wide figures so that while parts of cities might have qualified, only eight cities with populations over 250,000 met the criteria in 1966 (Pressman and Wildavsky 1984: 10).
9. The story of the Oakland project is told in *Implementation: How Great Expectations in Washington are Dashed in Oakland; or Why's It's Amazing That Federal Programs Work At All This Being a Saga of the Economic Development Administration* (Pressman and Wildavsky 1984).
10. These evaluations include USHUD (1982a) and GAO (1984).
11. If other federal funds and state and local funds are included, the total cost per job rises to $12,072.
12. HUD reports that 'for closed out and completed projects, more minority jobs were

created than planned (147 %). However, planned jobs are understated because, during the early years of the program, planned minority jobs were not included in applications as a separate category while jobs for minority persons actually created have always been reported by grantees' (USHUD 1987: 84).

13. Each job costs $15,089 if all public funds are considered.

14. As of 30 Sept. 1986, $4.249 billion of UDAG funds were expected to leverage $26.059 billion of private investment, a 6.1 to 1 ratio (Table 4.1). If other federal and state and local funds are included, the leveraging ratio drops to 3.9 to 1. Grantees reported that $21.7 billion had actually been expended by the end of FY 1986 (USHUD 1987: 77). This amount represented 83 percent of planned private expenditures. For completed and closed out projects, more private funds had been expended than actually planned (121 percent).

15. Susan and Norman Fainstein argue that 'business plays municipalities off against each other for subsidies and concessions, thereby increasing the average public subsidy to private accumulation while severely limiting the ability of even large municipalities to direct investment for socially desirable purposes' (1986c: 267).

16. Wilmington has the dual distinction of being the first community in the US to receive an Action Grant and to be among the top two or three cities in the per capita amount of UDAG funds received—about $600 for each resident and totalling over $40 million in 1986.

17. The property for the new Hercules office building was purchased with $3.9 million of UDAG funds and resold to Hercules for one dollar. The balance of the UDAG (about $12 million) was loaned to Hercules at 4 percent over 25 years with the requirement that only interest be paid back during the term of the loan and the principal to be due in the 25th year.

18. It is difficult to understand how maintenance of the Hercules building has created 424 jobs, but these figures were accepted by the evaluation team. It is also not clear that these are all full-time jobs. It is claimed that 496 of the jobs created to date have gone to low/moderate income workers and 400 have been filled by minorities. It is probable that there is significant overlap in the building maintenance jobs and the jobs that have gone to low/moderate income workers and to minorities.

19. While the ceiling on small issues effectively prevented use by large corporations some of the beneficiaries were large, profitable companies whose operations consisted of relatively low-cost branches or retail outlets.

20. Restrictions on the use of IRBs were progressively tightened until the Tax Reform Act of 1986 eliminated the tax exemption of small issue bonds as of 31 Dec. 1986, except for bonds issued exclusively to finance manufacturing facilities. The tax exemption for these issues was scheduled to expire three years later.

21. Source: *Editor and Publisher Market Guide* (New York: Editor and Publisher, 1964, 1969, 1974, 1979, 1984).

22. Baltimore, Boston, Buffalo, Cincinnati, Cleveland, Columbus, Detroit, Indianapolis, Milwaukee, Minneapolis, Pittsburgh, and St. Louis.

23. Case studies of New Haven (Fainstein and Fainstein 1986b; Stone and Sanders 1987b), Hartford (Neubeck and Ratcliff 1988), Houston (Kirby and Lynch 1987; Feagin 1988), Detroit (Hill 1986), New Orleans (Smith and Keller 1986), Denver (Judd 1986), and San Francisco (Fainstein, Fainstein, and Armistead 1986) have also documented the unevenness of urban development. While the economy and real estate values in these cities may have improved in the aggregate as a result of development, lower income areas often expanded and became poorer. The authors concluded that reliance on private development alone could not redress the imbalance. 'Only governmental action to channel the benefits of growth and the costs of decline can even out the development process' (Fainstein and Fainstein 1986a: 3).

5

The New Privatism and Urban America in the 1980s

WHEN Ronald Reagan entered the White House, he promised a new era of privatism in America. His first priority was to reverse the nation's economic decline by providing relief from decades of public interventions in the domestic economy which, he asserted, had failed to deliver prosperity. He proposed to restrict domestic spending, to relax or eliminate regulatory restrictions on private enterprise, and to restore balance to the federal system by ending Washington's domination of matters 'best left' to the states and localities (White House 1981). He also sought to encourage individual and community self-reliance, to stimulate a renewed commitment to voluntarism, and most of all to turn over responsibility for America's future to the institutions of private enterprise.

In many ways, President Reagan's domestic policy proposals echoed themes of earlier conservative administrations. The privatism of the 1980s, however, was more than a reaffirmation of ideological preferences for less government involvement in allocative decision making; it was proclaimed as the only viable national response to the problems of economic decline. In the context of urban policy this meant that cities must follow the lead of private enterprise. Rather than insulating cities from national and international market forces, both federal and local policies should encourage adaptation to the major technological changes that were reshaping the economic world. In order to prosper in this dynamic environment, cities had to capitalize on their competitive advantages; this, in turn, required that they depend upon the guidance of market-sensitive institutions (Savas 1983: 451).

In the Reagan administration's view, proposals to stimulate the privatization of urban America represented a radical departure from previous national urban policies. From a broader historical perspective, however, they were an extension of the long and continuous tradition of policy efforts to promote the private city. As we have demonstrated, policy initiatives to strengthen the private sector in urban areas and to focus the attention of cities on economic development were already well underway during the Carter administration. Rather than using the resources of the federal government to leverage private investment, however, the Reagan administration's approach was to minimize restrictions on private sector activity as much as possible. Towards this end, federal involvement in efforts to guide urban development had to be eliminated or at least dramatically reduced.

The novel characteristic of the Reagan administration's urban policy was its conception of the relationship between cities and the national economy. Since the 1930s, American urban policy had been based on the assumption that cities were vitally important to national prosperity. In the 1980s, the formulators of urban policy at the federal level no longer accepted this assumption as valid. As a result, revitalization of cities was not a priority; indeed, recovery of the national economy was thought to be possible only by improving market efficiency which, in turn, depended upon the ability of firms to operate as freely as possible from governmental constraints on investment decisions and locational choices. The urban dislocations and disinvestment that accompanied spatial realignment of economic activity were the necessary costs of national economic growth and national economic growth took precedence over the fortunes of particular urban places.

The New Urban Reality and the Urban Agenda

Many of the assumptions underlying the Reagan administration's orientation towards cities were articulated before the 1980 election by a group that was appointed by President Carter during the last years of his administration—the President's Commission for a National Agenda for the Eighties (PC). In its reports, *Urban America in the Eighties: Perspectives and Prospects* (PC 1980*a*) and *A National Agenda for the Eighties* (PC 1980*b*),[1] the Commission rejected the Carter administration's urban policy approach and provided a rationale for much of what was witnessed in urban policy after the election of Ronald Reagan (Barnekov, Rich, and Warren, 1981).

The most publicized aspect of the report was its call for public acceptance and encouragement of the transition of population, jobs, and industry from cities in the Northeast and Midwest to those in the sunbelt. This transition was viewed by the Commission as a clear sign that the old industrial city was an outmoded institution which inevitably was becoming less significant in American social and economic life. The Commission's assessment was consistent with a good deal of urban analysis in the late 1970s which depicted the more densely populated northeastern and midwestern regions as declining while the sunbelt and mountain rim states were growing; smaller towns and non-metropolitan areas were expanding at the expense of large cities and metropolitan areas; and within metropolitan areas, suburbanization and exurbanization were occurring at the expense of the central city (Berry 1981). The Commission pointed out that 'industrially based urban centers are gradually being unraveled' and the advantages of agglomeration and central location are being 'eroded by technological innovations and new production technologies that have given locational freedom to an ever wider array of industries' (PC 1980*b*: 24):

Much evidence exists to suggest that the economy of the United States, like that of many of the older industrial societies, has for years now been undergoing a critical transition from being geographically concentrated, centralized, and manufacturing-based to being increasingly deconcentrated, decentralized, and service-based. In the process, many cities of the old industrial heartland . . . are losing their status as thriving industrial capitals (PC 1980*b*: 66).

These trends were spatial expressions of the transformation of the United States from an industrial to a post-industrial society, a transformation that defined the path for the economic and technological revitalization of America. The future prosperity of the nation depended upon successful accommodation of the forces of post-industrial change. The Commission recognized that this change was producing acute economic and social dis-locations in hundreds of cities, and it acknowledged the distress and despair of those 'left behind' but it argued that attempts to restrict or reverse the pro-cess, 'for whatever noble intentions—is to deny the benefits that the future may hold for us as a nation' (PC 1980*b*: 66). Rather, the nation must recognize that urban distress resulting from the redistribution of population and economic activity is part of the process of renewal; the nation must 'reconcile itself to these redistribution patterns' (PC 1980*b*: 3–4).

The post-industrial transition, the Commission suggested, was breaking the economic bond between national and city prosperity. While urbanization as a process was still important to the development of the American eco-nomy, this economy was no longer dependent upon the economic growth of the older industrial cities. Indeed, the culture and amenities of city life were not confined to large city centers and were being diffused throughout the country by economic and technological forces. Because of this, the decline of older industrial centers did not signify a challenge to national prosperity but, rather, was a necessary part of the process of economic renewal.

In the past, the federal government allocated billions of dollars to aid declining urban areas in the hope that the endeavor would help their resid-ents but, according to the Commission, it was a short-sighted and ineffective strategy which achieved 'very little in upgrading those localities, let alone in helping the unemployed, underemployed, and dependent' (PC 1980*b*: 69). Indeed, it proved to be very difficult to shore up or 'revitalize' urban areas. More importantly, such a strategy actually exacerbated the problems of national economic revitalization because it tried to prevent the decline of some urban places at the expense of the growth of others and because it failed to assist cities to adjust to an emerging post-industrial era. 'Cities are not permanent', maintained the Commission, 'their strength is related to their ability to reflect change rather than to fend it off . . . In the long run, the fates and fortunes of specific places [should] be allowed to fluctuate' (PC 1980*b*: 65).

The Commission contended that in the transition to a post-industrial society, the overall social and economic welfare of the country depended on the vitality and adaptability of the national economy and not on the condition of specific places. Moreover, national economic revival and the economic revitalization of distressed cities were not necessarily compatible. On the one hand, 'national economic policies that seek to increase productivity, to expand markets, to create jobs, and to nurture new industries also have the potential for conflict with urban revitalization efforts'; such policies 'may well lead to the outmigration of firms or to their secondary expansion away from distressed locations, where the costs of doing business are prohibitively high'

(PC 1980*a*: 4). On the other hand, urban policies may obstruct national economic renewal; 'vigorous pursuit of a national urban policy—with its current emphasis on restoring economic vitality to distressed localities and regions—may undermine a more general effort to revitalize the national economy—with its relative deemphasis on what happens to specific places' (PC 1980*a*: 4).

The Commission concluded that 'the best national urban strategy is the restoration of steady growth in the economy' (PC, 1980*b*: 70). Indeed, 'the federal government's concern for national economic vitality should take precedence over the competition for advantage among communities and regions, (PC 1980*a*: 5). The principal role of the federal government should be to assist communities to adjust to redistributional trends rather than to attempt to reverse them. The Commission also turned to the instrument that traditionally had been relied upon in the US to produce economic prosperity—private enterprise. 'Public sector activity', the Commission advised, 'should endeavor to encourage private sector vitality, taking care to try to alleviate its undesirable consequences without hampering that vitality' (PC 1980*b*: 70).

While the Commission opposed direct efforts to assist distressed communities, it recognized that people in these communities needed help in making the transition to the new post-industrial order. Since people suffer as America is transformed, the primary responsibility of the federal government is to assist them as directly as possible.

The government should aim principally to remove barriers between people and economic opportunity. We believe that a people-to-jobs strategy based on vigorous government programs of assisted migration and skill acquisition should receive the emphasis that has been reserved in recent years for job-to-people strategics dependent upon local economic development (PC 1980*b*: 65).

Towards this end, the Commission pointed to the need for 'national social policies that aim to aid people directly wherever they may live' (PC 1980*a*: 102). It called for 'a guaranteed job program for those who can work and a guaranteed cash assistance plan for both the "working poor" and those who cannot work' (PC 1980*a*: 102). A guaranteed income program 'would effectively and properly shift the welfare burden to the federal government, which can administer it more efficiently and with a greater capacity for responding to equity considerations than subnational governments' (PC 1980*a*: 102). But while advocating strengthened social policy, the Commission was emphatic in concluding that the nation would be ill-advised to pursue a 'centrally administered national urban policy that legitimizes activities inconsistent with the revitalization of the larger national economy' (PC 1980*b*: 99).

The urban agenda proposed by the Commission was an unmistakable repudiation of the Carter urban policy. Rather than aiding individual cities, it proposed that federal policy have as its basic goal the efficient spatial allocation of resources in the marketplace. In effect, the Commission called for the abandonment of national urban policy because, for it, there were 'no "national urban problems," only an endless variety of local ones' (PC 1980*a*: 99). Thus, it proposed that national responses to the problems of local communities 'should evolve from a largely place-oriented, locationally sensitive, national urban policy, to more people-oriented, locationally neutral, national economic and social policies' (PC 1980*b*: 82).

James Fallows has described the Commission report as 'the first shot in the economic battle of this decade' (Fallows 1985: 48)—a battle about how the United States should view and respond to the economic changes that loomed ahead and about what, if anything, should be done with the urban residue of an industrial era bypassed by the forces of economic transition. As Fallows points out, for those persuaded by the Commission report, the policy choices for urban America are easy once the inevitability of 'ceaseless, churning change' is recognized.

Industries rose and fell—and so did empires, and so did cities. Nothing endured forever, and in the real world of economics, it was vain to hope that anything would . . . [T]he big, broadshouldered places from which America's twentieth century industrial wealth had been wrung—Chicago, Cleveland, Pittsburgh, Detroit—could not expect to survive in their current form . . . In the face of such a certainty . . . the government should stop trying to ward off the inevitable by subsidizing specific cities and regions. After all, its obligations were to people, not to places where they happened to live (Fallows 1985: 47).

Acceptance of this logic was anything but easy for the leaders of declining cities. The Commission report especially drew the wrath of urban leaders in the frostbelt and other economically distressed areas of the country who were outraged by the call for an end to special assistance for declining cities and regions and were anything but complacent about predictions of the inevitable demise of their communities.

Despite these protests, the logic underlying the Commission report remained influential throughout the 1980s, long after the report itself vanished from the arena of urban policy debate. While sometimes moderating and occasionally challenging some of the prescriptions of the Commission, studies sponsored by prominent institutions such as the Committee on National Urban Policy of the National Research Council (Hanson 1983) and the Brookings Institution (P. Peterson 1985) supported much of the analysis. Thus, Paul Peterson proclaimed that the industrial city had become an institutional anachronism and its demise signalled the emergence of a new urban reality.

If the great manufacturing centers of Europe and the American Snow Belt developed as by-products of the industrial revolution, their decline is no less ancillary to contemporary technological change . . . Two to three decades ago urbanists sought to save the industrial city by redeveloping central business districts, or creating model cities that would transform poverty-stricken neighborhoods, or 'energizing' citizens to participate in planning their community's future. Few would venture to propose such schemes today. Quite apart from political changes that have occurred in Washington, economic and social changes have moved so far that reversing their direction no longer seems feasible or even desirable. Industrial cities must simply accept a less exalted place in American political and social life than they once enjoyed. Policies must adapt to this new urban reality (Peterson 1985: 1).

Peterson and other analysts arrived at conclusions that were similar to those of the Commission: the best federal policy to assist urban areas is a 'non-urban policy'; efforts should concentrate on redressing the social and racial inequities attendant to the emergence of the new urban reality but federal policies should have 'no specifically urban component to them at all' (Peterson 1985: 25–6).

The themes of the Commission report and the vision of the new urban reality offered a rationale for the Reagan administration's efforts to end federal assistance to urban places. This rationale and its implications for cities were most explicitly and forcefully articulated by E.S. Savas, an Assistant Secretary in HUD who directed the Office of Policy Development and Research. Congruent with the Commission report, Savas argued that strengthening the national economy was the single most important action the federal government could take to help urban America because, he said, 'our economy is predominantly an urban one, what's good for the nation's economy is good for the economies of our cities' (Savas 1983: 447). The future of a city, he proposed, would depend not on grants from the federal government but on its ability 'to perform a useful role in its regional economy' (Savas 1983: 450). A city had to take stock of itself, understand the technological and market forces that were acting upon it, and capitalize on its competitive advantages.

Urban economic development, according to Savas, was an important component of a city's survival and growth strategy; it should be pursued by local government with encouragement but not direct intervention or assistance from the federal government. The private sector should be involved in this strategy; indeed, private institutions needed to become a more prominent part of local urban leadership because they 'provide the long-term perspective that is institutionally absent from the political process' (Savas 1983: 450). The private sector also offered an alternative system for delivery of urban services. Savas charged that 'municipal monopolies' often did not work effectively in the public interest; they should be broken up by introducing competition into the delivery of services through privatization, contracting out, franchising, issuing vouchers, and relying on voluntary institutions (Savas 1983: 452). In effect, municipal efficiency in the production and delivery of services required the discipline of the marketplace.

Urban Policy and the Standard of Economic Efficiency

In a message delivered by President Reagan to a Joint Session of Congress on 'A Program for Economic Recovery' on 18 February 1981, no mention was made of a strategy to deal with urban problems. The focus was entirely on general economic policy and on proposed limitations in the growth of federal expenditures, reductions in tax rates, relief of federal regulatory burdens, and the establishment of a monetary policy that was consistent with a more limited federal role in the economy (White House 1981: 2). Proposals were made for reducing or eliminating what the President regarded as counter-productive urban aid programs such as the Economic Development Administration (EDA), the Urban Development Action Grant program (UDAG), the Community Development Block Grant (CDBG) program, and subsidized housing.

The idea of an urban policy ran counter to the administration's governing philosophy which attributed no lasting value to federal assistance to urban areas. Under federal law, however, the President must send a national urban policy report to Congress every other year. This posed a dilemma since it would be embarrassing to issue a report that simply documented urban problems that the administration intended to do nothing about, and thus some argued that repeal of the report's authorizing legislation should be sought. Others pointed out that the Reagan administration had an urban policy—whether it recognized it or not—and the urban policy report pro-vided an opportunity to explain it (Ahlbrandt 1984: 479). The policy that was finally described in the 1982 *National Urban Policy Report* adopted much of the logic offered by the President's Commission for a National Agenda; particularly its justification for a reduction of federal aid to declining urban areas (USHUD 1982*b*). The administration adhered to only part of the Commission's framework, however; the call for a 'guaranteed job program' and a 'guaranteed cash assistance' program was ignored.

Savas was principal author of the early drafts of the *National Urban Policy Report*. Some members of the administration, however, regarded his lan-guage as too blunt and his economic view of the world too simplistic. As a result, the language of early drafts was softened and efforts were made to avoid depicting the administration as uncaring about cities and their resid-ents (Ahlbrandt 1984: 482). But, since Savas's views were consistent with the administration's efforts to fundamentally alter the federal government's responsibilities to distressed urban areas, his urban policy prescriptions remained relatively intact throughout the drafting process. Basic themes and priorities remained the same: the nation's first priority was to strengthen the economy; states and cities, properly unfettered, could manage themselves more wisely than the federal government; the private sector should be encouraged to assist urban communities; federal urban programs had not resulted in improving urban conditions; and there would be no significant increases in federal assistance to the poor (USHUD 1982*b*). Despite the continuity in policy orientation from early draft to final version, the President did not formally endorse the report nor did he choose to sign it before sending it on to Congress.

One of the distinctive aspects of the announced urban policy was the administration's commitment to remaining passive in the face of what were acknowledged as serious urban dislocations. The policy lacked a significant role for the federal government either to directly assist urban areas or to provide incentives for private sector activity. There was no room for target-ing federal resources to high cost, less productive, declining areas; instead, resources were to be directed to those areas the private sector had already determined to be productive and profitable (Myron Levine 1983: 17). Cities were 'instructed to wean themselves from dependence on federal aid and to prepare themselves for free-market competition' (Judd and Ready 1986: 210). Cities had primary responsibility for making themselves attract-ive to private investors; they had to find the mechanisms that would involve the private sector in local development; they, along with state government, were most responsible for meeting the welfare needs of their residents; and they should look to the private sector for alternative ways of efficiently delivering services to their citizens. Within this context, the administration encouraged a competition among cities for a share of national economic growth, and it called upon declining urban areas to 'form partnerships with their private sectors and plan strategically to enhance their comparative advantages relative to other jurisdictions' (USHUD 1982*b*: 3).

In effect, the Reagan urban policy was based on the conviction that society benefits most when both public and private actions are measured by the criterion of economic efficiency. By this criterion, the public sector was judged 'inherently inefficient'. According to Myron Levine the strategy was to minimize the scope of government activity in hopes that this, in itself, would stimulate a more efficient allocation of resources:

In the eyes of the Reagan administration, government action not only ties capital and labor to high cost areas, it also adds unnecessary paperwork and bureaucratic over-head costs to investment. Such added costs to production only exacerbate inflation at home and hurt American industry's competitive position relative to that of firms based overseas. Hence, the Reagan urban policy celebrates the themes of deregulation, decentralization and privatization. Wherever possible, efficiency-oriented private sector action is to substitute for intrusive federal action (Levine 1983: 17–18).

Given this view, most of the proposals introduced by the Reagan administration were designed to negate federal policy interventions. Only one new program was proposed for urban areas—the Enterprise Zone—a concept adapted from the British program which established areas in inner cities where economic activity was encouraged through relief from taxes, regulations, and other government burdens (see Chapter 7). Other than the Enterprise Zone idea, the Reagan urban policy cannot be found in any specific federal initiatives or set of programs. It was, to a large extent, the residual product of a national economic policy that exhibited little interest in the sub-national impacts of national change. As Norman Glickman has pointed out, simply describing the Reagan urban policy is a challenge because:

the administration has paid little explicit attention to cities, focusing its policies on the prosperity of firms and people, not places. Besides the 'New Federalism' and enter-prise zone proposals, there have been few federal urban initiatives since 1981. At the heart of [the] Reagan program is the goal of economic growth; accordingly, industrial development should proceed with little serious concern for spatial or interpersonal equity (Glickman 1984: 471).

The federal policy approach to urban areas in the 1980s might be described as a policy of 'spatial trickle-down' (Glickman 1984: 471). The underlying assumption was, in the words of the 1982 *National Urban Policy Report*, that 'ultimately, the key to healthy cities is a healthy economy' (USHUD 1982*b*: 1). But even the idea of spatial trickle-down incorporates an expectation that not all areas gain from national prosperity. As Savas wrote, 'not all cities will benefit equally, and some may not benefit at all' (Savas 1983: 447). Unfortunately, the prospects for enjoying the benefits of growth were especially dim for urban places that already experienced distress precisely because of their inability to adapt to the changing needs of the national marketplace. These areas did not figure significantly in the economic recovery of the nation and they were not likely to benefit from its achievement. In the face of this reasoning the president-elect of the National League of Cities described the administration's urban policy approach 'as a blueprint for surrendering America's cities ... the federal government admits it is incapable of winning the battle for the cities, and announces its intention to go AWOL (JEC 1983: 36).

The Urban Budget and the Attack on Local Economic Development

In his budget proposal for fiscal year 1982, President Reagan unveiled a series of federal program cuts totalling $44 billion (White House 1981). All expenditure categories, except defense, were marked for reduction but income security, education, training, employment, and social services accounted for more than half of the total. Over $18 billion dollars were to be cut in programs directly affecting cities (Table 5.1) including consolidation of the CDBG and UDAG programs into a single program at reduced funding levels; termination of the Comprehensive Employment Training Action (CETA) and Public Service Employment Program (PSE); phasing out of mass transit operating subsidies and substantial reduction in mass transit capital grants; termination of the Municipal Wastewater Treatment Program and restructuring of a new program at 50 percent below the current funding level; termination of EDA; reorganization of compensatory education programs at reduced funding levels; consolidation of categorical grants into a Local Education Block Grant and State Education Block Grant; consolidation of health categorical grants into a Health Services Block Grant and Preventive Health Block Grant at reduced funding levels; creation of a Social Service Block Grant; reduction in budget authority for subsidized housing and an increase in tenant rent contribution from 25 percent to 30 percent of income (White House 1981). From the pre-Reagan 'baseline' levels, the proposed reductions for FY 1982 amounted to a 30 percent decline in budget authority and an 18 percent decline in

TABLE 5.1. *Reagan's Proposals for Urban Programs for FY 1982 (in $M)*

	Budget authority FY 1982			Outlays FY 1982		
	Pre-Reagan baseline, FY 1982	Proposed reduction from pre-Reagan baseline	Percentage reduction	Pre-Reagan baseline, FY 1982	Proposed reduction from pre-Reagan baseline	Percentage change
CDBG and UDAG[a]	4,750	584	12.3	4,625	12	0.3
CETA–PSE[b]	3,955	4,644	117.4	3,771	3,566	94.6
Mass transit operating subsidies	1,208	103	8.5	876	96	11.0
Mass transit capital grants	3,650	950	26.0	2,800	270	9.6
Municipal wastewater treatment grants	3,610	3,610	100.0	4,220	125	3.0
Economic Development Administration[c]	1,034	769	74.4	1,023	440	43.0
Elementary and secondary education[d]	6,061	1,498	24.7	5,797	106	18.3
Health and social services[e]	9,491	2,697	28.4	9,334	2,540	27.2
Assisted housing[f]	27,123	3,536	13.0	6,894	10	0.1
TOTAL	60,882	18,391	30.2	39,340	7,165	18.2
TOTAL (excluding housing)	33,759	14,855	44.0	32,446	7,155	22.1

[a] Reagan's proposals called for an integration of CDBG and UDAG programs.
[b] Comprehensive Employment Training Act and Public Service Employment Program.
[c] Includes proposal to eliminate regional commissions.
[d] Includes Local Education Block Grant and proposed State Education Block Grant.
[e] Includes both Social Service Block Grant and various health block grants.
[f] Includes reduction in number of assisted units and proposed increase in tenant rent contribution.

Source: White House 1981 (as presented in Wolman 1985: 316).

budget outlay for programs of concern to urban areas. Excluding subsidized housing, the reductions were 44 percent in authority and 22 percent in outlay.

Ultimately, Congress overturned a number of the Reagan budget proposals or approved smaller reductions. EDA continued but at a substantially reduced funding level, UDAG and CDBG remained as separate programs but also at reduced levels, the CETA-PSE public service employment programs were terminated but mass transit assistance and wastewater treatment grants continued at reduced levels, compensatory education remained as a separate program and the local education block grant was not approved but other block grants in education, health, and social services were approved in a less sweeping form than Reagan had proposed (Wolman 1986: 315). Congress did not trim the FY 1982 budget authority for urban programs (excluding housing) at the level proposed by the President (44 percent), but this authority was set at 36.5 percent below the pre-Reagan baseline and outlays were reduced by 23 percent, slightly over Reagan's proposed 22.1 percent (Wolman 1986: 317).

While the administration's overall intent to dismantle the urban budget, and specifically its effort to withdraw federal support from urban social programs, was consistent with its general ideological position, the reasons for the sustained attack on federal programs designed to stimulate economic development through business expansion in urban areas were not as evident. After all, the administration was anything but restrained in its enthusiasm for privatism, and it urged urban areas to promote redevelopment through a greater reliance on the leadership and investment choices of the private sector. Nonetheless, federal assistance programs for local economic development were defined as ill-conceived and misguided and were systematically targeted for reduction or elimination. Reagan's February 1981 budget message declared that the Commerce Department's EDA program and HUD's UDAG program—both popular among local officials and business leaders—were wasteful and ineffective. The UDAG program, the President maintained, 'currently requires an excessive amount of Federal intervention in developing, selecting, and monitoring local economic development projects' (White House 1981: 151), and EDA was effective in 'creating an array of planners, grantsmen and professional middlemen' but there was no convincing evidence that it produced new jobs or capital investment or was actually needed to promote local and regional economic development (White House 1981: 4, 136). 'We believe we can do better', declared the President, 'just by the expansion of the economy and the job creation which will come from our economic program' (White House 1981: 4). He proposed to abolish the EDA program and incorporate UDAG into the CDBG program.

The administration clearly preferred not to have any federally funded programs directly aimed at local economic development. If there was to be government stimulation and guidance of private investment decisions, it should be 'through the less distorting national tax policy than through conditional federal grant and loan programs which allow federal bureaucrats to review the investment and operating decisions of private sector officials' (Myron Levine 1983: 19). Economic development programs, it was alleged, undermine the efficient operation of the market. David Stockman, Reagan's first Director of the Office of Management and Budget (OMB), testified before the House Public Works and Transportation Subcommittee on Economic Development that EDA doesn't create jobs, it reallocates them. Even when the program succeeds in inducing a firm to locate in a particular city, he observed, it does so only at the expense of overall national economic growth, shifting investments to high-cost or less economically efficient areas. 'I think you have got a great shell-game underway in which resources are being moved all over the country, but I'm not sure who is getting helped' (US House 1981: 25).

The administration's principal criticism of federally assisted economic development programs was that in macroeconomic terms they allocated resources inefficiently. There were several dimensions to this argument. First, economic development programs absorbed capital in the form of tax revenue from the private sector which otherwise might be invested in ways that would achieve larger long-run social benefits. Second, they retained capital and labor in locations which did not allow for their most productive use. Third, they discouraged the development of new capital and technologies by rehabilitating aging physical plants in distressed cities (Stephenson 1987: 26).

EDA, in particular, was charged with being ineffective and wasteful. Critics, in and out of the administration, argued that the agency had lost a large amount of money in delinquent loans, that it had not succeeded in advancing the development of chronically depressed areas, and that it wasted money because it promoted development that would have occurred anyway. Even when net new jobs were created, it was alleged, they cost the government too much money. Although there was a good deal of disagreement on this point, the administration claimed that the total cost per job directly created by an EDA development grant was in the order of $60,000 to $70,000 for a person-year of employment (White House 1981: 136).

The EDA program was especially vulnerable to Congressional log-rolling or what has been called 'politics by printout', a process in which legislators manipulate aid formulas to ensure that their districts receive a share of the expenditures of a federal aid program (Myron Levine 1983: 19). Given EDA's mission to relieve long-term economic distress in depressed regions, one would expect its expenditures to be concentrated disproportionately in states with low levels of economic development. Grasso's analysis of EDA expenditure patterns had found, however, that they were related more to the goal of a wide geographical dispersal of aid (Grasso 1986: 95). As a result, about 80 percent of the nation's population lived in areas that were eligible for participation in EDA's programs (Myron Levine 1983: 19).

While EDA was criticized for distributing money too broadly, the UDAG program was castigated for targeting too much assistance to areas that the private sector found to be uneconomical or inefficient locations for production

(Myron Levine 1983: 19). According to an OMB 'black book' of proposed budget cuts which circulated Congress in February 1981, 'the UDAG program compensates the private sector for shifting investments to high-cost or less economically efficient areas. This reduces the net economic (although not necessarily the social) gains from any given amount of investment' (*National Journal*, 21 Mar. 1981: 495).[2] In the administration's view, there was no justification for a federal program that interfered with local economic activity to the detriment of national economic growth. States and cities could do much better on their own, it was believed, but ultimately efficient private sector action was much preferred over wasteful and intrusive government action. Stockham argued:

If you want an economy that's productive, that maximizes growth, income, opportunity over time, you've got to encourage both investment and disinvestment. You've got to have adjustment. Government basically is a reactionary institution that tries to foster one and retard the other, and usually makes a botch of both. So that's why we want to have a kind of hands-off policy (*National Journal*, 21 Mar. 1981: 496).

The administration's initial proposal to do away with UDAG was met with bipartisan opposition in Congress which, combined with sustained lobbying by urban groups, convinced the Reagan White House to include the program in its fiscal 1982 budget revisions at a proposed one-third reduction in funding (from $675 to $440 million). The negative reaction to UDAG's abolition, however, did not change the administration's belief that the program misallocated resources. Stockman was a particularly vigorous opponent of UDAG and reported in his book, *The Triumph of Politics*:

If there was a single program in the 1981 budget we inherited that was both a statist abomination and something a Republican Administration had a chance to kill outright, it was the Urban Development Action Grant Program. It was called UDAG—a sincere-sounding acronym that covered a multitude of sins. PORK would have been more accurate (Stockman 1986: 142).

Despite a HUD report that positively evaluated UDAG's effectiveness (USHUD 1982a), and an endorsement of the program in the 1984 *National Urban Policy Report* (USHUD 1984), the President's fiscal 1986 budget once again targeted UDAG for abolition; and for the fifth time in as many years no new program authority was sought for EDA. While the administration had not yet been able to end the programs, by 1986 UDAG's budget authority had been cut by over 50 percent and EDA's by nearly 60 percent of the 1981 levels (Table 5.2).[3] The administration steadfastly adhered to the conviction that 'shifting responsibility for economic development programs to the State and local levels brings both economic development funding and priority decisions closer to the people', a belief that was reaffirmed in the White House budget proposals for fiscal 1988 (EO 1987a: 2–22). As part of its effort 'to reduce unnecessary subsidies and excessive Federal intervention in the economic decisions of private firms and individuals', the administration proposed termination and recision of most of the 1987 appropriations for EDA and UDAG (EO 1987a: 2–22). These programs, the White House maintained,

TABLE 5.2. *Trend in Funding of UDAG and EDA Programs, FY 1981–FY 1991*
(In $M)

Fiscal Year	UDAG			EDA		
	Proposed	Authority	Outlay	Proposed	Authority	Outlay
1980	400.0	675.0	225.0	609.0	553.0	629.0
1981	675.0	675.0	371.0	1,241.0	476.0	536.0
1982	675.0	474.0	388.0	674.0	224.0	412.0
1983	440.0	440.0	451.0	15.0	294.0	303.0
1984	196.0	440.0	454.0	—	294.0	216.0
1985[a]	440.0	440.0	496.7	15.0	230.7	262.6
1986	0.0	315.8	460.9	18.0	190.9	252.7
1987	0.0	225.0	354.0	22.0	217.0	341.0
1988[b]	0.0	216.0	400.0	15.0	205.0	268.0
1989[b]	0.0	50.0	366.0	0.0	40.0	226.0
1990[b]	0.0	—	310.0	0.0	—	144.0
1991[b]	0.0	—	168.0	0.0	—	91.0

[a] Proposed $196 M in new revenue along with $224 M in excess 1983 resources for a total request of $440 M.
[b] Budget Authority and Budget Outlay for 1988–91 are estimates.
Source: EO 1980–9.

'siphon productive resources from private investment projects to politically designed projects that may provide local benefits, but that are less efficient for the national economy as a whole' (EO 1987*a*: 2–22).

In place of federal support for local economic development, the administration encouraged cities to form partnerships with their private sectors to stimulate economic development, but it also informed them that such partnerships must be largely local affairs supported by local resources. While endorsing the partnership concept, it consistently opposed federal programs designed to implement this concept and, for the most part, limited its support to the sponsorship of periodic task force and panel reports that reminded localities of the immense benefits of a greater reliance on the private sector and listed partnership models that it regarded as successful. Thus, the Presidential Task Force on Private Sector Initiatives devoted considerable time to a 'community partnership division' which catalogued ways in which private organizations can play a more prominent role in local affairs. Similarly, the Governmental Capacity Sharing Division of HUD introduced the Community Partnership Resource Center to provide city officials with information on techniques suitable for stimulating private sector involvement in local programs. Beyond the process of cataloguing and disseminating information, however, the administration provided no substantive support for the partnership concept it so fervently endorsed.

Voluntarism, Community Self-Reliance, and the New Federalism

A primary justification for the substantial reduction in federal dollars available to cities was that these losses would be offset by the positive impacts of two key features of the Reagan administration's programs. First, the cutback in federal funding would reduce federal intrusion in areas of community social assistance that were traditionally the responsibility of voluntary and charitable institutions. The end of dependency on federal funds was expected to stimulate community self-reliance and unleash a massive increase in voluntarism and private philanthropy that would become even more substantial as the national economy improved. Second, the decentralization of decision making from federal to state and local authorities would give localities greater control over those funds that remained and induce the states to resume or expand their role in the assistance of local communities.

In the midst of the budget debates during President Reagan's first term, he suggested that the impacts of federal budget cuts would be moderated by sectoral substitution. The growth of government activities, he argued, had displaced private and voluntary activities: 'We've let government take away many things we once considered were really ours to do voluntarily . . . I believe many of you want to do these things again' (quoted in Bendick and Levinson 1984: 462). The President was particularly adamant about the administration's intent to restore 'the American spirit of voluntary service, of cooperation, of private and community initiative' and the tradition of depending more fully on private charitable resources and voluntary efforts to solve community problems (Salamon and Abramson 1982: 220).

Lester Salamon and Alan Abramson—who participated in the Urban Institute's three-year project to examine the shifts in economic and social policies occurring under the Reagan administration—argued that the President's commitment to promote private voluntary organizations was consistent with conservative political theory which

considers the relationship between government and such organizations as essentially competitive; it sees in the expansion of government the displacement of private organizations and the crowding out of charitable resources; and it views the impact of tax rates on private giving solely as a function of the amount of income left in private hands (Salamon and Abramson 1982: 230).

Analysts pointed out that there is little historical evidence to support this theory. Rather than a lid being placed on private charitable activity as a result of an overbearing and intrusive federal government, charitable giving actually increased dramatically in recent decades. Bendick and Levinson show that the level of charitable giving in 1983 was 86 percent higher than it had been in the late 1950s, and over the same period the rate of increase in giving actually was greater than the rate of increase of per capita income (Bendick and Levinson 1984: 468). Furthermore, despite the President's exhortations and the promotional activities of a number of administration task forces and panels, there was no evidence that the private sector—corporate or voluntary—could fill the gap created by federal budget cuts (Salamon 1984). Indeed, the studies conducted by the Urban Institute early in the administration's first term suggested that the evidence ran in the other direction: federal cuts would have significant negative consequences for voluntary organizations: public revenues would decline and individual and corporate giving would be discouraged by the administration's tax policies.

Salamon and Abramson maintain that, historically, the growth of federal support has broadened and stabilized the role of non-profit organizations, resulting in a complex partnership arrangement that constitutes a system of non-profit federalism (Salamon and Abramson 1982: 234). The withdrawal of federal funding threatened the stability of this partnership and, rather than expanding the initiative of non-profit organizations, would make it difficult for these organizations to maintain even existing levels of services. Their projections of the impact of federal cutbacks on the non-profit sector were vastly different from those of the administration.

Non-profit organizations' revenues from federal sources are estimated to decline by $3.7 billion (in 1981 dollars) between FY 1981 and FY 1982. Moreover, based on the administration's budget proposals for subsequent years these revenue losses would accelerate, to the point that they would total $35.3 billion over the entire FY 1982–1985 period. Particularly hard hit by these cuts would be social service and community development organizations, which would lose the equivalent of about 60 percent of their federal support between 1981 and 1985 ... [T]hese types of organizations receive the largest shares of their income from federal sources. Thus, they face the greatest potential increase in demand for their services as a consequence of the overall budget reductions (Salamon and Abramson 1982: 234, 236).

Private giving would have to increase by 30 to 40 percent over the 1983–1985 period just to maintain existing service levels, an increase of three to four times the previous record level of increase. Even if this were achieved, it would make no contribution towards non-profit organizations filling the gap created by overall federal cutbacks in social programs (Salamon and Abramson 1982: 236).

Adding to this bleak picture was a second study by the Urban Institute on charitable giving which concluded that, even under optimistic economic assumptions, the 1981 Economic Recovery and Tax Reform Act would inhibit the growth of charitable giving by individuals (Clotfelder and Salamon 1982). In fact, charitable giving by upper-income taxpayers would actually decrease. Since charitable giving by individuals constituted 83 percent of all private giving, the tax changes could translate into $9 billion dollars per year in reduced revenue for non-profit organizations. Further, the prospect of 'filling the gap' with contributions from corporate philanthropy or foundations was hardly more encouraging since these sources together made up no more than 10 percent of total US charitable contributions; indeed, the attention they received from the administration far outstripped their actual levels of activity (Bendick and Levinson 1984: 465). Corporate giving averaged only 1 percent of pre-tax income during the 1970s, even though the maximum allowable charitable tax reduction was 5 percent (CUED 1981). Put another way, it was estimated that in 1981 corporate giving came to far less than one tenth of the federal budget cuts (SRI 1981: 19).

In light of these analyses, the President and other administration officials denied that there was any expectation that the private sector would take up the slack for federal budget cuts. Even so, there was still strong encouragement for the private sector in general, and the corporate sector in particular, to do more through philanthropic contributions. Administration calls for cuts in public programs continued to be paired with praise for private efforts, leaving the impression, at least, that persons adversely affected by budget cuts would have alternative private assistance available to them (Bendick and Levinson 1984: 458). C. William Verity, Jr., chairman of Armco Steel and chairperson of the President's Task Force on Private Sector Initiatives suggested that corporate philanthropy was important to the nation and that an honor roll should be created for businesses that had pre-tax giving policies (Berger 1984: 194). Despite awareness of the Urban Institute studies, the administration 'never escaped the temptation of using the rhetoric of "filling the gap" ', even though, wrote Denis Doyle, 'the scale and scope of the proposed Reagan cuts were so enormous that there was simply no way the private sector could fill the gap, even if the economy had been robust' (Doyle 1984: 213).

In addition to increased private sector contributions, the administration argued that the impacts of the budget cuts would be moderated by the Reagan version of New Federalism. In effect, diminished federal intervention in local affairs was offered at the price of reduced federal assistance, and reduced assistance was rationalized, in part, on the basis of local control of policy decisions and implementation. This aspect of the Reagan program reflected a 'belief that states and cities can more wisely and efficiently handle programs affecting their citizens' (Tate 1981: 709). The administration maintained that as the federal government had assumed increasing responsibilities, state and local governments became 'administrative arms of Federal agencies to an alarming degree'; the federal government had 'swollen to unmanageable proportions' and 'policymakers have become more remote at the same time that Government itself has become more intrusive' (USHUD 1982b: 54). The President proposed that this pattern be drastically changed and that balance in the federal system be restored by transferring power and responsibilities from the federal government back to the states through consolidated block grants. These grants would enable localities to use federal funds as they determined, not as dictated by Washington. 'In a single stroke', the administration claimed in the 1982 *National Urban Policy Report*, 'we will be accomplishing a realignment that will end cumbersome administration and spiraling costs at the Federal level, while we insure these programs will be more responsive to both the people they are meant to help and the people who pay for them' (USHUD 1982b: 54).

Actually, the idea was not new. Nixon's New Federalism initiated just such a transfer of consolidated programs back to states.[4] Carter also wrestled with the problem of rationalizing the coordination and management of almost 500 federal aid programs for states and localities even though little reform was accomplished during his administration. In a sense, Reagan was picking up where earlier administrations had left off. He also was acting in an area where groups like the Advisory Commission on Intergovernmental Relations, the National Governors' Association, and the National Conference of State Legislatures had called for federal reform.[5] What was distinctive about the Reagan approach was the intent to carry the process of program decentralization further than his predecessors had envisioned and to couple program decentralization with general cutbacks in resources. Earlier efforts at reform had sought to simplify the management of intergovernmental programs while retaining a national commitment to the support of a broad array of state and local services. The Reagan administration aimed at reducing or eliminating national financial support as well as national rules and standards (Beam 1984: 418). 'It is my intention', Reagan declared in his inaugural address, 'to curb the size and influence of the federal establishment and to demand recognition of the distinction between the powers granted to the federal government, and those reserved to the states or to the people' (Reagan 1981).

The administration maintained that New Federalism would increase authority at the municipal level, but the extent to which local governments would be able to formulate their own policies was left unclear. In fact, the Reagan urban strategy had the potential to constrain the policy options of cities. The elimination or reduction of federal programs believed to be burdensome to business was not undertaken with the expectation that these programs would be reinstituted by local governments. Indeed, the administration did not look favorably upon cities that used their authority to 'interfere' with market decisions; such actions resulted in threats of legislative or administrative reprisals, the withholding of federal funds, or other punitive measures. In July 1981, for example, the Senate approved a housing program that increased the autonomy of local governments to administer federal grants and barred public rental housing funds to cities that engaged in rent control. Although the latter provision was rejected by the House of Representatives, the idea was formulated and promoted by the Reagan administration. One observer suggested at the time:

This apparent contradiction in the conservative ideology about local control now prevalent in Washington once again reveals that the administration is not really interested in bringing political power closer to the American people but is determined to subordinate the public welfare to corporate interests in housing as in everything else (editorial, *In These Times*, 17–30 June 1981: 14).

The Reagan New Federalism also signalled an increased dependence of urban areas on state government. The overall cutback in the funding of federal urban programs would require cities to look to state governments for aid. In fact, the actual turn back of domestic policy responsibilities was to the states, not the cities, substituting state for federal authority in the determination of which cities would receive funds and on what terms. Many local officials were uncomfortable 'with this outcome. Wayne Anderson, Executive Director of the Advisory Commission on Intergovernmental Relations, commented that while local governments recognized the need for change in intergovernmental strategies: 'they are reluctant to see the states acquire more control in areas in which they have not built competence. They also question how much the states can help when they have their own fiscal problems and their own tax and spending limits' (Kashdan 1981: 9).

Indeed, there was little reason to expect that state governments would provide additional support. As Jonathan Howes, mayor of Chapel Hill, North Carolina, pointed out, there are no more than 'half a dozen states with a truly distinguished record of helping urban communities, especially in the field of housing and community development' (Kashdan 1981: 8).[6] It was feared that the effect of Reagan's New Federalism would be to reduce rather than enhance the capacity of cities to control their own affairs. On the one hand, the substantial reduction of federal grant programs would restrict the ability of declining cities to maintain and improve their physical infrastructure, compete for job and revenue-producing business, and hold their populations. On the other hand, extensive investment of local funds combined with tax and regulatory concessions would be necessary to compete successfully with less distressed areas. Thus, Richard Hill has proposed:

Asserting the values of decentralized authority, community and local democracy, the New Federalism is designed to appeal to public distrust of a too-distant and too-intrusive state. But the New Federalism has less to do with strengthening communities than with restoring natural discipline on spending by imposing competition among state and local governments for scarce resources . . . The aim is to make local governments more responsive to the tax and expenditure demands of business enterprises, while the sharp drop in federal dollars to state and local governments is to come largely out of programs for the urban poor (Hill 1986: 16–17).

The Reagan administration was able to achieve the first absolute reduction in federal grant-in-aid expenditures recorded in decades (Beam 1984: 420). Federal spending fell from $94.8 billion in FY 1981 to $88.2 billion in FY 1982 (Table 5.3). Richard Nathan has pointed out, however, that there was a widespread tendency to exaggerate the impact of the budget cuts on states and localities—liberals overstated the impact in order to rally opponents while conservatives claimed credit for changes they did not achieve (Nathan *et al.* 1982: 320). While the administration succeeded in dramatically slowing the growth of federal aid, the achievements are less impressive when measured against its announced intentions. 'No large scale devolution of federal fiscal or regulatory functions has been accomplished,' notes David Beam; 'indeed, once the heat of battle dissipates, it is possible that the changes that have actually emerged from Congress since 1981 will be regarded as relatively moderate, incremental adjustments to the intergovernmental system' (Beam 1984: 440).

TABLE 5.3. *Federal Grant-In-Aid Outlays, 1960–1990*

Fiscal Year	Amount (in $ Billions)	As percentage of GNP
1960	7.0	1.4
1965	10.9	1.6
1970	24.1	2.4
1975	49.8	3.3
1980	91.5	3.4
1981	94.8	3.2
1982	88.2	2.8
1983	92.5	2.8
1984	97.6	2.6
1985	105.9	2.7
1986	112.4	2.7
1987[a]	109.9	2.5
1988[a]	106.3	2.2
1989[a]	106.5	2.1
1990[a]	107.9	2.0

[a] Estimated figures.

Source: EO 1987b: H-22.

Enterprise Zones and the Romance of Enterpreneurialism

Within the policy environment defined by the Reagan administration there was widespread acceptance of the view that cities with lagging economies must make substantial monetary and policy concessions to hold and attract business and jobs. This view was reflected in the advocacy of 'Enterprise Zones', one of the few specifically urban-related proposals made by the Reagan administration during its tenure in office, and the only urban initiative to be spatially targeted to distressed subareas. The Enterprise Zone concept—borrowed from Britain—was pursued as an ideologically acceptable means by which cities might seek to generate new private investment. While the specific provisions of the legislation introduced in Congress since 1980 differed from the British model (described in Chapter 7), the prescriptions were the same: promote a free market environment in designated urban areas by reducing taxes and relaxing or eliminating regulations on business activity.

The Enterprise Zone concept was a local-area analogue of 'supply-side economics' that the administration recommended for the nation as a whole (Bendick and Rasmussen 1986: 103). It epitomized the administration's faith that unfettered entrepreneurial capitalism would eliminate urban problems, produce jobs and internationally competitive products, and create harmonious and industrious communities (Walton 1982: 10). Enterprise Zone advocates believed that government intrusion into the economic life of inner cities was the root cause of urban distress: heavy taxation reduced the financial incentive to invest, government planning made cities incapable of adapting to changed circumstances, welfare payments reduced incentives to work, and government regulation stifled business initiative (Bendick and Rasmussen 1986: 101). It followed from this diagnosis that the elimination of governmental restraints and the reduction of the public presence would unleash a flood of latent entrepreneurial initiatives. 'People want to work, want to save, want to be productive,' argued Republican Representative Jack Kemp, who first introduced Enterprise Zone legislation in Congress in May 1980; but 'our economic policies just are not giving them the chance' (Kemp 1980: 3). According to Kemp, the country needed 'a program based on an understanding of what makes people—rich and poor—tick economically and what motivates them in the marketplace' (*Congressional Quarterly* 1981: 806).

The key to realizing the Enterprise Zone's ambitions, the advocates maintained, was to foster the development and survival of small businesses, a focus which seemed to be confirmed by David Birch's findings that small businesses were chiefly responsible for generating new jobs in the US (Birch 1980). 'We're trying to create a climate in inner cities,' said Representative Kemp, 'where small, independent, labor-intensive industries and manufacturing enterprises can flourish again' (*National Journal*, 14 Feb. 1981: 265). By lifting government barriers to entrepreneurialism, blighted areas could be rebuilt from the 'bottom up'.

President Reagan announced his commitment to the Enterprise Zone program in January 1982 and sent a proposal to Congress in March. For a combination of technical, procedural, and political reasons, the legislation remained lodged in the House Ways and Means Committee throughout his first term, although it passed the Senate twice. In numerous House and Senate hearings, Congress heard conflicting testimony from expert witnesses. Will the program create jobs or merely relocate businesses? Should small business be the focus for economic development when there is such a high failure rate? Can Enterprise Zones assist in closing the 'capital gap' that hinders small firm growth? Do tax credits really matter when studies showed that a two percent wage differential could have as much impact on a company as a 40 percent differential in tax rates? What happens to neighboring areas that cannot offer the same incentives? The main stumbling block to passage of the legislation, however, was Ways and Means Committee chairman Daniel Rostenkowski who doubted that Enterprise Zones would create jobs and shared the fears of other Democrats that it would become a substitute for existing urban programs.

Administration backed bills were introduced again in Congress in 1983 and 1985 and the 1986 *National Urban Policy Report* identified the Enterprise Zone as a central part of the administration's approach to urban economic development (USHUD 1986: 18). Some commentators maintained that the administration's tenacious support of the zone concept should be understood as part of its political strategy rather than its urban policy. The Enterprise Zone was politically appealing because it combined a simple interpretation of urban problems with an apparently pragmatic and purposeful means of resolution. A more cynical interpretation was that it provided 'a facade of concern for poverty and unemployment while mystifying the urban question and luring critics off the track' (Walton 1982: 14).

The 1985 legislation sought to designate seventy-five zones over three years, one-third to be in rural areas. Based on competitive selection, the severity of economic distress was not the key variable; preference instead was given to the zones with the strongest and highest quality courses of action and the broadest support and commitment from private entities, organizations, and community groups.[7] 'Courses of action' referred to the package of incentives offered by state and local governments. These could include relief from payment of property, sales, or local income taxes; relaxation of zoning, planning, and building regulations; and the improvement of public services including the use of private sector contractors.

In addition to the incentives offered by state and local government, the federal government would establish both capital and labor related incentives. In the first category were exemption from capital gains taxes on investments within the zones, additional investment tax credits for short-term personal property and for longer term investments, a 10 percent credit for expenditure on new construction or renovation of buildings, availability of small issue industrial development bonds within zones beyond 1986, and accelerated cost recovery for property financed by these bonds. The labor incentives included employer tax credits for hiring disadvantaged workers, employer credits on total zone payroll, and employee personal income tax credits. The 1985 proposal no longer included some of the more controversial ideas found in earlier versions—elimination of health, safety, and civil rights regulations, abolition of the minimum wage, or removal of specific employment regulations.

The failure to enact federal Enterprise Zone legislation did not prevent states from adopting the concept as an economic revitalization tool. By 1986, 32 states had designated 1,400 zones in 675 jurisdictions (USHUD 1986: 19). Many of these zone programs were initially established to enable a state to compete for a federally supported zone, but some were transformed into programs that were intended to operate solely on the basis of incentives provided by state and local government.

While there is considerable variation in these programs (Brintnall and Green 1988), several patterns can be identified: Enterprise Zones are generally used to complement, not replace, existing programs; the benefits offered are primarily tax incentives; deregulation measures are rare or insubstantial; large amounts of public resources are expended to establish and support zones; and there is sustained and significant government involvement in on-going zone operations. Thus, in the twenty-one states that had passed zone laws as of early 1984, Bendick and Rasmussen found that fifteen programs were 'essentially tax incentive efforts with little more than symbolic nods in the direction of deregulation' (Bendick and Rasmussen 1986: 114). These incentives were supplemented with extensive government activity within the zones:

far from creating an environment of 'no government' and 'unfettered free enterprise,' state enterprise zones typically are areas of concentrated public effort—in land use planning, infrastructure investment, public service improvement (especially in arson and other crime control), business loan funds, business technical assistance, training of disadvantaged workers, and similar efforts (Bendick and Rasmussen 1986: 114).

Other studies of programs within individual states confirm that the typical program encourages public involvement. DeLysa Burnier found that the invisible hand of the marketplace was not restored in 41 Ohio zones (Burnier 1987: 20). Instead, the program succeeded as a result of sustained government involvement and the expenditure of public resources:

Local governments designate the zone, negotiate with businesses, and follow-up on compliance. Public resources are used beyond the tax abatement for site preparation and infrastructure improvements. Finally new businesses do not spring into existence simply because taxes are reduced in a given area. Local governments must carefully market the zone, search for business prospects, build relationships with zone businesses, and monitor the actual number of jobs created by zone businesses (Burnier 1987: 20).

Similarly, in Indiana, according to Wilder and Rubin, public investment in ten zones totalled more than $59 million, while private investment approached $295 million, a five to one private to public leveraging ratio (Wilder and Rubin 1988: 6). In Indiana, as in Ohio, the Enterprise Zone 'is largely a tax abatement program with a substantial role for government, rather than a comprehensive free market approach to urban problems' (Burnier 1987: 2). It is apparent that the concept, as it has been applied in state programs, has moved from an experiment in de-planning to a package of incentives for industry to locate in particular areas (Jordon 1984: 146).

There is reason to suspect that Enterprise Zones cannot achieve the redevelopment benefits that advocates promise because they do not provide the type of assistance that is needed by small, new firms. The proposed tax credits provide aid to firms with tax liabilities but new firms, struggling to get established, often do not show a profit during the first years of operation. They need venture capital or other forms of start-up financing, a type of assistance that is not provided in the proposed federal Enterprise Zone program. Tax credits are also likely to attract firms that otherwise would locate in nearby sites—an outcome that Enterprise Zone advocates condemned in other economic development programs. Location studies indicate that crime, poor access to transportation, inadequate labor supply, local labor costs, proximity to markets or raw material are more important determinants of where firms locate than taxes (Harrison and Kanter 1978; Schmenner 1978: Wasylenko 1980).[8] Since zones do not directly address these factors, they are not likely to influence a firm to locate in a distressed community. Within an urban area, however, these factors are largely equalized, and therefore tax incentives could become important to a firm's choice among sites within a few miles of each other (Bendick and Rasmussen 1986: 107). Empirical studies have shown that firms are willing to move locally in response to tax incentives (Greison 1977; Oakland 1978; Small 1982). Thus, the firms that are most likely to move into an Enterprise Zone as a result of tax incentives are those that would have located near the zone in any case (Bendick and Rasmussen 1986: 108).

Advocates argue that the absence of burdensome regulatory restrictions would stimulate new business activity. In practice, however, deregulation does not play a significant role in Enterprise Zone programs—a conclusion reinforced by the experience of state programs. Regulations mandated by federal law—minimum wage levels, equal employment opportunity, occupational health and safety, and environmental protection—have been enacted because of concerns about the health and welfare of the general public. It would be politically unacceptable to exempt Enterprise Zones from their restrictions. Recognizing this reality, the administration's 1985 proposal had very little to say on the subject of federal deregulation. Since the same political obstacles apply at the state and local levels as well, it is difficult to conceive of any significant area of government regulation—federal, state, or local—that could be relaxed in an Enterprise Zone program.

It is too early to tell whether the Enterprise Zone will prove to be an effective economic development tool. In Indiana, for example, Wilder and Rubin found that job creation and retention were occurring, but the price for some cities was high public investment and only modest benefits to zone residents (Wilder and Rubin 1988: 7). In ten zones, 300 new businesses were initiated while 178 firms experienced expansion. This growth generated more than 6,600 new jobs with zone residents occupying from less than 5 percent to over 70 percent. Over all about one-third of the jobs went to zone residents (Wilder and Rubin 1988: 6). In Ohio, the Department of Development estimated that 4,024 new jobs had been created and 8,363 jobs retained in 41 zones but since record-keeping and monitoring of compliance varied from zone to zone, the accuracy of these figures cannot be confirmed (Burnier 1987: 11).

There is reason to question the reliability of the data used by Enterprise Zone advocates to make their case for success. A study of eight zones by Jones and Weisbrod, selected to represent a range of locations, settings, and programs throughout the country, found a substantial discrepancy between the reports of local Enterprise Zone administrators and Dun and Bradstreet records. The administrators reported that 12,756 jobs were created or retained in the zones between 1982 and 1984 while Dun and Bradstreet recorded only 1,244 employment changes (Jones and Weisbrod 1986: 18–19). The administrators counted retained jobs but few could distinguish between jobs that were actually threatened and those which were never in real danger. Only half of the zones required any certification concerning full-time employees or new jobs created. The Dun and Bradstreet data indicated that five of the zones gained employment since the start of the program but three zones actually lost employment (Jones and Weisbrod 1986: 19).

The federal Enterprise Zone initiative languished because in the administration's second term there was no strong political support for new urban policy initiatives of any type.[9] The federal agencies lost interest as it became clear that there were too many loose ends and too many areas of dispute to ensure a smooth passage for the bill. The Treasury Department was concerned about the 'cost' of the program—estimated at $12.5 million in tax revenues per zone, a total of almost $1 billion. Other parts of the federal bureaucracy, with not inconsiderable support from the urban lobby, feared with reasonable justification that Enterprise Zones would hasten the demise of other urban economic initiatives like UDAG. Even in HUD, which defined the Enterprise Zone legislation as a central priority, enthusiasm waned as the impact of general budget cuts—especially general revenue sharing—far out-weighed any potential benefits of Enterprise Zones. Whatever small element of bipartisan support the legislation enjoyed also evaporated when Democrats anticipated the replacement of politically important programs such as UDAG, the loss of their hold over urban initiatives, and further overall cuts in the urban budget. At the same time, the legislation no longer loomed as important even among many of the earlier conservative advocates since the overall cutbacks of urban and social programs were so extensive that there was no longer the need to search for acceptable ways to use government funds. Given the administration's objective of retrenchment from an active federal role in programs of urban redevelopment, the cutback in the urban budget was a larger, and most likely, more enduring victory, than the pas-sage of a particular piece of legislation. Moreover, given that victory, the administration largely succeeded in leaving cities to deal with their economic development problems with their own resources.

Privatization of Public Services

In late 1987, with what one national news magazine called 'a burst of hopeful rhetoric' (*Newsweek*, 21 Sept. 1987: 57), President Reagan appointed a Com-mission on Privatization to develop ways to turn government functions over to private business. In a statement for the press, the President declared that the Commission would help him 'end unfair Government competition and return Government programs and assets to the American people' (*New York Times*, 3 Sept. 1987). The Commission was the latest among a number of efforts made throughout the Reagan administration to promote the privatization of government functions. Starting in 1981, the Task Force on Private Sector Initiatives was directed to seek ways for business to take up the work of the diminished social welfare programs; the Asset Management Program was set up to sell large portions of federally owned land in the West; in 1982, the President's Private Sector Survey on Cost Control (known as the Grace Commission) was appointed to recommend ways to apply private sector principles and procedures to government operations; in 1983, the President's Advisory Council on Private Sector Initiatives was established to showcase examples of privatization; and it was told to report to the White

House Office of Private Sector Initiatives which coordinated and publicized the administration's privatization initiatives.

Despite this broad array of efforts, the Reagan administration succeeded in privatizing very few federal programs or assets. Only one significant asset was sold (Conrail, the national freight railway system), the effort to sell public lands was aborted, most of the recommendations of the Grace Commission were not implemented, and specific proposals, such as the idea put forward early in the administration's first term that the regulation of nursing homes and other health care facilities be turned over to a private organization, were withdrawn. On the positive side, the White House claimed that the services provided by 38,000 government positions were contracted out to private firms at an annual savings of $602 million (*New York Times*, 3 Sept. 1987).[10]

The administration's privatization failures at the federal level resulted from its underestimation of the forces opposed to privatization, its misunderstanding of the differences between public and private administration, its tendency to approach privatization in budgetary rather than political terms, and its propensity to toss the idea haphazardly into the political process without a clearly formulated policy design (Baber 1987; Smith 1987). Rhetorical support for privatization, however, coincided with and reinforced a trend towards privatization of some types of government activity at the local level. A comparison of a 1973 survey by the Advisory Commission on Intergovernmental Relations (ACIR) with a 1982 survey by the International City Management Association (ICMA) found that in seventeen service areas covered in both surveys, the percentage growth in contracting out ranged from 43 percent for refuse collection to 3,644 percent for data processing (Fixler and Poole 1987: 165).

The meaning of privatization is confusing because the term has been used by the administration and others to refer to several types of policy initiatives. These include the disengagement or withdrawal of government from specific responsibilities under the assumption that private institutions (firms, families, voluntary organizations) will take care of them, the shift from public to private provision of goods or services (through contracting out or voucher arrangements) while maintaining public financing, and the sale of public assets.[11] The thread that runs through these concepts is the idea that the inherent inefficiencies of government can be relieved by subjecting goods or services, traditionally provided by government, to the disciplines of the marketplace. Competition among firms, freedom from red tape and other procedural constraints, and flexibility in hiring, firing, and compensation practices, it is believed, create pressures for efficiency and cost savings that cannot be achieved in the public sector.

Two distinct and quite different objectives are pursued under the name of privatization: the improvement of the delivery of goods or services by taking advantage of marketplace efficiencies versus the reduction or termination of public support for particular goods or services altogether (sometimes called load-shedding). In the first case, privatization does not eliminate government accountability for the results of its expenditures, it simply shifts the locus of service delivery; the means of policy implementation is privatized but not the functional sphere of government action (Starr 1987: 125). What is relinquished, says James Sundquist, 'may be the easiest part—the doing. The conceiving, planning, goal-setting, standard-setting, performance-monitoring, evaluating, and correcting all remain with the government' (Sundquist 1984: 307). In the second case, government withdraws or reduces its role as a buyer, regulator, standard setter, or decision maker in particular service areas (Kolderie 1986: 288). According to some proponents, this is 'real' privatization because it breaks up 'public spending coalitions' and reduces the base of political support for government growth (Butler 1985). Others argue that it is 'false' privatization because for government to abandon a program or responsibility is not to privatize it—for privatization to occur, government must assure that something happens on the private side (Sundquist 1984: 307).

For the most part, efforts to privatize local services in the US have focused on shifting the delivery of public services to the private sector while maintaining public financing. The municipal services that are most frequently privatized—typically through contracting out—are solid waste collection and disposal, street lighting, electricity supply, engineering services, transportation, building and grounds maintenance, and data processing. Some jurisdictions are beginning to apply privatization to accounting and legal services, tax collection, the operation and maintenance of water-supply and treatment, and some health and human services such as hospitals, community mental-health services, and alcohol-drug rehabilitation (Fixler and Poole 1987: 167–71). Public safety—fire and police protection—is least likely to be privatized. Where life or property is concerned, the public prefers 'to maintain unambiguous lines of responsibility, and avoid any possible public–private conflict of interest, even at the loss of whatever increased efficiency and innovativeness might be attained through privatization' (Sundquist 1984: 310).

There is evidence that privatization in the US has yielded significant cost savings, for a variety of services. Bendick reports that 'where careful, controlled evaluations have been undertaken, verifiable cost savings were observed, if not universally, more often than not' (Bendick 1984: 157). For example, two studies of solid waste collection identified a cost savings of about 25 percent, although one study concluded that this result held only for communities of over 50,000 in population (Kemper and Quigley 1976; Savas 1977). A study of public and private provision of school-bus service in Indiana found that contractor-provided transportation was generally 12 percent less costly (McQuire and Van Cott 1984). A study of 595 transit agencies concluded that privately owned and operated systems were more efficient (more output per dollar) and generated more revenue than other types of systems (Perry and Babitsky 1986). A comparison of government versus contractor delivery of services in 120 Southern California cities found that contractor provision was significantly less expensive than direct government provision in seven of the eight service areas studied (Stevens 1984). A survey of California local governments found that 69 percent reported that contracting out led to reduced costs (Hatry 1982).

For a number of local services—those that 'are predominantly straightforward, immediate, measurable, monitorable, and technical in nature' (Bendick 1984: 157)—contracting out has led to improved service as well as reduced costs but 'as the mix of objectives in a program shifts toward more complex, long-range, holistic, and unmeasurable outcomes, and when the state of the art is more primitive concerning how to achieve those outcomes', the record of successful experience thins (Bendick 1984: 166). A federally funded study of educational performance contracts in twenty localities found that the results were universally disappointing. None of the participating school districts chose to renew their contracts; the private firms lost money; and relations between contractors and school boards often closed on an acrimonious note (Bendick 1984: 158–9). 'Purchase of service' arrangements have been used for some social services such as child day care, homemaker or chore assistance services, and vocational rehabilitation. A few studies have shown cost savings, but the majority of the contracts were with non-profit firms and operations that were too efficient or too low cost were viewed with suspicion on the grounds that service quality was being compromised in ways that could not be easily controlled by contract specifications or program monitoring (Bendick 1984: 159).

While there is evidence that the privatization of service delivery—at least for some local services—has led to improved efficiency and cost savings the studies hardly resolve basic concerns about the overall impact of privatization. Studies showing cost savings and efficiency improvements often overlook the tendency of private providers to service only the easy and profitable customers, while the difficult and unprofitable are neglected—a process called 'creaming'. When service delivery is privatized, government loses control of the operations it is financing. The result may be reduction or even termination of benefits to the poorest and neediest clients. In addition, studies that describe efficiency improvements from privatization usually lack evidence about the impact of privatization on the quality of services, thereby making it difficult to judge whether lower costs result from greater efficiency or deteriorating quality (Starr 1987: 129).

It is naïve to expect that, in the long run, privatization will decrease the costs of service delivery. The American experience with the defense industry, highway construction, and medical care should alert us to the potential of private contractors for manipulation of political decisions, exploitation of contract incentives, and cost overruns. Even a prominent advocate of privatization, Stuart Butler, has expressed concern about the 'cost-increasing' effect of contracting.

Moving the supply function out of government may simply replace muted bureaucratic pressure for bigger programs with a well-financed private-sector campaign clamoring for more federal spending. This significant drawback of contracting out means that it should be viewed with great caution as a means of privatization . . .

Contracting out can certainly lead to more efficient government, but it does not guarantee smaller government (Butler 1985: 56).

Advocates reply that these problems can be resolved if government is careful to specify the work it wants done and inspects the work to make sure it gets what it wants (Kolderie 1986: 287). Government, it is proposed, must develop detailed specifications and performance standards, monitor the performance of the contractor, and enforce the standards set forth in the contract. It may be true that with appropriate safeguards and quality control built into the contracting process, privatization may work better than public provision in some service areas, but, as Paul Starr points out, 'the difficulty of privatizing some public goods is that public administration is essential to their character' (Starr 1987: 133). In the administration of justice, the exercise of coercion, the collection of taxes, 'the very appearance of buying and selling undermines the claim of the state to be acting impartially on behalf of the entire community' (Starr 1987: 133). The public character of these services depends on government delivery.

A more serious concern is that privatization results in diminished access by removing decisions from the public realm where open discussion creates opportunities for criticism and mutual persuasion. In the marketplace, 'private firms have fewer obligations to conduct open proceedings or to make known the reasons for their decisions' (Starr 1987: 132). Starr reminds us that:

democratic politics is a process for articulating, criticizing, and adapting preferences in a context where individuals need to make a case for interests larger than their own. Privatization diminishes the sphere of public information, deliberation, and accountability—elements of democracy whose value is not reducible to efficiency (Starr 1987: 132).

Democratic politics also opens up choices that are not available in the market. In the marketplace, people with more money have more 'votes' while in the political process, each citizen gets one vote. When markets fail to provide particular goods and services, voting enables the public to purchase them (Starr 1987: 133).

Finally, there is a basis for serious concern about privatization's impact on government. As James Sundquist argues, privatization, at best, can contribute in only a minor way to resolving the problems of government (Sundquist 1984: 312). In fact, there is a real danger that privatization will weaken government by luring attention away from making governmental institutions work as they ought to work or, even more disturbing, by encouraging a turning away from governmental institutions altogether.

After all the dismantling possible has been accomplished, after every governmental function that can be privatized has been let out to contract, whoever is in power will still find that government is an instrument that must be used for an extensive and irreducible range of purposes and that to permit government to fail through sheer administrative incompetence is to imperil this country's unity and progress at home and its position in the world (Sundquist 1984: 318).

Entrepreneurial Cities and the Technology Chase

In the midst of the Reagan administration's attack on federal funding of local economic development, city governments continued to concentrate their attention on strategies that might improve their capacity to compete for a share of national economic growth. As Judd and Ready point out, city leaders accepted the fact that they could no longer depend on federal aid and that they had to strengthen their ability to compete for private investment (Judd and Ready 1986). While the decline in federal funding made the challenge of local economic development more demanding than before, civic entrepreneurship remained the key preoccupation of municipal government in the 1980s.

Economic development strategies have become much more elaborate and complex. Growth cities as well as cities in decline have turned to the national market and scrambled to make themselves attractive to footloose private firms. All cities are engaged in aggressive campaigns to secure their share of national economic growth . . . Entrepreneurial strategies make up the heart of the municipal agenda and municipal politics in the mid-1980s. Most cities have accepted the Reagan administration's mandate that city governments cooperate with the private sector and compete with one another to provide a favorable climate for business (Judd and Ready 1986: 210).

The Reagan administration expressed satisfaction with this new era of civic entrepreneurialism and claimed that it demonstrated the wisdom of its policies.

Cities have assumed more responsibility for their economic bases, negotiating specific commitments in exchange for private sector investment. No longer relying on Federal aid as the principal redevelopment resource, city officials have learned to transcend the traditional local means of delivering services and enforcing regulations. By developing more collaborative, entrepreneurial, self-reliant forms of management, these officials have been able to tailor development strategies to their cities' needs (USHUD 1986: 4).

The administration was not reluctant to identify successful local models. The partnership of business and government leaders in Indianapolis, for example, was attributed by HUD with creating a more diversified local economy, attracting over $1 billion in private investment, revitalizing the downtown, and creating 6,000 new manufacturing jobs. Similarly, the cooperative initiative of public and private leaders in Nashville, using a combination of public improvements, private investment, and federal incentives, was depicted as giving

new life to an old warehouse area on the Cumberland River, containing over 50 Victorian buildings with a million square feet of space. This area now includes a new Riverfront Park, new streets, sidewalks, streetlights, utilities, and a 1,200-car parking garage built under an innovative public–private partnership arrangement. The warehouse space has been renovated and is now occupied by a variety of new businesses. When the entire project is completed, it is expected to draw 1 million visitors a year, provide 2,000 jobs, and generate an additional $800,000 in property tax revenues (USHUD 1986: 5–6).

In sum, the administration claimed that, because of its policies, cities in America were making themselves more attractive to private investors and, as a result, in all regions were 'growing faster and showing greater vitality than they did in the 1970s' (USHUD 1986: 6).

In many respects the local economic development policies of the 1980s mirrored those launched in the 1970s. They continued to stress the need for communities to make concessions and provide incentives to leverage private investment, and they emphasized the importance of new public–private coalitions to promote redevelopment activities. But, in addition to the fact that local partnerships were increasingly funded by local resources, there also were important differences in the politics of local economic development and in the substantive emphasis of redevelopment strategies. The impact of some of these differences is still unclear. For example, the election of minority mayors in large urban centers in the mid-1980s, including four of the ten largest cities, is 'a political development that potentially challenges conventional growth politics' as well as traditional expectations about who should be the beneficiaries of local economic growth—but the actual impact of this political change on development policy is still difficult to evaluate (Judd and Ready 1986: 211). More substantively, Judd and Ready argue that while almost all cities embraced the broad outlines of a similar economic development agenda, the translation of that agenda into a municipal strategy exhibits significant differences among cities. In cities traditionally dedicated to unrestrained privatism, like Houston, there has been a continued commitment to creating a good business climate for private investment; in other cities, however, the pursuit of privatism through economic development has taken on different dimensions to meet local political demands. In Denver, the conventional pro-growth coalition has been reworked by minority and reform mayors to make development of the downtown acceptable to both dominant business interests and minority and neighborhood interests. In Chicago, old downtown-oriented development policies have been challenged, and efforts have been made to redefine economic growth objectives so as to give priority to job creation and neighborhood revitalization. In St Paul, the emphasis has been on economic self-reliance and local control of growth rather than simply promotion (Judd and Ready 1986). Nevertheless, within this diversity of political and policy emphasis, 'virtually all local public leaders consider economic development to be the linchpin that supports every activity undertaken by local government' (Judd 1988: 406).[12]

There have been some new themes in the 1980s. Among these, the most prominent is the emphasis cities have placed on programs to develop or attract high-technology industries. The economic development policies of the 1980s often have been translated into strategies to avert or reverse economic decline by attracting firms in the high-technology and service sectors of the economy and by encouraging local programs of technology development. In pursuing these strategies, cities participate in the creation of local technology development centers; small business incubators for new high-technology ventures; research consortia between local industry, universities, and public agencies; and an array of subsidy programs to attract firms producing advanced technology. Economic development analysts estimate that, as of 1985, 3,000 local development agencies in 42 states had put in place, or were planning, technology development programs as part of their strategies for economic regeneration (Farley and Glickman 1985). The strategic objectives have been to maximize local innovation opportunities and to form a base for localized control of technological and economic change. Towards this end, cities have tried to lure or create technology intensive firms, promote business ventures that concentrate specialized knowledge on the development of new product cycles and production processes, establish lasting development networks for technology transfer, and, in general, develop indigenous capacity for diffusing advanced technology. The new technology development strategies presumably demonstrate a city's progressive stature, its willingness and capability to change to meet market needs, and its determination to outbid civic rivals for a place in the post-industrial future (Dustin and Rich 1987).

In promoting technology development, cities have been able to capitalize on a growing number of state level programs and investments. In 1986, the National Governors' Association reported that 21 states had provided $317 million in grants, facilities, and risk capital for technology development (Science and Government Report, 15 Dec. 1986). Even the poorest states, such as Mississippi, plan high-tech futures based on public–private partnerships (Little, Inc. 1984).

Building on the expectations of local economic development strategies that came into vogue in the 1970s, it is assumed that the community as a whole will benefit from job creation and economic diversification if the city is successful in competing for the technology and service industries—in other words, the high-tech path to urban economic revitalization will make everyone a winner (US Congress 1982). As yet, there is little evidence to support this conclusion.

Technology development strategies are designed to pick technology winners. But the ability to pick winners presumes a detailed understanding of the dynamics of economic change at the local, national, and international levels, and a capacity to accurately anticipate and influence the course of technological development. In addition, such strategies presume that decision makers understand the likely effects of technology development on a local economy. To fulfill these requirements one must be able to forecast conditions such as plant shut-downs, relocations and contractions, industry multiplier effects, investment impacts on the tax base, and swings in the business cycle. One must also be able to identify which firms offer the best prospects for increasing productivity, profitability, and expansion. And, one should be able to determine which firms create new jobs that give the disadvantaged in the community a chance for employment and provide upward mobility opportunities (Pascal and Gurwitz 1983). Even these factors, do not include the immensely more complex variables operating at national and international levels in what advocates acknowledge is an era of massive trans-regional economic and technological transformation. The understanding of these conditions is recognized to be inadequate even by those who pursue technology development strategies. Commenting on the promotion of technology development centers, Robert Noyce, Vice-Chairman of Intel Corporation, said:

We must characterize our efforts by the statement of Harrison Ford as Indiana Jones in 'The Raiders of the Lost Ark.' As he jumps on his white horse and rides off to save the day he is asked 'Where do we go from here?' His reply: 'Hell, I don't know. I'm making it up as I go along.' Hopefully we can plan better as we progress down this road (Noyce 1982: 17).

A further dilemma is that what is meant by 'a technology winner' is ambiguous. Most often, it is suggested that high-technology industries are a city's best bets for future growth. There is, however, no reliable or consistent definition of high-technology; rather analysts rely on *post hoc* listings of whatever new technologies become fashionable. In addition, job growth performance among supposedly high-technology industries varies significantly (Riche *et al.* 1983; Glasmeier *et al.* 1985). New technologies often decrease the number of total jobs available, particularly skilled jobs that pay good wages (Rumberger 1984; Shapira 1984). The tendency to overestimate the economic contribution of high-technology industries was addressed in a 1984 US Office of Technology Assessment report on high technology and regional development (OTA 1984*a*). The report points out that jobs of all types in high-technology industries represented a relatively small share of total jobs: between 3 and 13 percent of total US employment, depending on the definition of high technology used. Further, employment in high-technology firms grew rapidly between 1972 and 1982, but future growth will not significantly increase the employment contribution of high-technology industries (OTA 1984*b*).

Dustin and Rich argue that picking technology winners or making concessions to 'companies seeking windows on technology with the expectation that these enterprises will prosper, continue to grow, and do so in the local economy, depends on an act of faith ... even if growth firms could be identified, there is no reason to expect, based on experience to date, that they could be successfully targeted for development in a particular local economy even with government help' (Dustin and Rich 1987: 11). Moreover, there is little evidence to support the belief that new economic activity created by technology development strategies will spill over into the local economy as a whole. Indeed, given the mobility characteristics of the post-industrial economy, the likelihood is slim that new products developed by local firms will be produced in the same locality or that new production processes will save local firms from relocation, contraction, or shut-down (Berney 1984; OTA 1984*b*). 'Increasing leadership in technological invention does not guarantee leadership in production, profits, or new jobs to the nations, much less the local communities which subsidized the invention' (Dustin and Rich 1987: 12).

Experience in the 1980s suggests that community-based technology development, even if it occurs, by no means assures a more balanced, stable and prosperous local economy. The semiconductor industry was cited as the most visible bright spot in the overall performance of US industry since the late 1970s, but by the mid-1980s it had become another industry laying off workers, shutting down plants, and seeking assistance and subsidy from the federal government (Ferguson 1983; LaDou 1984). Salt Lake City decided in the 1970s to add high-technology development to its copper mining based economy. After attracting dozens of national firms to the region, market shifts and company repositioning resulted in hundreds of laid-off workers and shattered community confidence in the new, supposedly recession-proof, economy (*New York Times*, 13 Dec. 1985).

Technology development strategies exhibit a fundamental logical contradiction. On the one hand, it is assumed that cities face economic decline if they do not heed the technology imperatives of post-industrialism. On the other hand, post-industrialism means that firms in the forefront of economic and technological change will be highly mobile and largely immune to lasting community commitments. Cities therefore are unlikely to capture the benefits of their investments in technology development. Indeed, as Dustin and Rich point out, 'the benefits of a city's search for a place in the high-tech future often are illusory but the costs of such a search may be immense' (Dustin and Rich 1987: 17). Despite this, city after city in the 1980s has oriented its economic development strategy so that it may participate in the technology chase, assuming that somehow this will benefit the entire community. Indeed, the question most often asked by local governments about technology development programs in the 1980s has been 'how' not 'why'.

Impacts of the New Privatism

Shortly after President Reagan announced his budget recommendations in 1981 a number of urban leaders predicted that an unprecedented crisis was in store for America's cities. Mayor Richard Hatcher of Gary, Indiana, called the program 'the first really serious threat to the existence of cities since World War II' (*National Journal*, 30 May 1981: 960) and Milwaukee Mayor Henry Maier said that 'the Reagan Administration's promised land of milk and honey may turn out to be a desert of rocks and dust for this city of Milwaukee and the other older central cities of America' (*National Journal*, 30 May 1981: 966). While the worst of these predictions for American cities have not materialized, seven years of Reagan budgets, on top of the reductions achieved at the outset of the first term, left many national urban programs in a state of near collapse. Indeed, the viability of the Department of Housing and Urban Development has been seriously threatened. According to an Associate Director of the National Association of Housing and Redevelopment Officials, HUD Secretary Samuel Pierce, Jr. presided over the dismantling of the department's major assistance programs (Nenno

1987: 105). In 1981, HUD ranked fourth among federal departments in the dollar amount of budget authority; in the proposed budget for 1988 it ranked eighth. Inclusive of the FY 1988 proposals, the cumulative impact on HUD's programs and budgets since 1981 are: a 69 percent reduction in total HUD budget (from $33.4 billion to $10.2 billion); a 23 percent decline in HUD employment (from 16,100 to an estimated 12,438); an 89 percent reduction in Assisted Housing (from $26.7 billion to $3.9 billion); a 29 percent reduction in the CDBG program (from $3.7 billion to $2.6 billion); and the elimination of UDAGs (Nenno 1987: 105). These cutbacks indicate that the Reagan administration's objective of federal disinvestment in urban areas has been substantially achieved.

At the city level, the impact of federal retrenchment on city budgets and services also has been severe but predictions of impending disaster for city government have not been borne out. Indeed, George Peterson points out that several measures of the financial condition of the thirty largest cities— the number and severity of general fund operating deficits and liquidity ratios[13]—reveal an improvement throughout the 1970s that 'continued, and perhaps even accelerated, through the first two years of the Reagan administration' (G. Peterson 1986: 27). Several studies of individual cities supported by the Urban Institute—Phoenix, Arizona; Rochester, New York; and Stamford, Connecticut—found only minor effects on city government resulting from the federal policy and budget changes (Shannon *et al.* 1986; J. Hall 1986; Liebschutz and Taddiken 1986). In Stamford, for example, 'although there had been a visible decline of federal support to the city government, reductions in service were modest and no regular employees had been laid off' (Shannon *et al.* 1986: 180).

A number of factors mediated the effects of the Reagan administration's retrenchment policies including the fact that after 1982 Congress rejected most proposals for further cuts and adopted measures to stimulate the economy and reduce unemployment. Cities also made fiscal adjustments by raising taxes, carrying funds over from previous years, introducing productivity measures, and in some cases receiving cushions from selective increases in state aid.[14] Additionally, federally assisted programs often 'proved readily detachable from the rest of a city's activities' (G. Peterson 1986: 31). The Boston city treasurer said:

We got out of running the city on basic federal funds five years ago. The fiscal problems of the city, since 1979, have not been attributable to decreases in federal aid. The federal cuts have simply meant that we provide far fewer special services than we used to provide. It's the service populations for these programs, not the city budget or the city taxpayers, that has [*sic*] had to make the adjustments (G. Peterson 1986: 31).

One local reaction to the budget cuts was to isolate federally assisted programs from regular city government. Both Boston and Los Angeles established separate agencies to administer major federal grant programs (G. Peterson 1986: 32) and in some communities, local officials explicitly distanced themselves from responsibility for programs and services that received federal support. John Stuart Hall reports that in Phoenix, Arizona, many local officials and constituents accepted the reasoning of a former mayor that 'the poor are a federal not a local responsibility. If Washington cannot afford these programs, we certainly can't. Local people do not feel the welfare programs should be financed by local taxes' (quoted in Hall 1986: 196).

Nonetheless, definitive evidence on the results of the Reagan administration's policies for cities is not yet available. Certainly the experience of Phoenix, Stamford, and Rochester should not be regarded as typical. These cities (particularly Phoenix and Stamford) are relatively well-off, having greater than average resources to meet public service needs, robust economic growth, and a tradition of minimal reliance on federal funding to support city services. Other cities have not been as effective in absorbing funding reductions by isolating federal aid programs. In the past, severely distressed cities frequently have been forced to convert federal grants into support for basic services and their success in this endeavor has made them particularly vulnerable to aid reductions. In Detroit, for example, the city finance director reported that in 1981 CETA workers were spread throughout the departments and used for essential services. When federal funding for the program was cut from the FY 1982 budget, the city lost 1,800 CETA employees, more than 10 percent of the city's work force (G. Peterson 1986: 32).

While some city halls may not have been seriously affected by the budget cuts, local institutions or agencies with federally assisted functional responsibilities have been significantly impacted. Cities lost resources for operating job training, education, health, social service programs, and for community development. Cuts in the Comprehensive Employment and Training Act (CETA) and education aid were particularly steep. Even in cities which generally fared well in the face of federal budget cuts, the impacts in these areas were significant. In Rochester, for example, the federal budget changes resulted in $2 million less for job training in 1984 than in 1981 and a similar decline in funds for community development (Liebschutz and Taddiken 1986: 136). In Phoenix, as well, retrenchment was relatively severe in a few important program areas such as employment and training and community services (J. Hall 1986: 199). These services have direct impacts on people and thus, as Harold Wolman, a senior researcher at the Urban Institute, pointed out while 'cities as units of government are probably doing better now than they were in the late '70s . . . [the] people who live in cities are worse off' (quoted in Marks 1984: 1513).

In analyzing the initial Reagan budget proposals, Danziger and Haveman warned that proposed cuts in social programs were likely to have the immediate consequence of reducing the incomes and work effort of the poor and near-poor without otherwise benefiting them. In the long run, they proposed, the ability of low-income youths and families to escape from poverty would probably diminish through the reduction in federal support for education and training programs (Danziger and Haveman 1981: 11).[15] The

Northeast–Midwest Coalition also expressed congressional concerns that the Reagan urban policies would put the poor in a double bind in older cities. 'On the one hand, they would be squeezed by cuts in federal funds for public service jobs, housing, food stamps, and Medicaid. Yet there would be no program to help them move to places where jobs are plentiful' (S. Lewis 1981: 13).

Research conducted at Princeton University based on fourteen states and forty local governments has shown that the cuts in domestic programs, in fact, have had a more adverse impact on people (notably the working poor) than on state and local government (Nathan *et al.* 1983; Nathan 1986). Cuts in funding for social services, coupled with changes in eligibility for Aid to Families with Dependant Children (AFDC), have been translated into losses of supplements to earned income and of subsidies for day care. Local inter-views conducted in Rochester with affected families—those headed by single mothers and concentrated in city neighborhoods—indicated that life has become more difficult. Less satisfactory day care arrangements, greater diffi-culty in meeting necessary housing expenses, and more medical, nutritional, and behavioral problems are common among the former beneficiaries of AFDC and Title XX day-care subsidies (Liebschutz and Taddiken 1986: 152–3).

While it is difficult to determine precisely how much impact the Reagan administration's policies have had on different income groups in the US, Marilyn Moon and Isabel Sawhill have calculated that payments from federal benefit programs—including cash payments, such as ADFC and Social Secur-ity, and in-kind transfers, such as Food Stamps and Medicaid—were about 7 percent lower than what they would have been for FY 1984 if the Reagan budget cuts had not been enacted. The net impact of the cuts, they conclude, has been to widen disparities in economic well-being.

The program cuts range from almost 8 percent of income for households with less than $10,000 in annual income to less than 0.2 percent for households with more than $40,000 in annual income. If Congress had acted affirmatively on all the president's budget proposals, the increase in inequality resulting from the program cutbacks would have been even greater, since relative to what was enacted, the proposed benefit reductions were more than twice as large and also more heavily concentrated on low-income assistance programs (Moon and Sawhill 1984: 324).

In addition, as a result of the Reagan cuts in federal personal income taxes the burden of paying for government shifted from higher-income taxpayers to lower-income taxpayers. In 1984, 'the bottom 40 percent of families [were] paying proportionally more of their income in taxes, with most of the increased burden falling on the poorest 20 percent of families, whereas the top 60 percent were paying proportionally less of their income in taxes' (Moon and Sawhill 1984: 327).

In contrast to the administration's view that 'the general improvement in the economy has been shared by the poverty population' and that 'gains have been made in reducing poverty' (USHUD 1986: 25), over the past decade poverty rates have increased, and the share of aggregate income received by the poorest two-fifths of the population has declined. For all races, poverty rates increased from 11.4 percent in 1978 to 14.0 percent in 1985; among whites, from 8.7 percent to 11.4 percent in 1985; among blacks, rates stayed relatively constant, rising from 30.6 percent in 1978 to 31.3 percent in 1985; among persons of Spanish origin, they rose sharply from 21.6 percent in 1978 to 29.0 percent in 1985; and among children under 18, rates rose from 15.7 percent in 1978 to 20.1 percent in 1985 (Table 5.4). These increases occurred primarily between 1980 and 1983; after 1983 some decrease in poverty occurred. Nonetheless, as of 1985, poverty rates were still substantially greater than in 1978 (except among blacks, however in both years nearly one out of every three black persons fell below the poverty level).

TABLE 5.4. *Persons below the Poverty Level, 1978–1985, by Race and Spanish Origin and Children under 18* (in percentages)

Year	All races	White	Black	Spanish origin	Children under 18
1978	11.4	8.7	30.6	21.6	15.7
1979	11.7	9.0	31.0	21.8	16.0
1980	13.0	10.2	32.5	25.7	17.9
1981	14.0	11.1	34.2	26.5	19.5
1982	15.0	12.0	35.6	29.9	21.3
1983	15.2	12.1	35.7	28.0	21.8
1984	14.4	11.5	33.8	28.4	21.0
1985	14.0	11.4	31.3	29.0	20.1

Source: US Bureau of the Census 1986: 22.

Between 1978 and 1985, the share of aggregate income received by the poorest two-fifths of the population declined from 16.8 percent to 15.5 percent (lower than any year since 1947 when the data was first collected) while the share of the wealthiest fifth rose from 41.5 percent to 43.5 percent (Table 5.5).

TABLE 5.5. *Percentage Share of Aggregate Income, 1978–1985, by Quintile and Top Five Percent of Families*

Year	Lowest fifth	Second fifth	Middle fifth	Fourth fifth	Highest fifth	Top five percent
1978	5.2	11.6	17.5	24.1	41.5	15.6
1979	5.2	11.6	17.5	24.1	41.7	15.8
1980	5.1	11.6	17.5	24.3	41.6	15.3
1981	5.0	11.3	17.4	24.4	41.9	15.4
1982	4.7	11.2	17.1	24.3	42.7	16.0
1983	4.7	11.1	17.1	24.3	42.8	15.9
1984	4.7	11.0	17.0	24.4	42.9	16.0
1985	4.6	10.9	16.9	24.2	43.5	16.7

Source: US Bureau of the Census 1987: 37.

Indeed, families in the bottom two quintiles actually lost all the ground they had gained over the two preceding decades (in 1959 the bottom two quintiles received 17.2 percent of aggregate income).[16] Families at the top of the income distribution gained substantially. Their share of total family income rose from 41.5 percent to 43.5 percent.[17] This 2.0 percentage point increase may not at first glance seem very large, but it represents a transfer of disposable income to the top quintile from other income groups of approximately $25 billion overall and translates into an extra $2,000 per family for this group.[18]

During the Reagan administration, income was redistributed away from lower-income families and individuals—particularly the poorest—and towards the most affluent. As Moon and Sawhill point out, some widening of the income distribution would have taken place irrespective of who had been President (in fact, the gap between low and high income families began to widen after 1974). Long-term structural changes—especially the shift from manufacturing to services—are a principal cause of the deteriorating position of low- and moderate-income families; but, unlike government policies in the 1960s and 1970s, President Reagan's mix of tax and benefit reductions exacerbated underlying economic trends. Instead of countering these trends by redistributing income towards the poor, his policies 'helped the affluent but not the poor or the middle class' (Moon and Sawhill 1984: 345).

The Reagan Legacy and the Politics of Urban Disinvestment

The Reagan administration's version of privatism produced no significant innovations in urban policy instruments and programs. At the beginning of the 1980s, federal urban programs were already focused on efforts to stimulate economic development through a reliance on private institutions. Much of what the administration proposed in order to promote privatism had been proposed before, but with less ideological consistency and zeal. It is true, nonetheless, that the administration enthusiastically embraced the model of the private city and sought to expand the scope of privatism by restricting the role of the public sector. Social programs, many of which provide service and financial assistance to the poorest segments of America's urban population, were subjected to budget reduction or elimination with the justification that they wasted public resources or were unworkable even when they were not wrongly inspired. Local economic development programs, like UDAG and EDA, were also targeted for elimination. Indeed, the administration, at least initially, was unapologetic about its efforts to achieve a federal withdrawal from urban affairs and about its intent to dismantle the federal bureaucracy that had been set up over three decades to maintain and direct programs of urban development.

In this regard, the meaning and implications of the Reagan version of urban privatism contrasts sharply with the pursuit of the private city by other administrations in the post-war period. The Carter administration, like its forerunners in both political parties, pursued privatism as a strategy of urban regeneration. It sought to use federal resources and authority to support private investments that would contribute to local economic development. As we have demonstrated, many of the programs launched to achieve this objective were based on questionable assumptions about the process of local economic development, the feasibility of targeting assistance to distressed communities and groups, and the outcomes of leveraging private investment. Even so, the emphasis was on enhancing the federal role in urban affairs.

By contrast, the Reagan administration pursued privatism as a strategy of urban disinvestment. While never fully bringing to fruition the complete federal withdrawal promoted at the outset, the reduction in federal funding was substantial and a wide array of urban and social policy programs were eliminated or drastically reduced in scope. The costs of federal disengagement fell especially heavily on subsets of the urban population that had already borne the heaviest burdens of economic distress. In the logic of the 'new privatism' the best option for these groups was to move to where the jobs are located. Yet restricted mobility is one of the principal characteristics of an urban underclass. Despite its challenges to established urban policy, the President's Commission for a National Agenda for the Eighties recognized these conditions and called for enhanced national social assistance to deal with racial and economic inequality (PC 1980b). Nonetheless, while pursuing a policy of federal disinvestment in urban places, the Reagan administration also turned away from assistance to the victims of this disinvestment. Instead, it added to their distress by terminating, cutting, or tightening eligibility requirements for federal programs that assist the urban poor—food stamps, the Comprehensive Employment and Training Program, Medicaid, and public housing assistance—and there is no evidence that the voluntary sector has been able to fill the gap. Voluntary institutions have struggled and, for the most part, succeeded in maintaining their fiscal solvency in the face of substantial losses of federal revenues (J. Hall 1986; Liebschutz and Taddiken 1986; Shannon *et al.* 1986); but even when they have made up for revenue losses, they have done so by increasing user fees, restraining service growth, and obtaining additional private contributions that otherwise might have been available to expand services rather than simply to maintain operating budgets.

In 1972, Norton Long proposed that large cities in America were becoming the home of the poor and socially marginal groups to such an extent that the only way they could stay afloat was for 'those who run the city's bureaucracies to persuade the outside society to pay them to run the city as an Indian reservation or a poor farm' (Long 1972: 160). The 'new privatism' fostered this role for cities but without compensation from the outside society. Federal disinvestment posed a serious dilemma for distressed cities. These cities were forced to choose between using scarce local resources to compete with other communities to lure or hold job-generating firms or to meet the service needs of large numbers of their citizens who suffered from the cutback of federal aid. Furthermore, federal withdrawal from urban programs sits uncomfortably against evidence that federal funding is often the critical factor in the promotion of public–private partnerships. For at least some cities, continuing cutbacks in federal aid have made economic development, public or private, a daunting challenge. Cities have been left to their own diminishing public and private resources while participating, as best they can, in the modern version of civic mercantilism. In this respect, the policy of privatism in urban America is, itself, one of the most serious problems many cities faced in the 1980s.

The 'new privatism' projects a vision of the competitive marketplace as the criterion by which to judge any action, public or private. In essence, the logic of the 'new privatism' assumes a form of Social Darwinism applied to cities and their residents as it was once applied, with pernicious consequences, to social classes. In this light, Mayor George Voinovich of Cleveland called upon the federal government to look at the unevenness of the economic recovery: 'what are they going to do about those cities that aren't responding . . . are they going to shrug their shoulders and turn their eyes in a different direction and hope we go away?' (*National Journal*, 11 Aug. 1984: 1516). The answer given by the 'new privatism' is that in the competition between cities for private investment, as in any other market, it is expected that there will be winners and losers. If Cleveland cannot compete with Houston for enterprises and jobs, it follows that it would be folly to try to bail out Cleveland. While some places may prosper at the expense of others, this is not a matter of national concern so long as the consequences contribute to the efficient spatial allocation of resources in the economy as a whole. The focus of urban policy attention in America in the 1980s was not so much on privatism for cities as it was on privatism for privatism's sake.

Notes

1. Ten reports were issued including the summary report. The subjects were: energy, the economy, science and technology, social justice, urban america, the regulation of corporate and individual decisions, the electoral process, the quality of life, and the US and the world community.
2. Max Stephenson's comparison of UDAG implementation during the Carter and Reagan administrations concludes that the growing competition for program resources resulting from Reagan's cuts in urban redevelopment funding and attempts to abolish UDAG outright has quickened a shift in the politics of the program away from an emphasis on targeting to defined need towards a more distributional focus. For program administrators, the chief result of the Reagan urban strategy has been a more competitive process of selection that has led to an increasingly conservative approach to project risk evaluation. 'Too zealous an adoption of that approach', concludes Stephenson, 'in turn, runs the risk of undermining the original rationale for the creation of the program' (Stephenson 1987: 33).
3. In July 1988 the Senate and the House voted to end the UDAG program.

4. President Nixon outlined his version of the New Federalism in 1969. He proposed that a number of narrow-purpose federal programs be combined into block grants and turned over to the states for administration. At the same time, programs that dealt with national problems, like welfare, would be placed under federal control. He also sought to reform the process by which remaining federal programs for state and local assistance would be managed and to reduce the time lag and administrative requirements of responding to local needs. Some of what was proposed, including the establishment of block grants to consolidate some programs, was carried out. Other efforts like welfare reform and standardizing federal grant management failed.

5. The report on *Urban America in the Eighties* had also called for the federal government to turn over responsibilities for many of its aid programs to state and local government (PC 1980a).

6. These conditions were not unknown in the national urban policy community. A one-year experiment was initiated under the Carter administration to evaluate the transfer of control for federal programs to the states. In Kentucky, authority over development block grants for cities and counties of under 50,000, otherwise administered by the Department of Housing and Urban Development, was delegated to the state. Apart from the obvious shift in the attention of local governments competing for the funds from Washington D.C. to the Department of Community and Regional Development in Frankfort, Kentucky, a summary of the experience indicated: 'that the states must hire more people to administer the federal programs and that the shift is not likely to put an end to the red tape and bureaucratic practices that have damaged many Federal programs. It is still an open question whether the states can administer the programs without fraud or abuse' (*New York Times*, 8 Sept. 1981).

7. To be eligible for Enterprise Zone selection, jurisdictions would have to satisfy a number of conditions: they must have a minimum population of 4,000 (1,000 in rural areas) or be entirely within an Indian reservation; they must be in an area already eligible for funding under the Urban Development Action Grant program; they must have 'pervasive poverty, unemployment—at least 1.5 times the national rate—and general distress'.

8. After studying business location studies conducted since the 1920s, Michael Wasylenko concluded that 'taxes and fiscal inducements have very little if any effect on industrial location decisions. Thus, state and local policies designed to attract business are generally wasted government resources' (1981: 155).

9. The 1987 Housing Bill did authorize Federal Enterprise Zones under Title VII and in its budget for FY 1989 the administration indicated that it would 'work with state and local governments to determine the most effective ways Federal enterprise zones can support and expand business development most effectively' (EO 1988: 5–85). In practical terms, no federal Enterprise Zones would be set up under the Reagan administration.

10. In its budget proposal for FY 1989, the Reagan administration announced that it would 'conduct a series of comprehensive studies on functions for which privatization offers the potential of improving the quality of the activity or reducing costs' and these functions would include the Postal Service and the in-house research laboratories of the National Institutes of Health (EO 1988: 2b–23). To provide an opportunity to test several different privatization techniques, pilot projects would be conducted on federal prisons, Customs commercial cargo inspection and regulatory audits, military commissaries, Coast Guard buoy

maintenance, and undeveloped lands (EO 1988: 2b–23). Full privatization efforts would be made to increase contracting out of services and in the sale of real assets such as the Alaska Power Administration and several oil fields.

11. The removal of controls on the private provision of goods or services (deregulation) is also described as privatization. The term, as it is used here, refers to the transfer of a government function or activity from the public to the private sector.

12. Judd points out that even the most unconventional mayors of the 1980s accepted the necessity to subsidize private sector activity in their cities. Coleman Young, Detroit's first black mayor and a Marxist labor organizer in the 1950s, has aggressively competed for corporate investment. 'Those are the rules,' he said; 'and I'm going by the rules. This suicidal outburst of competition . . . has got to stop but until it does, I mean to compete. It's too bad we have a system where dog eats dog and the devil takes the hindmost. But I'm tired of taking the hindmost' (Judd 1988: 407).

13. The ratio of cash and cash equivalents on hand to general fund spending.

14. George Peterson also suggests that the improvement in the fiscal condition of cities was, to a large extent, the result of cities taking financial management more seriously after the defaults of New York and Cleveland in the 1970s (G. Peterson 1986: 29).

15. Between 1978 and 1986 there was a sharp rise in the working poor. 'In 1986 two million adults—50 percent more than in 1978—worked full time but remained poor . . . A related development was the dramatic rise in the percentage of young people who reported no earnings at all. In 1985, 9 percent of young men ages twenty to twenty-nine reported no earnings, up from 6 percent in 1973. Among black young men, the comparable figures were 19 percent with no earnings in 1985, as compared to 9 percent in 1973' (Ford Foundation 1988: 2).

16. Moon and Sawhill estimate that 'the Reagan program cuts had a greater impact on the second than on the first quintile. This pattern reflects the administration's policy of targeting benefits on the most needy and reducing benefits most sharply for those with some earnings, even though most families in the second quintile also have incomes below the official poverty line, (Moon and Sawhill 1984: 336).

17. Surveys conducted by the Federal Research Board found that the net wealth holdings of the richest ½ percent of US families rose from 25.4 percent to 35.1 percent between 1963 and 1983. An analysis of these surveys by the Joint Economic Committee of the US Congress concluded by citing data which strongly suggested 'that the dramatic increase in the share of national wealth held by the richest Americans, which is documented by the two Federal Reserve surveys, did not begin until late in the 20-year period between the two surveys' (JEC 1986: 24).

18. This is an estimation based on Moon and Sawhill's calculations that a 1.9 percentage point increase in the top quintile's share of total family income between 1980 and 1984 represented a transfer of $25 billion in disposable income from other income groups an extra $2,000 per family (Moon and Sawhill 1984: 320).

6

The Redirection of British Urban Policy

AFTER World War II, the objectives, the principal actors, the programs and many of the key decisions that shaped British cities were developed as part of an extensive state apparatus that relied upon planning and social administration as the major instruments of urban policy. In 1979, proposals were made by the Conservative Government of Margaret Thatcher to reduce the role of these instruments in the formulation and execution of British urban policy. In line with a general effort to reorient domestic policy, the Conservatives argued that urban change should result primarily from the unplanned decisions of the marketplace. If government must intervene then it should do so only in a supportive role, to overcome the failures of recent economic history or to bolster the market when it is demonstrably weak. Sir Keith Joseph, a leading Conservative in the 1970s, who played a prominent role in articulating the philosophy of the Thatcher Government, proclaimed that: 'The blind, unplanned, uncoordinated wisdom of the market is overwhelmingly superior to the well-researched, rational systematic, well-meaning, cooperative, science-based, forward-looking, statistically respectable plans of government, bureaucracies and international organizations' (Joseph 1976: 17).

As in the case of US urban policy, the emergence of a commitment to privatization of urban Britain did not occur abruptly. For at least a decade prior to Thatcher's electoral victory in 1979, British urban policy moved in a direction which emphasized the economic dimensions of urban problems. By the early 1970s, the national welfare consensus that had prevailed since World War II was under attack. The expectation that government action, through the welfare state, could remove inequality and uniformly improve living standards was openly challenged. Despite post-war initiatives in planning and social policy, the economic and social conditions in many British cities, particularly as measured by unemployment, continued to deteriorate (Begg, Moore, and Rhodes 1986). This contributed to a belief that the state planning system was not only ineffective but dangerously inefficient. In 'economic and other affairs', Cherry suggests, 'it was abundantly clear that the State held no monopoly of wisdom, and centrally directed state programmes of economic, fiscal or land planning were disquietingly imperfect' (Cherry 1982: 67). By the late 1970s, urban policy was already oriented towards a more expansive role for the private sector and, in important respects, was compatible with the Conservative Government's ideological commitment to privatization.

Our analysis of the roots of privatism in British urban policy begins by tracing some of the key aspects of policy reformulation during the 1970s. The review concentrates on those aspects of urban policy that illustrate the gradual focusing of attention on the economic dimensions of urban problems. With this background we examine the domestic policy orientation of the Thatcher Government and explore what this orientation has meant for urban policy.

The Beginnings of Policy Redirection

By the mid-1960s, the deteriorated condition of British cities, especially inner-city areas, was unmistakable. The symptoms of urban decline had been recognized for decades but 'despite fifty years of municipal effort, especially in the field of housing, and despite redevelopment opportunities created by military destruction,' Paul Lawless points out, 'the problems of urban malaise could not be dismissed, and to many appeared more accentuated than ever' (Lawless 1981: 3–4). The visible signs of this malaise included the loss of inner-city population and jobs and the deterioration of inner-city housing. All of the large urban areas—London, Birmingham, Manchester, Liverpool, Newcastle, and Glasgow—lost population and employment in the 1950s and 1960s (Begg, Moore, and Rhodes 1986: 17–18). These areas also had a greater proportion of dwellings lacking physical amenities than the country as a whole, and residential overcrowding was particularly acute in certain inner-urban areas, notably inner Glasgow and inner London (DoE 1975, 1976*a*).

Some of these trends, specifically the decline of inner-city populations and the loss of inner-city jobs, were, in part, the intended result of government policy. Since 1945, regional and new towns policies had promoted the dispersal of population and economic activity away from the large, congested cities. The Barlow Report, produced in 1940, provided a rationale for these efforts by emphasizing the dangers of urban congestion, the need to help depressed areas and to achieve greater industrial efficiency, and the benefits of a policy of urban containment (Barlow Report 1940). In the post-war period the central government's approach to regional planning resulted in industrial location policies that attempted to achieve a 'proper distribution of industry' by reducing unemployment in development areas and at the same time restricting new industrial development in congested inner-city areas.[1] Cullingworth points out, however, that, despite the concern with employment, industrial location, and economic change, this policy was regarded 'in the main, as a social policy running alongside, but not supporting, economic policies' (Cullingworth 1985: 301).[2]

While government policy encouraged the out-migration of population and employment from urban areas in the 1950s and 1960s, planned dispersal of population and industry contributed 'only a modest amount to overall decentralization of people and jobs in the post-1945 period' (Stewart 1987: 131). Decentralization was also, and more significantly, a product of changes in the structure of the British economy. These changes included the trend to larger industrial plants and the declining competitive advantages of central city locations for manufacturing, as well as the impact of improvements in communications and transportation which increased the attractiveness of business locations outside the city (Evans 1980). In effect, then, government policies served to reinforce a deconcentration trend that was already underway and that, in the view of some analysts, was 'in any case dictated by economic necessity' (Eversley 1980: 461).

It was not government's intent, however, that the out-migration of people and jobs from the inner cities be accompanied by increased urban unemployment, physical dereliction of vacated areas, or social and economic deprivation for those left behind. In fact, the inner-city resident unemployment rate, already a third higher than the average for Britain in 1951, continued to rise through the 1950s and 1960s (Begg, Moore, and Rhodes 1986: 17–18). Added to the general problem of urban unemployment was the high concentration of impoverished racial minorities and immigrants in inner-city neighborhoods. Indeed, 'between 1951 and 1966 Britain's non-white population increased from an estimated 74,500 to 595,100, and the vast majority of these new immigrants settled in inner city areas or in areas whose housing stock was old and deteriorating' (McKay and Cox 1979: 234). While the minorities experienced 'acute problems in housing, education and employment—many of them deriving from racial discrimination', British governments, until the mid-1960s, did not 'make any special provision for the social and economic needs of immigrants'; 'instead debate tended to be focused on the question of immigration control' (McKay and Cox 1979: 234).

Positive Discrimination and the Community Development Project

The initiation of urban policies by the Wilson Government (1964–70) was both a response to the general social and economic decline of urban areas (the traditional political strongholds of Labour) and a reaction to the concentration of ethnic minorities in the inner city. The fear of racial violence was provoked by Conservative politician Enoch Powell. In response to the 1968 Race Relations Bill, Powell charged, in a speech at Birmingham, that the Bill 'would risk throwing a match into gunpowder', making Britons 'strangers in their own country'. He predicted considerable urban unrest: 'Like the Roman, I seem to see the River Tiber foaming with much blood' (quoted in Crossman 1977: 20). At least, in part, the Wilson Government's initiatives were a political reaction to Powell's provocation, a response that was intended to demonstrate the government's concern for the problems of ethnic minorities (Edwards and Batley 1978). Nevertheless, even before Powell's provocation, the government was already planning some financial assistance programs for areas of social deprivation (Fuller and Stevenson 1983).

The concern about urban decline arose amid growing criticism of the British welfare state. While the system of social services constructed after the war was envisaged as an application of universalistic principles of social and economic equity, there was mounting evidence that the welfare state had not eradicated poverty and social deprivation or insured equality of access to social services. A number of studies in the early 1960s contradicted the commonly held view that the post-war trend towards greater affluence was accompanied by greater equality and pointed out that, despite the increasing prosperity enjoyed by a substantial portion of the nation, the impoverish-ment of many British citizens remained acute (Abel-Smith and Townsend 1965; Lynes 1963; Lambert 1964). In addition, major social services, espe-cially education and housing, were the subject of criticism by official reports that pointed to the failure of these programs to reach some of those most in need and called for positive discrimination in favor of the most distressed areas (Milner Holland Report 1965; Plowden Report 1967; Seebohm Report 1968; Cullingworth Report 1969).

The 'rediscovery' of poverty and the growing criticism of social services, created an impetus for policy initiatives which departed from the principles of universalism and open access to social and economic support services. Instead, policies were proposed that were based on selectivism and positive discrimination. The challenge, Richard Titmuss argued, was to positively discriminate 'on a territorial, group or "rights" basis in favour of the poor, the handicapped, the deprived, the coloured, the homeless and the social casual-ties of our society' (Titmuss 1968: 134). Edwards and Batley point out that the 'move towards greater selectivity (rather than a reassertion of universalistic principles) in the application of services and benefits was the government response to the awareness that the Welfare State was not reaching all the poor' (Edwards and Batley 1978: 12).

The positive discrimination programs launched by the Wilson Government were intended to address the severe social deprivations of inner-city popula-tions through targeted public intervention. The idea of targeted intervention was a theme that ran through various commission reports issued in the late 1960s. The 1967 Plowden Report, *Children and their Primary Schools*, called for the establishment of priority areas where special assistance would be provided to children whose home backgrounds led to serious educational disadvantages (Plowden Report 1967). One response was the introduction of compensatory education programs similar in concept to the War on Poverty initiatives in the US such as Head Start. Of more lasting significance, the Urban Programme was established in 1968 to direct central government resources to areas experiencing severe deprivation, particularly the immigrant communities. A funding arrangement was devised whereby central government provided 75 percent of the cost (and local authorities the remainder) of projects that filled the gaps in existing urban and social service programs. Home points out that:

Until the Urban Programme arrangements were changed in 1977, several thousand projects (most of small scale), proposed by local authorities and voluntary organizations, were approved. The emphasis was initially on capital rather than recurring expenditure, on experimental or innovative projects supplementing the main programmes, and on educational projects (Home 1982: 7).

The activities supported were largely peripheral to the political and economic dimensions of urban distress: children's play groups, day care and nursery facilities, family planning and advice bureaus, legal and housing advice centers, community centers, accommodation for the homeless, assistance to the elderly, and health, social work, and compensatory education projects. In 1969, the Wilson Government also created the Community Development Project (CDP), which was announced as 'a neighborhood-based experiment aimed at finding new ways of meeting the needs of people living in areas of high social deprivation' (Home Secretary James Callahan speaking in Parliament; cited in Home 1982: 8). Project teams were established to assist the disadvantaged to analyze their needs, to encourage self-help and community participation, and to improve communication with local government.

While the assumptions underlying these programs were not always stated explicitly, Lawless points out that two major premises guided the development of the experiments.

It was generally assumed, first, that improved local government administrative and coordinating procedures would help to identify and assist those who might be considered members of the urban deprived. Secondly, there was a whole series of arguments relating to the concept of social and individual pathologies apparent in the operation of cultures of poverty. It was essentially these two ideas, and variations on them, which formed the intellectual basis for the early projects, governed their early evolution, and which were, ultimately and vitally, to be rejected (Lawless 1981: 5).

The concern with administrative management and coordination presumed the need for a *total* approach to the problems of urban malaise that was specifically targeted to deprived areas. The culture of poverty thesis—a concept in vogue in the US War on Poverty—assumed that some individuals and families were locked in a 'cycle of poverty' that perpetuated social deprivation from generation to generation (O. Lewis 1966).

The Community Development Project initially incorporated both assumptions. The CDP was established in 1969 with a mandate to discover new ways to assist the residents of inner-city neighborhoods who were the victims of the culture of poverty and who might benefit from coordinated and targeted community programs. It was conceived as a:

modest attempt at community action research into the better understanding and more comprehensive tackling of social needs, especially in local communities within the older urban areas, through closer coordination of central and local and unofficial effort, informed and stimulated by citizen initiative and involvement (Home Office, mimeo, n.d., quoted in Marris 1982: 15).

Yet the interpretation of urban problems that ultimately emerged from this experiment in action research fundamentally challenged the culture of poverty thesis and the expectation that deprivation could be effectively addressed through better coordination of services. Rather, the CDP offered an alternative understanding of urban problems, one that emphasized the economic and structural sources of poverty. 'The CDPs constitute something of a watershed in the development of British urban policy', suggests Martin Loney; 'concerns with social pathology gave way to an acknowledgement of the spatial dimensions of deprivation' and 'area-based approaches, directed to the residential and industrial infrastructure, replaced a narrow focus on the supposed characteristics of inner city residents' (Loney 1983: 164).

Between 1969 and 1972, twelve CDP teams were established in local areas designated as suffering from severe deprivation. Action research was used to formulate strategies for community development—to determine how to enhance local services for the disadvantaged, increase community participation in self-assistance, and facilitate coordination and responsiveness among government agencies. Local research teams, directed by the Information and Intelligence Unit in the Home Office, were supported by the researchers from nearby universities. Indeed, the idea of the CDP as an experiment conveyed 'the implication that the built-in research and evaluation components were to provide lessons for wider application in tackling social problems' (Fuller and Stevenson 1983: 175). Over a period of almost ten years, at an estimated cost of slightly less than five million pounds, the CDP involved some 120,000 people in communities throughout Britain who experienced the conditions of multi-deprivation: 'lower than average incomes, higher than average unemployment rates, high dependence on state benefits, poor standards of health (especially high infant mortality rates), poor housing, lack of basic amenities and general environmental squalor ... serious economic and industrial decline and loss of population' (Higgins *et al.* 1983: 13).

Over the course of the program, the focus shifted from a preoccupation with social pathology, the 'cycle of deprivation', the spatial concentration of poverty, and the personal and family characteristics of the poor to a concern for 'the problems of multi-deprivation to be redefined and reinterpreted in terms of structural constraint rather than psychological motivations, external rather than internal factors' (CDP 1974: 8). This shift resulted from analyses of selected urban projects which drew attention to institutionalized economic factors that contributed to and sustained deprivation. The central conclusion of these analyses was that the problems of urban poverty 'could only be understood in the context of a larger political economy'; a context which situated urban decline in the broader pattern of industrial development and decline (Loney 1983: 103). It was a structural analysis of the sources of social deprivation that directed attention to the causes rather than simply the symptoms of poverty. Donnison and Soto suggest that the entire frame of reference of the CDP initiative had changed dramatically over the course of the projects:

After trying fruitlessly—some would say too briefly and ineptly—to gain from central and local authorities the massive resources needed in deprived areas, they (the CDP) rejected the liberal–democratic assumptions on which their projects had been founded. Government, they argued, was ultimately the servant of the interests and classes which dominate society (Donnison and Soto 1980: 32).

Logically, the perception of deeply rooted and institutionalized deprivation called for more than better coordination of traditional welfare services or planning. This was especially the case insofar as the institutions of the welfare state and the planning system were themselves implicated by the more radical CDP analysts as serving the interests of capital rather than the interests of the working class and the urban poor. By providing social services and land and infrastructure development, the cost of capital investment—specifically corporate investment—was reduced and, thus, the material and political interests of the property class were promoted. The CDP activists called for fundamental changes in national politics that would reflect an understanding of the institutionalized economic sources of urban malaise and create a capacity for the disadvantaged to organize in opposition to dominant economic interests. This was stated in its starkest terms by John Benington, the leader of the Coventry CDP, who supported a move from policy dialogue to a conflict model of action and proposed that the community, including the city council, confront the manipulation of the city by corporate institutions (CDP 1977).

The CDP analysis introduced a structural economic perspective into British urban policy that directly challenged the conventional orientation of post-war urban policy. It also offered a forceful critique of the national welfare system that was reinforced in the early 1970s by social science documentations of the failure of British public policy to adequately address urban problems (e.g. N. Dennis 1970; Pahl 1970; Gower-Davies 1972; Rex 1973). The limited performance of housing and social service programs was catalogued, and, in many instances, researchers adopted a neo-Marxist framework similar to the Coventry CDP position: if urban poverty is the product of the interplay of national and international economic forces, aided and abetted by government policy, then government cannot be expected to adequately address declining urban economic performance and the resulting human problems without major structural realignment. Just what was to be involved in the radical realignment of the welfare state was not always clear. Despite frequent criticisms of local public services by both the CDP teams and the social science researchers, there was little evidence of serious examination of alternative delivery systems.

The CDP resembled, in part, the community action programs of the US War on Poverty (Lawless 1986). Yet, there were significant differences in the programs launched by the two countries. For example, the local private sector, which was an active participant in the US War on Poverty, played no obvious role in the CDPs other than as an object of analysis that was tainted with the same exploitative characteristics as the international corporations and the state. Moreover, whatever their apparent similarities, Marris points out that the Community Action Program and CDP were responding to fundamentally different types of challenges. The US program represented the 'tentative beginning of a federal social policy (that) . . . opened discussion of a national welfare system, a national health service—the kind of comprehensive insurance against hardship which Britain had already, in principle instituted' (Marris 1982: 17).

By contrast, the Community Development Project was a reaction to the failure of that [social welfare] system—a search for a way out of the impasse of rising social costs and declining economic performance; not the beginning of a national responsibility but an attempt to displace the burden on to the ingenuity of applied social science. In this sense, however unpretentiously it was presented, the Community Development Project and the inner city action-research which followed it carried a heavier load of expectations than their American counterparts. If they could not find a way, what direction was there left to take but revolution, or a demoralizing palliation of incurable hardship? (Marris 1982: 17).

The actual policy response to the CDP analysis was far removed from the radical prescriptions of the activists. While the CDP teams were not intended to conflict with local authorities, 'almost without exception', they 'experienced considerable resistance from authorities required to improve services' (McKay and Cox 1979: 243). Local authorities had misapprehensions about the CDP from the start, and the Home Office exacerbated this problem by failing to specify relationships in advance between the project teams and both local and central government (Fuller and Stevenson 1983: 182). The critical analysis of local and central government performance by the project teams further precipitated the demise of the program. In 1976 elimination of the CDP Information and Intelligence Unit removed central government analytic support for the Project teams and marked 'the beginning of the end for CDP' (Higgins *et al.* 1983: 40).

By the end of 1976 two of the projects (in Cleator Moor and Batley) had closed prematurely because of local difficulties. The local authorities in which they were based had, it appeared, gratefully slipped through the loop hole created [by a] . . . widely publicized letter of October 1975. In this the Home Office had advised local authorities that if—given the unfavourable economic climate—they felt unable to maintain their commitment to the local projects, the Home Office would accept proposals for their closure. The remaining ten projects drew to a staggered conclusion, most of them by 1978, with little fanfare or comment (Higgins *et al.* 1983: 41).

The direct and immediate influence of the CDP on British urban policy was minimal. While succeeding governments in the 1970s exhibited a concern for the problems of deprivation in Britain's inner cities and often accepted an economic interpretation of the sources of urban decline, inner-city programs were limited to local, piecemeal, and ameliorative measures while the major aspects of urban policy continued to translate into traditional physical renewal now often presented in the language of political economy. Much of the social science research that accompanied the CDP analysis was ignored by the policy community. Through the mid-1970s, the expenditures on positive discrimination programs such as the CDP and the Urban Programme were extremely small in comparison to total expenditure in the urban policy area. Further, these programs were operated from the Home Office and were effectively isolated from the DoE, which was the agency responsible for mainstream urban policy in the areas of housing, planning, and transport. In the early 1970s there was competition rather than coordination between these departments, and no central operational unit to bring together targeted and service-oriented urban programs (Stewart 1987: 141).

Nevertheless, the structural economic interpretation of urban problems introduced by CDP analysts changed the 'climate of opinion' and the terms of the inner-city debate throughout the 1970s (Higgins *et al.* 1983: 46). While generally rejecting the Marxist frame of reference adopted by some of the CDP analysts, the more traditional government understanding of urban deprivation as resulting from individual or group social pathologies was increasingly replaced with a focus on the institutional forces—national and international as well as local—that contributed to and sustained urban economic decline. Eventually, this shift in perspective found expression in policies specifically intended to reverse the deterioration of local, and especially inner-city economies, albeit in different ways from those proposed by the Community Development activists.

Cities and the Impact of National Economic Policy

The Conservative Heath Government (1970–4) maintained support for the policies and programs of positive discrimination initiated by the preceding Labour Government. Indeed, McKay and Cox suggest that the Conservatives were 'if anything more enthusiastic about combatting urban deprivation than were their Labour predecessors' and 'during the 1970–74 period expenditure on inner city programmes rose quite rapidly—even if it remained small in relation to spending on traditional policies' (McKay and Cox 1979: 247). The principle of selectivity in public assistance was consistent with Conservative proposals for distributing benefits in line with a test of need or means and, in fact, selectivity was proposed in the Conservative election campaign in 1970. As a result, the Heath Government 'was ideologically prepared to adopt the earlier Labour Government's more novel advances in the field—the programmes of positive discrimination' (Edwards and Batley 1978: 15).

There were some shifts in the emphasis on Urban Programme projects which reflected an interest in greater participation by the voluntary sector and an increasing concern for improving the public sector's efficiency and effectiveness in the delivery and management of urban services.[3] A small number of new initiatives were launched. In 1971, the DoE embarked on its own contribution to inner-city policy when Secretary Peter Walker commissioned the Inner Area Studies to determine how best to pursue 'a total approach' to the urban environment. An Urban Deprivation Unit was established in the Home Office in 1973 to facilitate coordination of the programs concerned with inner-city deprivation and to conduct research on the sources and nature of urban deprivation. In 1974, the Home Office also launched the Comprehensive Community Programme,[4] a series of experiments to improve the coordination and management of services in areas of intense urban deprivation.

In the early 1970s, as in the late 1960s, the inner-city programs continued to be modest in scale and largely isolated from mainstream urban policy in housing, planning, transportation, and other infrastructure development. The Heath Government's enthusiasm for dealing with the issue of urban deprivation did not result in a radically different approach to urban policy. Overall, the urban policy of the early 1970s did not depart far from the physical redevelopment approach (guided by a familiar 'bricks and mortar' philosophy) that had been the traditional basis of British policy.

Yet, if the Heath Government's imprint on inner-city policy was modest, there were other ways in which it laid the foundations for what was to become the growing economic focus of urban policy during the 1970s and 1980s. The government concentrated on efforts to stimulate economic growth and industrial investment and to enlarge the role of the private sector. The Heath Government entered office with an ideological commitment and a set of draft policies to stimulate industrial regeneration, with the private sector as the principal agent of change. A series of measures—such as 'Competition Credit Control'[5]—were introduced to encourage investment and reduce regulatory controls on private sector investment decisions. Success depended on the willingness of the financial sector to take advantage of investment incentives and reduced controls, and to direct increased funding to industrial redevelopment. While the intention was to stimulate industrial growth by freeing the market, the actual result was vastly different. The financial sector, Cox suggests, was 'much more concerned with short-term maximization of speculative gains than with the long-term viability of the British economy' (Cox 1984: 167). Such speculative gains were seen as more often lying in the property market than in industrial capitalization. Despite the government's intention to promote industrial redevelopment, the relaxation and removal of investment controls 'gave the green light to financial institutions to invest in property' (Cox 1984: 163). 'In the two years between 1971 and 1973 owner-occupied dwelling prices increased by 80 percent, house-building land prices by 160 percent and commercial offices by 250 percent' (Lichfield and Darin-Drabkin 1980: 169). The result was property speculation that weakened the national economy by stimulating inflation as well as aggravating conditions in those parts of urban Britain with marginal investment potential by encouraging the withdrawal of capital.

The impact of the 'property boom' was most quickly felt in the financial markets. In 1971, 96 property companies borrowed £382 million from the money market; in 1973, this rose to £796 million, leaving a debt to the banks of £2,330 million (Cox 1984). The speculation had an even more profound effect on the public sector. Unable to compete with the private sector and incapable of directing the funds flooding into the property market, the public sector was priced out. The property boom, encouraged by and eventually fueling inflation, also tended to attract investment in short-term, high-yield property and discourage investment in long-term projects, particularly those located in more marginal urban locations peripheral to city-center commercial areas (Ambrose and Colenutt 1975).

Heath labelled the property speculators 'the unacceptable face of capitalism' and reintroduced regulatory controls by the middle of 1973. The counter-inflation policy imposed a freeze on rents for business property, increased interest rates, and limited bank advances to non-industrial borrowers. But the effects of these controls were short-lived. By 1974, at the time of Heath's electoral defeat, commercial rents were once more on the increase, returning confidence to the property market. In essence, Heath's Government had been constrained by the market whichever way it turned. Relaxation of controls combined with the expansion of the money supply served to open the floodgates to speculators, 'more concerned with their own enrichment in the short term than with [the condition of the] nation in the long term' (Cox 1984: 154).

The debacle of the 1971–3 property boom clearly demonstrated the significant extent to which city development was impacted by national economic policy. The Heath policies did not bear the label 'urban' nor were their effects conceived in spatial terms, but the outcome of ostensibly economic and industrial policies had a devastating urban impact which, at least for a time, overshadowed the effects of many of the policies specifically designed to assist urban areas. As a result of the property boom and the attendant inflation, land prices and building costs for local authority housing more than doubled between 1970 and 1974 and the interest rate local authorities needed to pay for their housing investments grew from 6.6 percent in 1971/2 to 8.1 percent in 1973/4 (McKay and Cox 1979: 141). This price explosion had profound effects. Public sector housing construction fell from 187,884 units in 1970 to 134,405 in 1974 and total housing construction fell from 364,475 units in 1971 to 278,363 in 1974, the lowest since 1952 (McKay and Cox 1979: 141). Beyond specific impacts, the property boom graphically illustrated the vulnerability of cities to national economic events beyond their control. It also demonstrated, even to a Conservative Government, the risks of an unrestrained reliance on private institutions to achieve public benefits.

When Labour regained power in 1974, it called for a reassertion of public control of the economy. Labour proposed to nationalize some of the leading companies (particularly in high-technology sectors), to promote national economic regeneration through the creation of a National Enterprise Board,[6] to assist regional growth through development agencies for Wales and Scotland, and to address some of the urban problems created by Heath's property boom. In particular, the new government announced policies to strengthen community control of development. The 1974 White Paper on land advocated 'positive planning' that would be achieved by public ownership of development land; it would 'enable the community to control the development of land in accordance with its needs and priorities' and would 'restore to the community the increase in value of land arising from its efforts' (Cullingworth 1985: 187). Over the next five years, urban policy was a familiar topic in Westminster, achieving an unprecedented degree of attention in the media and attracting considerable academic interest. Despite this attention, there was a wide gap, if not an outright contradiction, between Labour's radical rhetoric and its actual urban policy.

Almost immediately, Labour's manifesto for change sent shock waves through the British financial community and ultimately led to a crisis in confidence in the British economy. In response to this, and even before the sterling crisis in 1975/6, Labour's concept of economic recovery through the mechanism of increased state control was significantly modified if not effectively abandoned. The prospect of radical shifts in urban policy faded just as quickly. Anthony Crosland, Secretary of State for the Environment, admitted that protection of property interests remained a government priority and lifted the freeze on business rents originally imposed by the Heath Government. 'By December 1974, then, the Labour government's radicalism had been fundamentally constrained' (Cox 1984: 181). The effects of this constraint were exhibited in the ways in which Labour's proposals for 'positive planning' were pursued. The government was able to establish a radical program for local control of land development, called the Community Land Scheme which, in principle, provided broad powers for compulsory land acquisition and created a capacity for taxation of the added value of development and its return to the community. Instead of becoming the flagship for public intervention, however, the Community Land Scheme[7] became a weak, confusing, under-financed imitation, far removed from the ideals that it was originally intended to pursue. Ironically, 'the Scheme was well on the way to being bent into shape by the development industry' before the legislation was repealed in 1979 (Ambrose 1986: 64). Moreover, the funding of the Scheme (imposed by the Treasury) was designed to allow local authorities only to deal in land transactions that would benefit private house building. In fact, the Land Authority for Wales, the only part of the Community Land Scheme that survived after 1979, eventually became a key actor in stimulating private property development throughout Wales. As a system of public control of land development, however, the Community Land Scheme was impotent, particularly in the inner city.

Despite the abortive efforts at policy reform in areas such as land ownership, inner-city problems remained high on Labour's urban policy agenda. In part, this reflected a political sensitivity to the vulnerability of Labour's urban constituency and a genuine concern for the plight of urban Britain. The result was new legislation. Inner-city programs, still modest in cost compared to more traditional areas of urban policy, were one of the few policy areas safeguarded from public expenditure cuts. Moreover, while urban deprivation policies no longer commanded the interest of the Home Office, Environment Secretary Peter Shore moved the inner-city issue up his departmental agenda and launched a broad examination of policy alternatives. This shift of responsibilities for inner-city issues from the Home Office to the DoE reflected an important substantive change in policy focus away from the social problems of urban deprivation and immigrant adjustment and towards the economic and environmental problems of industrial decline and business development (Home 1982: 16).

The Emergence of Inner-City Policy

Four influences shaped the objectives and direction of the emerging inner-city policy in the 1970s. First, statistics, initially from the 1966 sample Census, then more dramatically from 1971 data (Holterman 1975), showed that urban malaise—poverty, bad housing, low incomes, unemployment—was not confined to small, isolated pockets but instead covered large tracts of older urban Britain. In 1971, unemployment in the seven largest conurbations was 40 percent of the total for Britain (Corkindale 1980: 175). Second, unemployment, particularly male, long-term, urban unemployment, became a persistent and politically sensitive feature of the monthly labor statistics. The increase in urban unemployment and the loss of inner-city jobs were not new phenomena, but the figures for job loss and employment decline continued to grow through the 1970s (Begg, Moore, and Rhodes 1986: 18–20). Between 1965 and 1975, for example, there was a national decline of over 12 percent in manufacturing jobs, and the loss was especially acute in inner-city areas that had frequently been the targets of positive discrimination programs (Keeble 1980: 110). Fully 27 percent (390,000) of the manufacturing jobs in Greater London were lost between 1966 and 1974, with the greatest losses in the inner boroughs (N. Dennis 1970: 47–8). Manchester lost 3 percent of its manufacturing jobs every year between 1961 and 1971 (Keeble 1980: 109). By 1976 British unemployment at 5.5 percent—more than twice the level two years earlier (CSO 1987)—had risen to 1.4 million; a figure 'unprecedented since 1945' (Higgins *et al.* 1983: 118), although, as we shall see, it was still modest compared to what was to come in the next decade (over 13 percent unemployment in 1985; CSO 1987). And there was a correlation between urban unemployment and a third factor: the concentration of racial minorities in parts of British cities such as London, Birmingham, Leicester, and Bradford. Moreover, the Labour Government had become concerned about unrest in several areas of ethnic minority concentration and the May 1976 local elections resulted in Labour setbacks and gains for the National Front[8] in London (Stewart 1987).

The final and most significant influence on the evolution of inner-city policy came through the publication of the Inner Area Studies, originally commissioned in 1971 by Peter Walker, Environment Secretary during the Heath Government. All three studies, in Lambeth (London), Birmingham, and Liverpool, demonstrated the frailty of the urban economy and the importance of addressing the causes, not merely the symptoms of urban economic decline. When urban poverty and social deprivation were discussed they were firmly placed in an economic context; where urban decay was identified, the answer was conceived to be as much economic as physical. The Inner Area Studies confirmed the shifting focus of urban analysis from demographic and social problems to an explicit concern with the 'erosion of the inner city economy and the shortage of private investment which might assist the process of regeneration' (DoE 1977: para. 5). In short, the argument presented in the reports was that the problems of the older urban areas stem directly from their inherent economic weakness and that the policy response should be to promote local economic improvement—for both new and existing firms—and, commensurate with this, to improve the physical environment. Furthermore, the reports prescribed resource discrimination in favor of the inner city, better coordination and fuller cooperation between government departments, and involvement of the Departments of Industry and Employment.

Environment Secretary Peter Shore announced the new strategy for urban regeneration in a speech at Manchester in 1976 (DoE 1976*b*). Shore challenged the regional and new towns policies of the post-war period which had encouraged economic and population dispersal. The new policy would seek to reverse the pattern of out-migration while strengthening the economic base of inner-city areas.[9] In a later speech at Bristol, he proposed:

The first objective on my list would be to improve the local economies of the inner-city areas. In present-day conditions, when there is not much brand new commercial and industrial development, our top priority must be to preserve the jobs that at present exist—a vital task when one considers the high proportion of the loss of jobs arising from firms not moving out of the inner city but simply dying there (Shore 1977).

The reorientation of urban policy was officially articulated in the 1977 White Paper, *Policy for the Inner Cities*. It repeated many of the arguments of the Inner Area Studies and focused on 'the erosion of the inner city economy and the shortage of private investment which might assist the process of regeneration' (DoE 1977: para. 5). Although the White Paper was primarily concerned with improving the response of central government to urban problems, it nevertheless portrayed local governments as the natural agencies for urban renewal. But, in contrast with policies of local public control, it recommended that activities be directed towards stimulating 'investment by the private sector, by firms and by individuals in industry, in commerce and in housing' especially in small and medium-sized firms (DoE 1977: para. 39). Moreover, the White Paper suggested that financial institutions could and should play a more positive role in assisting the inner areas, and argued for a 'new and closer form of collaboration ... between government and the private sector' (DoE 1977: para. 103). McKay and Cox suggest that:

there can be no doubt that the White Paper represented an important change in policy. Area based positive discrimination measures with a primarily social service orientation were effectively dropped, and replaced with an emphasis on administrative coordination and economic revival. Mainstream urban policy including housing, planning and industrial location were in principle to be linked to inner city decline for the first time, and the postwar policy of dispersal, while not discarded, was accorded lower priority than ever before (McKay and Cox 1979: 253).

Most of the recommendations from the White Paper were implemented without new legislation; indeed the initiatives to assist industry came from provisions already contained in the 1969 Local Government (Social Need) Act.[10] These provisions were also used to establish seven 'Special Partnership Areas' in which central government would help to promote economic development with selected inner area local authorities. Indeed, the inner-cities policy 'represented the consolidation of the area-based approach to urban problems', and it placed emphasis on improved management of central–local partnerships (Stewart 1987: 131–2). The three guiding ideas behind the Inner City Partnerships were 'to concentrate limited resources in some of the worst problem areas, to co-ordinate action for dealing with the complex and inter-related problems faced by those areas and to tailor policies and action to local needs' (Home 1982: 113). In direct contrast to the experience with public–private partnerships in the US, however, and despite the recommendations of the White Paper for collaboration with the private sector, the Inner City Partnerships did not include representation from the business community or the voluntary sector.

The connection between the Urban Programme[11] and economic regeneration was made explicit in the 1978 Inner Urban Areas Act which provided broader powers for making loans available to private firms for the purpose of physical and/or economic improvements. In sum, the inner-city policy was 'to give additional powers to local authorities with severe inner area problems so that they may participate more effectively in the economic development of their areas' (DoE 1977: para. 1). As Stewart points out, the inner-cities policy clearly recognized and encouraged the role of local authorities in local economic development: 'efficiency values were supported rather than redistributive values' (Stewart 1987: 132).

Despite the 'total approach' advocated by the White Paper, urban policy remained fragmented. While the DoE was able to dictate the project focus and direction of the Urban Programme through its financial controls over local government and its ability to exercise authority through its planning powers, it was less than successful in involving other central Departments. Moreover, the plethora of programs begun under the 'new' urban policy were still modest initiatives when measured against the larger national and international forces impacting the fortunes of inner-city economies. Furthermore, the resources and institutional machinery needed to promote economic development were missing from the programs of inner-city revitalization. Neither the central nor the local government officials had direct experience with promoting local industry or commerce; business and the trade unions were not invited to be formal members of the partnerships; and representatives of the private sector had only peripheral involvement in the new economic programs. While calling for new, radical, inventive ideas targeted at local economic revival, the revised policy continued to finance traditional programs of urban renewal. The economic focus was soon diverted into property development, giving city planners the chance to dust off plans for physical improvements sometimes prepared a decade or more earlier. It proved to be far easier to rebuild infrastructure than to resurrect failing local economies. Moreover, the economic bias in the new urban policy clearly benefited some existing and new businesses, but there is little evidence that this had any short-term regenerative impact on declining urban economies.

Whatever the shortcomings of implementation, the inner-city policy articulated by the Labour Government reflected a significant redirection of urban policy that emphasized the economic dimensions of inner-city problems and the economic development function of local government. On leaving office in May 1979, Labour left an array of local economic policies and initiatives that were largely compatible with the Conservative interpretation of urban change. More than this, the previous five years of Labour Government had effectively redrawn the parameters of British urban policy. The definition of the urban problem had changed dramatically. The problems of cities—and particularly inner-city areas—were increasingly viewed as resulting from economic decline. The consequences were manifest in job loss, redundancy of skills native to an area, low incomes, below average employment opportunities, an outward flow of population in search of better employment prospects, and an inability of major cities to hold or attract industry. Not only was the urban problem now seen in a different light, but there was also a widespread reaction against government as the natural vehicle for urban reform. Indeed, by the late 1970s, the policy environment precluded 'any significant development of urban renewal policies reliant on state intervention' (Gibson and Langstaff 1982: 317). The Labour Government had set in motion a series of policy reformulations that would eventually become a wholesale movement towards central government encouragement and support of the private sector as the lead actor in the process of urban economic change.

Cities and the Strategy of Privatism

More than a decade before her 1979 electoral victory, Margaret Thatcher argued that British domestic policy needed to roll back the frontiers of the state and rekindle the furnace of the free market. 'What we need now is a far greater degree of personal freedom and decision, far more independence from the government and a comparative reduction in the role of government' (Margaret Thatcher, lecture to the Conservative Political Centre, 1968; quoted in Riddell 1985: 21). Later Conservative rhetoric echoed this theme. Sir Keith Joseph proposed that a prosperous future for Britain required a reassertion of the virtues of capitalism, the profit motive, and the entrepreneurial spirit. Without cuts in public expenditure, restriction on the money supply would 'strangulate the private sector and precipitate recession', and without some level of control over the state, there would be no incentives to produce 'the climate of entrepreneurship and risk-taking that will alone secure prosperity, high employment and economic health' (quoted in Riddell 1985: 25–6).

Shortly before the election victory, Sir Keith presented the nation with a list of the problems afflicting the country as seen by the Conservatives:

I reckon there are six; six poisons which wreck a country's prosperity and full employment: excessive government spending, high direct taxation, egalitarianism, excessive nationalisation, a politicized trade union movement associated with Luddism, and an anti-enterprise culture. Six of them. Now most of our rivals have one of these poisons, some of them have two, we're the only country in the world that has all six. And sometimes I think that the miracle is that with all these poisons in our system we still do as relatively well as we do (From the transcript of the 'Charlton Interview,' 30 July 1979, BBC; quoted in D. Heald 1983: 7).

To overcome or avoid these poisons, Thatcher developed a strategy to permanently realign the relationship between the state, the private economy, and individuals. In the words of John Moore, Financial Secretary during the second administration:

Our aim is to build upon our property-owning democracy and to establish a people's capital market, to bring capitalism to the place of work, to the high street, and even to the home, [and this in turn] will produce an irreversible shift in attitudes and achievements which will bring lasting benefits to the UK (*The Economist*, 21 Dec. 1985).

The building blocks of what became known as 'Thatcherism' were constructed around four beliefs: (1) government had grown too big, too expensive, too involved in economic affairs, and should be restricted and reduced in favor of the private sector; (2) more sensitive and effective guidance of growth could be exercised by the market than by planned intervention of the State—indeed, public ownership and control inhibited economic freedom to grow; (3) in almost all aspects of the economy, the private sector is more efficient than the public sector equivalent; and lastly, (4) by reducing the dependence on public sector support, firms, families, and localities would rediscover the traditional values and benefits of enterprise, initiative, and self-reliance. Given these beliefs, it followed that social change and social improvement could be achieved only by a transformation of the economy. If this transformation required personal hardship for some through dislocation or unemployment, then that must be accepted as a necessary price of progress and eventual prosperity. The market-driven transformation would ultimately create winners and losers; people and places who could not or would not compete or would not keep pace with the rate of change must no longer be permitted to restrict growth in hopes of cushioning themselves from the economic realities of the marketplace. Under the tenets of the Thatcher version of privatism, the benefits of the market order were contrasted with the inefficiency of government intervention, the impotence of government programs, and the frequently insidious results of government's encroachment on the free operation of the market; specifically, the suppression of individual initiative and the distortion of economic behavior.

In sum, the rediscovery and nurturing of an enterprise economy required that Britain liberate itself from the suffocation of decades of bureaucratic state control and trade union indulgence. While the foundations for this transformation were laid before the Thatcher Government, the scope and pace of privatization proposals were vastly accelerated by the infusion of Conservative ideology.

The Dimensions of Privatization

From 1981, and with added vigor after the 1983 election, the Thatcher
Government implemented a broad-ranging privatization program. Four
dimensions of this broad policy, spanning all major areas of domestic policy
and linking the objectives of liberalizing the economy, promoting a share-
owning population, and reducing the level of public borrowing, have had
implications for cities and served to create the conditions for specific urban
policy initiatives. First, privatization would involve the selling-off of state
assets and holdings to the private sector including nationally owned
industries and, of particular significance for cities, the disposal of public
housing. Second, services previously provided by the public sector would
increasingly be contracted-out to the private sector with local services such
as refuse disposal and cleaning services singled out for special attention.
Third, charges would be introduced for public goods or services that had
been funded through the welfare state; this included, particularly, the operations of the National Health Service but also road charges and market pricing
for public sector housing. Fourth, economic activity would be deregulated
through liberalization of state controls and protection, and, specifically,
planning and building codes would be relaxed.

Selling-Off State Assets. Undoubtedly the dimension of the privatization
strategy that has received the greatest public attention has been the selling-
off of government assets. This was intended to achieve a 'transfer of government owned industries to the private sector' and to assure 'that the
predominant share of assets on transfer lie with private shareholders'
(Peacock 1984: 3). Other terms, such as 'load-shedding', 'de-nationalization',
and 'people's capitalism', more graphically illustrate the ideological as well as
the economic objectives of this policy. From 1981 through 1987, the government sold-off state interests across the entire range of British industry. The
process began in modest fashion, raising £290 million from the first issue of
shares in British Petroleum, but eventually became an important source of
income, raising billions from the sale of British Telecom (£2.6 billion), British
Gas (£7.7 billion), and British Petroleum (a minimum of £5.7 billion). In
between, the government divested its interests in Britoil, British Airways,
and Jaguar cars as well as other lesser-known companies.

The widening share-ownership in newly privatized British industry was
criticized as being short-lived in that the small, individual shareholder often
would be tempted to take quick profits, and this ultimately would result in a
reconcentration of ownership in the financial institutions. In this regard, the
privatization strategy was criticized as merely transferring monopoly power
from the public to the private sector. Moreover, skeptics suggested that the
share price realized by many of the sales was generated by the temporary
excitement of this new environment and that the 'gloss will dull when the
next recession comes and enthusiasm has worn off' (*The Economist*, 21 Dec.
1985: 84). Other critics suggested that what began as an experiment in
'people's capitalism', soon became simply another governmental revenue

source. John Kay, Director of the Institute of Fiscal Studies, argued that while 'privatization began as an exciting and innovative attempt to restore market forces to areas of the public sector which had traditionally been . . . [subjected to] centralized co-ordination and control', the government quickly lost sight of the original, announced intent. In effect, Kay suggested, the government abandoned the commitment to market solutions and softened its policies 'in favour of getting a higher price for the Treasury' (*The Economist*, 21 Dec. 1985: 71). The original philosophic justification was also lost on some members of the Conservative Party itself, albeit from a very different position on the ideological spectrum. Speaking at the tenth anniversary dinner of the moderate Tory Reform Group, the Earl of Stockton (Harold Macmillan, Conservative Prime Minister between 1957 and 1963) criticized the government, mocking their policy of selling assets to pay for current spending: 'First all the Georgian silver goes, and then all that nice furniture that used to be in the saloon. Then the Canalettos go' (*The Times* (London), 9 Nov. 1985).

Notwithstanding such criticism, it is difficult to underestimate the impact of this aspect of privatization on the structure of the British economy. Commenting just prior to Mrs. Thatcher's election to a third term in office, *The Economist* reported that: 'In 1979, four times as many Britons belonged to trade unions as owned shares on the stock market. Since then the unionists have shrunk, the capitalists have blossomed; the two groups are now virtually identical in size' (*The Economist*, 16 May 1987: 15).

One of the most successful parts of the privatization strategy was the sale of public sector (council) housing to sitting tenants. Between 1979 and 1986, 1,060,085 houses were transferred from public to private ownership. Fully 87 percent of these dwellings were sold at discount price to 'sitting tenants' renting from local authorities or New Town development corporations. These sales increased home ownership in Britain from 53 percent in 1975 to 62 percent in 1985 (DoE 1987*b*). Indeed, by 1987, the proportion of private home ownership in Britain was larger than any other country except the US (*The Economist*, 16 May 1987: 15). It is estimated that the sale of council houses generated up to £2 billion per year for local authorities and other public landlords (Malpass 1986). Selling council houses proved to be an important political asset for the Conservative Party at the 1983 election and posed a serious dilemma for the Labour Party which had to reassess its policies on home ownership. Nonetheless, the success of this program was incomplete. First, the disposal of municipal housing was accompanied by severe cuts in the level of housing investment; in Britain as a whole, investment in public sector housing between 1976 and 1986 fell by 46 percent, from £3.76 billion to £2.02 billion, at 1980 prices. This resulted in a marked reduction in the construction of dwellings in the public sector. Over the same period, new house completions in the public sector fell from 135,000 per annum to just over 23,000 per annum (DoE 1987*b*). The building of new 'general needs'[12] housing in the public sector was effectively ended through what became known as the 'residualization' of local authority housing (Malpass 1986; Forrest and Murie 1984).

Second, there is debate about whether the policy of selling council housing removed, once and for all, the better quality stock. It is argued that this reduced choice within the public sector and left the worst housing, in the least attractive locations, to households unable or unwilling to join the property owning classes (English 1982). Hence the policy created a division between the more affluent classes who could afford to buy, and an important minority—often unemployed or in low paying jobs—who did not have the opportunity to cross the divide. The policy was spatially divisive, it is argued, further isolating, in social and economic terms, whole parts of British cities and locking residents into deteriorating council housing estates with little hope of escape or that the stock would be substantially improved.

Despite these and other problems of introducing privatism into the public housing market, the overall policy thrust was extended from the sale of council houses to a wider range of housing issues. There are four components of this policy development: (1) further sales of difficult-to-let flatted property by introducing extended discounts; (2) exhortation of local authorities to improve their management performance and to learn from the experience of private developers; (3) encouragement of owner-occupiers to increase their responsibility for home maintenance and improvement—hence reducing the level of public support; and (4) extension of the privatization strategy to include the wholesale disposal of entire public sector housing estates (Brindley and Stoker 1987: 13). The strategy involved central and local governments entering into sophisticated public–private partnerships with developers and financial institutions, employing new techniques of financial leverage to attract the private sector into the public market. What began as a modest program of selling council houses emerged as a coherent 'strategy for the privatization of housing renewal . . . : the containment of public expenditure; improved performance from public sector investment; increased responsibility for private owners; and a major role for the private corporate sector, especially volume builders and the building societies' (Brindley and Stoker 1987: 13).

Despite the sale of council houses to sitting tenants, followed by the disposal of whole estates to private developers, Britain still retains some 40 percent of housing in council or other public ownership. In some regions, notably in Scotland, the majority of housing is under the control of public landlords and in these areas the 'Right to Buy' legislation has been much less successful. In Glasgow, where 67 percent of all housing is owned and let by the public sector, less than 2 percent of the council-owned property had been sold to sitting tenants by 1986 (Grieve 1986). In part, this may reflect the large percentage of Glasgow dwellings that are flats rather than houses and are less attractive for purchase. But it is also a reflection of relative poverty in a city where 70 percent of all families had a principal household income of less than £5,200 (Grieve 1986).

The policy of encouraging the sale of council property was also used by government to justify reduction in subsidies to local housing authorities. Councils were allowed to retain a proportion of the receipts from council house sales for investment in the maintenance and improvement of the remaining stock. This policy had mixed results. In the more affluent areas, where there were substantial sales, local councils were able to use a proportion of their receipts for maintenance and other capital projects; in poorer areas, with a higher proportion of council houses and a lower percentage of sales, housing authorities had to maintain their existing—and often decaying—stock with fewer and fewer resources. Moreover, subsidies for building new council housing, even for 'special needs', was cut.

After Mrs. Thatcher's 1987 re-election victory, the government proposed to greatly extend the privatization of housing. A new housing bill was introduced in November 1987 that was designed to further reduce, and possibly eliminate, the role of local councils as providers of housing and encourage the provision of homes for rent by letting the market decide the price (*Guardian*, 21 Nov. 1987). Housing action trusts would be created by the Environment Secretary to manage run-down council housing estates and to prepare homes through rehabilitation and repair for disposal to other public or private landlords—but not the local councils that built them.[13] In addition to these provisions, the Housing Bill introduced a 'pick-a-landlord' scheme that would allow tenants to transfer council ownership of their home to another landlord—a housing association, a housing trust, a co-operative, or a private landlord. At the same time, it proposed that housing associations, which depend heavily on government financial support for capital, should increase their reliance on private sources of funding for new building. The result of this would be to greatly increase the rents on new properties to such an extent that the National Federation of Housing Associations believes they would be 'everywhere beyond the reach of the people for whom associations exist to serve' (*Guardian*, 21 Nov. 1987). Finally, government setting of 'fair rents' would be replaced by landlord–tenant agreements on new rents, effectively at the market rate. These policy proposals make it clear that, in its third term, the Thatcher Government intended to greatly expand its efforts at privatization of the housing sector.

Contracting-Out. A dimension of the privatization strategy that was firmly supported by the Thatcher Government is the contracting-out of services; that is, the use of private organizations to undertake services previously provided or delivered by the public sector. This dimension had both economic and ideological ends, with free-market pressure groups such as the Adam Smith Institute and the Institute of Directors drawing on the opinions of US public choice economists to support their claim that private production is inherently superior to public service. The actual evidence of the superiority of contracting-out was largely comprised of anecdotal experience from the US. Nonetheless, the Thatcher government found this an attractive option because it was ideologically consistent with its commitments to reduce the scale of government, cut public sector employment, and improve efficiency by replacing public goods and services with their private sector equivalents. For cities, the pressure to change came initially from the Local Government, Planning and Land Act 1980 which required that Direct

Labour Organizations (construction units operated by local government) compete with private companies for all building and maintenance work and establish a 5 percent rate of return on capital employed. Further pressure was applied when the Treasury, one of the keenest supporters of extending competition within local government, argued that 'the decision to contract out the provision of services is the responsibility of individual local authorities, however, they are being encouraged seriously to do so as a means of reducing costs to their ratepayers, while still maintaining standards' (Treasury 1982: 2). Moreover, a government consultation paper, *Competition in the Provision of Local Authority Services*, proposed extension of contracting-out to five key services—refuse collection and street cleaning, property cleaning, ground maintenance, vehicle maintenance, and catering services (DoE 1985*d*).

Local government has not generally shared the enthusiasm for privatizing local services. A survey of privatization in local government found that by 1984/5, less than 12 percent of all councils in Britain were engaged in contracting-out of local services (Whitehead 1985). Rodney Bikerstaffe, a leading trade union official, suggested that only 41 out of 456 local councils in England and Wales had chosen to use private contractors with large parts of the country preferring to retain the 'direct production model' (Bikerstaffe 1985). In fact, local government services that have been contracted-out tend to be relatively insignificant—small-scale maintenance, grass-cutting, hiring leisure equipment, and providing meals in day-care centers. Moreover, those authorities favoring contracting-out are most often located in the south and east, the Conservative heartland of Britain (Moor and Parnell 1986).

Despite the government's exhortation and the threat of further legislation making contracting-out compulsory, a privatization study in 1987 found fewer authorities looking to the private sector to deliver services previously provided by local councils.

The number of councils contracting services out has fallen sharply since the last [1986] survey from more than 16 percent to 10 percent of the total responding. The small scale of council privatization is further emphasized by the total value of contracts put out to the private sector: less than £34 billion a year. The amount councils report saving by contracting out was less than £1.5 million (Whitehead 1987: 4).

Charging for Services. The introduction, or increase in use, of charges for public services has been an alternative to contracting-out services to the private sector. Historically, charges have played an insignificant role in the financing of the British welfare system, constituting less than 5 percent of gross public expenditure (D. Heald 1983: 302). One of the central arguments of the advocates of privatization has been that inefficiency in social services was inevitable in the absence of charges for the services provided. The British National Health Service (NHS) has been a primary target of such criticism. Supporters of privatization argue that the 'demand side of the health market has consumers with preferences'; an extension of charges would leave households 'free to choose the pattern of consumption which suits their own preferences' (Bosanquet 1983: 147). The supply of medical services is expected to be adjusted accordingly. Throughout the Thatcher incumbency, the imposition of increased charges for the NHS was cause for frequent political debate and was seen by the opposition as a step towards dismantling the health service in pursuit of an American-style private health care system. The government increased the basic prescription charge for drugs by 600 percent between 1979 and 1983. There were also proposals to impose charges for overnight accommodation in hospitals and for visits to a general practitioner. Early in her third term, Mrs. Thatcher faced growing criticism of underfunding in the NHS yet her response was to examine ways of implementing a radical privatization of medical services. Health policy and the NHS was, by the summer of 1987, the responsibility of John Moore, a staunch supporter of the free market.

The impact of this dimension of privatization on services has been mixed. Even if charges improved the efficiency of service delivery, the overall impact, in the context of persistent and growing urban poverty, is regressive. Unless a complex system of allowances and rebates is introduced and publicized at the same time, lower income households may be unable to purchase some basic public goods or services. Like other facets of privatization, the imposition of charges, particularly in the NHS, poses significant equity issues and, in the extreme case, would withhold public services from the groups in British society who are the most dependent.

Deregulation and the Challenge to the Planning Regime. The removal or 'liberalization' of state protection and controls, more commonly known as deregulation, is perhaps the cornerstone of Thatcherism. The idea of removing government from the private activities of individuals and companies was perceived as basic to all domestic policy, with the notable exception of law and order. As Alan Walters, economic advisor to the Prime Minister from 1981 to 1983, put it, 'the objective was to get a market economy functioning efficiently without suffocating government intervention' and to free 'the economy from the complex and confusing network of controls' (Walters 1986: 4). This aspect of policy was also supported by a combination of supply-side economic analysis and moral, even evangelistic, fervor. Presenting his first Budget in June 1979, Sir Geoffrey Howe justified deregulation on the grounds that government action and law stand in the way of change, stifling enterprise, punishing success, and discouraging innovation (HANSARD, Session 1979/80, vol. 968, col. 239). Speaking on the defects of nationalized industries, Nigel Lawson argued that 'the time has come to liberate ourselves from this burden—and then to liberate the industries themselves from this condition' (Lawson 1981).

In 'creating a climate for enterprise' (Riddell 1985), the Conservative Party claimed at the 1983 election to have successfully achieved the following deregulation activities:

1. ending pay, price, and dividend control;
2. easing planning controls and removing the restrictions imposed through

Industrial Development Certificates[14] and Office Development Permits;[15]
3. creating Enterprise Zones and 'freeports' (duty-free trading zones);
4. reducing business taxation and the employers' National Insurance surcharge;[16]
5. assisting small business to avoid the worst excesses of government bureaucracy;
6. encouraging technological innovation; and
7. liberalizing public-sector monopolies to increase the size of the free-market economy.

The aspect of this program that is particularly relevant to urban policy has been the attempt to extend the liberalization of control over the use of land imposed through the town and country planning system. Free-market pressure groups had long been critical of the planning system, claiming it merely served to crowd-out the private sector, distort and delay the market, and impose additional costs on development. These views were championed by what Lloyd (1985, 1986) refers to as the 'libertarian planning school'. Critical of the over-extension of the planning system, Sorenson (1983), Sorenson and Day (1981), and others have argued that the planning system should return to its rightful role as a mechanism for controlling and minimizing the externalities associated with development. These opinions were most forcibly articulated in an Adam Smith Institute report, *Town and Country Chaos* (Jones 1982) whose recommendations also surfaced as an important part of the 'Omega Report', a blueprint for privatization also produced by the Adam Smith Institute (1985).

The advocates of libertarian planning have found little to commend in the statutory planning system in Britain. Their conclusion is that public planning directed towards the best interests of the community is a demonstration of collective failure. By contrast, the best examples of town planning are found in the early history of private development: Belgravia in London and Edinburgh's New Town are cited as examples of the superiority of private development over public planning. The conventional wisdom that public planning secures lasting social and environmental improvement is also questioned—rather than improving cities, the control of non-conforming uses has resulted in rigid partitioning and served to stifle new development; the imposition of planning control and conditions on development, far from achieving civic improvement, led instead to intolerable delay, increased building costs and monotonous, bureaucratically inspired architecture. Thus, Jones argues that:

what looks to middle-class eyes as the protection of a city's character and the imposition of order instead of chaos, might seem to working class eyes as the denial of opportunity and convenience. A bustling, growing and thriving city, changing and mushrooming with all kinds of vigorous developments, might seem more attractive than a quiet and planned stagnation (Jones 1982: 12).

The Omega Report concludes that 'there is no doubt at all that the removal of most of the planning restrictions and controls which are applied in Britain would bring major and lasting benefit to the community' (Adam Smith Institute 1985).

Some of the recommendations of libertarian and conservative critics of the planning regime, particularly those concerning the designation of non-planning zones, are similar to the views expressed by leading environmental commentators, not least Peter Hall (1977, 1983). Hall's concept of re-creating the conditions for initiative that exist in Hong Kong as a solution for Britain's depressed inner cities is explored in the next chapter, but there is little doubt that the realization of this idea in the Enterprise Zone and the groundswell of criticism against statutory controls by free-market pressure groups played a role in the government's proposals for deregulation of the planning system.

Following their election victory in 1983, the Conservative Government emphasized the benefits to society of further deregulation, especially the removal of controls on business. In 1984, a consultation paper was released proposing the introduction of 'simplified planning zones'—areas, designated by local authorities, where there would be a minimum of planning controls (DoE 1984). The justification for this experiment in deregulation was presented in a report from the Department of Trade and Industry, 'Burdens on Business', that catalogued the costs to business of 'complying' with government regulation (DTI 1985). The speed at which planning decisions were made (or not made) was the key issue and, hence, a form of automatic planning consent in particular areas was advocated as an alternative. These ideas were later contained in a White Paper, entitled *Lifting the Burden*, which articulated the government's position very clearly:

The amount of regulation which new and established firms face acts as a brake on enterprise and the wealth and job creating process. Deregulation means two things. First, freeing markets and increasing the opportunities for competition. Second, lifting administrative and legislative burdens which take time, energy and resources from fundamental business activity (HMSO 1985: para. 1.5).

The White Paper examined deregulation across a range of topics but 'Planning and Enterprise' was singled-out for the most comprehensive recommendations for legislative reform. These and other measures were part of a general simplification of bureaucratic control over development:

while deregulatory measures . . . are important, the key objective must be to keep the planning process simple—to avoid over-elaboration and unnecessary detail in development plans, and to concentrate on the essentials in dealing with applications . . . Deregulation does not imply only the abolition of unnecessary controls. It also means achieving simplicity and efficiency in the way that necessary control is carried out (HMSO 1985: para. 3.14).

Issuing draft guidelines, government reaffirmed its belief that deregulation was a key element in achieving urban regeneration:

Simplified planning zones are based on the planning regime successfully pioneered in the Enterprise Zones. They provide planning authorities with a new method of attracting private investment to areas in need of development or regeneration. For developers and landowners, they provide the certainty of knowing what types of development can be carried out in an area. They save the authority and developers the work and expense involved in making and processing individual planning applications (Waldegrave 1987: 6).

These changes effectively shifted responsibility for certain types of environ-mental change on to the developer, the property owner, and the individual. A high priority is thus given to private (often commercial) interests with a commensurate diminution in collective or community (often welfare) interests. Furthermore, these changes were intended to achieve a general relaxation of controls on the land and property market. Lloyd points to the significant implications for urban communities: 'Simplified planning zones are likely to be located according to market pressures, that is, areas which offer the greatest potential return for property developers' (Lloyd 1987: 10–11). Thus, the proposed planning policies were intended to encourage private property development but, at the same time, they may impose additional environmental and social costs on communities least able to respond.

The strategy of privatism, begun in 1979 then extended after 1983, had a dual purpose. On the one hand, measures were introduced to change atti-tudes and opinions and hence the climate within which British industry and commerce would develop. On the other hand, government policy and programs were carefully designed to support private enterprise and reduce the role and importance of the state as the guardian of community interests.

The Pattern of Policy Initiative

While the Thatcher Government's general domestic policy of privatization had significant implications for cities, there was also an intent to realign formal urban policy to correspond to the needs of a market culture. The proclaimed objectives, according to Conservative Secretary of State Michael Heseltine, were to inject commercial principles into city government and to 'encourage to the maximum possible extent the investment of private sector finance in profitable ventures that relate to the areas of (urban) deprivation' (Heseltine 1983: 3). Because the Conservative Government inherited an urban policy framework already compatible with its commitment to privatism, the instruments and mechanics of urban policy remained much the same after 1979. However, the principal actors and the policy objectives were often quite different.

The partnership between central and local governments was reinterpreted as a partnership between the government and the private sector, entities which presumably shared a common interest in economic growth and pros-perity. 'While the partnership of government continues to pay lip service to the deprivation-oriented strategy,' Stewart and Underwood point out, 'the partnership of interest pushes ahead with an economic development pro-gramme' (Stewart and Underwood 1983: 149). This orientation was reinforced by the election victory in 1983, and it has contributed to the erosion of local public authority *vis-à-vis* both central government and the private sector. By redefining the terms of partnership, the Thatcher Government has redefined and reduced the scope of local autonomy. In effect, the policy of privatization has resulted in increased centralization.

Given that the stage for policy redirection was set prior to 1979, it is not surprising that Secretary Heseltine did not immediately initiate a major review of urban policy. His first statement on the matter accepted much of the existing program and the available policy machinery but took the opportunity to emphasize the potential role of the private sector: 'there must be a place for individual initiative and enterprise to get on the move' (DoE 1979: 1). Concerning the details of the Urban Programme, he reaffirmed the need to 'ensure that the balance of programmes is influenced by people employed other than in the public sector' (DoE 1979: 1). His overall objective for inner-city policy was 'for local authorities to bring about in the depressed areas the conditions which will encourage the private sector to come in, on a large scale' (DoE 1979: 1). Moreover, he urged local government to give assistance to industry and commerce, and in particular to speed-up the development control system: 'thousands of jobs every night are locked away in the filing trays of planning departments' (Heseltine 1979: 27). The removal of bureaucratic blockage 'is vital to the economic future of this country as well as to the creation and maintenance of a satisfactory environment' (Heseltine 1979: 28).

Privatism became a constant theme running through Conservative urban policy. At every opportunity, in Parliament, in the press, and on public platforms, various Secretaries of State and an army of junior Ministers proclaimed the importance of the private sector in rebuilding urban Britain. In his forward to a booklet on urban redevelopment, Ian Gow, one-time Minister of State for Housing and Construction, stated that:

The task of renewal is not one for Government alone. The private sector has a key role to play. Governments or local authorities may own land, and they can often act as the catalyst, by providing financial help to bridge the gap between what is needed and what is commercially viable. But the private sector has the local knowledge and the market experience to plan and carry out new developments on the ground (Gow n.d.).

And three years on, concluding a debate on the inner cities introduced by a Conservative back-bencher who asked that the House recognize the need for a partnership between the private and the public sectors in urban renewal, Mrs. Rumbold, Under-Secretary of State for Environment, reaffirmed her government's faith in the private sector:

The Government are guided by four main principles in targeting assistance on inner cities. First, they seek to target assistance on the most needy areas where results can be seen, and stimulus given to wider regeneration. Secondly, the Government are convinced that it is of great assistance to keep regulation and intervention by central and local Government to a minimum. That concentrates activity on creating the right climate for investment and enterprise. Thirdly, we must build up business confidence by tackling dereliction, by pump-priming investment and by improving local labour skills. The Government have consciously made efforts to improve all these aspects.

Fourthly, we want to help to make urban areas places where people want to live and industry wants to be . . . At the heart of our urban strategy is the recognition that to achieve the regeneration of inner city areas, priority must be given to creating a climate in which the private sector is encouraged, and the spirit of enterprise and innovation is engendered (HANSARD, Session 1985/6, vol. 97, col. 1024).

The Thatcher Government's approach to privatizing urban Britain was reflected in the shifting priorities of the central government financing of both national urban programs and local governments. The pattern of funding after 1979 not only demonstrates the commitment to market-driven economic development but, equally important, the intent to alter the relationship between central and local government. The privatization of urban policy was pursued in a manner that increased the direct guidance of urban change by central ministries or their agencies and reduced the role of local authorities. This move towards centralization was reinforced by the imposition of central controls over local authority spending and local revenue raising powers. While seeking to reduce the level of public expenditure for cities, central government sought to retain maximum control over the distribution and management of the funds that remained.

Early in 1981, the government reaffirmed its commitment to an Urban Programme and, indeed, introduced a modest increase in funding from £232 million in 1980/1 to £283 million in 1981/2 and £418 in 1982/3 (Table 6.1). Once again, government emphasized the primary role that the private sector should play: 'Our aim remains to make these places [the inner city] where people want to live and work, and where the private investor is prepared to put his money' (DoE 1981*a*). A significant sharpening of policy was introduced through Ministerial Guidelines on the Partnerships issued in July of 1981. These made explicit the change from the original social/community objectives of the Urban Programme to that of economic regeneration allied to capital growth rather than revenue spending: 'The main thrust of inner area programmes must be towards removing obstacles to creating and sustaining a flourishing local economy, for on that all else depends. There must be a presumption in favour of projects which have as their objective the stimulation of economic activity' (DoE 1981*b*). And in evangelistic tones, the Guidelines exhorted local government, 'to seize imaginative projects which will lift the sights of people living and investing in inner areas' (DoE 1981*b*). Although the private sector was not formally integrated into the individual Partnership arrangement, these Guidelines made it very clear that government approval for Urban Programme funding depended on full consultation with a suitable representative of the private sector, normally a member of the local Chamber of Commerce. In evidence to the House of Commons Environment Committee, Heseltine went so far as to state that, 'we would not operate the Partnerships unless the private sector was brought in and consulted about the changes that took place' (Environment Committee 1983: 149). Heseltine's comment underscores the criticism that the Partnerships represented a highly bureaucratic response to urban problems (Parkinson and Wilks 1983). Despite the involvement of central and local politicians, the

TABLE 6.1. *Urban Programme and Derelict Land Grant (England and Wales): Resources in £M (Outturn), 1978/9–1986/7*

	1978/9		1979/80		1980/1		1981/2		1982/3		1983/4		1984/5		1985/6		1986/7[d]	
	£	%	£	%	£	%	£	%	£	%	£	%	£	%	£	%	£	%
Partnership Authorities[a]	37	31.4	110	53.1	116	50.0	118	41.7	143	34.2	133	28.2	131	27.3	125	26.0	127	—
Programme Authorities	2	1.7	32	15.5	47	20.3	50	17.7	77	18.4	86	18.2	97	20.2	96	20.6	102	—
Other Designated Districts	2	1.7	3	1.4	6	2.6	5	1.8	9	2.2	8	1.7	8	1.7	10	2.1	9	—
Traditional Urban Programme[b]	56	47.5	30	14.5	33	14.2	42	14.8	47	11.2	53	11.2	47	9.8	44	9.2	37	—
Urban Development Corporations	—	0.0	—	0.0	—	0.0	38	13.4	62	14.8	94	19.9	89	18.5	86	17.9	NA	—
Urban Development	—	0.0	—	0.0	—	0.0	—	0.0	—	0.0	7	1.5	15	3.1	22	4.6	25	—
Derelict Land Grant	21	17.8	22	10.6	30	12.9	30	10.6	61	14.6	68	14.4	70	14.6	78	16.3	83	—
Other[c]	—	0.0	10	4.8	—	0.0	—	0.0	19	4.5	23	4.9	23	4.8	20	4.2	19	—
TOTAL	118	100.0	207	100.0	232	100.0	283	100.0	418	100.0	472	100.0	480	100.0	481	100.0	402	—

[a] Estimated figures.
[b] Traditional Urban Programme figures for 1978/9 include allocation for Programme Authorities and Other Designated Districts.
[c] Includes funding for the Merseyside Task Force, Garden Festivals, inner-city research, etc.
[d] Final allocation.

Source: Data provided by the Inner-Cities Directorate, DoE.

TABLE 6.2.   *Balance of Planned Urban Programme Expenditure by Partnership and Programme Authorities, 1979/80–1986/7 (in percentages)*

	79/80	80/1	81/2	82/3	83/4	84/5	84/5[a]	86/7[a]	86/7[a]
Economic	29	30	31	37	37	38	(34)	33	38
Environmental	19	18	25	27	25	20	(18)	19	16
Social	51	52	44	36	38	42	(40)	39	38
Housing	NA	NA	NA	NA	NA	NA	(8)	9	9
TOTAL	99	100	100	100	100	100	(100)	100	101

[a] Figures from 1987 report which separated housing management innovations and external improvements, and special needs housing into a separate housing category.

Source: DoE 1986*a*, 1987*a*.

Partnership system came to be dominated by civil servants and local government officials, effectively preventing a wider involvement by other potential partners.

It is likely that the changes in the Urban Programme's focus were, in part, the result of a review of three Inner City Partnerships in 1980. Independent teams (with all but one member representing commercial organizations) scrutinized the efficacy of policy in Liverpool, Manchester/Salford, and Newcastle/Gateshead using criteria acceptable to business and private development interests. Called the 'Team of Three' reports, they offered Ministers a 'mix of laudatory and semi-critical comments on partnerships' (Stewart and Underwood 1983: 142). Their recommendations were to surface again and again over all seven Partnerships, so much so, that by 1986 research commissioned by the DoE 'highlighted the improvements in business confidence resulting from Urban Programme assistance, mainly in the form of environmental improvement and direct financial assistance'[17] (DoE 1986b: 13).

Table 6.2 shows evidence of modest financial redirection in Urban Programme support for the Partnership and Programme authorities between 1979 and 1987 with expenditure on social projects falling from 51 percent of the total budget in 1979/80 to 38 percent in 1986/7. By contrast, spending on economic projects grew from 29 to 38 percent over the same period. These aggregate figures obscure differences in the spatial allocation of funds for different types of projects. Expenditure was lower in Liverpool, Hackney, and Islington than in Manchester, Birmingham, and Newcastle. In addition, much expenditure on so-called economic projects, was used for buildings, often involving the construction of factories, improved access, site reclamation, and other physical projects. Training or other help for the unemployed, direct assistance to firms, and business promotion accounted for a small proportion of the overall total (less than 15 percent) and an even lower proportion of the expenditure on economic projects in specific Partnerships. Similar figures can be found in the shift in spending by the Scottish Development Agency in its program of Area Projects for some of the most distressed communities in Scotland.

This new emphasis was given further support in the recommendations of the Financial Institutions Group (FIG) established by Heseltine as one of his responses to the urban riots in the summer of 1981. The FIG proposals, allied with internal pressure from the Treasury to refocus the Urban Programme and introduce better monitoring of expenditure and measurement of output, served to realign the main component of urban policy firmly in support of private industry, and with particular benefits to the property development and construction industries.

The theme of assisting the private sector to improve the local economy re-emerged in 1985 when a new set of Ministerial Guidelines were issued for Partnership and Programme Authority areas. These stated that,

the unemployment, physical dereliction and social stress in the inner cities cannot be tackled by the public sector alone. Involvement of the private sector and the community is essential ... Ministers expect a continued presumption in favour of economic projects; those which stimulate wealth creation, increase economic activity and employment opportunities, bring idle assets of land and buildings back into use, remove obstacles to development and investment, and improve business confidence (DoE 1985c: 1).

Furthermore, the Guidelines made reference to the public sector crowding-out the market.

Urban Programme provision of industrial premises by conversion or new building will be limited to types of premises which the private sector cannot provide in the areas concerned without public sector support. Local authorities should carefully consider the effect of intervention in the property market and should avoid schemes which undercut or deter private sector provision (DoE 1985c: 2).

The efficiency of urban programs became a preoccupation of central government especially after 1982. The Treasury played a leading role in this through its insistence that the DoE introduce a more sophisticated 'Guidelines Monitoring System' in order that the Urban Programme might deliver better 'value for money'. The DoE eventually responded with its own Urban Porgramme Management Initiative (UPMI)—employing a complex set of output measures to evaluate the achievement of stated objectives within each project receiving public support. UPMI was introduced at a time when the whole Urban Programme was under threat. The National Audit Office (NAO) was far from complimentary about the cost effectiveness of the Urban Programme. In its search for value for money the NAO

could not satisfy itself ... that appraisal and monitoring by the department was adequate for it to be certain that the authorities have given sufficient attention to strategies for dealing with local problems, to the assessment of priorities for action, and to efficiency and cost effectiveness of projects against quantified or, as appropriate, qualitative but well-defined objectives (NAO 1985: 1).

These and other criticisms from NAO were repeated in a report from the Committee of Public Accounts that expressed dissatisfaction with the economic performance of the Urban Programme (Committee of Public Accounts 1986a). Hence, the DoE was under considerable pressure from a Cabinet striving to cut public expenditure and also from Treasury accountants and their relentless search for 'value for money'.

Pressures for expenditure cutbacks and greater cost-effectiveness from government allocations also directly impacted on the general financing of local government. Indeed, local government financing became one of the most intractable political issues of the Thatcher Government. Reducing the issue to the barest essentials, the Treasury and the DoE had two main priorities: to keep local authority expenditure within overall public expenditure targets and to keep down local rates (property taxes) as part of their counter-inflation policy. This led central government into direct and bitter conflict with local councils—initially the high-spending, mainly Labour, urban councils, then later Tory controlled Counties and Districts. Central government's pursuit of its two policy priorities had direct and immediate impacts on local government. First, government attempted to transfer the burden for local spending on to the local rates (tax), reversing a trend towards higher and higher central funding of local expenditure.[18] Local councils suffered a penalty if they set a tax rate beyond the level fixed by Whitehall, resulting in reduced central government financial support. The Local Government Finance Act of 1982 made raising a 'supplementary rate' illegal in England and Wales and, furthermore, local councils over-spending in one financial year were duly penalized in the next. Central government also introduced strict control over the amount of capital expenditure incurred by local councils. This was imposed through restricting the borrowing limits of local authorities. In summary, the impact of central policies on local government expenditure, since the mid-1970s, has been substantial cuts in local government capital spending, a small increase in revenue spending and cuts in central support for local spending. Between 1979/80 and 1985/6, average domestic rate bills doubled largely as a result of the withdrawal of central support. The net effect on cities was increased local taxation without improved local services.

The effects of the reduction in central support for local government was felt most keenly in major urban areas facing a wide range of social, economic, and physical problems. A number of studies demonstrated that urban policy, including support through the Urban Programme, had not been able to make up for the loss of basic revenue support. The analysis of the Archbishop of Canterbury's Commission report, *Faith in the City*, showed that between 1981/2 and 1984/5, Partnership authorities—the most deprived cities in England—suffered a 22 percent cut in RSG (Archbishop of Canterbury's Commission 1985: 177–85). At the same time, their share of the resources allocated through the Urban Programme barely increased at all (Table 6.3). Lawless (1981), Lansley (1982), Rees and Lambert (1985), and the TCPA (1986) offer similar analyses demonstrating that the impact of the Urban Programme was diluted by the sharp cuts in general public expenditure. At the individual city level, the same story is repeated. Between 1979/80 and 1983/4 inner London received £261 million through the Urban Programme while losing £865 in RSG and reduced housing subsidies; over the same period Manchester City gained, in real terms, an extra £9 million via the Urban Programme while losing some £100 million in reduced RSG settlements (TCPA 1986: 9). Taking just one example in Scotland, between the arrival of the Conservative Government in 1979 and the end of the financial year 1984/5, Motherwell—a major steel town in the declining industrial heartland—was effectively prevented from undertaking capital investment in the order of £30 million by central government imposition of limits on local authority borrowing. This was almost equivalent to the whole of the Scottish Development Authority (SDA) input to the 'Motherwell Project', the Scottish equivalent of an Inner City Partnership. And, over the same period, Motherwell lost a cumulative £33 million in RSG and Housing Support (Keating and Boyle 1986: 92–3).

TABLE 6.3. *Rate Support Grant to Partnership and Programme Authorities, 1981/2–1984/5* (in £M)

			Change in grant	
	1981/2	1984/5	Money terms	Real terms (DoE deflator)
Partnership Authorities	650	606	– 44	– 143 (– 0.22%)
Programme Authorities	1,012	1,056	44	– 127 (– 0.13%)

Source: Archbishop of Canterbury's Commission 1985: 178; based on submission from the DoE.

The outcome was perhaps inevitable. Councils involved with the Urban Programme redirected resources to fund mainstream spending. Capital programs were delayed or simply abandoned. At best, a proportion of the revenue raised by the sale of capital assets was maneuvered, where possible, into paying for a falling number of new capital projects, hence locking the most deprived cities into a downward spiral of resource depletion. The Archbishop of Canterbury's Commission (1985) reached the pessimistic conclusion that even a greatly enhanced Urban Programme would have little more than a marginal impact if the downward trend in mainstream government grant (RSG) was to continue. The Town and Country Planning Association called for an end to government's practice of giving to deprived cities with one hand and taking away with the other:

What is really needed is a conscious and coordinated strategy that will link the work of all Government departments and synchronize their goals, now so often at variance . . . There should be no more nonsense of [urban] programme authorities risking rate capping for taking money to spend on city problems. There should be no such absurdity as resource depleted local authorities in inner city areas facing the withdrawal of more and more of the support they need from national resources of finance (TCPA 1985: 37).

Central government was well aware of the cross-pressures being created for cities, but pinned its defense to the idea that by shifting the emphasis of the Urban Programme and initiating new policy it could thus attract private resources to fill the void. At the same time, the Thatcher Government reminded local authorities that the privatization of urban Britain meant that cities must help themselves. Self-help was a key theme as the Conservatives entered their third term, and cities in economic distress were warned that they could not simply wait for central government or the private sector to come to their rescue. Lord Young, appointed Secretary of State for Trade and Industry at the beginning of Mrs. Thatcher's third term, told poverty stricken areas shortly after coming to office:

You'll have to accept the world as it is. Any large employer faced with the choice of a green-field site or the inner city over the last 10 years has tended to choose the green field . . . We want to see managed workshops in which people in the inner city can start up small businesses, co-operatives and go into self-employment (*The Times*, (London) 24 June 1987).

Thus, the policy themes of the new privatism—the economic diagnosis of the urban problem, the concentrated attention on private sector regeneration, the emphasis on civic self-help, and the more dominant and directive role of central government in relationship to local authorities—combined to present British cities with a daunting task. On the one hand, Conservative urban policy assumed that a prosperous private sector would encourage the economic growth of the cities. On the other hand, cities were warned that neither the private sector nor the central government would bail them out of their predicaments and that they need to muster their own dwindling resources to pull themselves up through 'bootstrap' privatism. Just how this was to be done has not been at all clear. Indeed, the situation has not been designed to make cities more self-reliant but, rather, more dependent on central government. As *The Economist* pointed out shortly after Mrs. Thatcher's re-election for a third term in June 1987, 'already, around 45 percent of the money to pay for English councils' net current spending (55 percent in Scotland, 65 per cent in Wales) comes from central government' (*The Economist*, 27 June 1987: 14). Moreover, proposals introduced by the government at the beginning of the third term will surely make pressures on cities even more severe. The government proposed that local business rates be replaced with a uniform national rate. The money generated by the national rate would be disbursed by central government. At the same time, the government proposed that household rates be replaced with a community charge on all adults—in effect a poll tax.[19] It was argued that this new tax would be difficult and costly to administer, and more severely regressive; a tax on people rather than property. Whatever the outcome of these proposals, they clearly indicate the Thatcher Government's intent to gain greater control over local affairs. Nonetheless, the Conservative Government argued that if its privatization policies are effective, everyone will be winners.

Notes

1. Eversley notes that, until the late 1960s, 'good planning meant . . . an intensification of official attempts to persuade industries to move out of cities, to new and expanded towns, to development areas, or in suitable cases to almost any location where land was zoned for industry and labour was either available or likely to be attracted. The emphasis between these types of location changed; the movement did not' (Eversley 1980: 462).
2. Cullingworth points to a classic exposition of this view by the President of the Board of Trade, Reginald Maudling in 1959: 'We should start from the assumption that the economic and industrial expansion of the country should proceed freely in response to growing and changing consumer demand, and that it should proceed on the principle of the most effective use of our national resources . . . This principle of the most effective use of our resources must clearly be mitigated in

some cases by Government action to deal with certain social consequences which the nation does not regard as acceptable' (House of Commons Debates, 9 Nov. 1959, as cited in Cullingworth 1985: 301).

3. Not only were there shifts in emphasis, but there was increasing confusion regarding the Programme's conception and procedure. The objectives were never clearly specified and its extreme flexibility meant it could be used in any social field at anytime (Cullingworth 1985: 277).

4. The Comprehensive Community Programme (CCP), introduced by the Home Office in 1974, was an experimental attempt to coordinate service provision between government departments and improve coordination between the different levels of government in areas experiencing acute levels of urban deprivation. Despite plans to have 100 area-based initiatives spread throughout the country, only two, in Gateshead and Motherwell, were formally launched (Rees and Lambert 1985: 131). Lawless suggests that the CCP represented the beginning of a new 'partnership' in urban policy but that the experiment was severely under resourced. The CCP experiment was overtaken by the major urban policy initiatives announced in 1978 (Lawless 1981: 88–90).

5. Following the report of a Working Party chaired by Lord Crowther, the Chancellor of the Exchequer accepted their recommendation of competition credit control. In order to expand the economy and stimulate capital investment in industry, he instructed the banks to relax lending restrictions. 'As a direct result of these measures, the money supply . . . increased from the middle of 1971 to the middle of 1972 by 25 per cent' (Rose 1985: 233).

6. The National Enterprise Board (NEB) was established under the Industry Act of 1975 to intervene in areas of high unemployment, in shipbuilding, and in the emerging oil industry. The NEB was not as powerful as originally envisaged in the 1974 Manifesto. In particular, its funding of £250 million was considered well short of what was required for effective state intervention in the national economy. The introduction of Planning Agreements, however, did formalize the concept of developing industrial sectoral strategies.

7. The Community Land Act (CLP)1975 introduced the Community Land Scheme giving local authorities the power and the duty to acquire all land needed for 'relevant' development at a market value less Development Land Tax (DLT). If set at 100 percent, a local authority theoretically could acquire land at the original price paid by the vendor. The CLA was one of the first pieces of legislation repealed by the Conservative Government in 1979.

8. The National Front is a fringe party on the extreme right of the political spectrum in Britain. Its key policies are concerned with race, including support for strict immigration control and the repatriation of ethnic minorities. It has never secured a seat in Parliament but has, on occasion, won seats in local elections, mainly in the West Midlands and in London.

9. Murray Stewart notes this was a direct challenge to the dominant role of the Board of Trade/Department of Industry in job location policy in the post-war period (Stewart 1987: 131).

10. The Local Government (Social Need) Act 1969 was introduced through the (Traditional) Urban Programme. Projects were organized by local authorities themselves or by voluntary organizations. 'Urban aid' was allocated on a competitive basis to designated authorities. Central government funded 75 percent of the cost of the projects, initially for a period of four years. In the early years, the Urban Programme funded projects primarily in social work, health, and education but

later policy dictated a shift in emphasis that included supporting economic and employment projects.

11. Although the Urban Programme was originally designed to offer grant assistance to local authorities in urban areas of special social need, the legislation and the bureaucratic procedures were adapted to implement the organizational arrangements introduced after the 1977 White Paper on the *Inner Cities*. Moreover, the same arrangements were employed to fund an increasing proportion of economic projects (see Table 6.2). For the next ten years, the Urban Programme (in England) was composed of: (1) the Traditional Urban Programme (absorbing 11.6 percent of funding in 1986/7); (2) Partnership Authorities (39.8 percent); (3) Programme Authorities (32.0 percent); and (4) Other Designated Districts (2.8 percent).

12. Increasingly, the provision of local authority housing is not to serve 'general' needs but is to provide accommodation for 'special needs': the elderly, the infirm, the handicapped, or single people returning to the community after a period of institutionalization. The other main client of public housing will become those families unable to join the 'property-owning democracy'—the poor and unemployed, minority groups, and others whose income excludes them from the market (Donnison and Ungerson 1982: 160–3).

13. In effect, the housing assets represented by council estates would be transferred from council ownership to housing trusts funded directed by central government.

14. Industrial Development Certificates (IDCs) were established by government in 1945/7 to control the location of industry. To develop or expand, all companies were required to obtain an IDC from central government. For three decades, there was a policy of restricting the supply of IDCs in London and inner-Birmingham in an attempt to encourage the dispersal of manufacturing industry to the Assisted Areas in Wales, Scotland, and the north of England. In the late 1970s, there was a strong lobby from the West Midlands to repeal the Certificate or, at least, to remove the restrictions. It was argued that this policy had weakened the industrial competitiveness of the Midlands as firms had been forced to relocate (Lawless 1981: 21, 174–5). And there was a related argument that this arm of regional policy played some part in creating the urban problems of the 1980s, as policy acted against companies seeking to invest in the inner city. IDCs were abolished after the review of regional policy in 1984.

15. Control over office development in Britain was first imposed in 1964 by George Brown (Labour minister responsible), hence the term 'Brown Ban' on office construction in London. In 1967, the Office Development Permit (ODP) was formally introduced as part of regional policy in an attempt to control office expansion in London and 'push' service industries into the Assisted Areas. ODPs were abolished in 1979.

16. The National Insurance surcharge—effectively a tax on employment—was finally abolished in 1984.

17. 'Area focused approaches such as Industrial Improvement Areas (IIAs) proved to be most effective in this respect with about half of the firms questioned expressing confidence in area and over £1.1 million investment generated from the private sector in the IIAs studied. Environmental and direct support schemes which improved the sites and premises of inner city firms also helped to enhance the firms' images in between 80 and 90 percent of cases' (DoE 1986b: 13).

18. In 1975, rates accounted for 24.5 percent of Local Authority income; Rate Support Grant. (RSG) from central government accounted for 47.8 percent. In 1984, 31 percent of income came from the rates, 42.9 percent from RSG (CSO 1987).

Despite this shift, grants from central government are more critical to local funding in Britain than in other European countries (Karran 1986).

19. The Green Paper, *Paying for Local Government*, advocated increasing central control over non-domestic rates (property taxes), replacing local rates with a new poll tax: 'The Community Charge' (DoE 1986c). This is to be based on a flat rate paid by all adults in place of the existing tax that is only (directly) paid by home owners. The central premise is that there should be a clear link between local finance and local taxation and that a larger proportion of the electorate should face the taxation consequences of local spending. The Community Charge will be introduced first in Scotland (1989) then in England and Wales, phased over four years from 1991.

The Community Charge is likely to have a significant impact on household expenditure but will also have a macro effect on urban structure. At the personal level, it is estimated that 10 percent of all households will face increases in local taxes and as the rebate system has also been revised (the maximum rebate is set at 80 percent), the poorest adults in the community are likely to feel the regressive effects of this new tax (Helm and Smith 1987). Those families most likely to suffer will be resident in major cities, particularly in London.

Whatever the merits of the poll tax, Hughes has estimated that the abolition of domestic rates will lead to an average 25 percent increase in house prices, particularly in areas where larger owner-occupied properties currently attract a high rateable value (Hughes 1987).

7

Privatism and Urban Regeneration in Britain

THE severity of the economic recession in 1980–1 and its effect on British cities played a key role in creating a new urban economic agenda. By 1982, the national unemployment rate had risen to over 12 percent, more than double the rate which, only five years earlier, had helped to bring about the new inner-cities policy. Moreover, the rates of unemployment in traditional industrial areas of England and Scotland were much higher—14 percent in Scotland, nearly 15 percent in the West Midlands, and nearly 17 percent in the north of England (CSO 1987: 114). There was also a heavy concentration of unemployment among residents of the inner-city areas and the peripheral public housing estates[1] of cities such as Liverpool and Glasgow. Male unemployment was nearly 25 percent in Glasgow and 40 percent in the city's peripheral areas of Drumchapel and Easterhouse. In a major analysis of British inner cities, the Economic and Social Research Council concluded that despite fifteen years of initiatives in urban policy,

the issues confronted by inner cities policies remain. Recession has increased the number of those who have been drawn into an under-class of the unemployed and disadvantaged which is still disproportionately found in inner areas. Disinvestment, especially by manufacturing industry, has increased the state of dereliction faster than ameliorative policies have brought land into productive use (Hausner and Robson 1985: 34).

The recession was a contributing factor to the serious social disorders throughout areas of urban Britain in the spring and summer of 1981. There were riots and civil disorders in Brixton (London), Toxteth (Liverpool), and Moss Side (Manchester). The outbreak of violence was attributed to a variety of causes including 'over-aggressive policing (especially to the West Indians of Brixton), chronic high youth unemployment, and frustration at the ineffectiveness of inner city policies over more than a decade' (Home 1982: 15–16). The Scarman Report on the Brixton disorders focused on policing but social and economic circumstances, particularly housing conditions, were also considered. The report concluded that a coordinated attack on urban problems was required (1981).

The recession and its impact on British cities was a national problem, requiring national solutions. Not only did it lead to a concentration of national policy on economic issues, it had a profound effect on the implementation of urban policy and the role of local government. Based on earlier research material, the DoE advanced the view that without local economic development the future for the deprived British city would remain very bleak. Moreover, the concern with economic issues increasingly focused the attention of policymakers on questions of efficiency and competitiveness and on the failure of earlier urban policy to arrest urban economic decline (Stewart and Underwood 1983; Young and Mason 1983).

Not only was the emphasis on economic regeneration but the proposals to accomplish it were consistent with the Conservative Government's general policy of privatization. In the aftermath of the riots in Liverpool, Secretary of the Environment Michael Heseltine organized the Financial Institutions Group—a team of managers from leading banks, building societies, insurance companies, and pension funds—to 'develop new approaches and ideas for securing urban regeneration', and to increase 'private sector involvement in urban questions' (Environment Committee 1983: 5). The Group advocated a number of proposals: the Urban Development Grant (UDG), modelled on the US Urban Development Action Grant program; a property service company entitled Inner City Enterprises Ltd. to identify investment opportunities in the inner city which might not otherwise be considered by financial institutions; and the extension of the role of building societies in home repair and improvements through Agency Housing Services, a program similar to the neighborhood housing services widely used in the US.

While a variety of program initiatives were introduced by the government to carry forward the philosophy of injecting private resources into the inner city, few additional funds were made available to finance new programs. Rather, existing and amended legislation was used to shift the priorities of urban programs so that they focused more directly on economic issues. Ignoring cuts in the Rate Support Grant, government exhorted local authorities to direct their efforts at local economic regeneration, providing, that is, they kept strictly to the traditional areas of urban improvement in land and property development, access, and the environment. Central government promoted local programs that addressed economic distress but, at the same time, were ideologically compatible with Conservative commitments to privatization. Arguments about efficiency and privatization were also used to support the downgrading of traditional regional policy that was originally designed to assist manufacturing industry outside of London and the West Midlands. Following the 1979 recession, government announced a series of changes to its package of regional incentives: the size of the designated areas was reduced and the scale of funding narrowed; there was a shift from automatic to discretionary assistance; a cost per job ceiling was imposed on the level of grant made available; and new regional development organizations were encouraged to sponsor increased public–private cooperation (Lever 1987; Roberts and Noon 1987).

A long-term objective of the Thatcher Government's privatization policies for cities was to displace the influence of the planning regime on urban change. But Conservative antipathy towards planned urban development and its enthusiasm for the marketplace was not accompanied by a willingness to relax central control over the direction of urban policy. Rather, a major, if not always explicit, theme of urban policy under the Thatcher Government was policy centralization. Efforts intended to roll back the state, remove regulations, reduce planning requirements, and free the marketplace were accompanied by attempts to increase central government control over the implementation of urban redevelopment programs. The combination of privatization with policy centralization appears to be a contradiction. Yet, in light of its commitment to a facilitative economic policy requiring the state to intervene where and when the market dictates, government sought to justify specific and detailed involvement in urban projects. Moreover, the perceived connection between national economic policy and local economic development created an additional rationale for central government to increase direct control. Direct involvement also afforded central government an opportunity to insure that the private sector would be integral to both policy-making and implementation at the local level. Better to tighten control, the government reasoned, and win the support of the financial, business, and development communities than to encourage further profligacy and extremism by Labour controlled and socialist inspired urban authorities. The Conservative policy interests would be better served by direct control from Whitehall, than by giving additional resources and powers to a collection of, what many in the Conservative Party and the government considered to be, incompetent, left-leaning local councils.

Another theme running through urban economic development efforts was the encouragement and direct sponsorship of public–private partnerships by both central government and local authorities. The partnership concept enjoyed support not only from Conservative Government officials but often from leaders of opposition parties. In response to a new round of urban riots in 1985, David Owen, leader of the Social Democratic Party, argued that public–private partnerships were essential for urban regeneration. New local political and institutional arrangements were needed which would

enable new partnerships to be forged between business and the community at the local level, and between national government, local authorities and the private sector to work for the economic revival of inner city areas. This partnership is now the *only way* to revitalize the inner-cities . . . The UK urgently needs a long-term strategy for urban renewal which will mobilize public and private sector investment for the economic and financial revival of its major cities (Owen 1985: 24).

The enthusiasm for partnerships was based in large part on the frequently cited achievements of these arrangements in US cities. Partnership advocates argued that renewed entrepreneurial spirit enabled cities such as Baltimore, Pittsburgh, Minneapolis, and San Francisco to regenerate their local economies, and they cited American programs such as UDAG and the Reagan administration's Task Force on Private Sector Initiatives as models for Britain. Debates in the House of Commons, government reports, technical documents, professional conferences, and academic publications all promoted the benefits of the US style public–private partnership.

Public–private partnerships became a politically acceptable umbrella for rationalizing a wide array of different program initiatives at both the central and local government levels. The British interpretation of the public–private partnership was loosely based on the premise that the objectives of urban policy could be best achieved by combining scarce public resources with the much larger reserves of investment capital at the disposal of private institutions. In this way, government could not only maximize the impact of its own investment but, by acting in concert with the private sector, could induce private capital into locations and communities previously abandoned by the market. Furthermore, by attaching demands for partnership arrangements to central government support for local programs, central government could direct a broad pattern of privatization at the local level. In line with this, central government programs for local economic development encouraged a competition between communities for the limited central subsidies available. In addition, the promotion of partnerships was intended to foster a receptive attitude by local government in their dealings with the development industry.

The British promotion of public–private partnerships relied upon much of the logic and many of the program ideas already popular in US urban economic development programs. Of particular significance were British efforts to build urban economic development programs around the principle of leverage, using the UDAG program as a model. Our review of British urban economic development programs in the 1980s begins by examining these efforts.

Leveraging Urban Regeneration

The most notable US urban policy export to Britain in the 1980s was the concept of 'leverage', particularly as it was applied in the UDAG program. It is generally held that UDAG was introduced to the British government by the Financial Institutions Group as one of their responses to the urban riots in London and Liverpool in 1981. In fact, British civil servants had been interested in UDAG since the late 1970s. In April 1980 they organized a high-level US/British conference on urban policy and subsequently arranged for the short-term transfer of professional staff between HUD and the DoE to exchange ideas on techniques such as UDAG. Even earlier, Donna Shalala, Assistant Secretary for Policy and Development at HUD during the Carter administration, advised the British government on leveraging and public–private partnerships. In light of the British enthusiasm for the concept of leverage, she cautioned that program development was a 'tricky business' and that even with a sophisticated monitoring system, HUD could never measure precisely the impact of their investment (Nathan and Webman 1980: 63).

Despite this admonition, the British Urban Development Grant program (UDG), closely following the UDAG model, was introduced in 1982. UDG was intended to be a limited capital subsidy that would induce or 'leverage' additional net private investment—or prevent disinvestment—in economically disadvantaged or distressed urban areas. The government placed considerable faith in the technique stating that it 'aims to promote the economic and physical regeneration of inner urban areas' (DoE 1985*b*). UDG was central to the realignment of urban policy. It encouraged local authorities to shift the Urban Programme to a 70 : 30 capital to revenue ratio, to concentrate resources on the economic aspects of urban regeneration, and, in addition, to directly involve the private sector in policy implementation. In line with other Urban Programme funding, UDG was paid in the form of a 75 percent grant to selected local authorities—those designated as distressed areas under the 1978 Inner Urban Areas Act or having an Enterprise Zone within their boundaries. These, in turn, would then distribute the grant to private developers. The onus for generating appropriate projects and for combining the resources of the public and private sectors fell on local government which had to ensure that projects were viable and conformed to general guidelines laid down by the DoE.

Technically, UDG was more flexible than its American counterpart. There were no formal restrictions on the type or size of project eligible for UDG support nor was there a minimum leveraging ratio; that is, a minimum amount of private financing that had to be generated in relation to the size of the government grant. Instead, the public sector contribution

should be the minimum necessary to allow the project to go ahead . . . [T]he Department wishes to see urban problems attacked by attracting private sector investment which, by injecting a public sector contribution to cover the gap between the costs of the project, and the expected return, will render projects commercially viable (Jeffrey Jacobs 1985: 193).

Following the UDAG model, central government appointed a UDG Appraisal Team—drawn largely from the private sector—whose task was to evaluate the commercial viability of all schemes submitted by local authorities. Each project was evaluated on the basis of: the nature and amount of private sector risk investment proposed; the viability of the scheme; the practical feasibility of the project; and the contribution the development would make towards improving the economic, social, or environmental conditions of the urban area.

As the program proceeded, it became apparent that the criteria driving the selection of projects was increasingly determined by the private sector partner. A senior civil servant administering UDG, John Parker, sought to justify this situation by explaining that

the private sector will only invest in urban renewal if it is persuaded that there is a return to be earned on its investment. Thus it has to be persuaded that there will be a demand for the goods and services that would be produced, or for the property that would be built . . . [T]he private sector is most likely to be enthusiastic if it thinks that it has itself spotted a market opportunity that nobody else has seen. The need to respond to market opportunities, and to harness, or to generate, private sector enthusiasm has clear implications for local authorities who want to get derelict land or difficult sites back into use (Parker 1986: 60).

To attract UDG support, local authorities had to learn to appreciate market demand. Their planning policies and land designations had 'to be flexible and responsive', and they needed to openly invite 'potential developers to say what they would like to do with the land, and on what terms' (Parker 1986: 60). Hence, UDG (as well as a bundle of other categorical grant schemes including the Derelict Land Grant and the Tourism Development Grant) was not simply a mechanism to refocus government subsidy for urban redevelopment; it was part of the restructuring of policy. Despite statements that local government must determine individual regeneration strategies, Parker argued that it is market demand that will effectively shape the content and direction of local policy. Where public planning and public resources, such as UDG, have a role to play it is in support of decisions taken by private developers, guided by commercial criteria (Parker 1986).

By March 1986, 181 proposals had received UDG assistance amounting to £85.4 million (DoE 1986a: 10). In total, this was expected to generate an estimated £354.7 million of private investment, representing a 'gearing' or leveraging ratio of 1 : 4.2. The DoE calculated that when all these projects were completed, 540 acres of land would have been improved, 3,727 houses and flats built, and almost 20,000 jobs created. If the employment estimates were correct, then UDG would prove to be one of the least expensive job creation schemes operated by the British government. The projected cost per job of £4,332, based on UDG funds only, was far less than the cost per job of Enterprise Zones (£12,000), Urban Programme grants (£6,700), and, most clearly of all, traditional Regional Policy (£40,000).

Among the 181 UDG projects, 38 percent were industrial, 34 percent were commercial (of this category, a large proportion, two-fifths, were retail developments), and 28 percent were predominantly concerned with housing. But the distribution of UDG resources illustrates a different pattern. Commercial development (offices, hotels, shopping centers) attracted 46 percent of the funds available; industrial schemes (factory or warehouse developments and business expansion projects) obtained 31 percent; and housing developments absorbed 23 percent (DoE 1986a: 10). This pattern is similar to the distribution in the UDAG program where commercial projects accounted for the largest proportion of funds (Boyle 1985).

Although UDG was available only for development that occurred in areas designated as Inner City Authorities (and in those cities with an Enterprise Zone), there was still regional variation in the take-up and allocation of funding. Based on data released by the DoE in January 1986, the West Midlands, based around Birmingham, was at the top of the list, attracting £18 million of UDG finance and leveraging in excess of £100 million of private investment. While it is difficult to identify a particular pattern, gearing or leverage ratios varied across the country—Yorkshire and Humberside having the lowest average ratio (1 : 3.4) and the Northern Region, centered around Newcastle, achieving the highest (1 : 5.2). These figures need, however, to be read with caution. In the Northern Region, for example, the financial data includes investment in a major regional shopping center, the Metro Centre. This development, estimated at a total value of £40 million, obtained a UDG of £1.55 million which financed the cost of road construction into the shopping mall. What the published data do not reveal is that the mall was located in the Newcastle/Gateshead Enterprise Zone and hence the developer received considerable additional public subsidy by not paying local property taxes. Moreover, due to its location, political significance, and scale, the Metro Centre also benefited from other public subsidies that were not included in the final accounting for the UDG.

In Scotland urban policy often has evolved somewhat differently than in England and Wales. Indeed, the program for leveraging private sector investment, equivalent to the UDG, was given a different and very distinctive name in Scotland. It was called LEG-UP (Local Enterprise Grants for Urban Projects) and was administered by the Scottish Development Agency (SDA),[2] an economic development board that has responsibility for implementing related aspects of British urban policy in Scotland. In the case of LEG-UP, the US connection has been particularly strong since a HUD official with extensive UDAG experience was for a time seconded to the SDA.

The leveraging principle in LEG-UP is the same as in UDG but the administration is somewhat different. All urban areas in Scotland (defined as towns and cities with a population larger than 15,000) are eligible, although areas experiencing economic distress are given favorable treatment. Unlike the UDG, LEG-UP is designed to stimulate private investment without any mandatory involvement by local government. Any person or company can apply for a grant providing that their project is predominantly financed by the private sector; public support simply closes a 'gap' between capital requirements and available resources. The result is that no limits are imposed on the amount of financial assistance available, although in theory, but not in practice, no more than 28 percent of the cost of any project can be financed through LEG-UP.

As in England, bids for assistance are evaluated on a competitive basis. Four factors are employed: (1) leverage—all projects must have a minimum ratio of 1 : 2.5 but the larger the proportion of private finance realized by the grant the higher the evaluation; (2) employment—the number of jobs created; (3) location—the extent to which the project will benefit distressed areas; and (4) feasibility—the ability of individual schemes to be commercially viable (Zeiger 1985). In summary, LEG-UP is a competitive scheme where support is given to projects which deliver the greatest benefits for the lowest public subsidy.

A feature of LEG-UP that demonstrates its similarity to the UDAG program is that, despite the title, grants are rarely paid to individual developers. It is more common for assistance to be provided as a loan or in some form of equity participation. The loans tend to be set below the market interest rate. Other arrangements involve profit participation where the SDA gets a return on its investment as the project becomes commercially viable (Planning Exchange 1986). Between 1983 and 1986 the focus of LEG-UP was on property development, with some 53 percent of all funds being used to support projects concerned with shopping, leisure development, hotels, and offices. Residential projects absorbed 30 percent of all the resources; 17 percent of the funds were used for industrial projects.

In marked contrast to the availability of information on the UDAG program, project details and funding data for both UDG and LEG-UP remain confidential and even program descriptions have been superficial. Where specific information has been released it tends to be used as publicity for the government (DoE 1987c; Munday and Mallinson 1983; SDA n.d.). Hence, well-informed analysis or a measured critique of either program has yet to appear. On the basis of what is known, however, some of the strengths and weaknesses of UDG and LEG-UP can be identified.

As the US experience has shown, leverage strategies find support in almost all quarters. The Thatcher Government claimed that they are effective in attracting the private investor back into the city. At the same time, local governments have encouraged leveraging programs such as UDG and LEG-UP. New hotels or shopping centers have substantial political pay-offs for local officials, and developers are always pleased to accept a grant without strings or to negotiate a cheap loan. Only the financial institutions have remained wary. UDG money, for example, 'failed to entice the financial institutions into pre-funding investment projects and many traditional investment projects which ought to have attracted institutional investment have not done so' (Mallinson 1984: 2).

Yet even the most cautious institutions have begun to look at the profits that are available from using UDG or LEG-UP for low-risk housing development. In Scotland, this has taken the form of conversions of older warehouses and other out of use property into flats intended initially for the lower end of the private housing market.[3] In England, UDG has been used to convert hard-to-let local authority housing into properties ready for sale.[4] Developers have become adept at working with building societies (equivalents of US Savings and Loans), local authorities, and central government advisors in the transfer of stock from the public to the private sector. And the availability of UDG has transformed previously modest returns on property conversion investments into substantial profit margins. This is consistent with the aims of a policy intended to make private investments attractive. Yet who benefits from these developments? Experience in different British cities—Salford, London's East End, Glasgow and elsewhere—suggests that the privatization of public housing or inner-city conversions does not address the chronic housing problems of the poor. A study in Salford indicates that the majority of purchasers of low-priced flats had already been homeowners and that the redevelopment scheme did not significantly reduce the house-waiting list (Brindley and Stoker 1987).

In Scotland, where owner-occupation is very low, LEG-UP has been successfully employed to finance the rehabilitation of bleak public housing projects. LEG-UP has subsidized the conversion of old city-center property into new owner-occupied flats and houses. But these projects are often not in the most distressed communities and many of those who buy the rehabilitated property do not suffer from economic distress. Indeed, the projects may have an adverse affect on the poor by reallocating scarce public resources from badly-needed general services and special housing projects. Those who have gained the greatest benefit from the LEG-UP property conversions are the more affluent house-buyers and the property developers themselves.

Both UDG and LEG-UP have led to the development of new skills in local government. Local officials arrange financial packages, negotiate with financiers and accountants, and work directly with the development industry. In principle, these skills may be employed to extract maximum benefit for the community from the private development industry. In practice, the exact opposite often occurs. As in the US, the key decisions are taken by the private sector and the skills of the local economic development officer are used to smooth the passage of private development, ultimately benefiting the entrepreneur but not necessarily the city or its residents (Kilpatrick and Bender 1986). This situation means that local government sometimes actually encourages reverse leverage; assisting the private sector to obtain maximum public subsidies rather than attracting private investment for community benefit.

Leverage techniques also tend to distort urban policy objectives. Both UDG and LEG-UP were conceived as instruments to address economic malaise, particularly urban unemployment. Both were intended to create jobs. In practice, however, they enhance property development and physical renewal and new employment is relegated to an ancillary result but by no means an assured outcome. In the end, the priorities of these programs are defined by the private sector and not by the local community. Hence, Mallinson (DoE's UDG Appraisal Team leader) commented to the Brick Development Association in 1984. 'do not invest in inner cities because it is good for you; invest in inner cities because there is profit in it for you' (Mallinson 1984: 10).

Even before the results of the first review of UDG, the DoE established a modified program to take on some of the characteristics of LEG-UP. The Urban Regeneration Grant (URG), introduced in the 1986 Housing and Planning Act and launched in April 1987, was intended to redress some of the perceived weaknesses in UDG. It was also responsive to the recommendations of the government-sponsored Property Advisory Group which offered advice on the UDG appraisal process and in 1983 reported on *The Climate for Public and Private Partnerships in Property Development* (PAG 1983). This report urged government to sanction and support an urban policy that measured success in terms of private property development:

We urge local authorities to concentrate much more attention on the benefits to their localities of successful private development . . . If they see their tasks in this context, local councils will the more readily identify their role in 'partnership' as helping to create the circumstances in which the private development industry, while still satisfying its own commercial criteria, can contribute to an area's economic, physical and social improvement (PAG 1983: para. 12).

The Property Advisory Group proposed that property development was the essence of local partnership: 'a local authority leasing land on ground rental terms to a private developer who then has designed, financed, built and managed the complete project, any community benefits passing to the local authority' (PAG 1983: para. 2).

In keeping with this analysis, the Regeneration Grant offered a number of advantages. First, it gave the DoE greater flexibility in that grant assistance was no longer tied to areas designated under the Inner Urban Areas Act. Second, it was paid directly to private developers with no necessity for local authority involvement. Third, it only supported physical redevelopment. Finally, it was available for site improvement, often involving more than one building. Reflecting the interests of the development industry, Baldock suggests that the URG was designed specifically to meet the development requirements of the private sector by being available for sites that offer the greatest market advantage: a 'realistically sized enclave'; in areas where private and public investment offer a good prospect of self-sustaining economic regeneration; close to the city center; and with 'actual or potential environmental ambience appropriate to its uses, e.g. water frontage for mixed-use residential, commercial and leisure developments' (Baldock 1986: 1428). As justification for this emphasis, Baldock argues that the designation of a URG project should not be based on a measure of urban distress but instead should be determined by the attractiveness of an area to the market: 'It sometimes appears that areas are defined for improvement under the Urban Programme merely because they are in poor condition, and without regard to the likely willingness of the private sector to invest in implementation. Areas which are problem-led tend to show poor results [in terms of leverage]' (Baldock 1986: 1429). In a sense, the URG scheme represented the maturing of urban policy, returning it once more to a focus on property development, enabling direct central government subsidy for urban regeneration, and providing financial support for the promotion of public–private partnerships which are not necessarily in the most acutely deprived urban areas.

Leverage techniques have redefined the priorities of urban regeneration. The result is that local governments are placed in a dilemma. If local officials utilize these techniques they face the prospect of promoting the interests of capital investment rather than the needs of the community. If they choose not to cooperate, they must turn away from one of the few available sources of support for urban development, face being stereotyped by private investors as anti-development, and risk having their community defined, in comparison with other communities, as unsuitable for business growth.

As we have already argued in the US context, leverage techniques certainly encourage private sector investment but not always in the same place or for the same reasons as intended by those who seek to rehabilitate distressed areas. The same conclusion appears to be true in Britain. Early in 1987, the DoE announced that the largest Urban Development Grant, a £6 million subsidy, had been offered to support the cost of a 314 bedroom hotel in Birmingham (Planning 1987: 708). The company involved was Hyatt-Regency, one of the beneficiaries of the UDAG program in the US.

In January 1988, the government belatedly published the results of a consultant's evaluation study of UDG (PSMRU 1988). Originally commissioned in 1985, this study provided an impact assessment and an operational review of the grant scheme. The consultants concluded that, as in the US, development proceeds much more slowly than political ambition. Out of 514 project applications submitted to the DoE by the time the survey was completed, only 22 percent of the projects in receipt of UDG funding had reached implementation. Hence, it was 'apparent that the great majority of UDG proposals were not resulting in development on the ground, due either to their inherent deficiencies as development propositions, or because of the poor quality of the applications themselves' (D. Johnson 1987: 3). The leader of the research team went further, suggesting that the gap between concept and delivery was due to a combination of the haste with which the program was conceived, inadequate skills in local government, and the 'ineptness of the private sector in putting together cogent development propositions' (D. Johnson 1987: 3). These conditions resulted in the fairly modest annual expenditure for the UDG program, with a cumulative total of £44 million by 1985/6 (see Table 6.1). Despite this low level of spending, the study team found that the implemented projects resulted in a consistently high number of new jobs ('additionality'), more than was apparent from the various assessments of UDAG.

The UDG projects achieved a leverage (or gearing) ratio of greater than 4 : 1. But when discounted (only new jobs included), the ratio fell to between 2.4 : 1 and 3.4 : 1, considerably less impressive figures than government had been claiming. Again, the experience of UDAG is repeated in terms of employment impacts, with a discrepancy between anticipated employment benefits and the actual number of new jobs created. Nonetheless, in contrast with other urban employment initiatives, an 'encouragingly high proportion of those working on UDG projects actually live in or fairly close to the inner city' (D. Johnson 1987: 12). In general, the evaluation consultants concluded that UDG

does represent a modest improvement on a do-nothing scenario. Equally, however, it scarcely represents a major response to the regeneration needs of most inner city areas . . . [The program] should be strengthened and revised, in order to enhance the quality and quantity of UDG applications and their appraisal (D. Johnson 1987: 16).

Further, they rejected the suggestions that the involvement of local government delayed the grant decisions, arguing that to eliminate local government would simply reduce an already inadequate supply of good projects.

Urban Development Corporations and the Centralization of Policy

As we have noted, the Thatcher Government's pursuit of privatization was conducted at the same time that efforts were made to centralize control of urban policy. In the area of local economic development, the initiative that drew together privatization and central control of policy was the Urban Development Corporation (UDC), a new type of agency introduced by Michael Heseltine in his 1979 urban policy statement. Direct central government involvement in urban areas had been considered before, particularly for parts of inner London, and a form of direct intervention was already in operation in Glasgow. A new stimulus for the formation of a centrally controlled agency to promote local economic development came from Liverpool where the existing Inner Area Partnership—a managerial arrangement drawing together the different local authorities with the appropriate central department—was deemed incapable of handling the severity of the problems and the complexity of urban renewal in Liverpool. Pressure from the DoE and the Treasury led initially to the selection of two urban areas as sites for UDCs: one in Liverpool, the other in the London Docklands, a location where there were good prospects for private sector participation since the docklands are within two miles of the City of London, one of the most important financial districts in the world.

Powers to designate UDCs were introduced in the Local Government, Planning and Land Act of 1980 and in the following year the Merseyside and London Docklands Development Corporations were launched. Similar in many respects to the Development Corporations that had been set up to oversee the construction of British new towns, both UDCs were given sweeping powers of development: land acquisition, environmental improvement, provision of infrastructure, land use planning, and control of development as well as responsibility for the marketing and promotion of their area. In many respects, the UDCs replaced the duties and responsibilities of the elected local authorities in that they were able to exercise a variety of powers including assistance to industry, building control, fire fighting, even public health. Both UDCs were governed by an appointed Chairman and Board and administered by a Chief Executive and a team of professional and technical staff. Both were funded through a combination of grants and borrowing through the National Loans Fund.[5] The Secretary of State exercised control over the UDCs by setting annual financial limits, approving administrative expenditure on individual items in excess of £50,000, and approving annual corporate plans.

Despite similar administrative and financial arrangements, the Merseyside and London Corporations have operated in sharply contrasting locations and reflect different objectives and aspirations. The Merseyside Development Corporation (MDC) is confined to a number of small, dockland sites covering 865 acres in Liverpool and the Wirral. In 1981 the banks of the Mersey were one of Britain's graphic testimonials to the deindustrialization of the north. The redevelopment area was a decaying industrial landscape composed of vacant, redundant wharves, warehouses, and factories surrounded by acres of derelict land. Ninety-two percent of the land was already in public ownership and the area had no resident population (Wray 1987). Proposals for redevelopment of the docks focused largely on improving, then marketing, waterfront sites for a combination of residential, commercial, and leisure uses, and providing new or upgraded industrial units should the demand arise. The development strategy, determined and largely funded by the public sector through the Merseyside Development Corporation (MDC), was to create a new and very different local economy. In place of Liverpool's historic achievements in shipbuilding, manufacturing and cargo handling, the future of the city, as defined by the Development Corporation, would lie in tourism, the leisure industry, and the service sector.

The flagship of the MDC was the redevelopment of a 125-acre site on the Mersey for the 1984 International Garden Festival. Despite hostility from the Labour-controlled city council, the festival went ahead. Central government considered the event to be highly successful, attracting some four million visitors over the summer months. The long-term benefit to the city of the £31 million spent on the festival is questionable, however. While the festival site was transformed into an attractive park with associated leisure facilities, this highly visible economic development venture did not address the deep-seated economic problems of Liverpool. Three years after the event, a private company, Transworld, had failed in its effort to operate the site as a commercial venture and, as a result of rate capping, the city council had no surplus resources to properly manage the park as a public facility. In essence, Liverpool's International Garden Festival illustrates the weakness of a local economic development policy constructed around ephemeral, transient events that offer quick and visible results but little long-term value. Despite Liverpool's difficulties, however, the garden festival model of redevelopment became an established part of British economic development policy (Balsillie 1986). Even before the Liverpool event was completed, the DoE asked other cities to compete for similar national events throughout the 1980s. And with the incentive of additional public expenditure, local government duly obliged. The festival model was replicated in Stoke on Trent in 1986 and Glasgow in 1988, Gateshead was scheduled for 1990, and South Wales for 1992.

MDC's policy of diversifying the city's economy by developing the leisure and service industries was further extended with its investment, alongside the private sector, in the renovation of the Albert Dock. This effort closely paralleled waterfront development in US cities in the late 1970s and early 1980s. Officials from the MDC and the developers of the dock made numerous visits to Baltimore and Boston to examine the mix of commercial, leisure, and residential development, the type of financing used, and the management of different components of what has become known as the festival market: a facility, developed and promoted by the Rouse Corporation, which is a common feature of many eastern seaboard waterfronts in the US. Not surprisingly, what was created on the Albert Dock bears a striking resemblance to these festival markets. Its combination of tourist facilities, leisure shopping, offices, and cultural facilities—all with an urban heritage motif—closely reflects projects in Baltimore's Inner Harbor and Boston's Quincy Market. This similarity was used by the developers as part of their promotional scheme; if Baltimore or Boston can offer these attractions then why not Liverpool? Other British waterfront cities have also followed the example—Glasgow, Swansea, Hull, and Cardiff have investigated how to replicate Baltimore's and Boston's redevelopment 'miracles'.

Wray (1987), Parkinson (1986), and Adcock (1984) have examined the effectiveness of the Albert Dock project, a feature of the city that stands in sharp contrast to the deterioration encountered elsewhere in Liverpool. The short-term results of the Albert Dock redevelopment were encouraging. All the retail units were quickly let, and the first consumer surveys indicated a positive visitor reaction. It is less clear that this initial interest can be sustained or become a catalyst for a resurgent Liverpool economy. Unlike the waterfront redevelopment areas in Baltimore and Boston, the Albert Dock is not situated at the edge of a major complex of thriving central city offices which can provide a day-to-day market. Instead, the Dock is in a declining inner-city area within one of the most depressed regions in Britain and it is far removed from the concentration of high-income households in southeast Britain which have the spending power to sustain an urban tourist attraction. While Baltimore has one of the wealthiest market areas in the world, Liverpool has one of the poorest in northern Europe. Moreover, the limited success the project has achieved thus far has had little to do with the private sector. The Albert Dock and other renewal projects on the Mersey have been underwritten by a massive input of public resources, £80 million between 1981 and 1986. In a generally impoverished city such as Liverpool, it is questionable whether the development of an urban festival market is the best use of public resources.

In stark contrast to the isolation of the Liverpool redevelopment area, the London Docklands Development Corporation (LDDC) has jurisdiction over 5,100 acres of central and east London, including the major (but largely redundant) docks previously owned by the Port of London Authority. The docklands, located within three London Boroughs and (at the time the LDDC was formed) the Greater London Council, have had a long and protracted planning history, with central government involvement since the early 1970s (Ledgerwood 1985). The inner section, called the Isle of Dogs, was designated an Enterprise Zone in 1981.

Although located close to the central business district of London, the docklands suffered from industrial decline, high unemployment, and limited job opportunities which affected a number of important residential communities, many of which also suffered from poor housing. LDDC produced very ambitious proposals, with the stated aim of attracting private investment for office development from the nearby financial district. In evidence to the Environment Committee, LDDC proposed that:

It would use its powers and its resources of land and finance to create the economic infrastructure and physical environment which would attract considerably more private sector investment into the Docklands than had earlier been the case. In this way, it would gear up—or using American terminology—leverage private sector investment by making an initial and essentially short term injection of public sector resources . . . act as a promoter and publicist of Docklands . . . aimed particularly at developers and financial institutions (Environment Committee 1983: para. 6.1).

TABLE 7.1. *London Docklands Development Corporation Expenditure, 1981–1985* (in £M)

Land acquisition, reclamation, and treatment	
1. industrial/commercial	59
2. housing	50
3. other land uses	47
Administration and management	28
Promotion and consultants	10
Community expenditure	11
TOTAL	205

Source: LDDC 1985: 55.

Given its commercially desirable location, the scale of government financial support (£149 million up to the end of 1984/5), and the powers available (not least the Enterprise Zone in the Isle of Dogs), the LDDC was an example of a government policy that sought to 'pick winners'. The 1984/5 LDDC Annual Report announced that the public funding of £149 million had attracted £821 million in private investment, yielding a respectable leverage ratio of 5.5 : 1. By the year 2000, LDDC expected to attract £2.3 billion into the area, much of this in the form of investment in office development close to the city (LDDC 1985). Table 7.1 summarizes LDDC's expenditure up to 1984/5.

When compared with expenditure on the Urban Programme (£1,067 million over the same time period), these figures represent a considerable investment of public money, much of it focused on an area that already was attracting investment interest from private home builders, the financial leaders in the City, and the Fleet Street 'print' industry which began to relocate to the east end of London in the late 1970s. Nevertheless, the Chief Executive of LDDC argued that the use of public funds in the Docklands was justified because

It confirms that careful and constructive use of limited public sector investment can fuel inner-city regeneration, in contrast to the conventional view that it must always depend on heavy government funding. It also indicates that, if a market-led situation can be created, the pace of regeneration is that much faster (LDDC 1985: 14).

Despite his enthusiasm for market-led redevelopment, he also made a strong plea for sustained government support: 'there is a very sensitive level at which pump-priming expenditure has to be maintained, over a relatively short period, to avoid reducing the leverage ratio and slowing the momentum of development' (LDDC 1985: 14). One is left to ponder the definition of 'heavy government funding'!

From its inception, LDDC was not well received by dockland residents and the local authorities. The specific development policies of LDDC, however, widened criticism beyond nearby residents to include other Londoners as well as architectural experts and individuals concerned about the aesthetic character of the urban environment. LDDC's plan for Canary Wharf on the

Isle of Dogs was condemned by residents across the Thames in Greenwich as an architectural disaster and it attracted severe criticism from the Royal Fine Art Commission. The proposed project was originally on a scale worthy of mega-development in Manhattan: three towers, each 850 feet high, containing 8.8 million square feet of office and 'trading' space, 800 hotel rooms, 500,000 square feet of retailing, space for 8,000 cars, and the potential of creating upwards of 50,000 jobs. In opposition to LDDC, a number of local groups fought against the policy of encouraging such large-scale property development in the docks (Ambrose 1986: 241–5). Using the Docklands Consultative Committee (DCC) set up by the Greater London Council and the three boroughs, opposition groups such as the Docklands Forum and the more radical Joint Docklands Action Group (JDAG) led a vociferous community campaign, arguing that LDDC ignored the aspirations of the local community. They cited the failure to promote the creation of jobs that were suitable for local residents, the price of houses being built in the area, and the apparent lack of concern for existing small business (DCC 1985). They, like many who objected to Canary Wharf, were very critical of the undemocratic nature of LDDC and its failure to consult people living in the area. The alleged secrecy of the Corporation and its Board did little to allay the fears of residents (DCC 1985: 30).

With financial backing from Credit Suisse and First Boston, an American developer, G. Ware Travelstead, argued that office development on this giant scale could be justified because the 'Big Bang'—the deregulation of financial trading in Britain in the fall of 1986—would impose impossible demands on office space in the traditional Square Mile in the City of London where financial institutions were concentrated. The selection of the Isle of Dogs as an alternative site was not accidental. Located in an Enterprise Zone, the development would be exempt from rates for a number of years, attract substantial capital allowances against tax liabilities, and, crucially, would have almost complete freedom from normal planning restraints. The Canary Wharf site was 'approved' by the LDDC Board in less than six weeks. Despite the clamor from many organizations including English Heritage, the Royal Institutes of Architecture and Planning, and other august bodies, the Secretary of State refused to intervene, claiming that he had no jurisdiction over specific developments within an Enterprise Zone.

By early 1987 the Canary Wharf development had been approved but the developer was starting to have second thoughts about the scale of the project. Whatever the outcome, Canary Wharf is an example of government policy operating intentionally and openly in the interests of capital and implemented by a government agency prepared to ignore competing demands for resources in order to underwrite large-scale private development. As Ambrose concludes in his analysis of 'The Second London Blitz':

The area has been 'taken into care' by central government because its natural parents were too leftist, too committed to local needs and too sensitive to local feelings to carry out the kind of private sector led redevelopment strategy the Thatcher government had in mind. The pattern of redevelopment, the opportunistic philosophy and the divergence from democratically produced plans in almost every important respect has been demonstrated (Ambrose 1986: 251).

Despite Treasury reservations about the cost of the two original UDCs, immediate and direct state intervention through an extension of the development corporation model was considered as a government response to the 1985 riots in London and Birmingham. The need for the UDCs was attributed to the failures of local government. In a speech to the Conservative Central Party early in 1987, Nicholas Ridley, Secretary of State for the Environment, argued that:

The problem faced by people in many of our inner cities must be dealt with immediately. The problem is too serious to be left to Labour councils—indeed they have to take a large share of the blame, through sky-high rates, business-hostile attitudes, by tangled red-tape and chaotic bureaucracy and the waste of public capital (*Guardian*, 21 Mar. 1987).

Ridley's solution was for central government to take more cities 'into care.' Early in 1987, an additional five UDCs were selected in the more deprived cities in England and Wales: Trafford Park in Greater Manchester, in Tyne and Wear, on Teeside, in Sandwell in the West Midlands, and in Cardiff Bay in South Wales. These five new UDCs covered significantly larger areas than the Merseyside UDC. The development corporation for Teeside, for example, will have responsibility for some 12,000 acres stretching across four separate district councils. Despite the hostility of the city councils against the LDDC in London, and to lesser extent in Merseyside, this new round of UDCs was generally welcomed by local government. City councils were prepared to lose responsibility for major sections of their communities in return for additional government funding, the possibility of greater private investment, and the likelihood of modern commercial development. It appears that local accountability and community control over development was less important than success in the competition for urban development. This is precisely the response which central government has sought to encourage and, in this respect at least, the UDCs must be judged as a significant success. Towards the end of 1987, this success was recognized when UDCs were extended yet again. Five new 'mini' UDCs were announced for Bristol, Central Manchester, Leeds, Wolverhampton, and Sheffield. Here the parallel with earlier American experience with the urban development corporation is apparent. This 'third generation' of UDCs is beginning to move into the heart of urban Britain, taking on sites and projects adjacent, if not actually within, city centers. As in the US, this is where the market wishes to develop, hence policy has been adjusted accordingly. In Manchester, for example, the new mini-UDC will effectively take over one-third of the city center, including a number of commercial and tourist projects (such as a major exhibition center) which already were successfully developed by a public–private partnership led by local government. The participation of local government in the mini-UDCs has been left ambiguous; the central role of private developers has not.

The pattern of central direction of urban development has a longer lineage in Scotland which haš a different governmental system. The Scottish Development Agency (SDA), a regional economic development board, was created in 1975 by the Labour Government and given responsibility for British urban policy in Scotland. The SDA was part of a political response to the growing support for the separatist Scottish Nationalist Party and was intended to demonstrate the sincere interest of central government in Scottish redevelopment. The Agency was first given a remit to revive the Scottish economy and to coordinate its industrial strategy with efforts to improve the environment (Keating and Midwinter 1983). The SDA absorbed a number of agencies which functioned in the areas of industrial estates development, assistance to small firms, and clearance of derelict land. It was also given a mandate for direct intervention at the level of the firm.

Despite pressure from the central government in London to restrict interventions in urban policy, since 1979 the SDA has built on an existing Scottish 'tradition' of area-based intervention strategies intended to impact directly on local, mainly urban, economies (Boyle and Wannop 1982). Using a variety of different indicators (plant closure, industrial contraction, severe unemployment, or identifiable development opportunities) the SDA selected a number of locations as suitable sites for 'Area Projects'. While the Agency was initially reluctant to take on a spatial focus, as of 1984, it targeted some 60 percent of all its expenditure to identifiable Area Projects (Keating and Boyle 1986: 86).

The Area Projects were based on non-binding agreements, called Project Agreements, between the SDA, the respective local authorities (in Scotland, regional and district councils), other public agencies, and representatives of local companies. These agreements loosely determined the objectives, the timing, and the funding of each project (Keating and Boyle 1986; Lever and Moore 1986). Normally the SDA coordinated the activities of the different partners, but it did not remove or alter the legal responsibilities of other participants. Moreover, and in sharp contrast to the urban development corporations operating in England, the local councils retained all of their statutory powers.

Bending to government pressure, from 1984 on the SDA attempted to decrease its involvement in urban policy. In place of high profile public intervention, there was a shift towards a 'self-help' model where the local community—public and private—was expected to develop and organize renewal programs (Gulliver 1984). Two of the projects—in Inverclyde and the Glasgow City Center—moved away from the Project Agreement model entirely, introducing instead a more flexible arrangement and elevating, in theory at least, the role of the private sector. The aim was to increase the 'business' component in each initiative and replace scarce public funds by private investment.

There is some evidence, from the Inverclyde project in particular, that the lack of indigenous private sector resources in project areas has restricted the redirection of urban policy. The commercial objectives of the Inverclyde Project were to be guided by a series of Venture Groups, each focusing on a particular sector of the local economy which had been devastated by the decline in shipbuilding. The membership of these groups was to be drawn largely from the private sector so that program development could be integrated with a potential source of project finance. The evidence suggests, however, that neither sufficient finance nor manpower has been forthcoming (Hardie 1986). In order to mobilize the project and produce the desired results, the SDA has been forced back to its original interventionist mode. Nevertheless, the funding made available by the SDA has been welcomed by local government. Regional and district councils are eager to 'trade' a modest reduction in program control in return for the resources delivered by an area project. Furthermore, local councils have been quite prepared to follow the direction of the SDA, shifting the focus of policy away from traditional housing and environmental renewal and job creation towards support for market-led commercial development.

Such policy redirection, predominantly inspired by the SDA, has threatened to dilute effective urban policy. Under the influence of central government, the Agency has begun to de-emphasize urban renewal in favor of more limited commercial development. This change has profound implications for parts of Scottish cities. Not only is a focus on commercial criteria inappropriate for some local economies but the use of a central government agency along with the private sector to implement policy may effectively remove the necessary social support that traditional policies delivered (Boyle 1987).

Enterprise Zones and the Displacement of the Planning Regime

A central objective of the strategy of privatization has been to reduce the capacity of the British planning system to control market forces affecting urban change. Instead of directing market forces, it was intended that town and country planning play a supportive and facilitative role for private initiatives in local investment. In effect, the British planning regime was to be restrained, if not marginalized.

The Enterprise Zone experiment illustrates the interest in shifting the balance between planning and market forces. It has been among the most innovative aspects of British urban policy in the 1980s and, as described in Chapter 5, it inspired a parallel effort by the Reagan administration to introduce national Enterprise Zone legislation in the US. In Britain, the Enterprise Zone experiment was formally announced in 1980, launched in 1981, and extended in 1983.

The idea of an Enterprise Zone was first proposed in 1977 by geographer Peter Hall. He suggested that traditional urban policies for some of the most depressed areas in central Liverpool and Glasgow should be replaced by a 'highly unorthodox, free port solution'; in essence, an exercise in non-planning where 'small areas of inner cities would be simply thrown open to all kinds of initiative, with minimal control' (Hall 1977: 5). This concept of replicating in selected parts of British cities the economic conditions of Hong Kong in the 1950s was unconventional but not especially novel. Hall and Rayner Banham used the columns of the journal *New Society* to test these ideas (Banham 1969) and, in the early 1970s, held graduate tutorials on the validity of encouraging the 'black economy' and supporting deregulation of small firms as a response to economic strategies from the opposite end of the political spectrum. Likewise, the champions of the free-market and deregulation and the critics of state intervention in the spatial economy were very much in favor of a non-planning experiment and they supported the 'non-government-zone' proposal of the right-wing Center for Policy Studies.

Sir Geoffrey Howe, who became Chancellor of the Exchequer in 1979, also supported the idea, and, in a paper entitled *Liberating Free Enterprise: A New Experiment*, he suggested that test areas or laboratories be established where business could be nurtured in a free enterprise environment (Jordan 1984). Howe proposed to establish a series of zones, managed by a new type of agency, where land use planning would cease to apply: public authorities would be required to auction off their land holdings; firms would be exempt from taxes on land development and from rates; companies would not be able to claim government grant or subsidy; price control, pay policy, and employment protection legislation would not apply; and business would receive guarantees against tax changes and nationalization. Howe's proposal recognized the impossibility of withdrawing welfare, police and fire protection, and infrastructure services, especially as this would go against the idea of stimulating industry.

Nevertheless, it left government with a key dilemma: if businesses received public benefits, without having to pay local taxes, then the Enterprise Zone would simply amount to another form of public subsidy—quite the reverse of the original free-market idea and not exactly Hong Kong of the 1950s! Moreover, the ideal of confining benefits to defined zones interfered with a principal feature of the free market—namely the ability of private firms to locate in the best available sites without costs being distorted by government policy (Keating and Boyle 1986). Furthermore, the process of translating the Enterprise Zone concept into policy resulted in inter-departmental bargaining and additional modification (Jordan and Reilly 1981; Taylor 1981). There was considerable debate about the appropriateness of removing *all* planning controls. It was accepted that some restrictions on noxious industries were necessary, that it would be useful to plan for the development of infrastructure, and that activities which adversely affected neighboring areas, such as unlimited retail development, should be controlled. The Department of Employment refused to suspend the Employment Protection Act, and the idea of holding an auction of all public land was dropped as unworkable and very costly. On the other hand, in order to make the zones attractive to business, the proposal for rate relief[6] for a set period was incorporated. Rates were not abolished; they were to be paid by the Treasury, in essence a public subsidy to all zone occupants, new and old. When challenged about the anomaly of creating a windfall subsidy for firms already located in a zone, the DoE argued that it would be impractical to differentiate between old and new firms.[7]

Jordan ascribes the evolution of the Enterprise Zone proposal to five principal factors: interest group pressure; civil service hostility; theoretical deficiencies; the necessity of retaining government subsidy for industry in the zones, without it, 'the zones were bound to fail' (Jordon 1984: 150); and, despite disclaimers by the government, the location of zones in the most disadvantaged parts of the country resulting in the Enterprise Zone idea having to satisfy industrial policy (hence traditional regional policy) and welfare policy (hence aspects of traditional urban policy) at one and the same time. By the time the Enterprise Zone proposal emerged, the idea had come a long way from the original free market concept and was beginning to look like an instrument of traditional spatial policy—simply a means of subsidizing the location of firms in one area rather than another. It was not surprising, therefore, that the zones were generally welcomed by local government. At the cost of losing a modest degree of local planning control, communities would receive an additional national subsidy. In addition, local authorities could use the zones as marketing tools to attract firms to their areas as well as to improve their opportunities to obtain other forms of public support.

Howe announced the Enterprise Zone experiment—a pioneering 'approach to the question of industrial and commercial revival'—in his 1980 budget speech. Originally, six zones were to be selected, each around 500 acres, where industry would benefit from tax exemptions and reduced regulation for a ten-year period.[8] Enterprise Zone measures were then implemented through the Finance Act and the Local Government, Planning and Land Act, both in 1980. Although Howe's proposal was originally developed by the Treasury, the DoE was given general coordinating responsibility with administrative involvement by the Scottish, Welsh, and Northern Ireland Offices.

Following a complex selection process, 11 zones were designated in 1981 and a further 14 between 1983 and 1984 (Table 7.2). Virtually all of the zones were administered by local authorities (Howe's idea of a special management agency was dropped), and all but two zones were located in designated development areas or in other areas which also benefited from special financial assistance under other government policies.[9] The average size of the first round zones was 546 acres. In total, they covered 950 existing firms, employing 23,000 workers, with the rates exemption amounting to some £5 million per annum. The second round zones were drawn much tighter with an average size of 243 acres. These encompassed 425 existing companies, employing 6,600 people, and created an Exchequer cost for 'uncovenanted benefits' (exemption from Rates) of £2 million per annum (Table 7.2). In the second round selection, the DoE looked for a willingness on behalf of local government to enter fully into the spirit of the experiment by relaxing their powers of planning control, speeding their decision making, and cooperating closely with the private sector to ensure the continuous release of land for development and the promotion and marketing of the zones. The second

TABLE 7.2.   *Enterprise Zones in the UK: Characteristics*

Name[a]	Date[b]	Area[c]	Unemployment[d] (%)
Belfast	Oct. 1981	513	NA
Clydebank	Aug. 1981	570	15
Corby	June 1981	280	22
Dudley	July 1981	540 (+ 109)	14
Hartlepool	Oct. 1981	270	19
Isle of Dogs	Apr. 1982	362	7
Swansea	June 1981	735 (+ 40)	14
Salford/Trafford	Aug. 1981	875	12
Speke	Aug. 1981	340	17
Tyneside	Aug. 1981	1,120	12–17
Wakefield	July 1981	140 (+ 80)	10
Delyn	July 1983	293	20
Derry	Sept. 1983	270	NA
Glanford	Apr. 1984	124	19
Invergordon	Oct. 1983	148	18
Middlesbrough	Nov. 1983	190	20
Milford Haven	Apr. 1984	362	18–29
North-east Lancashire	Dec. 1983	282	13–18
North-west Kent	Oct. 1983	310 (+ 60)	17
Rotherham	Aug. 1983	260	21
Scunthorpe	Sept. 1983	260	19
Tayside	Jan. 1984	260	17–20
Telford	Jan. 1984	279	21
Wellingborough	July 1983	136	14
Workington	Oct. 1983	215	20

[a] Operating title only; the Local Authority responsible may have a different name
and the designated EZ may cover more than one local jurisdiction.
[b] Date of effective operation.
[c] Area measured in acres.
[d] Unemployment (total, adjusted) for First Round zones is taken at June 1981;
Second Round at Sept. 1982.

Source: NAO 1986 and Lloyd and Botham 1985: 42, 51–2.

round zones were generally in better condition, were less intensively
developed, and faced less competition from surrounding areas.

   Whatever else may be claimed for the Enterprise Zones, they did not result
in low cost job creation nor did they substantially replace public subsidy with
private investment. While the full costs remain hidden, the National Audit
Office (NAO 1986) reported that up to the end of the financial year 1984/5,
the Enterprise Zone program had cost the Exchequer about £180 million
including: transfer payments for loss of rates (£50 million); capital allowances
(£50 million); and public investment, covering site preparation, infrastructure,
and other development costs (£80 million). Even this is a highly conservative
estimate as the full costs have yet to be determined. In the Clydebank Enterprise Zone, for example, the SDA invested £25 million in its role as leader of

the Clydebank Task Force and only part of this investment is included in the above figures; while in the Tyneside Enterprise Zone, road access to a major retail development, the Metro Centre, was partly funded by a £1.5 million Urban Development Grant, again excluded from the NAO estimate.

The Enterprise Zone program provided serviced sites that were previously difficult to obtain in many older industrial areas. Building activity did increase in these sites, but it 'resulted from publicly financed programmes for land assembly and servicing rather than from a market response to the enterprise zone measures' (Tym *et al.* 1984: 145). Instead of creating non-intervention zones where market forces had a free rein, the outcome has been the opposite: planned, controlled, spatial intervention, led and financed by the public sector. British Enterprise Zones operate like traditional spatial policy measures consisting of a package of fiscal incentives and a heavy promotional effort, the latter undoubtedly motivated by the considerable political stake which central government has in showing results (Keating and Boyle 1986).

Assessment of the impact of zones on employment and the local economy is problematic because government evaluation is incomplete (a government sponsored monitoring exercise was ended in 1984) and efforts to measure results raise difficult problems of estimating substitution effects and added value. Within the Enterprise Zones some 18,000 jobs were created in 650 new or relocated companies (Table 7.3). These figures fail to show that there was a net loss of jobs in other areas from the relocation of firms that sought to take advantage of zone incentives. Of equal concern is the conclusion reached by the Tym Study that 85 percent of Enterprise Zone firms would be operating in the same region in the absence of a zone and that between 88 and 96 percent of the new firms would have started without the zones. The study also found that of the relocating firms, some 92 percent came from the same region (Tym *et al.* 1984). Hence, Enterprise Zones appear to influence firm location but have only a limited influence on the formation of new firms. Moreover, a study of the effects of Enterprise Zones on local property markets by the Royal Institute of Chartered Surveyors found that while many firms might be attracted by rate concessions, a large part of the benefits were paid away in higher rent. The NAO reports that this conclusion is supported by a DoE analysis which found that rents for new factory units were, in most cases, from 10 to 50 percent higher in the zones, essentially cancelling-out the financial benefits of the rates exemption (NAO 1986).

Despite its deficiencies as a policy for urban development, the Enterprise Zone program has proved to be a powerful marketing tool, giving local authorities and development agencies a definite 'edge' over their competitors for inward investment and new-firm formation. Firms have benefited from the tax advantages (Bromley and Morgan 1985); and, according to the Tym report, the simplified planning regime is welcomed by the development industry (Tym *et al.* 1984). There is evidence, however, that before the zones were established, planning controls were not a serious impediment to development, particularly in areas of high unemployment: 'the simplification

TABLE 7.3. *Enterprise Zones (England, Scotland, Wales): Firms, Employment, and Investment*

Name	Number of establishments		Number of employees[a]		Public investment[b] (in £M)
	Sept. 84	Change	Desig.	Sept. 84	Sept. 84
Clydebank	236	+31	2,825	5,500	6.0
Corby	91	+88	NA	4,100	5.5
Dudley	145	+18	2,671	2,800	1.1
Hartlepool	64	+23	299	1,100	NA
Isle of Dogs	235	+130	641	2,500	11.3
Swansea	162	+83	2,068	3,300	NA
Salford/Trafford	187	−18	2,254	3,100	1.3
Speke	59	+53	565	800	0.6
Tyneside	271	+106	10,363	12,500	NA
Wakefield	36	+18	1,196	1,600	0.4
Delyn	64	+6	933	1,200	0.6
Glanford	11	+5	41	200	0.2
Invergordon	15	+7	103	100	1.0

Middlesbrough	65	+18	1,356	700	0.5
Milford Haven	125	NA	1,200	1,200	NA
North-east Lancashire	32	−5	740	1.300	0.5
North-west Kent	78	+29	752	2,300	0.4
Rotherham	37	+8	531	1,100	0.2
Scunthorpe (data for Scunthorpe & Glanford amalgamated)					2.0
Tayside	25	+8	546	1.200	1.1
Telford	14	+14	—	600	1.5
Wellingborough	12	+8	32	300	1.1
Workington	54	+20	397	600	1.4
TOTAL	2,018	+650	29,513	48,100	36.7

[a] Companies employing large temporary and fluctuating work-forces are included in employment at designation stage but are excluded from employment at Sep. 1984.

[b] Public investment relates solely to the cost of service provision (gas, water, electricity, and sewerage) and general environmental improvement. It excludes all site preparation costs, land purchase, and roads as well as public expenditure on Regional or Urban Development Grants, Selective Financial Assistance, Derelict Land Grant, and any expenditure by government agencies.

Source: NAO 1986.

of planning idea on which Sir Geoffrey Howe had put so much faith, turned out to look less relevant than was assumed' (Jordan 1984: 132).

Far from vindicating the policy of 'non-planning', the experience with Enterprise Zones has confirmed the important role of public intervention and positive development policies when the local market fails to generate new industry and employment. The Enterprise Zone experiment represents a triumph of marketing and civic public relations; it has helped local authorities and central government to use free market rhetoric to justify reliance on a program that is in the mainstream of traditional, spatially-focused, government intervention. Rather than policy innovation, Grant Jordan suggests that Britain has invented the Enterprise Zones to serve as a symbol of 'ideologically acceptable job creation' (Jordan 1984: 146).

With little publicity, the government published the result of an evaluation of the Enterprise Zone program on Christmas Eve 1987 (DoE 1987*e*). The report was welcomed by Environment Secretary Nicholas Ridley and interpreted as proof that the Enterprise Zones had indeed been the flagship of deregulation and a critical factor in the rekindling of the entrepreneurial spirit in Britain. He announced that the program had resulted in 63,000 jobs in the 23 zones, 35,000 being attributed as a direct result of the incentives offered—the rate relief and the capital allowances. But, despite Ridley's encouraging portrayal, the evaluation was hardly cause for celebration. It found a high proportion of existing firms moving into the zones, thereby reducing the actual added benefits of the enterprise experiment. In fact, over five years, the Enterprise Zones had produced only 13,000 new jobs.

Further, the study estimated that up to 1986, the government had invested some £400 million (net £300 million) on the experiment, at a cost per job of £23,000, or £30,000 if construction costs are included. These costs, difficult to control due to 'uncovenanted' benefits (exemption from the payment of rates), were understandably distressing to the Treasury. In addition, the House of Commons Committee of Public Accounts had earlier expressed 'important reservations' about the experiment and was severely critical of the adverse effect it was having on firms located in areas close to the zones (Committee of Public Accounts 1986*b*). Indeed, in December 1987, it was ruled that companies just outside Enterprise Zones were entitled to a reduction in their rates. Hence, it was not surprising when the DoE announced that the 'experiment' would end in 1991.

Public–Private Partnerships and the Marketing of Cities

While enthusiasm for the Enterprise Zone experiment had dwindled by the mid-1980s, another idea for privatizing urban Britain—the public–private partnership—gained momentum. Indeed, the creation of public–private partnerships became the conventional answer of both government and business leaders to the physical, economic, and social problems of British cities. In the area of housing policy, for example, partnership arrangements were experimented with in virtually every aspect of housing provision: the rehabilitation of private inner-city stock and promotion of housing agency services; the extension of owner occupation through shared ownership; the private financing and construction of housing to satisfy special needs of the elderly, the young, and the mentally ill; cooperative building of new houses for private rental; and, notably, the private renewal and management of difficult-to-let public housing stock.

The promotion of public–private partnerships was, perhaps, the major continuing initiative in British local economic development policy in the 1980s. Partnership proposals exhibited a wide variety of organizational models and program arrangements, most of which reflected the influence of US experience. Much of the impetus for partnerships came from government agencies, both central and local, but there also was some initiative from British business organizations which borrowed ideas on partnership and corporate social responsibility from US groups such as the National Council for Urban Economic Development, the Committee for Economic Development, and even from the Department of Housing and Urban Development. Moreover, both government and the business community expressed support for corporate contributions to the non-profit sector (Newham 1980; Boyle 1983*a*). The widely-reported activities of US not-for-profit organizations, such as the Local Initiatives Support Corporation in the south Bronx, presented an attractive model for combining voluntary, corporate, and governmental activity in local economic development.

The idea of a partnership across the economic sectors was used by Business in the Community (BIC), a privately-funded body created with government support in 1981, as a 'focus and catalyst for the greater involvement of industry and commerce in the local community' (BIC n.d.). Through their Centre for Corporate Responsibility, BIC exhorted private enterprise to take an interest in urban affairs, and particularly in the inner cities, if only because: 'Strife and decay in the inner cities and associated threats to property and public safety carry a high political risk—neglect will eventually impose a high cost on the whole business community' (BIC n.d.). With reference to the needs of particular cities, BIC suggested corporate involvement could occur through all of the following mechanisms: targeted location of new business and finance; selective hiring policies and special training initiatives; local purchasing policies; direct corporate involvement in local affairs; participation in local partnerships; and enhanced community and charitable support. Given its commitments to privatization and partnership, the government enthusiastically endorsed BIC as a vehicle for urban economic development. In keeping with this, government promoted the spread of Enterprise Trusts to stimulate locally generated economic development by encouraging and applying the concept of corporate social responsibility and promoting mutual aid in the private sector. While the functions of Trusts vary from place to place, these organizations usually focus on assistance to new and expanding firms through business counseling, support services, and training (Keating and Boyle 1986).

One of the strongest advocates of partnerships has been the British property development industry which benefits greatly and directly to the extent that its conception of partnership arrangements is accepted as the norm for public policy. The major institutions in the industry have come together to form the Phoenix Partnership, an organization devoted to promoting local economic development partnerships. The Phoenix Partnership includes representation from the National Council of Building Material Producers, the Building Employers Confederation, the British Property Federation, Business in the Community, the Urban Investment Review Group, the Association of British Insurers, and the Building Societies Association. The organization has promoted new partnership arrangements as the only viable alternative to urban decline.

Throwing money into inner cities would not by itself halt the decline. Cities are living organisms . . . Before change can take place there has to be a vision of the future in which the local community participates and believes . . . There is an alternative to the present apathy which exists in too many of our towns and cities (Cowie 1985: p. v).

That alternative requires that Britain replicate the successes of partnership arrangements in such US cities as Baltimore, Pittsburgh, Oakland, and Minneapolis. Drawing on evidence from the US, the Phoenix Partnership has argued that the strength of the public–private arrangements lies in the 'depoliticization' of the development process: 'Public agencies are singularly ill-equipped to play a supporting role in the development process . . . their role in comprehensive development projects is counter-productive' (Cowie 1985: 31). In its view, local partnerships in Britain should more fully accommodate the initiatives of the private development industry. The nature of the accommodation needed has been made clear by the Phoenix Partnership's citation of the effect of the LDDC on land values in the London Docklands: 'The price of housing land has risen steeply from an average of £38,500 an acre to an average of £450,000 an acre today' (Cowie 1985: 33). According to the Phoenix Partnership, this measure of success should be applied to other parts of the Urban Programme so that urban development grants in Britain systematically favor economic development. The social component of urban policy can be left, it is argued, to the 'impressive commitment' of British commercial and financial companies. In 1985, with the approval of the DoE, representatives of the Phoenix Partnership began to pursue public support for the development activities of its members by visiting numerous cities throughout Britain to persuade local councils of the merits of its proposals. The Phoenix Partnership advocated a concept of urban public–private partnership that turned the objectives of urban policy on end. Instead of exploring ways in which the private sector could assist the public process of urban regeneration, the Phoenix Partnership sought to modify policy—national and local—so that it subsidized private development.

The success of Phoenix and the ability of the private sector to directly shape urban policy was most clearly evident in early 1988 in the *Action for Cities* initiative where private industry and commerce were identified as the key actors in Mrs. Thatcher's assault on the inner city (Cabinet Office 1988). Apart from the extension of initiatives focused on leveraging private sector investment in the inner city (such as the City Grant, mini-UDCs, new Enterprise Agencies, and education initiatives funded by private industry), this major publicity drive also launched what Hugo Young termed 'the letting out of social policy to big business' (Young 1988). In return for their continued support of the Conservative Party through three election campaigns, the Prime Minister invited private industry, and especially construction firms, to participate in her new program—not because of their social responsibility but because urban policy could now deliver profits, notably in subsidized property development. Eleven of the largest civil engineering and construction companies (including major sponsors of the Tory Party such as Robert McAlpine, Taylor Woodrow, John Laing, and Trafalgar House) joined forces to develop inner-city sites. Links with government and direct access to the Prime Minister would be sustained since the Director of this powerful group was appointed from the Downing Street Policy Unit! Moreover, the Confederation of British Industry, Business in the Community, and the 3i Group (Investors in Industry) all launched new programs targeted at the inner city. And these initiatives were supported by urban policy with improved coordination through an extension of the Task Forces (16 in operation by 1988) and further powers for the City Action Teams (CATs)—with 7 CATs coordinating the public expenditure of the Departments of Employment, Environment, and Trade and Industry throughout England (DTI 1988).

Despite this faith in the value of integrating the private and public sectors in urban social policy, the evidence of success is far from conclusive. Albeit with the best of intentions, the Task Force initiative to lever substantial support from local and national companies highlights the difficulties of attracting private investment. In a Parliamentary Answer, Kenneth Clarke, Minister at the Department of Trade and Industry, indicated that, apart from support in the form of secondees, only £200,000 had been contributed by private companies (Lloyds and Barclays Bank) to all sixteen Task Forces. Overall, Clarke estimated that the Task Forces were generating a public–private sector leverage ratio of 1 : 1.6 (Boyle 1988).

Many of the economic development partnerships created in British cities during the 1980s bear the unmistakable stamp of older partnership arrangements in American cities. The city of Glasgow offers a useful illustration. Glasgow Action, a partnership to strengthen the commercial core of the city, was established with the support of the Scottish Development Agency. This initiative, focused on promoting opportunities for business development in the service sector, radically departed from the substance and style of previous Scottish urban policy (Keating and Boyle 1986). The organization—formed around a group of prominent city businessmen—was a product of a major SDA funded study of the development potential of the city center. McKinsey and Company, the consulting firm which prepared the study, recommended that public action seek to strengthen Glasgow's role as a major service center and that this effort be led by a private organization (McKinsey and Company 1984, 1985; and SDA 1986). The result was Glasgow Action. Although two leading local politicians became board members, leadership, control, and direction were firmly located in the private sector, and the objectives of the organization reflected the needs and aspirations of the business community. The Chief Executive of the SDA used the US model to justify this private sector focus: 'the example of US cities suggests that actively involving business bodies in the regeneration of the city increases the business community's commitment to it' (McKinsey *et al.* 1985: 4).

The parallel between Glasgow Action and the public–private partnerships that guided US urban renewal in the post-war period was not accidental. The glistening hotels, convention centers, and festival markets built in older industrial cities such as Baltimore, Boston, and Detroit proved irresistible to city planners, SDA officials, and local politicians who sought a solution to their urban economic problems. Numerous field visits were organized to Baltimore's Inner Harbor, to the South Street Seaport in New York, and to Boston's Quincy Market. Two recurring images were brought back. First, urban renewal, especially waterfront revival, required outstanding development attractions that would act as tourist magnets; and the most popular of these attractions is the aquarium. Within months, an aquarium became a standard component of waterfront renewal plans. A second image that found its way across the Atlantic was promoted by consultants from the US, notably the American City Corporation, a subsidiary of the Rouse Company. To achieve urban regeneration, cities must become much more receptive to the demands of the development industry.

The SDA, and others concerned about finding a new approach to urban development, were influenced in no small way by the attractive combination of private leadership and private investment found in Minneapolis, Minnesota. Visitors from the SDA were particularly impressed by the activities of leading companies such as Dayton-Hudson and Control Data. These corporations promoted involvement in urban affairs and were highly influential in downtown commercial development (Boyle 1983*a*). The model for Glasgow Action was an organization that would combine the strictly commercial goals of downtown development interests with more altruistic objectives that could be achieved through private sponsorship of community development. Perhaps most important of all, Glasgow Action inherited the American belief that urban regeneration depends on creating the correct conditions for private investment. It is not surprising that its promotional literature repeats many of the themes used by the Pittsburgh Allegheny Conference forty years earlier:

Glasgow Action is the name of a group of leading business people and politicians—and of the visionary plan they have for Glasgow's future, for the Glasgow of the 21st Century. The thinking behind the plan is that the development of a strong business and consumer service industry base will stimulate the regeneration of the city as a whole; . . . it aims to recreate Glasgow's entrepreneurial spirit (Glasgow Action 1985).

The formation of organizations such as Business in the Community, the Phoenix Partnership, and Glasgow Action suggest that the US pattern of public–private partnership has become a model for Britain. That model implies that the city, first and foremost, is a place to do business and that politics, government, and administration must adapt to the needs of the business community and rely on the initiatives of the private sector to direct the process of urban change. It is apparent that this standard has been accepted at the national level in Britain and, increasingly in the 1980s, at the local level as well, even if sometimes by default rather than by design. As the focus of local attention shifts to economic development issues, and as public resources become more scarce, partnership arrangements become more attractive to local officials as a means of securing a place in an increasingly privatized urban Britain.

Despite the centralizing effects of the Thatcher Government's policies, local authorities have increased their involvement in economic development programs. For some cities there has been little choice. As traditional regional policy was diluted (Lever 1987), with rising unemployment, and stagnant local economies, provincial cities began to take a greater responsibility for dealing with the impact of the recession and the long-term implications of deindustrialization. Many local authorities outside the central government's designated areas for special assistance face severe dislocation of their local economies yet have found that little help was forthcoming from central government. Moreover, central government has been supportive, in principle but often not in revenue, of local policy that would encourage efficiency in local government and improve the 'business climate' for British industry. Part of the *Action for Cities* initiative, the new City Grant—combining UDG, the Urban Regeneration Grant, and the private sector Derelict Land Grant—will effectively bypass local government (Cabinet Office 1988). Nicholas Ridley, Environment Secretary, claimed that this streamlined grant will 'simplify and speed up assistance to private sector developers in urban areas, enabling developers to deal directly with the Government' (DoE 1988: 2F). Hence, the evolution of leveraging techniques in Britain—UDG, URG, and the City Grant—is further evidence that central government has sought to marginalize local government. Despite their proven expertise and their considerable track record in working with developers, local government has been ignored, 'sacrificed in the pursuit of Mrs. Thatcher's political crusade' (Hetherington 1988). As a result, many local authorities have taken action on their own.

Local government promotion of economic development has a long history in Britain where economic recession has been a depressingly recurrent event. The local response, however, has been limited largely to the promotion of locational advantage to attract mobile industry (particularly from overseas) and the provision of sites, services, and infrastructure to house new or expanding industry (Camina 1974). 'Economic development' commonly belonged to the planning and housing function in local government; hence the approach, the techniques, and the prevailing philosophy was dominated by land and property interests (Boddy 1983). By the early 1980s, this orientation to local economic policy had fallen from favor and in its place, local authorities promoted programs to enhance local economic development by directly assisting and accommodating industry and commerce. Chandler and Lawless refer to this as the 'revival of economic intervention' (Chandler and Lawless 1985).

Various surveys in the mid-1980s document the widening interest of local authorities in local economic development. Mills and Young (1986) surveyed 197 councils in England and Wales, and related their results to the findings of similar surveys by government, particularly research into the economic impact of the Urban Programme (DoE 1986b). They concluded that there was widespread acceptance of the need to develop local strategies for economic development despite the fact that political commitment and resources were not always forthcoming from central government. They also found that a significant amount of internal reorganization of local government activity had taken place to address local economic problems. These reorganizations included the creation of industrial promotion units in Conservative controlled cities where commerce had previously been left very much on its own and the development of sophisticated interventionist structures such as Enterprise Boards and Employment Departments in a number of Labor controlled authorities—notably the Greater London Council and the West Midlands County Council, Sheffield, and selected London Boroughs (Mawson and Miller 1983, 1986). It is important to note that the Thatcher Government was originally less than pleased with these more activist interpretations of local and regional economic development and that this dissatisfaction undoubtedly reinforced the government's intention to disband metropolitan governments like the Greater London Council,[10] an objective which was accomplished in 1986 (Boddy and Fudge 1984). Finally, Mills and Young found that despite much of the rhetoric, a significant proportion of local economic development remained grounded in the provision of site and services. Fully four-fifths of the 197 responding authorities were directly involved in the provision and/or improvement of sites and commercial premises (Mills and Young 1986: 102). A similar study conducted in Scotland found that 96 percent of local authorities that had local economic development powers were involved in the acquisition and servicing of sites (Keating and Boyle 1986: 79).

The largest growth area in local economic development has been the extension of direct financial assistance to firms—not merely to attract new industry but to keep indigenous firms in the local economy and encourage them to expand. The scale of this intervention has been modest since the annual budget for financial assistance of most local authorities is less than £100,000. Indeed, it appears that the main constraint on local economic development has been financial. Outside the major cities, particularly where Urban Programme monies are not available, local government must operate with very limited resources. Even taking into account additional assistance from national and international bodies (such as the European Regional

Development and Social Fund [11]), local economic development in Britain has operated on a small and precarious financial base. Mills and Young found that while 'economic development is a concern of many more authorities than might have been imagined, [its success] must be qualified by the very modest resources that the great majority devote to its achievement. Economic development operations typically enjoy only slender resources' (Mills and Young 1986: 140).

Central government policies that address problems of the spatial economy—Enterprise Zones, the enhanced Urban Programme, assistance for small business, support for new technology—increasingly set one locality against another. Local government, in turn, responded to this emerging competition by actively seeking to strengthen their locational advantage, accepting whatever central assistance was available. Moreover, their own policies, which may have been stimulated by a serious concern about unemployment and issues of welfare, were subject to distortion whereby matters of distribution, equity, and disadvantage took second place to the quest for economic growth. The pressure on cities, particularly in the north of Britain, to find economic alternatives has been relentless, and increasingly local economic policy became synonymous with marketing the city.

As the marketing of place became an accepted and commonplace activity of local government, it advanced from simply a promotional exercise (Bath 1986; Clark 1986) to a key component of local development strategy. As cities continue to seek an alternative economic base—often some variant on high technology industry, service employment, retailing, tourism, or leisure services—they have become increasingly involved in a hunt for investment from outside their community—from London, Los Angeles, Tokyo, or elsewhere. This has forced local governments into the world of municipal marketing and public entrepreneurship and has produced some novel, often unusual, and occasionally illogical, decisions in British town halls. Glasgow launched a vigorous campaign of self-promotion under the slogan 'Glasgow's Miles Better' that included every conceivable means of publicity, including advertisements on the sides of London double-decker buses and on the London Underground—all with the intent of convincing a skeptical British public and tourists from abroad that Glasgow is no longer a city of slums, religious bigotry, and uncontrolled street violence but, rather, one of culture and investment opportunities. Other city promotion campaigns have been more specifically focused on a particular renewal strategy. Industrial cities, such as Bradford in Yorkshire, developed a forceful tourist campaign, selling the name of the Brontë Family to the travel industry. Nottingham sponsored ice-dancing, eventually boasting a world champion in Torvill and Dean. Birmingham spent substantial sums yet eventually failed to attract the 1992 Olympic games to the 'Heart of England'. Gateshead in the north-east also used athletics to promote their city. Famous architecture, industrial heritage, sporting or pop heroes have been pressed into service to promote the advantages, the benefits, or the attractiveness of particular towns and cities (Chandler and Lawless 1985: 37–75).

Thatcher's Divided Kingdom

> The new initiatives being taken by the Government and announced by
> the private sector show that we all mean business and that we are
> releasing the talent, enterprise and energy that is at the service of our
> inner cities . . . We are embarked on a great enterprise which will leave
> its mark on Britain for decades and carry our towns and cities into the
> 21st century in much better shape.
>
> (Cabinet Office 1988: 2)

With these stirring phrases, the Prime Minister launched the revised *Action
for Cities* report in March 1988. As we have already noted, however, there
was no substantive policy innovation and precious little additional central
government funding attached to her call for a '£3,000 million attack on the
host of problems covered by the inner cities label' (Cabinet Office 1988). Yet,
despite the paucity of ideas and the lack of new money, this glossy package of
policy promises and program rearrangements—linking the activities of six
Departments of State—was, at least symbolically, a bench-mark of contemporary British urban policy. Perhaps for the first time in two decades,
there was evidence of urban policy and program coordination, with Departments that normally pull in very different directions apparently agreeing to a
common cause. The underlying basis for common commitment is not difficult
to understand. Most, if not all, the senior Ministers who participated in *Action
for Cities* shared Margaret Thatcher's vision of the challenge ahead; a
challenge that recognized urban Britain—with its Labour controlled councils,
its public sector housing, its comprehensive State-run schools, and its legacy
of planning control—as the last and most enduring monument to state socialism. The interest of the government in urban policy cannot be separated from
the Conservative's crusade against the last bastions of Attlee's welfare state.
A keynote of this crusade was that urban Britain must be liberated from the
vestiges of state socialism and the 'inner cities should be given a chance to
share in the nation's prosperity' (Cabinet Office 1988: 28).

The Conservative strategy for achieving these objectives varied little since
the privatization initiatives were launched in 1979. Throughout the 1980s the
central message of urban policy was that local adaptations to the forces of
economic and social change must be consistent with national efforts to
stimulate economic growth.

> Cities are changing, and change can bring economic and social problems as well as
> new opportunities . . . The problems of structural change have been made worse by
> failed experiments in social engineering . . . Effective policies and programmes are
> required to help meet today's challenges. Government action must be coordinated.
> Priority areas must be carefully selected so that effort is not wasted. The aim is to
> encourage investment and job opportunities (DoE/DE 1987: 2–3).

And it was clear that, in addressing the problems of structural change, the
stimulation of and the reliance upon private enterprise was to be regarded as
the solution for cities as well as the nation. 'Cities grew and flourished

because of private enterprise. It is private enterprise backed by well-directed Government action, that will renew them. The emphasis is on coordinated effort to involve local communities and the private sector in the task of regeneration, and to build on their initiative' (DoE/DE 1987: 28).

Clearly, the assumptions and expectations which guided this strategy in the 1980s were far removed from the ideas which inspired and shaped the Urban Programme and the Community Development Project in the decade before. Then local industry and commerce were defined as part of the problem; in the 1980s they became the solution. The main variables of urban change—the economy, land, housing—were all targets for privatization. Public–private partnerships, corporate social responsibility, the release of public land holdings, the sale of public assets, Enterprise Zones, urban development grants, urban development corporations, and the municipal competition for new industry, technology, and jobs were all activities directed towards changing the traditional public–private balance. But the distinctive aspect of the pursuit of privatism in British urban policy in the 1980s was not the number and variety of privatization proposals but the substantive shift in the general policy orientation. In the pursuit of a business society the policy dialogue shifted away from issues of public sector responsibility and towards issues of private sector investment. Attention moved from welfare and redistribution to a concern with industrial decline, the weaknesses of the British economy, and the management of Britain's transition to a post-industrial society. Urban policy was guided by an economic imperative that elevated the importance of growth and diminished the value of equity.

Whatever else may be claimed for this urban strategy, it did not secure prosperity for inner cities; either for the industrial towns throughout northern Britain, which were surely a target of Tory political interests, or for the large peripheral housing estates where male unemployment remained stubbornly high. After eight years of the Thatcher privatization program, and despite the government's claims of success in creating 'people's capitalism', there were few signs of substantial regeneration in the most economically distressed parts of urban Britain. Rather, Mrs. Thatcher's urban policy formula proved to be both spatially selective and socially divisive. In 1987, the British unemployment rate was 13 percent, a figure more than double the 1979 rate of 5.3 percent when she entered office. Moreover, the highest concentrations of unemployment continued to be in areas which, since the late 1970s, had been the targets of local economic development initiatives—the inner cores and the peripheral estates of declining cities, and the industrial regions. While the national economic policies of the Conservative Government, specifically privatization, enhanced the prosperity of the British middleclass and improved conditions in some parts of Britain, they also exaggerated the spatial divisions within the economy—between the north and south, between the commercial city-center and the depressed peripheral housing estates, between the deteriorated inner-city areas and the prosperous market towns, between the old, declining industrial regions and the new regional concentrations of post-industrial services and high-technology firms.

At the beginning of 1986, the Department of Employment released figures that reflected the spatial divisions in Britain. Between 1979, when the Conservative Party regained power, and 1986, 94 percent of jobs lost in Britain were in northern England, Scotland, Wales, the Midlands, and Northern Ireland with the remaining 6 percent in the Tory heartland of the south of England. Manufacturing industry was particularly affected with the loss of some 1.94 million jobs over the same period (DoE 1987*d*). In the industrial north there was little evidence that the job loss was compensated by the growth of new industries. In contrast, and with the support of government policy, more than two-thirds of the new jobs created in the service sector were located in the prosperous south-east, with banking and finance recording the largest increases (Huhne 1987). This 'North–South' divide is graphically illustrated by Champion and Green whose analysis of the 1984 Census of Employment, combined with other data, clearly shows a 'growth crescent' around London (1988). While their statistics also illustrate modest improvements in central cities such as Birmingham, Glasgow, and Newcastle, the overall pattern that emerges is one of sharp spatial division, with even relatively stable centers in the industrial north failing to enjoy the prosperity of the south. Further, in looking to the future, Tyler and Rhodes suggest that of a projected increase of 900,000 jobs between 1985 and 1995, almost half will be in the south, reinforcing regional inequalities (Tyler and Rhodes 1987).

To a significant extent, the advocacy of urban privatism in the 1980s surpassed its implementation. The pursuit of the private city in Britain has, to a large extent, been a matter of promoting concepts, experiments, and expectations rather than putting in place a full-scale alternative urban program. In this context, there is a need to differentiate between the rhetoric of policy advocates and the reality of urban policy performance. Despite the Thatcher Government's pursuit of the private city, British urban policy remained firmly rooted in the public domain. The policy framework, both national and local, the planning and delivery of many urban services, the provision of infrastructure, and much of the funding of inner-city programs continued to be directed and implemented by the state. Whatever yardstick is employed, privatization within British cities in the 1980s still constituted a marginal addition to an essentially public activity. This public activity often served private interests but urban development policy remained a public enterprise; privatization initiatives took place within a comprehensive, continuous, and complex framework of public institutions and public controls.

Even under the best of circumstances, the privatization of urban Britain involves substantial transition costs. Reliance on the private sector as the central agent of urban development requires that fundamental changes occur in the institutional arrangements that have developed through decades of public sector activism and public responsibility for urban change. The costs of transition to a privatized system fall most heavily on communities and populations that are already faced with major economic dislocations and which, historically, have been dependent on the public sector rather than the private sector to direct urban development. In the peripheral estates, for example, there may be considerable benefit in the break-up of public monopoly, and these communities would obviously benefit from encouraging entrepreneurship and attracting new local enterprise but these initiatives do not carry the same implications as a sudden withdrawal of state support and a substantial reduction in the traditional forms of public expenditure.

In the midst of a policy environment dedicated to accommodating the requirements of the marketplace, there is little that local public authorities in depressed economic areas can do to reverse the pattern of spatial inequity. They lack native capital and the local public resources to attract capital investment. In fact, central government reduced local authority revenue, and, indeed, there is scant evidence that central government viewed privatization as requiring strong leadership by local public authorities. Many distressed communities in the 1980s depended even more on central government programs to launch economic development initiatives and those communities that were not selected for special subsidies from central government were placed in an even more severe bind.

Despite these constraints, in responding to the pressures of economic and technological change, city officials in Britain, like those in the US, have focused on issues of economic development and increasingly redefined the responsibilities of municipal governance to place public entrepreneurship in a central role. The entrepreneurial enthusiasm among civic leaders has made them boosters of local characteristics that can be considered marketable. In pursuit of investors, firms, technology, and tourists, cities in Britain now consider municipal marketing to be an essential activity.

Unlike the manufacturers of soap or toothpaste who can change the color of the stripes if the product does not sell, cities are not easily transformed to suit shifting market tastes. Cities and communities in Britain, like those in the US, have found that, in the short-term, they often can do little more than make costly cosmetic changes that may conceal but not redress underlying economic problems (Clark 1986: 125). Promotion strategies assume the existence of some untapped market potential but the economic condition of a number of British cities is itself a graphic testimonial to the lack of market appeal. While some areas—usually downtown commercial districts—may benefit from promotional campaigns, it is difficult to imagine how depressed urban areas can turn their fortunes around through advertising, image management, and greater concessions to footloose firms. Even if city promotion succeeded for the commercial center of Glasgow, for example, the problems of peripheral estates such as Drumchapel or Easterhouse would not be addressed.

In the midst of municipal competition, communities are forced to bid-up the incentives that they offer to corporations. Rather than creating new economic activity, cities use subsidies to lure firms from other locations, but the number and magnitude of the economic rewards that can be obtained is limited. Even the Secretary of State for Trade and Industry, Lord Young, acknowledged that 'there aren't that many mobile large employers around any more' (*The Times* (London), 24 June 1987). Nevertheless, the Thatcher Government promoted municipal competition. Local governments were encouraged to compete for whatever external resources are found on the horizon—firms, tourists, government grants, and public–private partnerships. Moreover, local policies, that began with a genuine concern about unemployment and issues of welfare, were modified so that they are more compatible with the economic criteria of business choice.

The policy of urban privatization in Britain manifests a number of contradictions that were persistent in the 1980s. First, efforts to bring the private sector back into the city were expected to reduce the role of public investment in urban development. In fact, government often adopted programs that depended on continuing and substantial public sector allocations to stimulate private investments. What was distinctive about these allocations was that the private sector became the principal beneficiary. Moreover, public subsidy of private investment increased at the same time as public expenditures for cities were reduced.

This relates to a second contradiction. While privatization was promoted by government as a strategy of urban regeneration, it often had, in fact, many of the earmarks of a strategy of urban disinvestment. On the one hand, programs like the Urban Regeneration Grant aimed at strengthening cities by using government resources to induce private investment. These programs were often pursued in an *ad hoc* manner that lacked any general coherence as a comprehensive urban policy but the emphasis was nonetheless on regeneration. By contrast, the selling off of public assets, the privatization of governmental functions and services, and particularly the reductions in public expenditures for cities represented a pattern of state withdrawal from responsibility for meeting the needs of distressed urban areas and disadvantaged urban populations. If privatization programs are to be successful in urban regeneration, then the benefits of those strategies must be shared by those urban areas and groups within urban areas that manifest chronic and severe distress. In the 1980s, the record ran in the other direction, with privatization programs exacerbating social and spatial divisions.

Finally, and perhaps most importantly, rather than reducing the role of central government, privatization of urban policy in the 1980s was accompanied by increased direct guidance of urban change by central ministries or their agents. At the same time, the role of local government was restricted. The trend was reinforced by the imposition of central controls over local authority spending and local revenue raising and by development programs such as the Urban Development Corporation which bypassed local authorities. This situation suggests that one of the most consequential long-term results of British urban policy in the 1980s is that it contributed to what some observers have called a 'half a century of municipal decline' (Loughlin *et al.* 1985). In seeking to redefine public and private responsibilities for urban change, government reshaped the balance of central–local government authority in a manner which threatened rather than strengthened the integrity of local institutions and thereby 'severely damaged urban government' (Hambleton 1988: 29). If privatization initiatives are to be effective in urban regeneration then the pressure for centralization must be brought to an end, and the state's objective of stimulating redevelopment through privatism must be matched by a commitment to the public funding and effective civic leadership necessary to make local redevelopment a success. As David Donnison warned:

> The determination of the Tories to destroy the metropolitan counties, to break down and disperse the powers of housing and education departments, to cut local spending, and to create centrally funded agencies, not accountable to local electors, which intrude on local territory, has helped to weaken responsible civic leadership and provoke a destructive politics which may wreck the Government's own programmes for renewing the inner cities (Donnison 1987).

When, after her third election victory, Margaret Thatcher committed her government to a concerted assault on the problems of the inner city some interpreted this as a signal of substantive policy change; a compassionate government response to the social and economic problems faced by many living in the poorest parts of urban Britain. But, Thatcher's interest in the inner city was primarily political. The remaining effective opposition to her policies was dug deeply into the Labour strongholds of northern urban Britain and, to a lesser extent, in London itself. Her interest in urban policy was intended, therefore, to remove this opposition and replace socialist authorities with a more 'enlightened' source of policy guidance from private enterprise and from central authority in London. As part of this effort, the government looked to replace the influence of local elected city councils with support from 'new groups, perhaps chaired by prominent local businessmen and broadly representative of the community, to harness the resources of industry, commerce, local enterprise agencies, the Government and local authorities' (Hetherington 1987). In effect, the policy proposals offered as part of the assault on inner-city problems were extensions of policies and programs pursued over the previous decade. These policies and programs have not resulted in widespread economic revival of previously depressed urban centers. Rather they have contributed to erosion of local authority and resources, and the worsening of Britain's spatial and social divisions.

Notes

1. In the 1950s and 1960s, with the support of central government, municipal housing authorities developed extensive 'schemes' of public housing, often located on the periphery of cities. These communities—frequently housing more than 20,000 people—were built in response to chronic housing problems with the result that quantity was more important than quality. Untested system-building techniques and inadequate site planning and design quickly resulted in environmental deterioration. Moreover, commercial and social facilities were often lacking and sources of employment were not seen as being relevant to the overall needs of these new communities. Hence, by the late 1970s, some of the

worst urban conditions in Britain were to be found in these peripheral estates.

Policies and programs designed for the inner city were soon adapted to fit the specific circumstances found in these areas. In particular, the DoE sponsored the Priority Estates Project, a management-based solution to the problems found in high-density, often high-rise, housing schemes (Power 1984). In the mid-1980s, government launched their Urban Housing Renewal Unit (renamed Estate Action in 1987), designed to help local housing authorities remodel their problem estates. This physical response to multifaceted urban problems was in no small way influenced by the work of Alice Coleman, a fierce critic of public housing in Britain and supporter of private enterprise: 'far better to phase the DoE Housing Development Directorate quietly out of existence and return housing initiatives to the free market, with minimum regulation and maximum consumer choice' (Coleman 1985: 184).

2. While LEG-UP is administered by the Scottish Development Agency (see ch. 6), final authority to grant money rests with the appropriate Minister, in this case the Secretary of State for Scotland. He is advised by a triumvirate of senior officials from the SDA itself, the Industry Department for Scotland, and the Scottish Development Department.

3. In areas of low owner-occupation, as in the west of Scotland, property subsidies like LEG-UP are used to promote local housing markets. Public support is targeted at developers providing new-build and conversions at a relatively low price. In Glasgow, this policy has resulted in some 800 units per annum being added to the city's private housing stock with three apartment flats costing between £19,500 and £17,500 [1985 prices] (Maclennan and Munro 1986).

4. Working in collaboration with Estate Action, a number of builders have successfully employed UDG funds to subsidize the conversion and improvement for sale of previously empty public housing. From the government's perspective, this use of UDG is particularly significant in that it satisfies the objective of spatial targeting.

5. Capital programs of a commercial nature undertaken by government agencies are financed through borrowing from the National Loans Fund (previously known as the Public Works Loan Board). This represents a small proportion of total investment by the UDCs. By March 1986, the Merseyside UDC had secured seven loans amounting to £1,054 million as against Grant in Aid in 1985/6 of £28,816 million.

6. 'Rate Relief' is the term applied to the incentive of a 10-year period when companies would not be liable for the payment of property tax. The local authority is, however, not penalized as the loss of revenue is made good by an additional transfer from the Treasury.

7. This resulted in the boundaries of the second round zones being more carefully drawn. In the Tayside Enterprise Zone in Scotland, the designated area was carefully selected to avoid including too many properties within an existing industrial estate.

8. These included: (1) exemption from development land tax (now abolished); (2) 100 percent capital allowances (for income and corporation tax purposes) on industrial and commercial buildings; (3) exemption from general rates on industrial and commercial property; (4) simplification of planning procedures; (5) exemption from the requirements of industrial training boards; (6) speedier customs procedures; (7) abolition of requirements for industrial development certificates; and

(8) reduction to bare minimum of the government's requests for statistical information (NAO 1986).

9. All Enterprise Zones are administered by local authorities with the exception of the Scottish zones: Clydebank and Tayside (administered by the SDA), and Invergordon (Highlands and Islands Development Board); and the Isle of Dogs in London (the responsibility of the LDDC).

10. In 1986, the Greater London Council and the Metropolitan County Councils (Tyne and Wear, West Yorkshire, South Yorkshire, Greater Manchester, Merseyside, and West Midlands) were abolished and their remaining functions distributed to the district tier of government or to special boards. The implication of this reorganization, and the increasing centralization implied, is usefully explored in a series of papers collected by West Yorkshire County Council shortly before its demise (Goldsmith 1986).

11. The European Regional Development Fund (ERDF) can, in theory, direct EEC resources to distressed areas in the Community. Funds are mainly used for infrastructure projects—roads, water supply, environmental improvement. In Britain, however (as in other member states), there is a 'non-additionality' rule whereby spending on ERDF schemes should not amount to additional public expenditures. This effectively means that ERDF money, received by a private concern or by a local authority, is simply replacing an existing subsidy (Keating and Waters 1985; Keating and Boyle 1986). In contrast, the European Social Fund (ESF) can offer additional funds for distressed areas; with grants commonly used for employment subsidy schemes and for retraining programs (Chandler and Lawless 1985: 214–17).

8

Urban Policy and the Limits of Privatism

WHILE similarities in British and American urban policy in the 1980s were readily apparent, the promotion of privatism in the two countries took place in very different institutional environments. The contrast is particularly striking when the enthusiasm for privatism is examined against the background of earlier policy traditions. The institutional framework for urban policy and the balance of public and private responsibilities in urban areas are significantly different in Britain and the United States. Furthermore, the magnitude, scope, and continuity of post-war policy experience with privatism have been substantially greater in the US than in Britain. These differences have important implications for the practical and political challenges to implementation of a strategy of urban privatization.

Despite these differences, and disregarding earlier warnings about the dangers of exchanging policy instruments across the Atlantic without substantive assessment of their effectiveness, a recurring feature of British urban policy throughout the 1980s was the attempt to replicate US urban redevelopment programs. The borrowing from US program initiatives (particularly economic development programs such as UDAG) was carried out with little systematic knowledge of the US record of performance and with scant regard for the consequences of inappropriate policy transfer. The physical improvements resulting from redevelopment efforts in Baltimore or Pittsburgh were understandably attractive to British politicians and planners. But the wider implications of seeking to replicate these models in a different social, political, and economic environment were usually ignored. Moreover, little attention was paid to the failures of US redevelopment which remain a prominent legacy of privatism. While these failures are rarely acknowledged by the proponents of transfer, they ought to be an important part of the policy experience that accompanies the exchange of program initiative and organization.

More important than recognition of the limits of transfer, however, are the general lessons to be learned about privatism and urban policy from the experience of both countries. In this regard, the differences of institutional contexts should not obscure the similarities of outcomes that have accompanied the reliance on the private sector for urban development. In our view, the strengths and weaknesses of privatism as an instrument of urban policy, a strategy of urban regeneration, and a community standard are much the same in Britain and America. In concluding our analysis we review the logic that has sustained an enthusiasm for privatism on both sides of the Atlantic and discuss the limits of that logic based on the experience with privatism in both Britain and the United States.

222

The Promise of Privatism

Advocates of privatism claim that the well-being of urban communities is linked to a greater reliance on private initiatives. This claim is seductive not only because it appeals to traditional values in market-oriented societies but also because it offers the prospect that business skills and resources can be mobilized to find harmonious solutions to urban problems. Further, since the 1970s, many government leaders in the US and Britain have assumed that privatism is a necessary condition for national development. Attention has focused on national economic renewal, and, for the conservative governments of both countries in the 1980s, national renewal required a market-led transformation of the economy.

As national economic decline is defined as the overriding problem facing urban areas, the fate of local economies is assumed to depend on the outcome of national efforts to improve market efficiency. These improvements are possible, it is believed, only if the private sector is relied upon to make allocative decisions and if the public sector resists interventions which distort the efficient choices of firms and individuals. Urban regeneration must be pursued in ways that are consistent with national economic needs and policy must concentrate on enhancing the role of the private sector in urban change. Local actions are appropriate, and likely to be successful, only when they run with rather than against the interests of private institutions. In short, privatism is the key to national recovery as well as local prosperity.

The commitment to privatism as an instrument of urban policy and a strategy of urban regeneration has translated into local economic development strategies that are similar in the US and Britain. These strategies have been used to justify the concentration of local economic development efforts on privatizing municipal functions and services and enlarging the reliance on the private sector for bringing about urban change. They are based on a rationale (identified in earlier chapters) which ties community well-being to local economic development and local economic development to privatism:

1. Cities which hope to prosper must concentrate their efforts and resources on local economic development in a manner consistent with national needs for economic growth.
2. Local economic development programs should reflect a commitment to privatism; ways must be found to stimulate the expansion of private activity since the private sector has the pivotal role in urban economic innovation and development.
3. The best way to stimulate the expansion of private activity in urban areas is to use public funds to 'leverage' private investment.
4. Local economic development efforts can and should be 'targeted' to disadvantaged groups and/or distressed communities.
5. Because economic prosperity increasingly lies with technological leadership, cities should concentrate efforts on those sectors likely to be in the forefront of a high-technology, post-industrial future.

6. Social programs cannot dominate the attention of local government since these programs are too expensive, frequently ineffective in improving the economic prospects of the poor and put cities at a competitive disadvantage *vis-à-vis* areas which adopt a more progressive economic development posture. Social problems can be best addressed through economic development.
7. Urban development is always spatially selective. Cities which hope to prosper must learn to compete effectively for economic growth with other urban areas.
8. Cities must increasingly rely on their own resources in creating economic development, and, therefore, the most prudent strategy is for local governments to form partnerships with their private sectors to enhance their comparative advantages relative to other jurisdictions. To be successful, local governments must develop an entrepreneurial attitude and new skills in municipal marketing.
9. Local economic development is a technical rather than a political issue; there is a community of common interests around which local economic development policy and programs can be organized.
10. Communities can capture the benefits of investment in local economic development.
11. Everyone in the community shares in the benefits of local economic development and the costs are not concentrated in any one segment of the population.

These ideas have been persuasive in both the US and Britain. Some of this appeal is obvious. There is ample evidence to support the belief that the future of most urban places is bleak unless they possess or can develop a viable and productive economic base. Glasgow and Liverpool, like Newark and the south Bronx, would be substantially better off if they had strong private sector infrastructures. These observations are basically truisms, however. They neither demonstrate the effectiveness of local economic development programs nor confirm that general benefits accrue from a commitment to privatism. More to the point, there is evidence that, through efforts to promote private sector activity, some urban areas have successfully leveraged private investment, mobilized public–private partnerships, and created new prospects for economic growth. In the 1980s, increased reliance on the private sector in urban development improved the economic prospects of some cities and some segments of the urban population in both Britain and the United States. Indeed, in the US the successes of privatism were portrayed by the federal government as part of a new urban renaissance and cited as proof that reliance on private institutions is the most prudent course for cities. In Britain, the emphasis on privatism also was credited as benefiting urban areas: by strengthening the institutional capacity for local economic development, breaking down the inertia of traditional bureaucratic structures in local government, and developing new governmental arrangements and public–private partnerships to stimulate and support locally-based economic initiatives. In both Britain and the US, the achievements to date are seen by advocates as only a preview of even better things to come from continued confidence in the promise of privatism.

The Limits of Privatism

Despite the achievements of privatism in Britain and the US, it does not follow that the prevailing ideas about local economic development have broad validity or that community development can be achieved by any locality that follows its prescriptions. In both the US and Britain, advocates of privatism as a strategy of urban regeneration have exaggerated its benefits and largely ignored its costs. Calls for business leadership, economic growth, and community self-reliance are understandably attractive but they are no substitute for evidence that privatization helps to regenerate depressed urban economies.

Our analysis demonstrates that privatism does not offer a reliable guide for urban regeneration in substantial portions of either the US or Britain. Indeed, in a number of respects privatism exacerbates the difficulties of urban communities. These conditions do not reflect technical failures that can be overcome by improved design of local economic development programs; rather, they signify the underlying limits of privatism as a strategy of urban development.

Reliance on the private sector for urban economic development often is portrayed as a pragmatic choice; a selection of institutional means to achieve presumably agreed upon social ends. In a privatized system, however, the substance and direction of efforts at urban regeneration, as well as the forms and instruments, must be structured to meet the demands of private investors. These efforts depend largely on what the private sector sees as its priorities and is willing to accept as investment risks. In both the US and Britain, despite periodic proclamations of corporate social responsibility, there is little evidence of sustained business interest in urban social investments. In the US, with the exception of brief excursions into urban social programs in the aftermath of the urban riots in the late 1960s, the business community has been disinterested and uninvolved in urban social programs, generally seeing these activities as the responsibility of voluntary organizations or government. In fact, experiences with social programs convinced many business leaders that they possessed neither the skills nor the incentives to play an active role in the social regeneration of cities. In Britain, despite occasional proclamations of corporate social responsibility, the private sector has been even less involved and there is no record of a sustained interest, or even willingness, to broadly participate in local public–private partnerships.

. For the most part, the activities which the private sector considers as sound investments, and as within their domain of expertise, have been property development projects in areas selected for their commercial potential and profitability. The injection of public powers and resources has sometimes induced the private sector to take a more active role in development projects, but it has not altered the pattern of investment choice. Property development has a place in the process of urban regeneration and sometimes it has mobilized substantial private capital. But even when the physical and commercial face of a city is dramatically changed, general benefits for the community are not necessarily the result. Proponents of property development point to new jobs and increased economic activity but often large segments of the urban population—particularly racial minorities, the poor, and the unemployed—are not among the beneficiaries.

Even if communities are prepared to accept the bias in development priorities, opportunities to rely upon the private sector as the key instrument of local economic development often are limited. This situation is particularly disconcerting in Britain where private infrastructure is not only unevenly distributed but largely absent in parts of many urban areas. In these areas, calls for a reliance on the private sector ring hollow. The older inner-city areas and the peripheral housing estates generally lack the local business networks that are essential to a partnership strategy. Yet it is precisely these areas that exhibit the most acute and chronic urban problems—high levels of joblessness, declining job opportunities, and falling wages. Attracting private resources into these areas assumes the presence of a supply of local capital. The reality is vastly different. Thus, leveraging private investment must be translated into efforts to import capital into areas traditionally viewed as poor investment risks. To accomplish this, the public sector must play a central role. Indeed, drawing private investment to the weaker parts of the economy in either the US or Britain requires more, not less, public expenditure, and the scale is inevitably staggering. One must question the meaning of privatism when supposedly market-led development is driven by massive public subsidy of private development interests.

Even when the desire is to target the benefits of privatism to distressed communities and populations, there are significant obstacles. In the US, the targeting of economic development programs to distressed communities has been limited by political pressures at both the federal and state levels which encourage a broad spatial allocation of resources. Moreover, directing the benefits of economic development to disadvantaged groups conflicts with the desire to create maximum incentives for private sector participation. The thrust of the privatization policies in both the US and Britain has been to remove limitations on private investment decisions not to increase them. One result is that subsidies are sometimes obtained for projects already planned or underway rather than for new initiatives in targeted economic development. Moreover, there is evidence (from the UDAG program in the US and the Enterprise Zone experiments in Britain) that investment presumably induced by subsidies would have occurred in any case; thus, firms receive windfalls for investment decisions made independent of community needs. Furthermore, once subsidies have been granted, compliance with targeting requirements (the provision of job opportunities to low-income or minority groups or response to particular community needs) is difficult to monitor and rarely are sanctions applied when obligations are neglected or substantially ignored. The difficulty of targeting resources to distressed urban populations has been a chronic dilemma of public assistance and urban policy programs in both Britain and the US, but the evidence suggests that it is made even more acute when policy is designed to accommodate private develop-ment interests.

In this context, it is important to examine closely the idea of leverage that has been in fashion on both sides of the Atlantic. Rather than public authority shaping private decisions, the reverse is often the case. US policy experience suggests that what is launched as an effort to stimulate private investment for public purposes frequently becomes a program of private leverage of public funds. The long-term result is the inversion of public and private priorities and the substitution of a private planning system for a public one without the establishment of an equivalent means of accountability—and the costs in public revenues can be substantial. In Britain, this inversion of priorities has been increasingly apparent in the 1980s. Urban policy that originally was conceived to address issues of social and economic dislocation and inequality instead has been used to launch and finance a series of property development projects where success is measured in terms of physical change and the return on private investment. Moreover, what began as public policy—with local government being the natural agents of change—has become a 'vehicle for the articulation of private sector interests' (Stewart 1987: 141).

The profit motive may be a powerful incentive, but it is not easily harnessed to achieve publicly defined policy objectives. Experiences with public–private partnerships in urban redevelopment demonstrate this difficulty. In the US, partnerships have often formed the basis for local leadership coalitions that are instrumental in general redevelopment planning and implementation. The creation and maintenance of public–private coalitions, however, requires a string of public concessions to business interests and a concentration of public resources on services and development ventures that are priorities of the local business community. Moreover, when a community makes use of local business leadership it often cannot avoid being captured by it. At times this has meant that local governments have turned over general responsibility for the guidance of development to institutions which represent only a small fraction of the community and which operate as private governments, effectively insulated from direct public accountability.

Market-led urban development has always resulted in an uneven distribu-tion of benefits and recent experience in the US and Britain is no exception. Distributive inequities apply not only to different groups within the urban community but also to different sections within cities and to different cities within the nation. Advocates of privatism point out that this unevenness reflects a responsiveness to the changing spatial needs of private enterprise which leads to greater market efficiency. But even if this logic is accepted, it hardly resolves the problems faced by deteriorated urban areas or reduces the hardships experienced by the poor. While greater market efficiency may significantly improve the conditions of many cities and urban subareas, it will, for the most part, further disadvantage those areas which the market has rejected.

Advocates of privatism claim that despite short-term dislocations, the benefits of market-led economic growth ultimately will trickle down through the community. But for many economically depressed communities in the US and Britain, there is little evidence of trickle-down. Despite more rapid national economic growth in both countries in the 1980s and a logic of economic development that concentrates on job creation and links local prosperity to national economic recovery, the British unemployment rate in 1987 was more than twice the rate when Mrs. Thatcher was elected in 1979. In the US, the employment record is more favorable but in many urban areas there continue to be high concentrations of unemployment and, as we previously described, in the nation as a whole, poverty rates and inequities in the distribution of income have increased.

In addition to its divisive social and spatial impacts, the commitment to privatism has brought forth a narrow vision of the responsibilities of local government. City officials throughout the US and Britain have adopted an approach to local responsibilities that redefines municipal governance as public entrepreneurship. In the chase for technology, tourists, and footloose firms, civic leaders in the US and Britain elevated municipal marketing to a central role of local government. But in the municipal competition that ensues, losers always outnumber winners and the cost of participation is significant. Firms play one city off against another, forcing communities to bid-up the incentives they are prepared to offer. At the same time, the resources available for other facets of urban development more directly consequential for depressed areas and their residents are reduced.

In the spirit of public entrepreneurship, privatism is promoted as if it were simply a technical reform; one which implements 'positive work programs' and creates the initiative for 'getting things done'. This reformist perspective presumes the existence of a community of common goals and values and the possibility of establishing a standard level of municipal services beneficial to all residents, an assumption that is contradicted by experience. In both America and Britain the definition of 'positive work programs' is a matter of political dispute, and the zeal for 'getting things done' is often a public rationale for the pursuit of private advantage. Turning to entrepreneurship and commercial initiative as a solution to the decline of urban areas represents not only an unjustified acceptance of the private sector's expertise but, more importantly, an imposition of artificial and premature closure on the definition of community interests.

In the pursuit of economic development, urban priorities are matched to the demands of private investors in ways that neglect other community interests. Even when communities are prepared to pay the price, privatism is no substitute for public investment. As Paul Starr points out, this is not to suggest that every activity in the public sector ought to remain there forever.

A pragmatic public policy must recognize where private alternatives work better and, by the same token, where new forms of public provision may ameliorate endemic shortcomings of the market. Most of all, it must recognize that markets are not natural creations; they are always legally and politically structured. Hence the choice is not public or private but which of the many possible mixed public–private structures works best. And 'best' cannot mean only most efficient, for a reasonable appraisal of alternatives needs to weigh concerns of justice, security, and citizenship (Starr 1987: 125.)

In both Britain and the US, reasonable appraisal of privatization alternat ives as policy options is obstructed by the pursuit of privatism as an end in itself. This distinction between means and ends may never be easy to sustain but it has all but been abandoned in the 1980s. Indeed, the distinction cannot be preserved when privatism is accepted as a self-sealing ideological imperat ive. It is one thing to experiment with different combinations of public and private responsibilities in the delivery of urban services; it is something quite different to confine possibilities for urban change to what the criterion of market efficiency allows.

In sum, while privatism may contribute to national economic growth and increase the aggregate wealth of some urban places, it does not ensure an equitable distribution of that wealth. There are many urban areas and groups whose circumstances testify to the failure of privatism's powers of urban regeneration and its inability to deal with the dislocations of urban social change. In his analysis of the historical effects of privatism on American cities, Sam Bass Warner, Jr. put the issue simply: 'What the private market could do well, American cities have done well; what the private market did badly, or neglected, our cities have been unable to overcome' (Warner 1968: p. x). The British and American experience with privatism in the 1980s confirms this assessment.

Post-Industrialism and the Politics of Privatism

The commitment to privatism represents an underlying complementarity in British and American policy directions that is likely to extend beyond the conservative governments of the 1980s. Increasingly, the pursuit of the pri vate city and the withdrawal of national resources from urban areas are rationalized by the perceived requirements of a market-led, post-industrial transition. Continued acceptance of this line of policy rationalization threatens to trivialize urban governance and to encourage a view of cities as disposable commodities of an enterprise culture. Addressing these threats means, first of all, the development of a more critical intellectual posture towards the cultural tradition of privatism.

Increasingly, the urban policy dialogue in both the United States and Britain has been framed in terms of the requirements for a transition to a post-industrial, service-oriented, technologically advanced society. The pre vailing expectation has been that economic progress depends on policies that respond to the demands of a market-led, post-industrial transition. In practice this expectation is translated into proposals that have gained allegiance across a wide political spectrum: loosen the reins of public policy traditions that have sought to preserve industrial prominence; develop new and differently balanced public–private arrangements to promote economic realignment; and do not resist or impede the social and spatial adaptations to changing technological and market forces.

Privatism and post-industrialism are emerging as complementary dimensions of the definition of social and economic progress. In the longer term, the concentration of national attention and resources on achieving a post-industrial transition may be more consequential in encouraging privatism than the specific policy measures undertaken by the Reagan or Thatcher Governments or other similarly inclined administrations. In fact, conservative zeal for privatism for its own sake may well be replaced by seemingly more pragmatic justifications for designing policies and institutions to accommodate the marketplace. While the ideological rationale for privatism may be moderated, the strength of national commitment to post-industrialism is likely to be intensified, and as a result the political base of support for a greater reliance on market institutions will significantly expand.

In a fundamental sense, post-industrialism represents an extension of the cultural tradition of privatism, and as such it adds new dimensions to that tradition. A central premise of this 'new privatism' is that shifts in spatial organization reflected in the movement of population and economic activity are natural and largely irresistible outcomes of a changing marketplace. In this context, the fortunes of cities in both America and Britain are and should be determined by a technologically driven economic transition that is neither the result of public policy nor susceptible to modification by government interventions.

This logic implies that national economic prosperity is no longer dependent in any direct manner on the prosperity of cities. In this context, the overriding purpose of privatizing urban policy is not the regeneration of cities but rather the adaptation of the urban landscape to the spatial requirements of a post-industrial society. Prosperity, it is assumed, does not depend upon the revival of economically depressed cities and, if achieved, would not necessarily entail the revival of flagging city economies.

The symbiosis of privatism and post-industrialism poses a profound challenge to municipal governance. Since the process of social change is increasingly seen to depend upon market and technological forces, the responsibilities of municipalities become largely reactive. In this sense, the value of municipal governance is limited to its ability to facilitate efficiency and productivity in the new post-industrial growth sectors. So viewed, municipalities, at best, can serve as multi-purpose service districts or public works authorities that administer decisions of central government and provide the physical infrastructure in locations favored by the spatial choices of private firms. This subordination of local government to markets and technology challenges the very meaning of urban governance. What effective governing authority at the local level can exist if a community's first responsibilities are to market itself as a commodity in a commercial sweepstakes and refrain from any actions that might modify market decisions or technological demands?

Ultimately, the logic of post-industrialism trivializes the city as a political and economic community. What is taken to be distinctive about post-industrial change is that it signifies the declining importance of central places as barometers of, and contributors to, economic and social progress and, by extension, as political institutions. In a world driven by the idea of post-industrial change, the value of cities becomes ephemeral. Indeed, there is no good reason why any city should exist, except by happenstance of rising or declining economic activity, within a national, and increasingly, international marketplace. The implication is that cities are to be regarded almost entirely as transient economic artifacts whose importance in the larger scheme of economic organization has been and will continue to decrease.

In America, the diminished role of cities is openly proclaimed under the heading of the 'new urban reality' and it is rationalized as a necessary fact not only by ideological polemicists but by a significant portion of the urban analysis community (G. Peterson 1986). Norton Long has aptly summarized the logic of this emerging view and the central question it raises:

In this view aging cities should be treated in much the same way as worn out mines and obsolete factories. They should be phased out as rapidly, and painlessly as possible in the interest of the efficient functioning of the national economy, and resources should not be squandered in a counter-productive effort to keep losers afloat ... There can be little objection in principle to phasing out obsolete mines or factories, though the process in practice is fraught with difficulty and suffering since the costs of economic adjustment fall heavily on its victims. An argument can be made and has been made that society, which is the supposed gainer from the readjustment, should share the cost of easing the transition. But one may ask, are cities organizations on a continuum with mines and factories whose fates should be decided by the unhampered play of market forces as they alter the terms of trade and comparative locational advantage? (1983: 21–2).[4]

Under the prevailing logic of post-industrialism, this question is itself viewed as irrelevant; a matter that will be decided by the natural forces of change.

While recognizing that post-industrialism is socially and spatially disruptive, urban analysts have warned that it would be folly to try to resist the forces of change or to ignore the beneficial outcomes that ultimately will result from the market-led transition (Bradbury, Downs, and Small 1981). But if one accepts the idea of a post-industrial imperative, Byrne, Martinez, and Rich (1985) have argued, it is easy to rationalize any costs of social change as the necessary price of progress.

What is being delivered as a post-industrial future may exhibit chronic instability and massive social burdens. From the vantage point of the post-industrial imperative, however, no degree of instability and no level of social burden is sufficient to call into question the path to progress. So long as we accept markets and technology as the appropriate and necéssary substitutes for social choice, we must conclude that whatever conditions they deliver are for the best. It makes the matter of social progress seem so simple: all we need is the will to face post-industrial reality—markets and technology will deliver the rest (1985: 134–5).

This rationalization encourages national policies that have no specific urban content at all and it encourages governments to avoid interventions to deal with the dislocations of economic change. In this context, perhaps the strongest parallel in the urban policy directions of the United States and Britain is not the common emphasis on the private sector but the mutual turning away from the social and economic dislocations affecting urban areas and the communities within these areas. So viewed, the central question for urban policy in Britain and America is not what can the private sector do, but, rather, what does the state no longer accept as its responsibility?

In our view, the fate of cities in Britain and America has been, to a significant extent, the result of political choice rather than economic necessity. That political choice is manifested in the dedicated pursuit of the private city. As Ted Gurr and Desmond King have pointed out, 'it is not plausible to regard the decline of some of our cities and the growth of others as the irreversible result of economic processes . . . [T]he continued decline of most of the old industrial cities of Britain and the United States is the result of public decisions to allow the economic fate of those cities to be determined in the private sector' (Gurr and King 1987: 190). Our examination of privatism and urban policy has described and evaluated many of these public decisions. It has demonstrated that the public choice of privatism is the dominant characteristic of contemporary urban policy in both the United States and Britain.

What is remarkable about this public choice is that its political character is rarely acknowledged or openly examined; it is disguised by rationalizations which themselves reflect the influence of the cultural tradition of privatism. The idea of a post-industrial imperative is only the most recent of these disguises. Yet, commitment to the cultural tradition of privatism remains a cardinal political choice and its political character is not erased by government decisions to exercise diminished public responsibility for urban areas and their residents. British and American governments, both national and local, should be held accountable for the consequences of this political choice. Such is the power of the tradition of privatism, however, that it acts to persistently erode any sense of public responsibility or accountability.

Privatism serves as an intellectual and cultural prism that defines ideas in accord with its assumptions as natural, inevitable, and politically neutral while dismissing alternative views as unrealistic, unworkable, and infused with politics. In this manner, privatism and its recent expression in the idea of a post-industrial imperative sustain a one-dimensional image of social and economic progress that has narrowed our vision of the possibilities for urban development. And so it will remain as long as the underlying political character of this cultural commitment is denied or ignored and thereby insulated from evaluation against alternative criteria of social value.

What is needed is what John Kenneth Galbraith has called an emancipation of beliefs (1973). Essential to this is an acknowledgment of the social impacts of privatism and the consequences that arise from its dominance as a cultural tradition. Equally important, however, is the recognition that the influence of privatism and its limitations do not constitute unalterable constraints on public choice. In our view, the forces shaping urban development in both Britain and the United States remain subject to influence through public intervention. In this regard, we need a theoretical posture and policy orientation that encourages public learning; one that subjects the dominant tradition of privatism to critical assessment and, thereby, identifies the alternative possibilities for public choice and public action.

References

Aaron, Henry (1978). *Politics and the Professors*. Washington, DC: Brookings Institution.

Abel-Smith, B., and Townsend, P. (1965). *The Poor and the Poorest*. London: Bell.

Abrams, Charles (1965). *The City is the Frontier*. New York: Harper and Row.

ACIR [US Advisory Commission on Intergovernmental Relations] (1970). *Eleventh Annual Report*. Washington, DC: GPO.

Adam Smith Institute (1985). *Privatisation*. London: Adam Smith Institute.

Adcock, Brian (1984). 'Regenerating Merseyside Docklands: The Merseyside Development Corporation, 1981–1984.' *Town Planning Review* 55: 265–89.

Adrian, Charles R., and Press, Charles (1977). *Governing Urban America*. New York: McGraw-Hill.

Ahlbrandt, Jr., Roger S. (1984). 'Ideology and the Reagan Administration's First National Urban Policy Report.' *Journal of the American Planning Association* 50 (4): 479–84.

Ambrose, Peter (1986). *Whatever Happened to Planning?* London: Methuen.

Ambrose, Peter, and Colenutt, Bob (1975). *The Property Machine*. Harmondsworth: Penguin.

Anderson, Martin (1964). *The Federal Bulldozer: A Critical Analysis of Urban Renewal, 1949–1962*. Cambridge, Mass.: Massachusetts Institute of Technology Press.

Archbishop of Canterbury's Commission (1985). *Faith in the City*. London: Church of England Commissioners.

Baber, Walter F. (1987). 'Privatizing Public Management.' In *Prospects for Privatization*, ed. Steve H. Hanke. New York: Academy of Political Science.

Bachrach, Peter, and Baratz, Morton S. (1970). *Power and Poverty: Theory and Practice*. New York: Oxford University Press.

Bailey, Robert W. (1987). 'Uses and Misuses of Privatization.' In *Prospects for Privatization*, ed. Steve H. Hanke. New York: Academy of Political Science.

Baldock, Jonathan (1986). 'Development Grants and Area Improvement.' *Estates Gazette* 278 (June): 1428–30.

Balsillie, Donald (1986). 'Garden Festivals.' Unpublished M.Sc. thesis. University of Strathclyde.

Banfield, Edward C. (ed.) (1965). *Big City Politics*. New York: Random House.

Banfield, Edward C., and Wilson, James Q. (1963). *City Politics*. New York: Vintage.

Banham, Rayner (1969). 'Non-Plan: An Experiment in Freedom.' *New Society* (Mar.): 435–42.

Barlow Report (1940). *Report of the Royal Commission on the Distribution of the Industrial Population*, Cmnd. 6153. London: HMSO.

Barnekov, Timothy K., and Rich, Daniel (1972). 'The Corporation as a Social Welfare Institution.' *American Behavioral Scientist* 15 (5): 749–63.

—— (1977). 'Privatism and Urban Development: An Analysis of the Organized Influence of Local Business Elites.' *Urban Affairs Quarterly* 12 (4): 431–60.

Barnekov, Timothy K., Rich, Daniel, and Warren, Robert (1981). 'The New Privatism, Federalism, and the Future of Urban Governance: National Urban Policy in the

1980s.' *Journal of Urban Affairs* 3 (4): 1–14.

Bath, David (1986).'Marketing Towns and Cities: A Case Study of Peterborough.' *Planner* 73 (2): 89–93.

Beales, H. L. (1967). *The Industrial Revolution, 1750–1850: An Introductory Essay*. New York: Kelly.

Beam, David R. (1984). 'New Federalism, Old Realities: The Reagan Administration and Intergovernmental Reform.' In *The Reagan Presidency and the Governing of America*, ed. Lester M. Salamon and Michael S. Lund. Washington, DC: Urban Institute Press.

Begg, Iain, Moore, Barry, and Rhodes, John (1986). 'Economic and Social Change in Urban Britain and the Inner Cities.' In *Critical Issues in Urban Economic Development, Volume I*, ed. Victor A. Hausner. Oxford: Clarendon Press.

Bell, Daniel (1971). 'The Corporation and Society in the 1970s.' *Public Interest* (Summer): 5–32.

Bendick, Jr., Marc (1984). 'Privatization of Public Services: Recent Experience.' In *Public–Private Partnership: New Opportunities for Meeting Social Needs*, ed. Harvey Brooks, Lance Liebman, and Corrine S. Schelling. Cambridge, Mass.: Ballinger.

Bendick, Jr., Marc, and Levinson, Phyllis M. (1984). 'Private Sector Initiatives or Public–Private Partnerships?' In *The Reagan Presidency and the Governing of America*, ed. Lester M. Salamon and Michael S. Lund. Washington, DC: Urban Institute Press.

Bendick, Jr., Marc, and Rasmussen, David W. (1986). 'Enterprise Zones and Inner-City Economic Revitalization.' In *Reagan and the Cities*, ed. George E. Peterson and Carol W. Lewis. Washington, DC: Urban Institute Press.

Berger, Renee A. (1984). 'Private Sector Initiatives in the Reagan Era: New Actors Rework an Old Theme.' In *The Reagan Presidency and the Governing of America*, ed. Lester M. Salamon and Michael S. Lund. Washington, DC: Urban Institute Press.

Berle, Adolph, A., and Means, Gardiner C. (1932). *The Modern Corporation and Private Property*. New York: Macmillan.

Berney, Karen (1984). 'Expanding Firms Are Flocking to North Carolina, but Start-ups Elude State's Efforts to Draw Them.' *Electronics Week* (Sept. 10): 38–44.

Berry, Brian J. L. (1981). *Comparative Urbanization: Divergent Paths in the Twentieth Century*. New York: St. Martin's Press.

BIC [Business in the Community] (n.d.). *Business and the Inner Cities*. London: Business in the Community.

Bikerstaffe, Rodney (1985). 'NUPE Pledged to Defeat Evils of Privatisation.' *Local Government Chronicle*, (July 5): 14–15.

Birch, David (1980). *Job Creation in Cities*. Cambridge, Mass.: Program on Neighborhood and Regional Change, Massachusetts Institute of Technology.

Blumenfeld, Hans (1969). 'Criteria for Judging the Quality of the Urban Environment.' In *The Quality of Urban Life*, ed. Henry J. Schmandt and Warren Bloomberg, Jr. Beverly Hills: Sage.

Boddy, Martin (1983). 'Changing Public–Private Sector Relationships in the Industrial Development Process.' In *Urban Economic Development*, ed. Ken Young and Chris Mason. London: Macmillan.

Boddy, Martin, and Fudge, Colin (eds.) (1984). *Local Socialism? Labour Councils and New Left Alternatives*. London: Macmillan.

Boorstin, Daniel J. (1967). *The Americans: The National Experience. New York: Random House.*

Bosanquet, Nicholas (1983). *After the New Right*. London: Heinemann.

Bourne, Richard (1973). 'The Urban Coalition: Consensus and Cleavage in an Agent of Social Change.' Unpublished Ph.D. dissertation. Harvard University.

Boyle, Robin (1983a). *Privatising Urban Problems: A Commentary on Anglo-American Policy*, Studies in Public Policy, No. 117. Glasgow: University of Strathclyde.

—— (1983b). *UDAG: The Urban Development Action Grant*, Strathclyde Papers on Planning, No. 1. Glasgow: University of Strathclyde.

—— (ed.) (1985). 'Leveraging Urban Development: A Comparison of Urban Policy Directions and Programme Impact in the United States and Britain.' *Policy and Politics* 13 (2): 175–210.

—— (1987). 'Urban Initiatives in Scotland—Measuring the Tartan Factor.' *Planner* 73 (6): 27–30.

—— (1988). *LEDIS Overview: Urban Policy—City Action Teams and Task Forces.* Glasgow: Planning Exchange.

Boyle, Robin, and Wannop, Urlan A. (1982). 'Area Initiatives and the SDA: The Rise of the Urban Project.' *Quarterly Economic Commentary* 8 (1): 45–7. Glasgow: Fraser of Allander Institute, University of Strathclyde.

Bradbury, Katherine L., Downs, Anthony, and Small, Kenneth A. (1981). *Futures for a Declining City: Simulations for the Cleveland Area*. Washington, DC: Brookings Institution.

Bradford, Amory (1968). *Oakland's Not For Burning*. New York: McKay.

Brandl, John, and Brooks, Ronnie (1982). 'Public–Private Cooperation for Urban Revitalization: The Minneapolis and Saint Paul Experience.' In *Public–Private Partnership in American Cities*, ed. R. Scott Fosler and Renee A. Berger. Lexington, Mass.: D.C. Heath.

Briggs, Asa (1963). *Victorian Cities*. London: Odhams.

Brindley, Tim, and Stoker, Gerry (1987). 'Housing Renewal Policy in the 1980s.' Paper presented to the Political Studies Association, Aberdeen.

Brintnall, Michael, and Green, Roy E. (1988). 'Comparative State Enterprise Zone Programs: Variations in Structure and Coverage.' *Economic Development Quarterly* 2 (1): 50–68.

Bromley, R.D.F., and Morgan, R.H. (1985). 'The Effects of Enterprise Zone Policy: Evidence from Swansea.' *Regional Studies* 19 (5): 403–13.

Buches, David William (1980). 'Observations on the City of Wilmington's Brandywine Gateway Development Project.' Unpublished internship report. University of Delaware.

Burnier, DeLysa (1987) 'Urban Policy in the New Federalism Era: The Emergence of Enterprise Zones.' Paper presented at the Urban Affairs Association Annual Meeting, April 22–5, Akron, Ohio.

Butler, Stuart M. (1985). *Privatizing Federal Spending: A Strategy to Eliminate the Deficit*. New York: Universe Books.

Byrne, John, Martinez, Cecilia, and Rich, Daniel (1985). 'The Post-Industrial Imperative: Energy, Cities and the Featureless Plain.' In *Energy and Cities*, ed. John Byrne and Daniel Rich. New Brunswick, NJ: Transaction.

Cabinet Office (1988). *Action for Cities*. London: Cabinet Office.

Cafferty, Pastora San Juan, and McCready, William C. (1982). 'The Chicago Public–Private Partnership Experience: A Heritage of Involvement.' In *Public–Private Partnership in American Cities*, ed. R. Scott Fosler and Renee A. Berger. Lexington, Mass.: D.C. Heath.

Camina, M.M. (1974). *Local Authorities and the Attraction of Industry.* Oxford: Pergamon.

Castells, Manuel (1977). *The Urban Question.* Cambridge, Mass.: Massachusetts Institute of Technology Press.

—— (1978). *City, Class and Power.* London: Macmillan.

CDP [Comprehensive Development Project] (1974). *The National Community Development Project: Inter-Project Report, 1973.* London: Information and Intelligence Unit.

—— (1977). *Gilding the Ghetto: The State and the Poverty Experiment.* London: Inter-Project Evaluation Team.

CED [Committee for Economic Development] (1971). *Social Responsibilities of Business Corporations.* New York: CED.

Cervantes, Alfonso J. (1967). 'To Prevent a Chain of Super-Watts.' *Harvard Business Review* 45: 55–65.

Chamber of Commerce (1972). *A Survey of Socio-Economic Programs in 347 Local Chambers of Commerce.* Washington, DC: US Chamber of Commerce.

Champion, Tony, and Green, Anne (1988). *Local Prosperity and the North–South Divide.* Coventry: Institute for Employment Research, Warwick University.

Chandler, J.A., and Lawless, P. (1985). *Local Authorities and the Creation of Employment.* Aldershot: Gower.

Checkland, S.G. (1981). *The Upas Tree: Glasgow 1875–1975 ... And After 1975–1980.* Glasgow: University of Glasgow Press.

Cheit, Earl F. (1964). *The Business Establishment.* New York: Wiley.

Cherry, Gordon E. (1972). *Urban Change and Planning: A History of Urban Development in Britain since 1750.* Henley-on-Thames: Foulis.

—— (1979). 'The Town Planning Movement and the Victorian City,' *Transactions, Institute of British Geographers* 4: 306–19.

—— (1982). *The Politics of Town Planning.* London: Longmans.

—— (1984). 'Britain and Metropolis: Urban Change and Planning in Perspective.' *Town Planning Review* 55: 5–33.

Claggett, William E. (1982). 'Dallas: The Dynamics of Public–Private Cooperation'. In *Public–Private Partnership in American Cities*, ed. R. Scott Fosler and Renee A. Berger. Lexington, Mass.: D.C. Heath.

Clark, Douglas (1986). 'Place Marketing—Marketing for Investment.' Unpublished M.Sc. thesis. University of Strathclyde.

Clark, Gordon L., and Dear, Michael (1984). *State Apparatus: Structures and Languages of Legitimacy.* London: George Allen & Unwin.

Clawson, Marian, and Hall, Peter (1973). *Planning and Urban Growth: An Anglo-American Comparison.* Baltimore: Johns Hopkins University Press.

Clotfelder, Charles, and Salamon, Lester M. (1982). *The Federal Government and the Nonprofit Sector: The Effect of Tax Cuts on Charitable Contributions.* Washington, DC: Urban Institute.

Cloward, Richard A., and Piven, Francis F. (1967). 'Corporate Imperialism for the Poor.' *Nation* 205: 365–7.

Cockburn, Cynthia (1977). *The Local State: Management of Cities and People.* London: Pluto Press.

Cohn, Jules (1971). *The Conscience of the Corporations: Business and Urban Affairs, 1967–1970.* Baltimore: Johns Hopkins Press.

Coleman, Alice (1985). *Utopia on Trial: Vision and Reality in Planned Housing.* London: Hilary Shipman.

Coleman, Bruce I. (1973). *The Idea of the City in Nineteenth-Century Britain*. Boston: Routledge & Kegan Paul.

Committee of Public Accounts (1986a). *Tenth Report, Session 1985/86: The Urban Programme*. London: HMSO.

—— (1986b). *Tenth Report, Session 1985/86: Enterprise Zones*. London: HMSO.

Controller General (1969). *Review of Economic Opportunity Programs*. Washington, DC: GPO.

—— (1971). *Evaluation of Results and Adminstration of the Job Opportunities in the Business Sector (JOBS) Program in Five Cities*. Washington, DC: GAO.

Corkindale, J.T. (1980). 'Employment Trends in the Conurbations.' In *The Inner City: Employment and Industry*, ed. Alan Evans and David Eversley. London: Heinemann.

Cowie, Harry (1985). *The Phoenix Partnership: Urban Regeneration for the 21st Century*. London: National Council of Building Material Producers.

Cox, Andrew W. (1984). *Adversary Politics and Land: Conflict Over Land and Property Policy in Post-War Britain*. Cambridge: Cambridge University Press.

Crossman, Richard (1977). *The Diaries of a Cabinet Minister*, Vol. 3, Secretary of State for Social Services, 1968–1970. London: Hamish Hamilton.

CSO [Central Statistical Office] (1987). *Annual Abstract of Statistics, 1986 Edition*. London: HMSO.

CUED [National Council for Urban Economic Development] (1981). *Corporate Social Responsibility: Examples of Private Sector Initiatives in Economic Development*. Washington, DC: CUED.

Cullingworth, J. Barry (1962). '*New Towns for Old: The Problems of Urban Renewal*,' Fabian Research Series No. 229. London: Fabian Society.

—— (1985). *Town and Country Planning in Britain*. London: George Allen & Unwin.

Cullingworth Report (1969). *Council Housing Purposes, Procedures and Priorities: Ninth Report of the Housing Management Sub-Committee of the Central Housing Committee*. London: HMSO.

Dahl, Robert (1961). *Who Governs? Democracy in an American City*. New Haven: Yale University Press.

Danziger, Sheldon, and Haveman, Robert (1981). 'The Reagan Budget: A Sharp Break with the Past.' *Challenge* (May–June): 5–13.

DCC [Docklands Consultative Committee] (1985). *Four Year Review of the LDDC*. London: Greater London Council.

Dennis, Norman (1970). *People and Planning: The Sociology of Housing in Sunderland*. London: Faber.

Dennis, Robert (1980). 'The Decline of Manufacturing Employment in Greater London, 1966–74.' In *The Inner City: Employment and Industry*, ed. Alan Evans and David Eversley. London: Heinemann.

DoE [Department of the Environment] (1975). *Census Indicators of Urban Deprivation: Great Britain*, Working Note No. 6. London: DoE.

—— (1976a). *Census Indicators of Urban Deprivation: Areas of Housing Deprivation*, Working Note No. 13. London: DoE.

—— (1976b) *Local Government and the Industrial Strategy*, Circular 71/1977. London: DoE.

—— (1977). *Policy for the Inner Cities*, Cmnd. 6845. London: HMSO.

—— (1979). *Inner City Policy*, Press Release No. 390. London: HMSO.

—— (1981a). *Review of Inner City Policy*, Press Release No. 59. London: DoE.

—— (1981b). *Ministerial Guidelines to Partnership and Programme Authorities*, July 1981. London: HMSO.

DoE [Department of the Environment] (1983). *The Climate for Public and Private Partnerships in Property Development*. London: HMSO.
— (1984). *Simplified Planning Zones*. London: DoE.
— (1985a). *City Action Teams: Your City and Your Government*. London: DoE.
— (1985b). *Urban Development Grant: Making Things Happen*. London: DoE.
— (1985c). *Urban Programme Ministerial Guidelines*. London: DoE.
— (1985d). *Competition in the Provision of Local Authority Services*. London: DoE.
— (1986a). *The Urban Programme 1985*. London: DoE.
— (1986b). *Assessment of the Employment Effects of Economic Development Projects Funded Under the Urban Programme*. London: HMSO.
— (1986c). *Paying for Local Government*, Cmnd. 9714. London: HMSO.
— (1987a). *The Urban Programme 1986/87*. London: DoE.
— (1987b). [Welsh Office]. *Housing and Construction Statistics 1976–1986: Great Britain*. London: HMSO.
— (1987c). *Urban Development Grant*, Information Note. London: DoE.
— (1987d). '1984 Census of Employment and Revised Employment Estimates.' *Employment Gazette* 95 (1): 31–53.
— (1987e). *An Evaluation of the Enterprise Zone Experiment*. London: HMSO.
— (1988). *Press Release—The City Grant*. London: DoE.
DoE/DE [Department of the Environment/Department of Employment] (1987). *Action for Cities: Building on Initiative*. London: HMSO.
Donnison, David D. (1987). 'The New Tory Frontier.' *Observer*, Sept. 20.
Donnison, David D., and Soto, Paul (1980). *The Good City: A Study of Urban Development and Policy in Britain*. London: Heinemann.
Donnison, David D., and Ungerson, Clare (1982). *Housing Policy*. Harmondsworth: Penguin.
Doolittle, Frederick C. (1983). 'Federal Grants for Urban Economic Development.' In *State and Local Finance: The Pressures of the 1980s*, ed. George F. Break. Madison: University of Wisconsin Press.
Downs, Anthony (1970). *Urban Problems and Prospects*. Chicago: Markham Publishing Company.
Doyle, Denis P. (1984). 'Private Sector Initiatives: Straw or Strong Men?' In *The Reagan Presidency and the Governing of America*, ed. Lester M. Salamon and Michael S. Lund. Washington, DC: Urban Institute Press.
Drucker, Peter (1954). 'The Responsibilities of Management.' *Harpers* 209. No. 1254 (Nov.): 67–72.
DTI [Department of Trade and Industry] (1985). *Burdens on Business: Report of a Scrutiny of Administrative and Legislative Requirements*. London: DTI.
— (1988). *White Paper: DTI—The Department for Enterprise CM 278*. London: HMSO.
Duncan, Simon, and Goodwin, Mark (1988). *The Local State and Uneven Development*. Cambridge: Polity Press.
Dunleavy, P. J. (1981). *The Politics of Mass Housing in Britain, 1945–1975: A Study of Corporate Power and Professional Influence in the Welfare State*. Oxford: Oxford University Press.
Dustin, Jack L., and Rich, Daniel (1987). 'Cities and the New Technology Movement.' Paper presented at the Urban Affairs Association Annual Meeting, Apr. 22–5, Akron, Ohio.
Edgar, Richard E. (1970). *Urban Power and Social Welfare: Corporate Influence in an American City*. Beverly Hills: Sage.

Edwards, John (1987). *Positive Discrimination, Social Justice, and Social Policy: Moral Scrutiny of a Policy Practice*. London: Tavistock.
—— and Batley, Richard (1978). *The Politics of Positive Discrimination: An Evaluation of the Urban Programme 1967–77*. London: Tavistock.
Eells, Richard S. (1962). *The Government of Corporations*. New York: Free Press.
Elliott, Brian, and McCrone, David (1982). *The City: Patterns of Domination and Conflict*. New York: St. Martin's Press.
English, John (ed.) (1982). *The Future of Council Housing*. London: Croom Helm.
Environment Committee (1983). *Third Report: The Problems of Management in Urban Renewal* (Appraisal of Recent Initiatives in Merseyside). Volume I: Report (HC 18-I); Volume II: Minutes of Evidence (HC 18-II); Volume III: Appendices (HC 18-III). London: HMSO.
EO [Executive Office of the President, Office of Management and Budget] (1972, 1980–1986, 1987*a*, 1988). *Budget of the United States Government*, Fiscal Years 1972, 1980–1989. Washington, DC: GPO. This is an annual publication.
—— (1987*b*). *Special Analyses, Budget of the United States Government, Fiscal Year 1988*. Washington, DC: GPO.
Evans, Alan (1980). 'An Economist's Perspective.' In *The Inner City: Employment and Industry*, ed. Alan Evans and David Eversley. London: Heinemann.
Eversley, David (1980). 'A Planner's Perspective.' In *The Inner City: Employment and Industry*, ed. Alan Evans and David Eversley, London: Heinemann.
Fainstein, Susan S., and Fainstein, Norman I. (1986*a*). 'Economic Change, National Policy, and the System of Cities.' In *Restructuring the City: The Political Economy of Urban Development* with Richard Child Hill, Dennis R. Judd, and Michael Peter Smith. Rev. edn. New York: Longman.
—— —— (1986*b*). 'New Haven: The Limits of the Local State.' In *Restructuring the City: The Political Economy of Urban Development* with Richard Child Hill, Dennis R. Judd, and Michael Peter Smith. Rev. edn. New York: Longman.
—— —— (1986*c*). 'Regime Strategies, Communal Resistance, and Economic Forces.' In *Restructuring the City: The Political Economy of Urban Development* with Richard Child Hill, Dennis R. Judd, and Michael Peter Smith. Rev. edn. New York: Longman.
—— —— and Armistead, P. Jefferson (1986). 'San Francisco: Urban Transformation and the Local State.' In *Restructuring the City: The Political Economy of Urban Development*, ed. Susan S. Fainstein, Norman I. Fainstein, Richard Child Hill, Dennis R. Judd, and Michael Peter Smith. Rev. edn. New York: Longman.
—— —— Hill, Richard Child, Judd, Dennis R., and Smith, Michael Peter (1986). *Restructuring the City: The Political Economy of Urban Development*. Rev. edn. New York: Longman.
Fallows, James (1985). 'America's Changing Economic Landscape.' *Atlantic Monthly* (Mar.): 47–68.
Farley, J., and Glickman, N.J. (1985). 'R & D as an Economic Development Strategy: The Microelectronic and Computer Technology Corporation comes to Austin, Texas.' University of Texas at Austin.
Feagin, Joe R. (1988). 'Tallying the Social Costs of Urban Growth under Capitalism: The Case of Houston.' In *Business Elites and Urban Development: Case Studies and Critical Perspectives*, ed. Scott Cummings. Albany: State University of New York Press.

Ferguson, C. H. (1983). 'The Microelectronics Industry in Distress.' *Technology Review* 86, No. 6 (Aug./Sept.): 24–37.

Fixler, Jr., Philip E., and Poole, Jr., Robert W. (1987). 'Status of State and Local Privatization.' In *Prospects for Privatization*, ed. Steve H. Hanke. New York: Academy of Political Science.

Ford Foundation (1988). 'The New Permanence of Poverty.' *The Ford Foundation Letter* 19, No. 2 (June): 1–9.

Forrest, Ray, and Murie, Alan (1984). *Measuring the Right to Buy*. Bristol: School for Advanced Urban Studies, University of Bristol.

Fraser, Derek (1979). *Power and Authority in the Victorian City*. Oxford: Blackwell.

Frederic, William C. (1960). 'The Growing Concern Over Business Responsibility.' *California Management Review* 2, No. 4 (Summer): 54–61.

Frieden, Bernard J., and Kaplan, Marshall (1975). *The Politics of Neglect: Urban Aid from Model Cities to Revenue Sharing*. Cambridge, Mass.: Massachusetts Institute of Technology Press.

Friedland, Roger (1980). 'Corporate Power and Urban Growth: The Case of Urban Renewal.' *Politics and Society* 10 (2): 203–24.

—— (1983). *Power and Crisis in the City: Corporations, Unions and Urban Policy*. New York: Schocken.

Friedman, Lawrence Meir (1968). *Government and Slum Housing: A Century of Frustration*. Chicago: Rand McNally.

Friedman, Milton (1962). *Capitalism and Freedom*. Chicago: University of Chicago Press.

Frug, Gerald E. (1980). 'The City as a Legal Concept.' *Harvard Law Review* 93, No. 6 (Apr.): 1059–1154.

Fuller, Roger, and Stevenson, Olive (1983). *Policies, Programmes and Disadvantage: A Review of Literature*. London: Heinemann.

Galbraith, John Kenneth (1973). *Economics and the Public Purpose*. Boston: Houghton Mifflin.

GAO [General Accounting Office] (1984). *Insights into Major Urban Development Action Grant Issues*, RCED-84-55. Washington, DC: GAO.

Gardner, John W. (1968). Speech by the Chairman of the Urban Coalition before the Seventy-third Congress of American Industry, sponsored by the National Association of Manufacturers, 4 Dec. 1968.

Geddes, Patrick (1971). *Cities in Evolution: An Introduction to the Town Planning Movement and to the Study of Physics*, originally published 1911. New York: Harper and Row.

Gelfand, Mark I. (1975). *A Nation of Cities: The Federal Government and Urban America, 1933–1965*. New York: Oxford University Press.

Gelfand, M. David (1985). 'Comparative Reflections and Projections.' In *Half Century of Municipal Decline: 1935–1985*, ed. Martin Loughlin, M. David Gelfand, and Ken Young. London: George Allen & Unwin.

Gibson, Michael S., and Langstaff, Michael J. (1982). *An Introduction to Urban Renewal*. London: Hutchison.

Gist, John R., and Hill, R. Carter (1984). 'Political and Economic Influences on the Bureaucratic Allocation of Federal Funds: The Case of Urban Development Action Grants.' *Journal of Urban Economics* 16: 158–72.

Glaab, Charles N., and Brown, Theodore (1976). *A History of Urban America*. New York: Macmillan.

Glasgow Action (1985). *Glasgow—The Need for Action*. Glasgow: Scottish Development Agency.

Glasmeier, A., Hall, P., and Markusen, A.R. (1985). 'Metropolitan High-Technology Industry Growth in the Mid-1970s: Can Everyone Have a Slice of the High-Tech Pie?' *Berkeley Planning Journal* 1: 131–42.

Glass, R. (1959). 'The Evaluation of Planning: Some Sociological Considerations.' *International Social Science Journal* 11 (6): 393–409.

Glickman, Norman J. (1984). 'Economic Policy and the Cities: In Search of Reagan's Real Urban Policy.' *Journal of the American Planning Association* 50 (4): 471–501.

Goldsmith, Michael (ed.) (1986). *Essays on the Future of Local Government*. Salford: University of Salford.

Goodman, A.C., and Taylor, R.B. (1983). *The Baltimore Neighborhood Fact Book*. Baltimore: Center for Metropolitan Planning and Research, Johns Hopkins University.

Goodman, Robert (1979). *The Last Entrepreneurs: America's Regional Wars for Jobs and Dollars*. New York: Simon and Schuster.

Goodrich, C. (1960). *Government Promotion of Canals and Railroads, 1800–1890*. New York: Macmillan.

Gow, Ian (n.d.). *The Writing is on the Wall: The Challenge of the Inner Cities*. Newcastle: Barratt.

Gower-Davies, John (1972). *The Evangelistic Bureaucrat*. London: Tavistock.

Grasso, Patrick G. (1986). 'Distributive Policies and the Politics of Economic Development.' In *Revitalizing the U.S. Economy*, ed. F. Stevens Redburn, Terry F. Buss, and Larry C. Ledebur. New York: Praeger.

Greenberg, Edward S. (1974). *Serving the Few: Corporate Capitalism and the Bias of Government Policy*. New York: Wiley.

Greenleigh Associates, Inc. (1970). 'The Job Opportunities in the Business Sector Program—An Evaluation of Impact in Ten Standard Metropolitan Statistical Areas.' Report prepared for Office of Policy, Evaluation and Research, Manpower Administration, US Department of Labor.

Greer, Scott (1962). *The Emerging City: Myth and Reality*. New York: Macmillan.

—— (1965). *Urban Renewal and American Cities: The Dilemma of Democratic Intervention*. New York: Bobbs-Merrill.

Greison, Ronald (1977). 'The Effect of Business Taxation on the Location of Industry,' *Journal of Urban Economics* 3 (Sept.): 21–35.

Grieve, Sir Robert (1986). *Report of the Inquiry into Housing in Glasgow*. Glasgow: Glasgow District Council.

Gulliver, Stuart (1984). 'The Area Projects of the Scottish Development Agency.' *Town Planning Review* 55 (3): 322–34.

Gurr, Ted R., and King, Desmond S. (1987). *The State and the City*. London: Macmillan.

Haar, Charles M. (ed.) (1984). *Cities, Law, and Social Policy: Learning from Britain*. Lexington, Mass.: D.C. Heath.

Hall, John Stuart (1986). 'Retrenchment in Phoenix, Arizona.' In *Reagan and the Cities*, ed. George E. Peterson and Carol W. Lewis. Washington, DC: Urban Institute Press.

Hall, Peter (1977). 'Green Fields and Grey Areas.' Proceedings, Annual Conference of the Royal Town Planning Institute. Chester.

—— (1983). 'Should We Privatise Planning?' Annual Conference of the Royal Institute of Chartered Surveyors. Stratford-upon-Avon.

Halsey, A. H. (1973). *The Times Education Supplement* (London), 9 Feb.

Hambleton, Robin (1988). 'Urban Government in the 1980s: The Recent British Experience.' Urban Affairs Association Annual Conference, St. Louis, Missouri, Mar. 9–12.

Hammond, J. L. (1935). 'The Social Background: 1835–1935.' In *A Century of Municipal Progress*, ed. Harold J. Laski, W. Ivor Jennings, and William A. Robson. London: Allen & Unwin.

Hanke, Steve H. (ed.) (1987). *Prospects for Privatization.* Proceedings of the Academy of Political Science. Vol. 35, No. 3. New York: Academy of Political Science.

Hansard (1980). *Parliamentary Debates*, Session 1979/80, Vol. 968, Col. 239.

—— (1986). *Parliamentary Debates, Session 1985/86,* Vol. 97, Col. 1024.

Hanson, Royce (ed.) (1983). *Rethinking Urban Policy: Urban Development in an Advanced Economy.* Washington, DC: National Academy Press.

Hardie, John (1986). 'The Organisation and Management of Planning for Employment and Economic Regeneration in Inverclyde.' Unpublished M. Sc. dissertation. University of Strathclyde.

Harrington, Michael (1962). *The Other America.* New York: Macmillan.

—— (1968). 'Can Private Industry Abolish Slums?' *Dissent* 15: 4–6.

Harrison, Bennett, and Kanter, Sandra (1978). 'The Political Economy of States' Job-Creation Business Incentives.' *Journal of the American Institute of Planners* 44: 425–35.

Hartman, Chester (1974). *Yerba Buena: Land Grab and Community Resistance in San Francisco.* San Francisco: Glide.

—— (1980). 'The Politics of Housing'. In *Housing Urban America*, ed. Jon Pynoos, Robert Shafer, and Chester W. Hartman. Chicago: Aldine.

Hatry, Harry P. (1982). *Alternative Service Delivery Approaches Involving Increased Use of the Private Sector.* Washington, DC: Urban Institute.

Hausner, Victor, and Robson, Brian (1985). *Changing Cities: An Introduction to the ESRC Inner Cities Research Programme.* London: Economic and Social Research Council.

Hayes, Edward (1972). *Power Structure and Urban Policy: Who Rules in Oakland?* New York: McGraw-Hill.

Hays, Samuel P. (1964). 'The Politics of Reform in Municipal Government in the Progressive Era.' *Pacific Northwest Quarterly* 55: 157–69.

Headey, Bruce W. (1978). *Housing Policy in the Developed Economy: The United Kingdom, Sweden, and the United States.* New York: St. Martin's Press.

Heald, David (1983). *Public Expenditure: Its Defence and Reform.* London: Martin Robertson.

Heald, Morris (1970). *The Social Responsibilities of Business: Company and Community, 1900–1960.* Cleveland: Case Western Reserve University Press.

Heap, Sir Desmond (1984). 'Town Planning: Yesterday, Today and Tomorrow.' In *Cities, Law and Social Policy: Learning from the British*, ed. Charles Haar. Lexington, Mass.: D. C. Heath.

Heidenheimer, Arnold J., Heclo, Hugh, and Adams, Carolyn Teich, (1983). *Comparative Public Policy: The Politics of Social Choice in Europe and America.* New York: St. Martin's Press.

Helm, Dieter, and Smith, Stephen, (1987). 'The Assessment: Decentralization and the Economics of Local Government.' *Oxford Review of Economic Policy* 3 (2): pp. i–xxi.

Hennock, E. P. (1973). *Fit and Proper Persons: Ideal and Reality in Nineteenth Century Government.* London: Arnold.

Henson, M. Dale, and King, James, (1982). 'The Atlanta Public–Private Romance: An Abrupt Transformation.' In *Public–Private Partnership in American Cities*, ed. R. Scott Fosler and Renee A. Berger. Lexington, Mass.: D. C. Heath.

Heseltine, Michael (1979). Secretary of State's Address. *Proceedings of the Annual Meeting of the Royal Town Planning Institute*. York.

—— (1983). *Reviving the Inner Cities*. London: Conservative Political Centre.

Hetherington, Peter (1987). 'Focus on Regions in Drive for Urban Revival.' *Guardian*, 17 Aug.

—— (1988). 'A Political Crusade Cloaked in Victorian Philanthropy.' *Guardian*, 7 Mar.

Higgins, J., Deakin, N., Edwards, J., and Wicks, M. (1983). *Government and Urban Poverty: Inside the Policy-making Process*. Oxford: Blackwell.

Hill, Richard Child (1983). 'Market, State, and Community: National Urban Policy in the 1980s.' *Urban Affairs Quarterly* 19, No. 1 (Sept.): 5–20.

—— (1986). 'Crisis in the Motor City: The Politics of Economic Development in Detroit.' In *Restructuring the City: The Political Economy of Urban Development* with Susan S. Fainstein, Norman I. Fainstein, Dennis R. Judd, and Michael Peter Smith. Rev. edn. New York: Longman.

HMSO [Her Majesty's Stationery Office] (1985). *Lifting the Burden*, Cmnd. 9571. London: HMSO.

Hofstadter, Richard (1955). *The Age of Reform: From Bryan to F. D. R.* New York: Vintage Books.

Holterman, Sally (1975). 'Areas of Urban Deprivation in Great Britain: An Analysis of the 1971 Census Data.' *Social Trends 6*. London: HMSO.

Home, Robert K. (1982). *Inner City Regeneration*. London: Spon.

Howard, Ebenezer (1965). *Garden Cities of Tomorrow*. London: Faber.

Howell, James M. (1979). 'The Evolving National Urban Policy: The Role of the Private Sector—Moneychangers of the Northeast.' *Urban Lawyer* 11 (2): 270–83.

Hughes, G. A. (1987). 'Rates Reform and the Housing Market.' In *The Reform of Local Government Finance in Britain*, ed. S. J. Bailey and R. Paddison. London: Croom Helm.

Huhne, Christopher (1987). 'Census Shows South's Grip on Jobs.' *Guardian*, 8 Jan.

Jacobs, Jane (1961). *The Death and Life of Great American Cities*. New York: Random House.

Jacobs, Jeffrey (1985). ' "UDG": The Urban Development Grant.' *Policy and Politics* 13 (2): 191–9.

Jacobs, Susan S., and Roistacher, Elizabeth A. (1980). 'The Urban Impacts of HUD's Urban Development Action Grant Program or, Where's the Action in Action Grants?' In *The Urban Impacts of Federal Policies*, ed. Norman J. Glickman. Baltimore: Johns Hopkins University Press.

JEC [Joint Economic Committee of the US Congress] (1983). Hearings, Ninety-seventh Congress, Second Session, Pt. 1, 13–20 July 1982. Washington, DC: GPO.

—— (1986). *The Concentration of Wealth in the United States: Trends in the Distribution of Wealth among American Families*. Washington, DC: JEC (July).

Johnson, David (1987). 'An Evaluation of the Urban Development Grant Program.' Mimeo, University of Aston, Birmingham.

Johnson, Lyndon B. (1964). 'Annual Message to the Congress on the State of the Union,' 8 Jan. 1964. In *Public Papers of the Presidents: Lyndon B. Johnson, 1963–64*. Washington, DC: GPO.

—— (1968). 'To Earn a Living: The Right of Every American,' Special Message to

Congress, 23 Jan. 1968. In Public Papers of the Presidents: Lyndon B. Johnson, 1968–69. Washington, DC: GPO.

Jones, Robert (1982). *Town and Country Chaos*. London: Adam Smith Institute.

Jones, Susan, and Weisbrod, Glen (1986). 'Urban Enterprise Zones: How Have the Panaceas Panned Out?' *National Council for Urban Economic Development Commentary* 10, No. 2 (Summer): 16–21.

Jordon, Grant (1984). 'Enterprise Zones in the U.K. and the U.S.A.: Ideologically Acceptable Job Creation?' In *Unemployment*, ed. J.J. Richardson and Roger Henning. Beverly Hills: Sage.

—— and Reilly, G. (1981). 'Enterprise Zones—The Clydebank EZ and Policy Substitution.' In *The Scottish Government Yearbook 1982*, ed. H.M. and N.L. Drucker. Edinburgh: Paul Harris.

Joseph, Sir Keith (1976). *Monetarism Is Not Enough, The Stockton Lecture*. Delivered to the London Business School. London: Centre for Policy Studies.

Judd, Dennis R. (1979). *The Politics of American Cities: Private Power and Public Policy*, 1st edn. Boston: Little, Brown.

—— (1986). 'From Cowtown to Sunbelt City: Boosterism and Economic Growth in Denver.' In *Restructuring the City: The Political Economy of Urban Development* with Susan S. Fainstein, Norman I. Fainstein, Richard Child Hill, and Michael Peter Smith. Rev. ed. New York: Longman.

—— (1988), *The Politics of American Cities: Private Power and Public Policy*, 3rd edn. Boston: Little, Brown.

Judd, Dennis R., and Ready, Randy L. (1986). 'Entrepreneurial Cities and the New Politics of Economic Development.' In *Reagan and the Cities*, ed. George E. Peterson and Carol W. Lewis. Washington, DC: Urban Institute Press.

Kantor, Paul (1987). 'The Dependent City: The Changing Political Economy of Urban Economic Development in the United States.' *Urban Affairs Quarterly* 22, No. 4 (June): 493–520.

Kaplan, Morton (1973). *Urban Planning in the 1960s: A Design for Irrelevancy*. Cambridge, Mass.: Massachusetts Institute of Technology Press.

Karran, Terrence (1986). 'Financing the System.' In *Essays on the Future of Local Government*, ed. Michael Goldsmith. Salford: University of Salford.

Kasarda, John D. (1985). 'Urban Change and Minority Opportunities.' In *The New Urban Reality*, ed. Paul E. Peterson. Washington, DC: Brookings Institution.

—— (1986). *The Regional and Urban Distribution of People and Jobs in the United States*. Paper presented before the National Research Council Committee on National Urban Policy Workshop, July 1986. Washington, DC.

Kashdan, Sandra (1981). 'Washington Report: Can States Handle Block Grant Load?' *Planning* 47 (8): 8–9.

Keating, Michael, and Boyle, Robin (1986). *Remaking Urban Scotland: Strategies for Local Economic Development*. Edinburgh: Edinburgh University Press.

—— and Midwinter, Arthur (1983). *The Government of Scotland*. Edinburgh: Mainstream.

—— and Waters, Nigel (1985). 'Scotland in the European Community.' In *Regions in the European Community*, ed. Michael Keating and Barry Jones. Oxford: Oxford University Press.

Keeble, David (1980). 'Industrial Decline in the Inner City and Conurbation.' In *The Inner City: Employment and Industry*, ed. Alan Evans and David Eversley. London: Heinemann.

Keegan, V. (1982). 'The Gap Between Industry's Needs and Those of Britain Still Seem to be Growing.' *Guardian*, 4 May.

Kemp, Jack F. (1980). 'Greenlining Urban America: "Enterprise Zones" for Economic Growth.' *National Council for Urban Economic Development Commentary* 4, No. 3 (July): 3–6.

Kemper, Peter, and Quigley, John M. (1976). *The Economics of Refuse Collection*. Cambridge, Mass.: Ballinger.

Kennedy, Robert F. (1967). *To Seek a Newer World*. Garden City: Doubleday.

Kilpatrick, Jay I., and Bender, Lewis G. (1986). 'Real Estate Joint Ventures: Examining the Myths.' *National Council for Urban Economic Development Commentary* (Summer): 7–11.

Kirby, Andrew (1985). 'Nine Fallacies of Local Economic Change.' *Urban Affairs Quarterly* 21: 207–20.

—— and Lynch, A. Karen (1987). 'A Ghost in the Growth Machine: The Aftermath of Rapid Population Growth in Houston.' *Urban Studies* 24: 587–96.

Kolderie, Ted (1986). 'The Two Different Concepts of Privatization.' *Public Administration Review* (July/Aug.): 285–91.

Kolko, Gabriel (1963). *The Triumph of Conservatism: A Reinterpretation of American History, 1900–1916*. New York: Quadrangle.

Kysiak, Ronald C. (1983). 'City Entrepreneurship: Institutionalizing the Process.' *National Council for Urban Economic Development Commentary* 7, No. 3 (Winter): 20–3.

LaDou J. (1984). 'The Not-So-Clean Business of Making Chips.' *Technology Review* (May/June): 23–36.

Lakoff, Sanford A., and Rich, Daniel (eds.) (1973). *Private Government: Introductory Readings*. Glenview, Ill.: Scott, Foresman.

Lambert, R. (1964). *Nutrition in Britain 1950–1960*, Occasional Papers in Social Administration No. 5. Welwyn: Codicote.

Lansley, S. (1982). 'The Road to Toxteth.' *New Society* (22 Apr.): 17.

Lash, J. E. (1973). *Businessmen's Urban Improvement Organizations*. New York: Institute of Public Administration.

Lawless, Paul (1981). *Britain's Inner Cities: Problems and Policies*. London: Harper and Row.

—— (1986). *The Evolution of Spatial Policy: A Case of Inner City Policy in the United Kingdom, 1968–1981*. London: Pion.

Lawson, Nigel (1981). *The New Conservatism*. London: Conservative Political Centre.

LDDC [London Docklands Development Corporation] (1985). *Annual Report 1984–85*. London: LDDC.

Ledgerwood, Grant (1985). *Urban Innovation*. Aldershot: Gower.

Lee, E. C. (1985). 'Reflections on Local Government and Politics in England and the United States.' *Local Government Studies* (Sept./Oct.): 49–67.

Lever, W. F. (1987). 'Strategic Policy-making in the UK: Lessons and Results,' Conference Paper. Manchester: University of Manchester.

Lever, William, and Moore, Chris (eds.) (1986). *The City in Transition: Policies and Agencies for the Economic Regeneration of Clydeside*. Oxford: Clarendon Press.

Levine, Marc V. (1987). 'Downtown Redevelopment as an Urban Growth Strategy: A Critical Appraisal of the Baltimore Rennaissance.' *Journal of Urban Affairs* 9 (2): 103–23.

Levine, Myron A. (1983). 'The Reagan Urban Policy: Efficient National Economic Growth and Public Sector Minimization.' *Journal of Urban Affairs* 5: 17–28.

Levitan, Sar A., and Mangum, Garth L. (1969). *Federal Training and Work Programs in the Sixties*. Ann Arbor: Institute of Labor and Industrial Relations, University of Michigan.

—— and Taggart, III, Robert (1971). *Social Experimentation and Manpower Policy: The Rhetoric and the Reality*. Baltimore: Johns Hopkins Press.

Levy, John M. (1981). *Economic Development Programs for Cities, Counties, and Towns*. New York: Praeger.

Lewis, Oscar (1966). 'The Culture of Poverty,' *Scientific American* 215 No. 16 (Oct.): 19–25.

Lewis, Sylvia (1981). 'Urban Policy on the Cheap.' *Planning* 47 (6): 12–18.

Lichfield, Nathaniel, and Darin-Drabkin, Haim (1980). *Land Policy in Planning*. London: George Allen & Unwin.

Liebschutz, Sarah F., and Taddiken, Alan J. (1986). 'The Effects of Reagan Administration Budget Cuts on Human Services in Rochester, New York.' In *Reagan and the Cities*, ed. George E. Peterson and Carol W. Lewis. Washington, DC: Urban Institute Press.

Little, Inc., Arthur D. (1984). *Feasibility Study of the Mississippi Institute for Technology Development*. Cambridge, Mass.: Arthur D. Little.

Livingood, J.W. (1947). *The Philadelphia–Baltimore Trade Rivalry*. Harrisburg: Pennsylvania Historical and Museum Collection.

Lloyd, M.G. (1985). 'Privatisation, Liberalisation and Simplification of Statutory Land Use Planning in Britain.' *Planning Outlook* 28 (1): 26–49.

—— (1987). *Releasing Private Enterprise: Lifting the Burden of Planning*, Strathclyde Papers on Planning No. 8. Glasgow: University of Strathclyde.

—— and Botham, R.W. 1985). 'The Ideology and Implementation of Enterprise Zones in Britain.' *Urban Law and Policy* 7: 33–55.

Loney, M. (1983). *Community Against Government: The British Community Development Project: 1968–1977*. London: Heinemann.

Long, Norton E. (1960). 'The Corporation, Its Satellites, and the Local Community.' In *The Corporation in Modern Society*, ed. Edward S. Mason. Cambridge, Mass.: Harvard University Press.

—— (1967). 'Political Science and the City.' In *Social Science and the City: A Survey of Urban Research*, ed. Leo F. Schnore. New York: Frederick and Praeger.

—— (1972). *The Unwalled City: Reconstituting the Urban Community*. New York: Basic Books.

—— (1983). 'Can the Contemporary City be a Significant Policy?' *Proceedings of the 1983 Annual Meeting of the Urban Affairs Association*. Newark: University of Delaware.

Loughlin, Martin, Gelfan, M. David, and Young, Ken (eds.) (1985). *Half a Century of Municipal Decline 1935–85*. London: Allen & Unwin.

Louis, Arthur (1975). 'The Worst American City.' *Harper's* (Jan.): 67–71.

Lowe, Jeanne R. (1967). *Cities in a Race with Time: Progress and Poverty in America's Renewing Cities*. New York: Random House.

Lubove, Roy (1969). *Twentieth-Century Pittsburgh: Government, Business and Environmental Change*. New York: Wiley.

Lyall, Katharine (1982). 'A Bicycle Built-for-Two: Public–Private Parnership in Baltimore.' In *Public–Private Partnership in American Cities*, ed. R. Scott Fosler and Renee A. Berger. Lexington, Mass.: D.C. Heath.

Lynes, A. (1963). *National Assistance and National Prosperity*, Occasional Papers in Social Administration No. 5. Welwyn: Codicote.

McFarland, M. Carter (1978). *Federal Government and Urban Problems. HUD: Successes, Failures and the Fate of Our Cities.* Boulder, Colo.: Westview Press.

MacGregor, Robert W. (1977). 'Privatism and Urban Development: A Response.' *Urban Affairs Quarterly* 12 (4): 461–8.

McKay, David H. (1987). *Politics and Power in the USA.* Harmondsworth: Penguin.

McKay, David H., and Cox, Andrew W. (1979). *The Politics of Urban Change.* London: Croom Helm.

McKelvey, Blake (1963). *The Urbanization of America: 1860–1915.* New Brunswick, NJ: Rutgers University Press.

McKie, James W. (1974). *Social Responsibility and the Business Predicament.* Washington, DC: Brookings Institution.

McKinsey and Company (1984). *Glasgow's Service Industries—Current Performance: A Report to the SDA.* Glasgow: Scottish Development Agency.

—— (1985). *The Potential of Glasgow City Centre.* Glasgow: Scottish Development Agency.

Maclennan, D., and Munro, M. (1986). 'The Development of Owner-Occupation.' In *Housing Policy under the Tories*, ed. P. Booth and A. Crook. London: Croom Helm.

McQuire, Robert A., and Van Cott, Norman T. (1984). 'Public vs. Private Activity: A New Look at School Bus Transportation.' *Public Choice* 43: 38–40.

Mallinson, Howard (1984). *Urban Regeneration*, Paper presented to the Brick Development Association. Gleneagles.

Malpass, Peter (ed.) (1986). *The Housing Crisis.* London: Croom Helm.

Marks, Marilyn (1984). 'The New Urban Journal: The Focus is on Helping Cities Help Themselves' *National Journal* 17, No. 32 (11 July): 1513–16.

Marlin, Matthew R. (1985). 'Evolution of a Subsidy: Industrial Revenue Bonds.' *Growth and Change* 16 (1): 30–5.

Marris, Peter (1982). *Community Planning and Conceptions of Change.* London: Routledge & Kegan Paul.

—— (1987). *Meaning and Action: Community Planning and Conceptions of Change*, 2nd edn. London: Routledge & Kegan Paul.

—— and Rein, Martin (1973). *Dilemmas of Social Reform: Poverty and Community Action in the United States.* Chicago: Aldine.

Martin, Curtis H., and Leone, Robert A. (1977). *Local Economic Development: The Federal Connection.* Lexington, Mass.: D.C. Heath.

Masotti, Louis H. (1974). *Private/Public Partnerships: The Only Game in Town?* Evanston: Center for Urban Affairs, Northwestern University.

Mawson, John, and Miller, David (1983). *Agencies in Regional and Local Development*, Occasional Paper No. 6. Birmingham: Centre for Urban and Regional Research.

—— (1986). 'Interventionist Approaches in Local Employment and Economic Development: The Experience of Labour Local Authorities.' In *Critical Issues in Urban Economic Development, Volume I*, ed. V.A. Hausner. Oxford: Clarendon Press.

May, Judith (1981). *Leveraging Performance of Federal Economic Development Programs*, Office of Community Planning and Development, Department of Housing and Urban Development. Washington, DC: GPO.

Mills, Liz, and Young, Ken (1986). 'Local Authorities and Economic Development: A Preliminary Analysis.' In *Critical Issues in Urban Economic Development, Volume I*, ed. V. A. Hausner. Oxford: Clarendon Press.

Millspaugh, Martin (ed.) (1964). *Baltimore's Charles Center: A Case Study of Downtown Renewal*, Technical Bulletin No. 51. Washington, DC: Urban Institute.

Milner Holland Report (1965). *Report of the Committee on Housing in Greater London*, Cmnd. 2605. London: HMSO.

Mollenkopf, John H. (1977). 'The Post-War Politics of Urban Development.' In *Cities in Change: Studies in the Urban Condition*, ed. John Walton and Donald E. Carins. Boston: Allyn and Bacon.

—— (1983). *The Contested City*. Princeton: Princeton University Press.

Molotch, Harvey (1976). 'The City as a Growth Machine: Towards a Political Economy of Place.' *American Journal of Sociology* 82 (2): 309–32.

—— (1988). 'Strategies and Constraints of Growth Elites.' In *Business Elites and Urban Development: Case Studies and Critical Perspectives*, ed. Scott Cummings. Albany: University of New York Press.

Monkkonen, Eric H. (1985). 'What Urban Crisis? A Historian's Point of View.' *Urban Affairs Quarterly* 20 (4): 429–47.

Moon, Marilyn, and Sawhill, Isabel V. (1984). 'Family Incomes: Gainers and Losers.' In *The Reagan Record: An Assessment of America's Changing Domestic Priorities*, ed. John L. Palmer and Isabel V. Sawhill. Cambridge, Mass.: Ballinger.

Moor, G., and Parnell, R. (1986). 'Private Sector Involvement in Local Authority Service Delivery.' *Regional Studies* 20 (3): 253–7.

Mott, Paul E. (1970). 'The Role of Absentee-Owned Corporations in the Changing Community.' In *Structure of Community Power*, ed. Michael Aiken and Paul E. Mott. New York: Random House.

Mumford, Lewis (1961). *The City in History: Its Origins, Its Transformations, and Its Prospects*. New York: Harcourt, Brace and Javanovich.

Munday, Neil, and Mallinson, Howard (1983). 'Urban Development Grant in Action.' *Public Finance and Accountancy* (Dec.): 32–5.

NAB [National Alliance of Businessmen] (1969). Advertisement in the *New Yorker* (15 Mar.): 96–7.

NAO [National Audit Office] (1985). *Report of the Comptroller and Auditor General—Department of the Environment: Urban Programme*. London: HMSO.

—— (1986). *Report of the Comptroller and Auditor General—Department of the Environment, Scottish and Welsh Offices: Enterprise Zones*. London: HMSO.

Nathan, Richard P. (1986). 'Institutional Change under Reagan.' In *Perspectives on the Reagan Years*, ed. John L. Palmer. Washington, DC: Urban Institute Press.

—— and Webman, Jerry A. (eds.) (1980). *The Urban Development Action Grant Program: Papers and Proceedings on Its First Two Years of Operation*. Princeton: Urban and Regional Research Center, Princeton University.

—— Doolittle, Fred C., and Associates (1983). *The Consequences of Cuts*. Princeton: Princeton University Press.

—— Dearborn, Philip M., Goldman, Clifford A., and Associates (1982). 'Initial Effects of the Fiscal Year 1982 Reductions in Federal Domestic Spending.' In *Reductions in U.S. Domestic Spending: How They Affect State and Local Governments*, ed. John Elwood. New Brunswick, NJ: Transaction.

Nelson, Richard R. (1977). *The Moon and the Ghetto*. New York: Norton.

Nemore, Arnold L., and Mangum, Garth L. (1969). 'Private Involvement in Federal Manpower Programs.' In *Public–Private Manpower Policies*, ed. Arnold R. Weber, Frank H. Cassell, and Woodrow L. Ginsburg. Madison: Industrial Relations Research Association.

Nenno, Mary K. (1987). 'Reagan's '88 Budget: Dismantling HUD.' *Journal of Housing* 44 (3): 103–8.

Neubeck, Kenneth J., and Ratcliff, Richard E. (1988). 'Urban Democracy and the Power of Corporate Capital: Struggles Over Downtown Growth and Neighborhood Stagnation in Hartford, Connecticut.' In *Business Elites and Urban Development: Case Studies and Critical Perspectives*, ed. Scott Cummings. Albany: State University of New York Press.

Newham, R. (1980). *Community Enterprise: British Potential and American Experience*, Occasional Paper No. 3. Reading: School of Planning Studies, University of Reading.

Noyce, R. N. (1982). 'Competition and Cooperation: A Presentation for the Eighties.' *Research Management* 25, No. 2 (Mar.): 13–17.

NRC [National Resources Committee] (1937). *Our Cities: Their Role in the National Economy*, Report of the Urbanism Committee to the National Resources Committee. Washington, DC: GPO.

Oakland, William (1978). 'Local Taxes and Intra-Urban Location: A Survey.' In *Metropolitan Financing and Growth Management Policies*, ed. George F. Break. Madison: University of Wisconsin.

OTA [Office of Technology Assessment, Congress of the United States] (1984a). *Technology, Innovation, and Regional Economic Development: Background Paper No. 1*. Washington, DC: GPO.

—— (1984b). *Technology, Innovation, and Regional Economic Development: Background Paper No. 2*. Washington, DC: GPO.

Owen, David (1985). 'Urban Decay.' Press Release, Oct.

Pack, Janet Rothenberg (1987). 'Privatization of Public-Sector Services in Theory and Practice.' *Journal of Policy Analysis and Management* 6 (4): 523–40.

PAG [Property Advisory Group] (1983). *The Climate for Public and Private Partnerships in Property Development*. London: HMSO.

Pahl, Raymond E. (1970) *Whose City?* 1st edn. Harlow: Longmans.

—— (1975). *Whose City?* 2nd edn. Harmondsworth: Penguin Books.

Parenti, Michael (1970). 'Power and Pluralism: A View from the Bottom.' *Journal of Politics* 32, No. 3 (Aug.): 501–30.

Parker, John (1986). 'Urban Renewal: Using Grants to Make Things Happen.' *Planner* 72 (2): 59–61.

Parkinson, Michael H. (1986). 'On Liverpool's Waterfront.' *New Society* (July): 10–12.

—— ., and Wilks, S. R. M. (1983). 'Managing Urban Decline: The Case of the Inner City Partnerships.' *Local Government Studies* 9 (5): 23–39.

Pascal, A. and Gurwitz, A. (1983). *Picking Winners: Industrial Strategies for Local Economic Development*, Prepared for the US Department of Housing and Urban Development. Santa Monica, Calif.: Rand.

Pascarella, Thomas A., and Raymond, Richard D. (1982). 'Buying Bonds for Business: An Evaluation of the Industrial Revenue Bond Program.' *Urban Affairs Quarterly* 18 (1): 73–89.

Patten, John (1987). 'Inner City Big Bang.' *Guardian*, 17 Apr.

PC [President's Commission for a National Agenda for the Eighties] (1980a). *Urban America in the Eighties: Perspectives and Prospects*. Washington, DC: PC.

—— (1980b). *A National Agenda for the Eighties*. Washington, DC: PC.

Peacock, Alan (1984). 'Privatisation in Perspective.' *Three Banks Review* 144: 3–25.

Peirce, Neal R. (1986). 'Is Baltimore Unique?' *Baltimore Magazine* (Oct.): 69–71.

Perry, Charles R. (1976). 'Job Opportunities in the Business Sector.' In *The Impact of Government Manpower Programs*, by Charles R. Perry, Bernard E. Anderson, Richard L. Rowan, and Herbert R. Northrup. Philadelphia: Wharton School.

Perry, James L., and Babitsky, Timlynn T. (1986). 'Comparative Performance in Urban Bus Transit: Assessing Privatization Strategies.' *Public Administration Review* 46 (1): 57–66.

Peterson, George E. (1986). 'Urban Policy and the Cyclical Behavior of Cities.' In *Reagan and the Cities*, ed. George E. Peterson and Carol W. Lewis. Washington, DC: Urban Institute Press.

Peterson, Lorin Wescott (1961). *The Day of the Mugwump*. New York: Random House.

Peterson, Paul E. (1981). *City Limits*. Chicago: University of Chicago Press.

—— (ed.) (1985). *The New Urban Reality*. Washington, DC: Brookings Institution.

—— (1987). 'Analyzing Developmental Politics: A Response to Sanders and Stone.' *Urban Affairs Quarterly* 22, No. 4 (June): 540–7.

Peterson, Paul E., Rabe, Barry G., and Wong, Kenneth K. (1986). *When Federalism Works*. Washington, DC: Brookings Institution.

Petshek, Kirk R. (1973). *The Challenge of Urban Reform: Policies and Programs in Philadelphia*. Philadelphia: Temple University Press.

Piven, Francis Fox, and Cloward, Richard A. (1971). *Regulating the Poor: The Functions of Public Welfare*. New York: Pantheon.

Planning (1987). 'Largest Urban Grant Goes to Hotel.' 6 Mar.: No. 708.

Planning Exchange (1986). 'Local Enterprise Grants for Urban Projects (LEG-UP).' LEDIS A240. Glasgow: Planning Exchange.

Plowden Report (1967). *Central Advisory Committee for Education: Children and their Primary Schools*. London: HMSO.

Power, Anne (1984). *Priority Estates Project*. London: DoE.

Pressman, Jeffrey L., and Wildavsky, Aaron (1984). *Implementation: How Great Expectations in Washington Are Dashed in Oakland; or, Why It's Amazing That Federal Programs Work At All This Being a Saga of the Economic Development Administration*, 3rd edn. Berkeley: University of California Press.

PSMRU [Public Sector Management Research Unit] (1988). *An Evaluation of the Urban Development Grant Programme—A Report to the Department of the Environment*. London: HMSO.

Raskin, Eugene (1971). 'Are Our Cities Doomed? Yes.' *New York Times* (12 May.)

Reagan, Michael (1963). *The Managed Economy*. New York: Oxford University Press.

Reagan, Ronald (1981). 'Inaugural Address.' 20 Jan. Washington, DC.

Rees, Gareth, and Lambert, John (1985). *Cities in Crisis: The Political Economy of Urban Development in Postwar Britain*. London: Edward Arnold.

Rex, John (1973). *Race, Colonialism and the City*. London: Routledge & Kegan Paul.

Riche, R.W., Hecker, D.E., and Burgan, J.U. (1983). 'High Technology Today and Tomorrow: A Small Slice of the Employment Pie.' *Monthly Labor Review* (Nov.): 50–8.

Riddell, Peter (1985). *The Thatcher Government*. London: Blackwell.

Rivlin, Alice M. (1983). 'CBO's Position on Tax-Exempt Financing for Private Activities.' *Municipal Finance Journal* 4 (4): 303–13.

Roberts, P., and Noon, D. (1987). 'The Role of Industrial Promotion in the Process of Regional Development.' *Regional Studies* 21 (2): 167–73.

Robson, William A. (1935). 'The Public Utility Services.' In *A Century of Municipal Progress*, ed. Harold J. Laski, W. Ivor Jennings, and William A. Robson. London: Allen & Unwin.

Rogers, David, and Zimet, Melvin (1968). 'The Corporation and the Community:

Perspectives and Recent Development.' In *The Business of America*, ed. Ivar Berg. New York: Harcourt, Brace and World.

Rose, Jack (1985). *The Dynamics of Urban Property Development*. London: E. and F.N. Spon.

Rumberger, R.W. (1984). 'High Technology and Job Loss.' Palo Alto: Institute for Research on Educational Finance and Governance, Stanford University.

Salamon, Lester M. (1984). 'Nonprofit Organizations: The Lost Opportunity.' In *The Reagan Record*, ed. John L. Palmer and Isabel V. Sawhill. Cambridge, Mass.: Ballinger.

— and Abramson, Alan J. (1982). 'The Nonprofit Sector.' In *The Reagan Experiment: An Examination of Economic and Social Policies under the Reagan Administration*, ed. John L. Palmer and Isabel V. Sawhill. Washington, DC: Urban Institute Press.

Salisbury, Robert H. (1964). 'Urban Politics: The New Convergence of Power.' *Journal of Politics* 26, No. 4 (Nov.): 775–97.

Sanders, Heywood T., and Stone, Clarence N. (1987a). 'Developmental Politics Reconsidered.' *Urban Affairs Quarterly* 22, No. 4 (June): 521–39.

— (1987b). 'Competing Paradigms: A Rejoinder to Peterson.' *Urban Affairs Quarterly* 22, No. 4 (June): 548–51.

Sapolsky, Harvey M. (1969). 'On the Ballistic Missile Solution to the Urban Crisis.'

Saunders, Peter (1979). *Urban Politics: A Sociological Interpretation*. London: Hutchison.

— (1986). 'Reflections on the Dual Politics Thesis: The Argument, Its Origins and Its Critics.' In *Urban Political Theory and the Management of Fiscal Stress*, ed. Michael Goldsmith. London: Gower.

Savas, Emanuel S. (1977). 'An Empirical Study of Competition in Municipal Service Delivery.' *Public Administration Review* 37 (Nov.–Dec.): 717–24.

— (1982). *Privatizing the Public Sector: How to Shrink Government*. Chatham, NJ: Chatham House.

— (1983). 'A Positive Urban Policy for the Future.' *Urban Affairs Quarterly* 18: 447–53.

Scarman, L.G. (1981). *The Brixton Disorders, April 10–12, 1981*, Cmnd. 8427. London: HMSO.

Schmenner, Roger W. (1978). *The Manufacturing Investment Decision: Evidence from Cincinnati and New England*. Washington, DC: Economic Development Administration.

Schulze, Robert (1961). 'The Bifurcation of Power in a Satellite City.' In *Community Political Systems*, ed. Morris Janowitz. Glencoe: The Free Press.

Science and Government Report (1987). 'Lot of Talk But Actually Few New Research Centers,' 1 Mar. Washington, DC.

SDA [Scottish Development Agency] (1986). *Annual Report: Agency of Opportunity*. Glasgow: Scottish Development Agency.

— (n.d.). *Local Development Grants for Urban Projects*. Glasgow: Scottish Development Agency.

Seebohm Report (1968). *Report of the Committee on Local Authority and Allied Personal Social Services*, Cmnd. 3703. London: HMSO.

Shannon, W. Wayne, Feree, Jr., C. Donald, Ladd, Everett Carll, and Lewis, Carol W. (1986). 'The Public Sector in Stamford, Connecticut: Responses to a Changing Federal Role.' In *Reagan and the Cities*, ed. George E. Peterson and Carol W. Lewis. Washington, DC: Urban Institute Press.

Shapira, P. (1984). 'The Crumbling of Smokestack California: A Case Study in Industrial Restructuring and the Reorganization of Work.' Berkeley: Department of City and Regional Planning, University of California.

Sharkansky, Ira (1975). *The United States: A Study of a Developing Country*. New York: David McKay.

Sharpe, L. J. (1973). 'American Democracy Reconsidered: Part I.' *British Journal of Political Science* 3: 1–28.

Shore, Peter (1977). Address by the Secretary of State for the Environment to the Save Our Cities Conference. Bristol.

Simmie, James M. (1974). *Citizens in Conflict: The Sociology of Town Planning*. London: Hutchinson.

Small, Kenneth A. (1982). *Geographically Differentiated Taxes and the Location of Firms*. Princeton: Urban and Regional Research Center, Princeton University.

Smith, Jr., Fred L. (1987). 'Privatization at the Federal Level.' In *Prospects for Privatization*, ed. Steve H. Hanke. New York: Academy of Political Science.

Smith, Michael Peter, and Keller, Marlene (1986). ' "Managed Growth" and the Politics of Uneven Development in New Orleans.' In *Restructuring the City: The Political Economy of Urban Development*, with Susan S. Fainstein, Norman I. Fainstein, Dennis Judd, and Michael Peter Smith. Rev. edn. New York: Longman.

Smout, T. C. (1986). *A Century of the Scottish People: 1830–1950*. London: Collins.

Sorenson, A. D. (1983). 'Towards a Market Theory of Planning.' *Planner* 69 (3): 78–80.

Sorenson, A. D., and Day, R. A. (1981). 'Libertarian Planning.' *Town Planning Review* 52 (4): 390–402.

Squires, Gregory D. (1984). 'Industrial Revenue Bonds and the Deindustrialization of America.' *Urbanism Past and Present* 9 (1): 1–9.

SRI [International] (1981). *Developing Public–Private Approaches to Community Problem-Solving*. Menlo Park, Calif.: Public Policy Research Center, SRI International.

Starr, Paul (1987). 'The Limits of Privatization.' In *Prospects for Privatization*, ed. Steve H. Hanke. New York: Academy of Political Science.

Stephenson, Jr., Max O. (1987). 'The Policy and Premises of Urban Development Action Grant Program Implementation: A Comparative Analysis of the Carter and Reagan Presidencies.' *Journal of Urban Affairs* 9 (1): 19–35.

Stevens, Barbara J. (ed.) (1984). *Delivering Municipal Services Efficiently: A Comparison of Municipal and Private Service Delivery*. A report prepared by Ecodata, Inc. for the US Department of House and Urban Development (June).

Stewart, Murray (1987). 'Ten Years of Inner Cities Policy.' *Town Planning Review* 58 (2): 129–45.

Stewart, M., and Underwood, J. (1983). 'The Private Sector in the Inner City.' In *Urban Economic Development: New Roles and Relationships*, ed. Ken Young and Charlie Mason. London: Macmillan.

Stewman, Shelby, and Tarr, Joel A. (1982). 'Four Decades of Public–Private Partnerships in Pittsburgh.' In *Public–Private Partnerships in American Cities*, ed. R. Scott Fosler and Renee A. Berger. Lexington, Mass.: D. C. Heath.

Still, Bayrd (1941). 'Patterns of Mid-Nineteenth Century Urbanization in the Middle West.' *Mississippi Valley Historical Review* 28: 187–206.

Stockman, David A. (1986). *The Triumph of Politics: How the Reagan Revolution Failed*. New York: Harper and Row.

Stoker, Robert P. (1987). 'Baltimore: The Self-Evaluating City?' In *The Politics of Urban*

Development, ed. Clarence N. Stone and Heywood T. Sanders. Lawrence: University Press of Kansas.

Stone, Clarence N., and Sanders, Heywood T. (eds.) (1987a). *The Politics of Urban Development*. Lawrence: University Press of Kansas.

—— (1987b). 'Reexamining a Classic Case of Development Politics: New Haven, Connecticut.' In *The Politics of Urban Development*, ed. Clarence N. Stone and Heywood T. Sanders. Lawrence: University Press of Kansas.

Sundquist, James L. (1984). 'Privatization: No Panacea for What Ails Government.' In *Public–Private Partnership: New Opportunities for Meeting Social Needs*. ed. Harvey Brooks, Lance Liebman, and Corrine S. Schelling. Cambridge, Mass.: Ballinger.

Taab, William K. (1969). 'Government Incentives to Private Industry to Locate in Urban Poverty Areas.' *Land Economics* 45: 392–99.

Talbot, Allan R. (1967). *The Mayor's Game: Richard Lee of New Haven and the Politics of Change*. New York: Praeger.

Tate, Dale (1981). 'New Federalism No Panacea for State and Local Governments.' Congressional Quarterly Weekly Report, 25 Apr. Washington, DC: GPO.

Taylor, Stan (1981). 'The Politics of Enterprise Zones.' *Public Administration Review* 59: 421–39.

TCPA [Town and Country Planning Association] (1980). *Town and Country Planning* 49 (10): 370–1.

—— (1985). 'Saving the Cities.' *Town and Country Planning* 54 (2): 37.

—— (1986). *Whose Responsibility? Reclaiming the Inner City*. London: Town and Country Planning Association.

Titmuss, Richard (1968). *Commitment to Welfare*. London: Allen & Unwin.

Treasury (1982). 'The Public Sector for the Public.' *Economic Progress Report*, No. 145: 1–4.

Ture, Norman B. (1980). 'Economic and Federal Revenue Effects of Changes in the Small Issue Industrial Development Bond Provisions,' in US Senate Committee on Finance, Hearing on Tax Cut Proposals, Ninety-sixth Congress (July).

Tyler, Peter, and Rhodes, John (1987). *South East Employment and Housing Study*, Discussion Paper 15. Cambridge: Department of Land Economy, University of Cambridge.

Tym, Roger, and Partners (1984). *Monitoring Enterprise Zones: Year Three Report*. London: DoE.

URPG [Urban and Regional Policy Group Report] (1978). *A New Partnership to Conserve America's Communities: A National Urban Policy*. Washington, DC: USHUD. S-297. This report is divided into section P (for preface), sections I, II, and III. Citations are given by section and page number.

US Bureau of the Census (1960, 1970, 1980). *Characteristics of the Population*. Washington, DC: GPO.

—— (1980). *Journey to Work Census*. Washington, DC: GPO.

—— (1983). *Annual Housing Survey, Baltimore*. Washington, DC: GPO.

—— (1986). Current Population Reports, Series P-60, No. 154. *Money Income and Poverty Status of Families and Persons in the United States: 1985*. Washington, DC: GPO.

—— (1987). Current Population Reports, Series P-60, No. 156. *Money Income of Households, Families, and Persons in the United States: 1985*. Washington, DC: GPO.

256 *References*

US Conference of Mayors (1984). *The Baltimore City Loan and Guarantee Program: A Trustee System*. Washington, DC: US Conference of Mayors.

US Congress, Joint Economic Committee (1982). *Location of High Technology Firms and Regional Economic Development*. Washington, DC: GPO.

US House (1981). *Overview and Assessment of Economic and Regional Development Programs Under the Jurisdiction of the Subcommittee on Economic Development. Hearings Before the Subcommittee on Economic Development of the Committee on Public Works and Transportation, House of Representatives, 97th Congress, 1st Session (March 11–13)*. Washington, DC: GPO.

USHUD [US Department of Housing and Urban Development] (1978). *The President's 1978 National Urban Policy Report*. Washington, DC: GPO. HUDCPD-328.

—— (1980a). *The President's 1980 National Urban Policy Report*, HUD-583-1-CPD. Washington, DC: GPO.

—— (1980b). *Urban Development Action Grant Program: Second Annual Report*. Washington, DC: GPO.

—— Office of Policy Development and Research (1982(a). *An Impact Evaluation of the Urban Development Action Grant Program*, HUD-PDR-694. Washington, DC: GPO.

—— (1982b). *The President's 1982 National Urban Policy Report*, HUD S-702-1. Washington, DC: GPO.

—— (1983). *Consolidated Annual Report to Congress on Community Development Programs*. Washington DC: GPO.

—— (1984). *The President's 1984 National Urban Policy Report*. Washington, DC: HUD.

—— (1986). *The President's 1986 National Urban Policy Report*, HUD-1068-PDR. Washington, DC: GPO.

—— (1987). *Consolidated Annual Report to Congress on Community Development Programs (CDBG, UDAG, Rental Rehabilitation, Section 312, Urban Homesteading*. Washington, DC: GPO.

US Senate (1970). *The Jobs Program (Job Opportunities in the Business Sector): Background Information*, Prepared for the Subcommittee on Employment, Manpower, and Poverty of the Committee on Labor and Public Welfare, Ninety-first Congress, Second Session, Apr. 1970. Washington DC: G.PO.

—— (1973). *The Central City Problem and Urban Renewal Policy*, Prepared for the Subcommittee on Housing and Urban Affairs of the Committee on Banking, Housing and Urban Affairs, Committee Print, Ninety-third Congress, First Session. Washington, DC: GPO.

US Treasury Department (1977). *Working Paper on the National Development Bank*.

Wade, Richard C. (1958). 'Urban Life in Western America, 1790–1830.' *American Historical Review* (Oct.): 14–30.

—— (1959). *The Urban Frontier: The Rise of the Western Cities, 1790–1830*. Cambridge, Mass.: Harvard University Press.

Waldegrave, William (1987). 'Simplified Planning Zones to Assist Urban Regeneration.' *Planner* 73 (8): 6.

Walters, Alan (1986). *Britain's Economic Renaissance: Margaret Thatcher's Reforms, 1979–1984*. Oxford: Oxford University Press.

Walton, John (1982). 'Cities, Jobs and Politics.' *Urban Affairs Quarterly* 18 (1): 5–17.

Wannop, Urlan (1985). 'Introduction: Leveraging Urban Development.' *Policy and Politics* 13 (2): 176–79.

Warner, Jr., Sam Bass (1968). *The Private City: Philadelphia in Three Periods of its*

References

257

Growth, 1st edn. Philadelphia: University of Pennsylvania Press.
—— *The Urban Wilderness: A History of the American City*. New York: Harper and Row.
—— (1987). *The Private City: Philadelphia in Three Periods of its Growth*, 2nd edn. Philadelphia: University of Pennsylvania Press.
Wasylenko, Michael (1980). 'Evidence on Fiscal Differential and Intra-Metropolitan Firm Location.' *Land Economics* 56: 339–49.
—— (1981). 'The Location of Firms: The Role of Taxes and Fiscal Incentives.' In *Urban Government Finance: Emerging Trends*, ed. Roy Bahl. Beverly Hills: Sage Publications.
Watkins, Alan (1988). 'Mrs T, Our American PM.' *Observer*, 15 May.
Webman, Jerry A. (1981). 'UDAG: Targeting Urban Economic Development.' *Political Science Quarterly* 96: 189–207.
Weicher, John C. (1972). *Urban Renewal: National Program for Local Problems*. Washington, DC: American Enterprise Institute for Public Policy Research.
Whitehead, Mark (1985). 'The LGC Privatisation Survey 1984–85.' *Local Government Chronicle* (July): 3–15.
—— (1987). 'The LGC Privatisation Survey, 1987.' *Local Government Chronicle* (July): 3–18.
White House (1981). *America's New Beginning: A Program For Economic Recovery*. Washington, DC: White House.
Wilder, Margaret, and Rubin, Barry (1988). 'Targeted Redevelopment Through Urban Enterprise Zones: Indiana as a Case Study.' *Journal of Urban Affairs* 10 (1): 1–17.
Wilson, James Q. (ed.) (1966). *Urban Renewal: The Record and the Controversy*. Cambridge, Mass.: Massachusetts Institute of Technology Press.
Wolfinger, Raymond E. (1974). *The Politics of Progress*. Englewood Cliffs: Prentice-Hall.
Wolman, Harold (1986). 'The Reagan Urban Policy and Its Impacts.' *Urban Affairs Quarterly* 21: 311–35.
Wood, Robert (1975). 'Suburban Politics and Policies: Retrospect and Prospect.' *Publius* 5: 45–52.
Woolridge, J. Randall, and Gray, Gary (1981). 'The CBO Study on Small Issue IRBs: Fact or Fiction.' *Municipal Finance Journal* 2 (2): 83–9.
Wray, Ian (1987). 'The Merseyside Development Corporation: Progress Versus Objectives.' *Regional Studies* 21 (2): 163–7.
Young, Hugo (1988). 'The Shameless Hype of Inner-City Policy is a Way of Saying Thanks to the Developers.' *Guardian*, 8 Mar.
Young, Ken, and Mason, Chris (eds.) (1983). *Urban Economic Development: New Roles and Relationships*. London: Macmillan.
Zeiger, Harvey (1985). 'LEG-UP: Local Enterprise Grants for Urban Projects.' *Policy and Politics* 13 (2): 199–204.

Index

cost savings 126–7
creaming 127
criticisms 127–8
definition 4–5, 125, 142, 160
deregulation 165–8
of education 127
Grace Commission [US] 124, 125
of housing 161–3
load-shedding 125, 160
of local services 126–7, 164
of medical services 164–5
objectives 3, 125–6
and quality of services 127
Reagan initiatives 124–5, 141–2
of school bus services 126
selling off of state assets 160–3
of solid waste collection 126
Task Force on Private Sector Initiatives 124
and Thatcher government 160–8, 182–3
of transit services 126
of vocational rehabilitation 127
Property Advisory Group (PAG) 189–90
property boom of 1971–3 [UK] 152–3
Public Housing Administration [US] 50
public–private partnerships 38–49, 183–4,
    206–13
and BIC 207
in Britain 183–4, 206–13
City Action Teams (CATs) 209
City Grant [UK] 211
in Detroit 48–9
and Enterprise Trusts [UK] 207
Glasgow Action 210–11
in housing 162, 206–7
in Indianapolis 129
limits of 227
and local authorities 211–13
in Nashville 129
and Phoenix Partnership 208
in Pittsburgh 48–9
proposals for [UK] 206–8
and Reagan administration 113, 129
and renewal of CBD 46–7
and Thatcher Government 183–4
and Urban Development Corporation (New
    York) 49
and urban renewal 38–49
and URG 190
US models 210–11
Public Works and Economic Development Act
    (1965) [US] 71
Pullman, George 37

quasi-public economic development
    Corporation 75–6
in Baltimore 90, 92
in Detroit 76
in New Orleans 76

race relations [UK] 145, 155
Rand Corporation 19
Rasmussen, David 121
Rate Relief 220
Rate Support Grant (RSG) 175–6, 179–80, 182
Ready, Randy 129, 130
Reagan, Michael 62
Reagan administration 100–40
    domestic policy proposals 100
    and EDA 110–11, 112–13
    enterprise zone proposal 107, 119–21
    and HUD 133–4
    impacts of budget cuts 133–8, 142
    legacy 138–40
    new federalism 116–18
    and President's Commission for a National
        Agenda for the Eighties 101–5
    privatization initiatives 124–5, 141–2
    Program for Economic Recovery 105–6
    and public–private partnerships 113, 129
    and UDAG 110, 111–13, 140
    urban budget 108–13
    urban policy 100–1, 106–8
    and voluntarism 114–16
Rees, Gareth 175
regional planning [UK] 144–5, 182–3
Rein, Martin 51
revenue sharing 63–4
reverse leverage 83–6, 189
Rhodes, John 216
Rich, Daniel 62, 132, 133, 231
Ridley, Nicholas 197, 206, 211
Rivlin, Alice 88–9
Rochester (New York) 135
Rockefeller, David 54
Rockefeller, Nelson 53
Rostenkowski, Daniel 120
Rouse Corporation 92, 193, 210
Royal Institute of Chartered Surveyors 203
Rubin, Berry 122, 124
Rumbold, Mrs 169–70

St Louis 43, 62
St Paul 130
Salamon, Lester 114, 115
Salford 188
Salisbury, Robert 45
Salt Lake City 133
Sanders, Heywood 91
Sapolsky, Harvey 55–6
Savas, E.S. 3, 6–7, 105, 106, 108
Sawhill, Isabel 136, 138, 142
Scarman Report 181
Schäefer, Donald 62, 90, 93, 95
Scottish Development Agency (SDA):
    Area Projects 173, 175, 198–9
    and enterprise zones 202–3
    formation 197–8
    and Glasgow Action 210–11